Indigenous Australia
for
kids

by Larissa Behrendt

Foreword by Cathy Freeman

A Wiley Brand

Indigenous Australia For Kids For Dummies®

Published by

John Wiley & Sons Australia, Ltd

42 McDougall Street

Milton, Qld 4064

www.dummies.com

Copyright © 2021 John Wiley & Sons Australia, Ltd

The moral rights of the author have been asserted.

ISBN: 978-0-730-39033-6

A catalogue record for this book is available from the National Library of Australia

Cover image: © Myra Nungarrayi Herbert / Copyright Agency, 2021

Typeset by SPi

READERS OF THIS BOOK SHOULD BE AWARE THAT, IN SOME ABORIGINAL AND TORRES STRAIT ISLANDER COMMUNITIES, SEEING IMAGES OF DECEASED PERSONS IN PHOTOGRAPHS MAY CAUSE SADNESS OR DISTRESS AND, IN SOME CASES, OFFEND AGAINST STRONGLY HELD CULTURAL PROHIBITIONS. THIS BOOK CONTAINS IMAGES OF PEOPLE WHO ARE DECEASED.

Contents at a Glance

Table of Contents

Foreword by Cathy Freeman

The Italian, Leonardo da Vinci, gave the world a better understanding of the human body through his extensive studies of living organisms. His drawings of human organs were the first of their kind in the world.

Another of his other remarkable feats was to devise a way for humans to take to the skies, which he did 400 years before the first plane ever took off.

Da Vinci achieved remarkable feats as an artist, engineer, inventor and scientist, and his contribution to humankind continues to have an impact on our lives today.

There is another man named David Ngunaitponi, also known as David Unaipon, who, like Leonardo da Vinci, made remarkable contributions that still have an impact on society today.

Unaipon, was a very proud man of the Ngarrinjeri people of South Australia's Coorong Region. He was a preacher, author, poet, inventor, philosopher and political activist whose name continues to stand for a rare kind of exceptionalism and excellence.

One of Unaipon's most noted accomplishments is in the area of invention with his innovations leading to the creation of a mechanical hand tool for shearing sheep.

Marking and celebrating this most unique man and his significant contribution, Unaipon's name and image has appeared on the Australian $50 bank note since 1995.

Like Da Vinci, Unaipon acquired a marvellous interest in science and in 1914 he commented regarding his scientific breakthrough regarding his helicopter design:

> 'An aeroplane can be manufactured that will rise straight into the air from the ground by application of the boomerang principle. The boomerang is shaped to rise in the air according to the velocity with which it is propelled, and so can an aeroplane.'

Unaipon, 22 years previous to its invention, had conceptualised the world's first helicopter and this achievement only added ever greater weight to the title publicly bestowed upon him as 'Australia's Leonardo.'

Da Vinci said that the noblest pleasure is the joy of understanding, and that the truth of things is the chief nutriment of superior intellects.

Unaipon had a curious and bright intellect. He read, studied and researched for innumerable hours and this genius habit was attributable to the fact that he is Australia's first published First Nations writer.

Professor Larissa Behrendt's book, *Indigenous Australia For Kids* is a means of nourishment and sustenance for all curious minds that seek a kind of intellectual grounding in a world that is often unknowing and unwise.

I would imagine that if they were both still alive, both Da Vinci and Unaipon would see themselves in each other, just as we too might see ourselves in them also.

To willingly seek information and to build on our own genius habits is the way to deepening our own sense of meaning and connection to our own lives and the world we live in.

Behrendt gives us a tremendous opportunity to learn about the world's oldest living culture that is Australia's First Nations people.

She enables us to gain deeper insight into our own view of who we are as individuals and, equally, who we are as a collective.

Indigenous Australia For Kids inspires readers to flex their creative and imaginative thinking muscles so we can all contribute to a world we aspire to live in some day.

Cathy Freeman
Kuku Yalanji woman and
Olympic Champion
August 2021

Introduction

Understanding the history and culture of Australia is impossible without understanding the country's Indigenous peoples. And to understand Australia's Indigenous peoples, you need to understand their history, traditional and modern cultural values, worldviews and experiences.

Indigenous Australia For Kids looks at the experiences of Indigenous people, including their political actions and dreams, and seeks to debunk some of the myths, especially the negative stereotypes, that are still around in Australian society about Indigenous people. Indigenous history and modern issues are very political matters in Australia. This book often looks at these matters from an Indigenous perspective, as well as covering different views.

About This Book

Indigenous Australia For Kids is a book for kids and teenagers who don't know much about Australia's Indigenous peoples but really want to know more. It looks at both historical and modern issues. The book helps give you a good general knowledge of all the relevant issues. Hopefully, you'll be inspired to then read more on the topics that interest you. Some of these topics can get very complex. So having a good basic understanding first helps. This book can be read straight through (from Chapter 1 to Chapter 20!). Or you can select a chapter based on the topic you want to read about. Each chapter is self-contained, or makes sense by itself.

Australia's Indigenous peoples are made up of Aboriginal people — who live all around the country. They also include Torres Strait Islanders, who settled the many small islands to the north of Cape York Peninsula in Queensland.

Names and terms are complex when it comes to Indigenous identity in Australia. The term *Indigenous* is used in this book to describe both Aboriginal people and Torres Strait Islanders. The term *Aboriginal* is used when I talk about matters that apply only to Aboriginal people.

Similarly, I use the term *Torres Strait Islanders* for matters that apply only to this group of people.

Also remember that some Aboriginal people don't like to be called 'Indigenous'. The term *First Nations* is being preferred more and more. Others prefer to be known through their nation or clan.

Because Indigenous languages in Australia were originally oral languages — not written — nation or clan names often have multiple spellings. Regional variations on how words were said have also led to more than one spelling for other words. Throughout the book, when I talk about specific nations or clans, I use the most common spelling.

Note: As both the author of this book and an Aboriginal person myself, if it sounds like I'm telling the story as an insider, I am.

On a different note, to help you get the information you need as quickly as possible, this book uses several conventions:

- **Bold** words make the key terms and phrases in bulleted lists jump out and grab your attention.

- *Italics* signal that a word is an important defined term.

- Monofont is used for web addresses.

- Sidebars, or the text separated from the rest of the type in grey boxes, are interesting but generally extra reading. You won't miss anything important if you skip the sidebars. If you choose to read the sidebars, though, you can benefit from some additional and interesting information.

Foolish Assumptions

This book assumes the following about you, the reader:

- That you have some basic understanding of Australian history — such as that Britain set up a colony in Australia in 1788

⌐ That you have a basic knowledge of Australian geography — or that at least you're able to look up different places on a map!

Icons Used in This Book

Throughout this book, the following icons are used to help you know when you're about to learn something special, quirky or significant.

CULTURAL PROTOCOLS

This is important information about Indigenous cultures that allows you to better understand Indigenous people.

MYTH BUSTER

Many myths, misunderstandings and stereotypes about Indigenous people have become widespread since European settlement of Australia. This information straightens out a few of those things.

PROJECT

Next to this icon are activities and ideas for finding out more about the information included in the chapter. You'll see these icons at the end of every chapter.

REMEMBER

Information next to this icon helps to give a deeper understanding of the topic being discussed.

TECHNICAL STUFF

This is specialised information, often legal in nature, that explains terms or gives the background to a topic.

TIP

This icon denotes a piece of advice about the subject matter being discussed that helps you to learn more.

Where to Go from Here

You can approach this book any way you like. You can read from start to finish — and perhaps skip some things along the way that you already know or are less interested in. Or you can go straight to the topics you're most interested in and dive right in there. For an overview of the diversity and richness of Indigenous cultures both before and after colonisation, for example, head to Chapters 1 to 4.

Chapters 5 to 9 look at the growth of the British colonies in Australia and how this affected Indigenous people. They also cover how Indigenous people reacted to colonisation. The chapters in Part 3 are all about Indigenous activism. Chapters 11 to 15 highlight the rich tradition of sport, art, storytelling, dance and music that's as vibrant today as it was before colonisation.

And if it's the current issues you'd like to jump in and tackle, head to Chapters 16 and 17.

You can use the table of contents to find topics quickly. The glossary lets you cut to the chase on any terms you may want to clarify.

Indigenous Australia For Kids is meant to be fun to read as well as informative, so go ahead and enjoy! Hopefully, this is just the start of a long, enjoyable and inspiring journey to find out more about the world's oldest living culture.

Part 1
An Ancient People: Then and Now

In This Part . . .

☐ Understand the long history of Indigenous peoples, going back over 65,000 years.

☐ Work out why it's important to understand rich and diverse Indigenous history, cultures and values, both traditional and contemporary.

☐ Find out about Indigenous worldviews, bush tucker and languages.

☐ Get to know customs when addressing Indigenous people or holding an event on traditional lands.

Understanding Indigenous Australia

The Aboriginal people of Australia are the caretakers of the world's oldest living culture. Indigenous Australians are Aboriginal people and Torres Strait Islanders. Their worldviews focus on the connections between people and their environment, and the bonds people have with each other. Indigenous Australians are also an important part of the Australian story. You can't understand modern Australia without considering the importance of its Indigenous peoples and their cultures in that story.

The colonisation of Australia devastated Indigenous people and cultures. Populations were destroyed, and traditional lands and means of self-support were taken away. Government policies were aimed at assimilation. These policies made official the taking of Indigenous children from their families so they could grow up like 'white' Australians. Even though this was a destructive period, the story of how Indigenous people — and their cultures — survived is inspiring.

In this chapter, I provide an overview of Australia's history through Indigenous eyes. You also see what issues they face today and some solutions they are using to meet these challenges.

REMEMBER

Understanding these aspects of Indigenous history and cultures lets you gain greater insight into who Indigenous people are and what Aboriginal and Torres Strait Islander cultures are like.

Indigenous Cultures: Then and Now

More than 500 different Aboriginal nations existed at the time the British colonised Australia. These nations had possibly up to one million people in total. These people had lived on this land for over 65,000 years, adjusting to big changes in the environment and landscape. But the arrival of the British in 1788 fundamentally affected Indigenous cultures. Over the next century, as colonies spread, Aboriginal people were separated from their traditional lands. This separation affected their ability to care for their country, support themselves and their families, and practise traditional ceremonies. But Indigenous cultures were strong. Even in the face of such big change, they still adapted.

Today, Indigenous people live across Australia in urban, rural and remote areas. They were once considered by non-Indigenous Australians to be a dying, inferior race. But their growing populations and continuing cultural practices show that modern Indigenous cultures are vibrant and alive. (Chapter 2 outlines the initial impact and later growth of the Indigenous population since colonisation.)

Ancient traditions

Indigenous cultures across Australia had strong connections to their traditional land. They depended on it to provide them with everything they needed to survive. This included food, shelter, tools and medicine. And they needed each other as well. Nations were divided into *clans*, which were large extended families, perhaps as small as 30 people in some cases. In such small groups, everyone had to pitch in, and people depended a lot on each other.

Cultural values focused on connection with nature, each other and ancestors. Indigenous peoples believed in respect and responsibility for country. They also valued respect for the wisdom and authority of Elders. Chapter 4 goes into traditional practices and beliefs. Chapter 18 describes some cultural sites that are important for Indigenous peoples today.

Diversity, diversity and more diversity

Indigenous cultures around Australia shared many values and had similar worldviews. But great diversity was also present because of the different environments and climates across Australia. Indigenous communities living by the ocean had different ways of life, technologies and practices from Indigenous communities living in desert areas. But across the country, large gatherings of several clans took place for ceremonies, and trading routes spread across the continent. See Chapter 3 for more on this cultural diversity.

REMEMBER

Indigenous cultures have remained strong and vibrant across Australia. Even in modern forms, they have a strong connection to traditional practices. Indigenous peoples do so by using new technology or including aspects of other cultures. Chapter 20 breaks down some myths about Indigenous people.

Contemporary painting, singing and dancing

Art, song and dance were key aspects of traditional cultural practice. They were mostly used for ceremonial purposes, and they still have a main position in modern cultures:

- ✔ Indigenous art has become a worldwide sensation. Some pieces attract prices in the tens and even hundreds of thousands of dollars. But this industry hasn't turned into wealth for the artists. Chapter 12 looks in detail at the Indigenous art world.

- ✔ Indigenous songs were some of the first things that were lost with colonisation. Today, though, Indigenous people are strongly involved with music — particularly country and western music! Younger Indigenous people have also embraced hip-hop music and rap to express their views and aspirations.

↙ Indigenous dance is now a leading contemporary Indigenous art form. It blends traditional dancing with more modern styles. Indigenous dance companies have grown around Australia. See Chapter 13 for some of the best of Indigenous Australia's musicians and dancers.

Old and new ways of storytelling

Indigenous cultures have a storytelling tradition, and Indigenous people have welcomed new ways of getting their message across. Indigenous playwrights, theatre directors and filmmakers have employed Indigenous actors to tell Indigenous stories. Indigenous people have also set up their own national radio service and television service. The national service works well with the many regional radio and television services set up by Indigenous communities. See Chapter 15 for more on these media.

Indigenous cultures originally had an oral tradition with no written languages. But Indigenous storytellers have now turned to the written word. For a long time, Indigenous people had stories written about them by white *anthropologists* (people who study aspects of humans within past and present societies), *linguists* (people who study different languages), historians and writers. But since the 1970s, Indigenous people have had a growing desire to tell their own stories themselves. Since then, Indigenous writing has crossed over into many genres, including crime novels and women's popular fiction. Chapter 14 covers Indigenous writing and publishing in detail.

And they can kick a ball!

Australia's Indigenous peoples lived as hunter-gatherers. This meant they spent a lot of time moving and had a nutritious, balanced diet. This way of life kept people strong and healthy. Perhaps because of this traditional way of life, Indigenous people have been excellent athletes. Across many codes — but especially football and athletics — Indigenous people have made a big contribution to Australia's sports.

Sportspeople are good role models for Indigenous young people. They often work in Aboriginal and Torres Strait Islander communities as mentors. They help with building confidence and self-esteem, and they encourage young people to be active, fit and healthy. You can find more information on leading Indigenous sportspeople in Chapter 11.

There Goes the Neighbourhood

Understanding modern Indigenous cultures and worldviews largely depends on understanding how Australia's Indigenous peoples have been treated during the country's rather short European history.

Lieutenant James Cook (later Captain) claimed the eastern coast of Australia for the British in 1770. At the time, the large, powerful colonising countries such as Britain, Spain and France had an agreement. They agreed that lands such as Australia, populated only by 'natives' who were seen to be inferior, could be claimed by the colonial power that found them first. This was known as the *doctrine of discovery.* (Chapter 5 talks about this concept.) Indigenous people could have had no idea that, after 1770, their world would change as it did.

The takeover begins

In 1778, the First Fleet arrived in Sydney Cove from Britain and started a penal colony. The settlement was designed to help with the problem of overcrowding in British prisons. It was also designed to set up a claim to the territory against other colonial powers, especially the French. With the start of the colony, life for Indigenous Australians would never be the same again. Chapter 6 explores the effects of this first colony.

The colony spreads

The colony at Sydney Cove soon spread. It needed agricultural industries such as wheat, sheep and cattle to survive, and for that it needed land. The British eventually set up colonies around the country, including

- Van Diemen's Land, which became known as Tasmania

- Port Phillip District, in what is now Victoria

- Moreton Bay, near what is now Brisbane

- Adelaide, in South Australia

REMEMBER

One initial problem for Aboriginal people was the effect of the diseases brought by the British. Aboriginal people couldn't fight smallpox, colds, flu and measles because their bodies had never fought them before and so had no immunity to them. Populations were destroyed as these diseases spread. Chapter 7 looks at the impact of this expansion.

Loss of land

As the colonies were built and spread out from their initial boundaries, Aboriginal people were pushed off their land. They lost their ability to feed and shelter themselves and their families. Cultural practices also were disturbed. This led to often violent conflict as Aboriginal people fought against, as best they could, the attempts to move them from their land. This resistance consisted mostly of setting fire to buildings and infrastructure and killing stock. It did slow down the growth of the frontier in some places. But eventually the colonists, with their greater firepower and growing numbers, gained the upper hand.

In many places, Aboriginal people were pushed to the margins of towns and forced to live on specially designated reserves. In some cases, Aboriginal people could live on their traditional lands on pastoral stations and were given basic rations. They did so in exchange for work for the station owner. See Chapter 7 for more on this uneasy alliance.

And children taken too

The colonists tried to *assimilate* Aboriginal people into European cultural ways. This meant they wanted Aboriginal people to act more like European people and adopt their values and ways of living. They believed that one effective way to do this was to remove Aboriginal children from their families and bring them up away from them and their culture. Sometimes they placed the children in institutions. Other times the children were adopted into white families. This also affected Torres Strait Islander people after missions were started in the Torres Strait in the late 1800s. The practice continued as Torres Strait Islanders began to settle on the mainland.

All states and territories had laws that allowed the removal of Indigenous children from their families. Some people carrying out the policy genuinely believed that removing Indigenous children from their families would give them a better life. Despite those good intentions, the practice often had devastating consequences for the children taken away and the families and heritage they left behind. Chapter 8 goes over this painful issue in detail.

Fighting Back

From the start of colonisation, Aboriginal people fought against the attacks on their rights to their lands and the impact on their communities and cultures. Over the years, Aboriginal communities continued to clearly state their rights to their lands and to protest their unequal treatment. Torres Strait Islanders soon joined them.

The right to be equal

When the British started their colony at Sydney Cove, they brought their laws as well as their people. They said the laws and their protections applied equally to Aboriginal people and colonists. But this mostly didn't happen.

Aboriginal people's rights to their lands were denied. They were also rarely offered protection from frontier violence. They had to follow rules about where they could live, who they could marry, and whether and where they could work. They couldn't get the same wages as other workers doing the same jobs. In most places, they couldn't vote.

Aboriginal people challenged these restrictions by appealing to governments and even the British Crown. A key focus was equal treatment. They fought particularly for the rights to own and farm their own land and to have the same rights to citizenship as other Australians. Chapter 9 covers citizenship rights in more detail.

Changing the playing field

By the 1960s, Indigenous communities around Australia were living in developing-world conditions, with lower access to health care, education and housing. Many Australians — black and white — believed that this was unacceptable. Over 90 per cent of Australians voted in 1967 to change the Constitution to let the federal government make laws for Indigenous people. At the time, people genuinely believed that this change would lead to a new era of non-discrimination. People also thought that the federal government would act in a way that would help Indigenous people. This assumption was later proved wrong, but the vote was a big moment in Australia's history. Most Australians believed that the improved treatment of Indigenous people was important for the country. Chapter 9 looks at the referendum in more detail.

'We want our land back'

Land rights have been a key focus for Indigenous political movements ever since 1788. The land rights movement gained steam in the 1960s and 1970s. Several land rights regimes were set up — in the Northern Territory and New South Wales, in particular. But hopes for a national scheme never came about. These schemes were set up by governments under different legislation. They were different in how they set up land councils and the terms they made for the return of land to Indigenous people. Rights to land were also given a boost in 1992. That's when the High Court of Australia recognised that, in some situations, Indigenous people could claim a 'native title' right to their traditional land.

Reconciliation, practical reconciliation and intervention

Governments still struggle to work out how to address system-wide problems of Indigenous disadvantage. In the early 1990s, a national agenda of reconciliation was set out. This agenda aimed to, over a ten-year period, consult with Indigenous people about the best ways they could work together to overcome Indigenous disadvantage. This aim was replaced by a later government with a program of 'practical reconciliation'. This program said it would focus on the areas of health, housing, education and employment. This approach didn't produce major results, though. In 2007, the federal government began a policy of intervention in the Northern Territory. Using this policy, the government tried to make further changes in Northern Territory Aboriginal communities.

REMEMBER

To date, no major inroads have been made into reducing the difference between the disadvantaged circumstances of the broad Indigenous community and the living standards of other Australians.

'Sorry' — and then what?

On 13 February 2008, Prime Minister Kevin Rudd gave a historic speech in the federal parliament. He apologised to Indigenous Australians for past wrongs committed by governments against them, particularly for the removal of children from their families. This apology was seen as an act of huge symbolic importance. Since then, the Australian government has also supported the United Nations Declaration on the Rights of Indigenous Peoples. This declaration supports self-determination for Indigenous peoples. Indigenous people continue to fight for that right in practice by seeking to be centrally involved in the policies and programs that affect their community.

Whether the symbolic changes will bring about actual changes in the lives of Indigenous Australians remains to be seen. Chapter 10 looks at the effects of the apology. Chapter 17 looks at the concept of self-determination.

New Problems for an Old Culture

The impact of colonisation on Indigenous peoples was huge. Traditional ways of life were completely broken up. Dispossession, segregation and racist policies left an unhappy legacy. Statistics show that Indigenous people are much more disadvantaged in areas of health, education outcomes and employment. These statistics pose a challenge to the goal to create a level playing field for all Australians. Indigenous communities are playing an active and effective role in trying to find solutions. Chapter 19 looks at some of the achievements of Indigenous people.

Breaking the cycle of poverty

Indigenous life expectancy is lower than that of other Australians. Their health is poorer. Their home ownership levels are lower. Their housing conditions are worse than those of other Australians. Indigenous people also have lower levels of education and higher levels of unemployment than non-Indigenous people. Much has been done to try to fix this situation. Indigenous people have set up their own medical services. They also are training to be nurses and doctors to work on health needs in their communities. Chapter 16 has more information on Indigenous health.

Indigenous disadvantage won't be overcome without improving the education levels of Indigenous people. Literacy levels and school attendance rates are a key focus in this area. Indigenous people have developed special programs that help Indigenous children learn how to read and write. Programs also have been designed to improve the education of Indigenous adults.

Of course, a link exists between education levels and unemployment levels. The remoteness of some communities is also a barrier to some Indigenous people entering the workforce. Chapter 16 explores education and employment.

Challenging the rules and regulations

Aboriginal and Torres Strait Islander communities had their own laws and government structures. Some of these survive today. But when the British colonised Australia, they brought their rules and governance systems. They didn't recognise the rights of Indigenous Australians.

British law claimed it would keep Indigenous people safe. In practice, British law became a weapon that sped up their dispossession. This law was also used to control Indigenous people. It told Indigenous people where they could live, the conditions of their employment, whether they could vote and sometimes even if they could marry. The laws also legalised theft of Indigenous people's land and removal of their children.

Indigenous people also came into contact with the criminal justice system. They were targeted by the police and charged with offences that non-Indigenous people wouldn't have been charged with. They were more likely to be refused bail (conditions that allow the release of an accused person while they await trial) and given longer sentences compared with non-Indigenous people.

All this led to an overrepresentation of Indigenous people in prisons. It also led to the charge that racism exists right through the criminal justice system. The Royal Commission into Aboriginal Deaths in Custody confirmed the bias in the legal system and made many recommendations.

REMEMBER

Very few of the recommendations made by the Royal Commission have been put into place. Indigenous Australians are still overrepresented in prisons.

Setting up Indigenous enterprises

Indigenous people aren't resting in the face of the problems in their communities. This book describes many instances of Indigenous people developing effective solutions to their own problems. One area in which Indigenous people are trying to find new opportunities is in business and economic development.

These opportunities range from ecotourism and cultural tours to partnerships with mining companies, bush tucker restaurants and Indigenous-owned holiday resorts. This is an important plan in overcoming Indigenous disadvantage. You can find more detail about this strategy in Chapters 3 and 16.

Doing It for Ourselves

Serious disadvantage is seen throughout the history of Indigenous Australia. But communities across the country have also had their successes in finding solutions to tough problems. These solutions are often simple. They include providing drying-out shelters or rehabilitation programs to deal with issues of alcohol abuse and violence, bilingual language models (using Indigenous languages as well as English) that help to improve educational outcomes, and community night patrols that keep the peace in Indigenous communities.

REMEMBER

All along, Indigenous people have said that, if they had the tools to deal with the issues within their own communities, they would do a better job than governments. Lots of evidence shows that this is the case. This is known as *self-determination.* Indigenous claims to the right to self-determination are a main part of their political agenda. Chapter 17 looks at these issues in more depth.

PROJECT

Find out who the traditional owners of the country you live on are. Learn more about them from local resources such as libraries, land councils and local Indigenous community organisation websites.

Rich Past, Strong Traditions

IN THIS CHAPTER

- ✔ Working out the age of the oldest living culture
- ✔ Looking at some evidence through art and tools
- ✔ Defining an Indigenous person and finding out where Indigenous people live
- ✔ Checking out how the Torres Strait Islands have developed
- ✔ Addressing ways to describe Aboriginal people and Torres Strait Islanders
- ✔ Using the right rules for acknowledging Aboriginal land or Torres Strait Islander land
- ✔ Understanding identity and busting stereotypes

Aboriginal culture is described as the world's oldest surviving culture. Its rich traditions and spiritual beliefs come from tens of thousands of years of living history. So does its complex social structure. Despite the destruction of populations after colonisation, the social unity and cultural strength of Indigenous communities has survived.

The Torres Strait Islands have an equally rich culture. Cultural practices and values have been affected by dependence on the sea. They were then influenced by trading with the Macassans, from the islands of what is now Indonesia, to the north. Life began to change for Torres Strait Islanders with the start of European missions on the islands from the late 1800s.

Today, a lot of confusion surrounds the make-up of the Indigenous population and the correct rules in addressing Indigenous people. This chapter sets out a little of the history of Indigenous Australia. It also tackles the issue of the correct terms for the diverse communities around the country.

The First Australians

Australia is the oldest continent in the world. So the fact that the country is also the home of the world's oldest surviving culture and religion is perhaps not surprising. Aboriginal people believe that they and their ancestors have occupied Australia since the beginning of time. 'Dreamtime' stories relate to a creation period — when the Earth was shaped, stars were made and animals developed. These stories explain, for example, how an echidna got its spikes or how a particular bird became flightless.

Archaeological findings and developments in DNA technology have led to current estimates that modern humans evolved in Africa about 190,000 years ago. They moved to the Middle East about 120,000 years ago and arrived in Australia via Asia over 65,000 years ago. Europe was populated about 40,000 years ago and the American continent about 14,000 years ago.

The discovery at Lake Mungo of 'Mungo Lady' in 1969 and 'Mungo Man' in 1974 challenged the 'out of Africa' theory of the spread of modern humans. Their remains are thought to be around 40,000 years old. DNA tests showed that they didn't share their origins with modern human beings. Some scientists think that this means humans' move to Australia didn't occur in one wave. (See Chapter 18 for more on this site.) More recently, Madjedbebe, a sandstone rock shelter in Arnhem Land in the Northern Territory, dates human presence to over 65,000 years ago.

The Torres Strait Islands are to the north-east of Australia — between the mainland and Papua New Guinea. They have been part of Queensland since 1879. More than 270 islands dot this area, though only 17 have people living on them. The Torres Strait Islands are believed to have been first settled by people moving from Papua at least 2,500 years ago. Evidence may be found in the future that dates settlement earlier, possibly up to around 4,000 years ago.

65,000 Years of Tradition

Archaeological evidence shows that Aboriginal people arrived in Australia at least 65,000 years ago. Three areas have been named as likely places where people travelling from South-East Asia arrived in Australia:

- The Kimberley region in the north of Western Australia

- Arnhem Land in the Top End of the Northern Territory

- Cape York at the northern tip of Queensland

These areas have rock shelters that have been used as places to live. Their floors are covered with charcoal and ash from campfires. They also have the remains of food such as shells and bones, and other pieces of human life such as tools and ochre. Stone tools and ochre are the toughest of these materials. They can be used to figure out the dates human activity occurred. (*Ochre* comes from soft varieties of iron oxide minerals. It ranges in colour from pale yellow to deep rust red. Ochre was used in ceremonies such as the painting of rockfaces and the painting of faces and bodies.)

Australia is relatively isolated. The technology of Aboriginal people and Torres Strait Islanders didn't evolve in the same way as it did in other parts of the world. Aboriginal people didn't develop through ages of pottery, bronze and iron. Stone technology was used into the 1960s. The use of stone technology and painting with ochre pigments date back to at least 60,000 years ago. This is supported by the dating of ochre fragments from the floor of a rock shelter in Arnhem Land.

Aboriginal cultures in Australia were the first to develop ground edges on cutting tools and the first to grind seeds. Archaeological work at Madjedbebe (once referred to as Malakunanja II) and Nauwalabila I has uncovered pieces of ground ochre, bone fragments, shells, tool fragments and signs of food processing. Carbon dating of the lowest layers that showed human activity places them at 65,000 years ago.

A cave on Barrow Island, off the coast of Western Australia, shows human presence from 50,000 years ago. Ochre found at other sites around Australia has been dated from 10,000 to 40,000 years ago. A piece of painting was found in a limestone rock shelter at Carpenter's Gap, near Windjana Gorge National Park in the Kimberley (Western Australia). It was dated at 40,000 years using carbon-dating technology. Rock art dating back 30,000 years exists on the Burrup Peninsula, also in Western Australia.

MYTH BUSTER

Aboriginal people were once thought to have been in Australia for as long as 40,000 years. After more recent archaeological work, that was moved to 50,000 years. It is now accepted to be *at least* 65,000. But this might even prove to be longer in the future.

REMEMBER

Signs of the length of Aboriginal presence in Australia come from many sources. Rock art was a common way of recording cultural practices. Some examples of rock art show animals that became extinct up to 40,000 years ago. Some of the oldest rock paintings, found in shelters in northern Australia, show ceremonies that are still performed and ceremonial decorations that are still worn today. This shows the continuation of Aboriginal cultural practices.

In the Torres Strait Islands, technology focused on using materials from the sea. These materials include fish bones, turtle shells, pearl shells and other shells. They were carved for use in ceremonies and as ornaments, and for tools, spearheads and fishhooks.

THE GREAT SOUTHERN LAND: HOW DID IT GET THERE?

Australia is the world's largest island as well as a continent. It has rocks that date to over 3,000 million years ago. Experts estimate Australia began its journey across the Earth's surface as an isolated continent between 55 million and 10 million years ago. Australia continues to move to the north by about seven centimetres per year.

Australia's shape is largely due to the movement of the Earth's tectonic plates and long-term changes to sea levels. But the landscape has also been shaped by wind and water erosion. About half of Australia's rivers run inland and end in salt lakes.

These draining patterns have a long history. Some valleys have kept their positions for millions of years. For example, the salt lakes of the Yilgarn region in Western Australia are the remains of a river drainage system that was active before the continental drift separated Australia from Antarctica.

The land mass that is now Australia started near the South Pole and was covered in ice caps. When the ice melted, parts of the continent subsided and formed basins. By the Cretaceous Period (145 million to 65 million years ago), Australia was so flat that rising sea levels created a shallow sea. This sea spread across the continent and divided it into three land masses.

During the Paleogene Period (65 million to 23 million years ago) and the Neogene Period (23 million to 2 million years ago), Australia had volcanic activity that continued in what is now Victoria and Queensland up until several thousand years ago. The most recent volcanic activity was at Mt Gambier in South Australia. It erupted about 6,000 years ago.

Around 30,000 years ago, Australia had a pleasant climate with lots of water, plenty of plants, snow-covered mountains and large animals roaming around. This changed 10,000 years later, when the most recent ice age came. This ice age lasted about 5,000 years. The middle of Australia was covered in large sand dunes during this time. Rainfall levels were half what they are today. The temperature was about ten degrees lower.

During its lowest level, the sea receded. Then Australia, Tasmania and New Guinea formed one large land mass. When the ice age ended and temperatures rose, a surge in plant growth took place. This meant the area where people could live as hunter-gatherers increased. During this rise in sea level, Tasmania was created. (That's about 11,000 years ago!) The island was separated from the mainland. New Guinea was cut off from Australia by rising sea levels around 8,000 years ago.

(continued)

(continued)

> By around 5,000 years ago, the islands of the Torres Strait looked like those that now exist — the Torres Strait Islands. They include high islands of volcanic rock to the west and small flat islands typical of the central and eastern areas. They also include sand cays and small volcanic islands in the far north of the strait, and large silt islands near the Papuan coast.

Aboriginal and Torres Strait Islander Populations Today

Aboriginal peoples and Torres Strait Islanders are still identified as distinct populations within the Australian community. Aboriginal peoples and Torres Strait Islanders live in diverse places across Australia. They adapt to different environments and situations. This is just as they did long ago.

Torres Strait Islander culture is also distinct from Aboriginal cultures. It's largely focused on the sea. Various languages are spoken throughout the Torres Strait, including English and Torres Strait Creole. The traditional languages of the Torres Strait are divided between Meriam Mir in the eastern islands and Kala Lagaw Ya in the central and western islands. The latter has four dialects, including Mabuiag. (See Chapter 3 for more on Indigenous languages.)

Defining who is an Indigenous person

A person's identity is a personal thing. Identity goes to the heart of how all people feel about their ancestry and the environment in which they grew up. Many Aboriginal people and Torres Strait Islanders have mixed heritage. But they choose to identify as being an Aboriginal or a Torres Strait Islander person.

When governments and organisations must figure out whether a person is Aboriginal or Torres Strait Islander, they generally use three criteria. All three criteria must be fulfilled. In their view, the person must

↙ Be of Aboriginal descent or Torres Strait Islander descent

↙ Identify as an Aboriginal person or as a Torres Strait Islander

↙ Be accepted as an Aboriginal person or as a Torres Strait Islander by the Aboriginal or Torres Strait Islander community in which they live

REMEMBER

The benefits of these criteria are that they include a part that looks at the way the person defines themself, as well as giving the community a role in determining who's considered to be Aboriginal or Torres Strait Islander for official purposes. Importantly, the test doesn't look at the percentage of Aboriginal or Torres Strait Islander heritage that a person has. If a person meets the criteria, what 'percentage' of Aboriginal or Torres Strait Islander heritage they have doesn't matter. This definition gives some power to the Indigenous community about who is considered to be Aboriginal and Torres Strait Island.

Aboriginal and Torres Strait Islander peoples don't embrace the term 'half-caste'. Even Aboriginal people of mixed ancestry usually say, 'I am Aboriginal' — rather than 'I am part-Aboriginal', for example. For this reason, it may offend Aboriginal people and Torres Strait Islanders if asked, 'What percentage of Aboriginal blood are you?'

RECOGNISING THE FLAGS

The Aboriginal flag was designed by Harold Thomas in 1971. The flag was displayed on 12 July 1971, National Aborigines' Day, at Victoria Square in Adelaide. It was also used at the Tent Embassy in Canberra in 1972. The flag has a horizontal stripe of black to represent Aboriginal people and a red stripe to represent the land and the blood that has been spilt on it. It also has a large yellow circle in the middle that represents the sun and symbolises the eternal joining of Aboriginal people to their land. It was given legal status as a flag of Australia in 1995.

(continued)

(continued)

In 2019, conflict grew about the use of the flag on products. In 2020, negotiations continued to allow the flag to be used more freely. This process also took commercial reasons into account.

The Torres Strait Islander flag was designed by Bernard Namok of Thursday Island. The flag has a representation of a white Dhari — a ceremonial headdress — which represents the people of the Torres Strait. It has a five-pointed star to symbolise peace and the five major island groups. A green horizontal stripe represents the land, a black stripe the people and a blue stripe the sea. It was also given legal status as a flag of Australia in 1995.

Counting the Indigenous population in Australia

In the 2016 Australian census, the Indigenous population was noted to be 798,365 people. This is about 3.3 per cent of the Australian population. The Australian Bureau of Statistics (ABS), which collects population data, understands that keeping accurate statistics has problems. This is because not all Indigenous people fill in the census form and not all enrol to vote. For this reason, the actual number of Indigenous people is thought to be higher than the official population.

Estimates of the Indigenous population across Australia at the time Britain established its colony in Sydney Cove are between 750,000 and 1 million people.

A national referendum in 1967 voted to change the Constitution to allow Indigenous people to be included in the census. (See Chapter 9 for more on the referendum.) But before 1971, the census didn't look to include Indigenous people who lived beyond settled areas. Estimates from authorities responsible for the welfare of Indigenous people were given. But accurate numbers weren't available. However, Indigenous people were identified as part of population counts from 1901. This information was collected, but Indigenous people 'of more than half blood' weren't included in the official figures.

After shrinking since the colonisation of Australia began, the national Indigenous population has been steadily climbing since the 1950s. Table 2-1 shows population figures from the ABS.

Table 2-1   National Indigenous Population since 1901

Year	National Indigenous Population
1901	93,000
1921	72,000
1933	81,000
1947	76,000
1954	75,000
1961	84,000
1966	102,000
1971	115,953
1976	160,915
1981	159,897
1986	227,645
1991	265,492
1996	386,000
2001	458,500
2006	517,200
2011	548,400
2016	798,365

Indigenous populations had been greatly reduced from the arrival of the British colonists. This was due to the impact of disease, forced moves from traditional country and from food and water supplies, frontier killings and the separation of families. By 1901, many non-Indigenous Australians thought that Aboriginal and Torres Strait Islander peoples were dying races. This trend started to change in the mid-1950s. Not all Indigenous people were included in the census figures until after 1967. But the increases before that suggest the population had already begun to grow.

After 1967, it still took many years to have the total population recorded accurately. Apart from having more Indigenous people in the census, the growth in population is chalked up to a higher reproduction rate within the Indigenous community. Indigenous families have more children on average than other Australians. The increase is also linked to more people identifying with their Indigenous ancestry. In 2016, 798,365 people identified as Indigenous. Of that number, 727,485 (91 per cent) identified as Aboriginal, 38,660 (5 per cent) identified as Torres Strait Islander and 32,220 (4 per cent) identified as both Aboriginal and Torres Strait Islander.

REMEMBER

The age of Aboriginal and Torres Strait Islander communities is much younger than that of the rest of the Australian population. The median age of the Indigenous population is 23; for the total Australian population, it's 37.8. For Aboriginal and Torres Strait Islander populations, 274,333 are under 15 years of age, and 34,012 are over 65 years. This means that Indigenous Australians under 15 are 34 per cent of the Indigenous population (compared to 18 per cent for non-Indigenous Australians). Over 65s are 4 per cent of the Indigenous population (compared with 16 per cent for non-Indigenous Australians).

The Indigenous population of Australia is projected to be 1.1 million by 2031.

Locating where Indigenous people live today

Indigenous populations were spread across Australia and the Torres Strait Islands when the Sydney Cove colony was started. But with the spread of settlement, many Aboriginal communities were moved off their traditional lands. They were eventually grouped together on missions and reserves, the edges of larger towns and in communities within cities. Torres Strait Island communities were left largely in place. But the start of missions on the Torres Strait Islands from 1871 also affected their cultural practices.

Today, many people imagine that most Indigenous people live in remote communities. However, the reality is quite different. Of the total Indigenous population, 37.4 per cent live in the cities (the largest Aboriginal community in Australia is in western Sydney). Another 45 per cent live in regional parts of Australia and 17.6 per cent live in remote areas.

The Torres Strait Islander population in 2016 was 70,880. This is about 9 per cent of the total Indigenous population. Only 28 per cent of Torres Strait Islander people live in the Torres Strait. A large group of Torres Strait Islander people live on the mainland, largely in Queensland but also in other parts of Australia. Torres Strait Islander people finish high school at higher rates than Aboriginal people. They also have higher employment rates and higher household incomes on average than Aboriginal people. And Torres Strait Islander people who live in the Torres Strait are more likely to finish high school and be employed than Torres Strait Islanders living in other parts of Australia.

Table 2-2 shows Australia's Indigenous population by state. The largest Indigenous populations are in New South Wales and Queensland. But in the Northern Territory, Indigenous people are by far the highest percentage of total population compared with other states. Interestingly, Tasmania has a relatively high percentage (given the common false idea that Tasmanian Aboriginal people were wiped out in the 1800s — see Chapters 7 and 20). Victoria has the lowest.

Table 2-2   Indigenous Population by State

State or Territory	Indigenous Population	Total Population	Percentage of Total Population	Percentage of Australian Total Indigenous Population
Australian Capital Territory	7,513	403,104	1.9%	0.9%
New South Wales	265,685	7,732,858	3.4%	33.3%
Northern Territory	74,546	245,678	30.0%	9.3%
Queensland	221,276	4,845,152	4.6%	27.7%
South Australia	42,265	1,712,843	2.5%	5.3%
Tasmania	28,537	517,514	5.5%	3.6%
Victoria	57,767	6,173,172	0.9%	7.2%
Western Australia	100,512	2,555,978	3.9%	12.6%
Total	798,365	24,190,907	3.3%	

Source: All data from the Australian Bureau of Statistics.

MYTH
BUSTER

Many people think that Aboriginal people and Torres Strait Islanders who live in cities have been *assimilated* into Western culture. In other words, people think that they have lost their connection with Indigenous community and culture. But even in Australia's cities, cultural relationships are strong.

Culture is important to the wellbeing of Indigenous Australians. This is according to data from the ABS and appears in the National Aboriginal and Torres Strait Islander Social Survey. This data shows that, among Indigenous Australians aged 15 years and over:

- 18 per cent spoke an Indigenous language. Another 20 per cent spoke some words of their language. And 11 per cent spoke an Australian Indigenous language at home as their main language. (See Chapter 3 for more on languages.)

- 62 per cent of Indigenous people knew the name of the clan they're descended from (79 per cent in remote areas; 58 per cent in other areas).

- 63 per cent of Indigenous people over 15 years and 70 per cent of children aged between 3 and 14 were involved in cultural events, ceremonies or organisations.

- 31 per cent of Indigenous children aged 3 to 14 years spent at least one day a week with an Indigenous Elder or leader.

A Note about the Torres Strait Islands

Possession Island, in the Torres Strait, is where Lieutenant James Cook 'took possession' of the whole of the east coast of Australia. This was 'together with all the . . . islands situated upon the said coast' in 1770. So the Torres Strait Islands were always part of the territory claimed for Britain. But the Islanders were mostly left alone until the London Missionary Society started its first mission on Erub (Darnley) Island in 1871. Queensland formally took over the Torres Strait in 1879. Communities in the Torres Strait Islands had to follow all the laws of Queensland, even though many of the islands are just off the coast of New Guinea.

Today, each island community elects its own council to run affairs on that island. This is a product of Queensland legislation from 1939. The administration for the region is based on Thursday Island. Fishing is the main economic activity, and many families also have small farms. Pearl shells, turtle shells, feathers and canoes were traditionally traded with neighbours. This trade still forms a basis for economic activity.

In 1978, Australia and Papua New Guinea signed a treaty to mark the boundary between the two countries. (Papua New Guinea had gained its independence from Australia in 1975.) The Torres Strait Islands Treaty allows for the free movement — without visas or passports — of Torres Strait Islanders and people from specific coastal villages in Papua New Guinea for traditional activities such as fishing, hunting, ceremonies and traditional trade within a defined zone of the Torres Strait Islands. Business and employment aren't considered traditional activities under the treaty and some quarantine limits apply.

REMEMBER

In 1982, a group of Torres Strait Islanders, including Eddie Mabo, made a claim for native title over their lands on the island of Mer. This island is part of the Murray Islands group in the Torres Strait. The case became known as the Mabo Case and it went all the way to the High Court. It succeeded in 1992 and gave a basis for Aboriginal people across Australia to make similar claims for their land.

In 1994, a Torres Strait Regional Authority was started to give Torres Strait Islanders greater ability to manage their own affairs. This body has representatives elected from the islands and allows management of affairs according to *ailan kastom* ('island custom' in Torres Creole). And freedom for the region is still on the political agenda.

In 2010, Justice Paul Finn of the Federal Court recognised the native title rights of Torres Strait Islanders over about 37,800 square kilometres of sea between the Cape York Peninsula and Papua New Guinea. These rights include the right to access, remain in and use the sea in those areas and to take resources, but not for commercial purposes. The finding doesn't keep others from using the sea.

Saying G'Day

Many non-Indigenous Australians are confused about the correct terms to use when addressing, or talking or writing about, Indigenous people. And that's understandable. Many different terms have been used by and about Indigenous people over the years. Some are downright offensive. Some reflect changing political attitudes and contexts. Some are simply a matter of personal preference.

When you meet and get to know an Indigenous person, the most appropriate thing to do is ask how that person prefers to be described or addressed. Sometimes mentioning a person's race isn't appropriate at all. But if you do need to refer to it, verbally or in writing, it's good to know what may or may not cause offence.

'Aboriginal', 'Torres Strait Islander,' 'First Nations' or 'Indigenous'?

Torres Strait Islanders come from the Torres Strait to the north of Cape York in Queensland. The term *Aboriginal* applies to Indigenous people from all other parts of Australia.

REMEMBER

The term *Indigenous* is commonly used to group together both Aboriginal people and Torres Strait Islanders. When writing this term, using a capital 'I' is important to designate that it's a nationality. Always capitalising *Aboriginal* is also important.

The letters *ATSI* are often used in abbreviations of organisations such as the Aboriginal and Torres Strait Islander Commission. However, using '*ATSI*' as an abbreviation when speaking of 'Aboriginal and Torres Strait Islanders' can cause offence.

Some Aboriginal people don't like the term *Indigenous* because it doesn't distinguish between Aboriginal and Torres Strait Islander cultures. They prefer to be called Aboriginal — or to use their Aboriginal nation. This can require the use of the term *Aboriginal people and Torres Strait Islanders* rather than *Indigenous people.* Increasingly, some Indigenous people are using the term *First Nations* to describe their unique relationship between themselves and the Australian state.

Some Aboriginal people prefer the use of the term Aboriginal *peoples,* rather than Aboriginal *people.* This notes the diversity of Aboriginal cultures across the country. And some Aboriginal people don't like the term *Aboriginal* either. They prefer to be referred to by their tribe or nation name or by an Aboriginal word (read on).

TIP

If you are addressing or introducing an Aboriginal or Torres Strait Islander person, ask how they would like to be referred to. They'll most likely appreciate the chance to define themselves rather than having someone do it for them.

'Aboriginal' or 'Aborigine'?

Although 'correct English' would have you believe otherwise, when describing an individual, saying, 'They are an Aboriginal' instead of 'They are an Aborigine' is more acceptable. Generally, Aboriginal people say, 'I am an Aboriginal person' or 'I am Aboriginal' instead of 'I am an Aborigine'. Think of it in terms of the use of the word *Australian*; for example, 'I am an Australian' or 'I am Australian' are quite acceptable in 'correct English'.

Aboriginal people and Torres Strait Islanders generally find the term *native* offensive. And, although Aboriginal and Torres Strait Islander people may call each other *blackfellas,* it's generally not a term used by anyone else.

Us mob: Koori, Goori or Murri; Noongar or Nunga?

Across Australia, Aboriginal people refer to themselves using words from Aboriginal languages. These are terms that refer to Aboriginal people collectively and are words that usually translate to terms like *us people,* such as:

- *Koori, Goori* or *Murri,* used in New South Wales

- *Koori,* used in the Australian Capital Territory

- *Koorie,* used in Victoria

- *Noongar* or *Nyoongar,* used in southern Western Australia

- *Nunga*, used in the southern part of South Australia

- *Murri*, used in Queensland and northern New South Wales

- *Palawa*, *Punta* or *Paganna*, used in Tasmania

- *Yolngu*, used in central and eastern Arnhem Land in the Northern Territory and *Anangu* in Central Australia

In New South Wales, Aboriginal people sometimes refer to white people as *gubbas*. Experts believe this came from the term *governor*. Another word used to describe white people in the south-east is *wundas*. This is an Aboriginal word for *ghost*. In the Top End of the Northern Territory, white people are sometimes called *balanda* (originally referring to the Hollanders — the Dutch — known to the Macassans who visited the region from Indonesia). In the Kimberley, *watjella* (which perhaps came from whitefella) is used.

Opening an Event: Welcome to Country

A *welcome to country* is a common custom whereby the traditional owners welcome people onto their land. *Traditional owners* are those who are recognised as being of direct descent of the original caretakers of that land. The welcome can take many forms. Usually the welcome comes through a speech, but it can also include dance or a smoking ceremony. The welcome is often in traditional language.

Having a welcome to country at public events has become a part of mainstream Australian protocol in the last decade. But Aboriginal people have been practising this custom for thousands of years. They clearly knew where the boundaries for their traditional lands were. Crossing onto someone else's land required permission — like a visa. In some Aboriginal societies, for example, lighting a fire on the boundary was the custom if you wished to pass over someone else's land. If members of the other group agreed to let you enter, they'd light a fire in return. Another custom was for gifts to be exchanged as a welcome to country.

Chapter 2: Rich Past, Strong Traditions

Permission to enter the land of another group was given with the understanding that that group's rules and customs would be respected.

Welcome or acknowledgement?

Often, a traditional owner of the area isn't present at an event to deliver the welcome to country. This means that a welcome to country can't be given because only the traditional owners can give that. Instead, an *acknowledgement of country* is given. This shows respect for the traditional owners and their relationship to their land.

REMEMBER

Not all Indigenous people can give a welcome to country. Indigenous people can give a welcome only on their own traditional land. If they aren't on their traditional lands, they must give an acknowledgement of country.

What do I say?

Many Australians and visitors give an acknowledgement of country before they begin the business of the event. A simple form of words for an acknowledgement of country would be

> *I acknowledge that I am on the land of [insert name of traditional owners] and pay my respects to their Elders past and present.*

Or

> *I would like to acknowledge that the traditional lands we are meeting on today are the lands of the [insert name of traditional owners] and pay my respects to their spiritual relationship with this country. I acknowledge their cultural beliefs and heritage and that they are the custodians of this land.*

If the traditional owners aren't known, a generic acknowledgement is acceptable:

> *I acknowledge the original inhabitants of this land, the traditional owners, and pay my respect to their Elders past and present.*

Or

> *I would like to acknowledge that this meeting is being held on Aboriginal land and recognise the strength, resilience and capacity of Aboriginal people in this land.*

Or

> *We acknowledge and respect the traditional custodians whose ancestral land we are meeting on today. We acknowledge the deep feelings of attachment that Aboriginal people have to country.*

TIP

Acknowledgement of country sometimes also includes a mention that this land and/or sovereignty was never ceded or that 'it always was and always will be Aboriginal land'. See Chapter 17 for more on these ideas of sovereignty.

Whose land am I on?

No maps of Aboriginal nations were drawn up in 1788 and many of these nations were dispossessed in the following decades. So exactly who the traditional owners of a particular area are and what its actual boundaries were isn't always clear. Sometimes disagreements arise. But even in the cities, traditional owners are identified.

Here's a list of some of the prominent language groups in the capital cities:

- **Adelaide:** You're on the land of the Kaurna people.

- **Brisbane:** You're on land of the Turrbal or the Jagera (also spelled Yuggera) people.

- **Canberra:** You're on the land of the Ngunnawal people.

- **Darwin:** You're on the land of the Larrakia people.

- **Hobart:** You're on the land of the Nuenonne people.

- **Melbourne:** You're on the land of the Wurundjeri people of the Kulin nation.

✓ **Perth:** You're on the land of the Noongar people.

✓ **Sydney:** You're on the land of the Gadigal people of the Eora nation. (This is only in the CBD area — it's a big city! The Eora nation is made up of 29 clans in total.)

One way to find out the traditional owners of a place is to check the website of the local Aboriginal and Torres Strait Islander organisations, particularly the land council. The website of the local council will often have information about the local Aboriginal community. In New South Wales, you can also phone the local Aboriginal Land Council. In the Northern Territory, you can contact the Northern Land Council or the Central Land Council. In north Queensland, contact the Cape York Land Council. In the north of Western Australia, contact the Kimberley Land Council. Land councils, as such, don't exist in every state but some Indigenous cultural groups may be able to help.

TIP

Another way to find the traditional owners is to check the *Aboriginal Australia* map published by the Australian Institute of Aboriginal and Torres Strait Islander Studies (AIATSIS). It's a large map and by no means easy to read in this format. But this gives you an idea of just how many nations and clans have existed. To buy a copy of the map, go to www.aiatsis.gov.au (under the Explore tab, click on the A Map of Diversity option).

REMEMBER

Indigenous languages were oral languages so correct spellings didn't exist. That's why more than one spelling of an Aboriginal nation or a Torres Strait Island people is often used. Variations in pronunciation among similar dialects also add to the confusion. For example, the Sydney people are the Gadigal people, also sometimes spelled Gaddigal or Cadigal.

Defining the Identity of an Aboriginal Person or a Torres Strait Islander

Governments have tried to define Aboriginal peoples and Torres Strait Islanders to figure out whether they should follow certain laws and rules. In the past, this practice has been mostly to control Indigenous people. Governments wanted to control where they could live, whether they could marry and whether their children should be removed.

However governments defined Aboriginality in the past and however they treated Aboriginal people and Torres Strait Islanders, Indigenous people have their own way of defining themselves. Identity is a product of family history and experience, languages and heritage, treatment by the rest of society and acceptance by the Indigenous community as being an Aboriginal person or a Torres Strait Islander. Aboriginality for Aboriginal people and Torres Strait Islanders is much more about their relationships than their percentage of blood.

The definition of Aboriginal people and Torres Strait Islanders for official purposes has changed over time. Three criteria are used today. (See the earlier section 'Defining who is an Indigenous person'.) But for decades, definitions were based on percentages of blood. 'Full-bloods' and 'half-castes' were treated very differently. From 1910 to the 1940s, people were defined as 'full-blood' if they had no white blood. They were defined as 'half-caste' if they had one white parent. They were defined as a 'quadroon' or 'quarter-caste' if they had an Indigenous grandfather or grandmother. They were defined as an 'octoroon' if their great-grandmother or great-grandfather was Indigenous. Today, these terms are considered offensive and racist by Indigenous people.

Proposals that genetic testing be used to identify who is Indigenous have been rejected on the grounds that race and ethnicity are social, cultural and political constructs so they can't be tested in this manner.

ABORIGINAL OR NOT?

Consistency wasn't always a hallmark of how Aboriginal people were treated. In 1996, at the Aboriginal Citizenship Conference in Canberra, historian Peter Read described the experiences of one Aboriginal person who was caught between two worlds:

In 1935, a fair-skinned Aboriginal man of part-Indigenous heritage was ejected from a hotel for being Aboriginal.

He returned home on the mission station to find himself refused entry because he was not Aboriginal. He tried to remove his children but could not because he was told they were Aboriginal. He walked to the next town where he was arrested for being an Aboriginal vagrant and placed on the local reserve. During World War II he tried to enlist but was told he could not because he was Aboriginal. He went interstate and joined up as a non-Aboriginal. After the war he could not acquire a passport without permission because he was Aboriginal. He received exemption from the Aborigines Protection Act — and was told he could no longer visit his relations on the reserve because he was not Aboriginal. He was denied entry to the RSL Club because he was Aboriginal.

This example shows how people could be refused access to services or other opportunities because they were Aboriginal, while also being controlled in other ways because they were 'not Aboriginal enough'.

Even when the laws were changed to remove these barriers, discrimination can be encountered. For example, a law now exists that bans landlords from refusing to rent places to people simply because they're Indigenous. However, Indigenous people in some areas still find renting a house hard. They're always turned down and told that a place is unsuitable or that it went to someone else. In some instances, to prove that the basis of the discrimination is their race, Indigenous people have gone into a real estate office and asked if rentals were available. After being told nothing was available, they have sent a white relative in to ask the same question, with that person handed a list of available houses. This situation is a breach of the law but that doesn't stop these practices of discrimination.

Stereotypes of Indigenous people

Stereotypes are caricatures of a group of people — often races or nationalities — that oversimplify and declare that those people display certain inherent characteristics. They're usually negative. Because they generalise and are meant unkindly, they are usually considered offensive.

Indigenous culture is seen as positive for tourism. Overseas visitors are interested in learning more about Indigenous cultures. Aboriginal peoples and Torres Strait Islanders and their cultures feature heavily in tourism commercials and other material. On the other hand, Indigenous people hear many negative comments from people who don't really know them.

MYTH
BUSTER

These negative stereotypes have no link to the lived experiences of most Indigenous people. Some Indigenous communities do have social problems. But these generalisations are wrong and offensive. Table 2-3 looks at the reality of some of these labels. See Chapter 20 for more on these and other myths about Indigenous people.

Table 2-3   Negative Stereotypes versus Reality

The Negative Stereotype	The Reality
Indigenous people are lazy and don't want to work.	Indigenous people are successful in areas as diverse as medicine, design and architecture, art, law, the public service and stockbroking.
Indigenous cultures are primitive and violent.	Indigenous cultures teach positive values such as respect for country and respect for Elders. They frown on violence, especially against women and children. These are the world's oldest living cultures.
Indigenous people, especially in the cities, have lost their culture.	Indigenous people, even in the cities, keep the positive values of their culture and keep cultural practices alive and vibrant.

The Negative Stereotype	The Reality
Indigenous people get more than whites.	Indigenous people have poorer health, lower levels of education, lower life expectancy, higher levels of poverty and lower incomes than other Australians. They don't get free houses and free cars.
Indigenous people are alcoholics.	Problems with alcohol do exist within Indigenous communities. But the communities themselves are at the front line of dealing with this social problem. Many have banned alcohol from their communities. They also have community-based programs to deal with alcohol abuse and its related problems. Per capita, more Indigenous people are teetotallers than are white people.

REMEMBER

Stereotypes aren't always negative. Positive stereotypes are caricatures that oversimplify and assert positive characteristics. Some positive stereotypes made about Indigenous people describe them as a kind of 'noble savage'. These stereotypes say that they're very spiritual, untouched by materialism, in touch with nature and can communicate with animals! Most people find these positive stereotypes just as offensive as negative stereotypes. Even though they're not meant unkindly, they're still generalisations, so are misleading and untrue.

But some of us have blond hair and blue eyes!

Some Aboriginal people from mixed heritage are very light-skinned. Some even have blond hair and blue eyes! This means that they aren't easily identified as Aboriginal people by non-Indigenous people.

Some Aboriginal people find guesses about their genetics offensive — and understandably so. In the past, genetics was explored only so it could be used to prove theories of white racial superiority. Some Australians say that light-skinned Aboriginal people aren't 'real' Aboriginal people. Some say that they just choose to be Aboriginal people because they can get benefits or it's trendy. These views don't consider the complexity of Aboriginal and Torres Strait Islander identities.

For Aboriginal people, their heritage is not just about skin colour. Their Aboriginality is also defined by their feeling part of the Aboriginal community and the Aboriginal community accepting them as Aboriginal. These additional aspects of being Aboriginal are recognised by the three criteria now used to define Aboriginality (refer to the earlier section 'Defining who is an Indigenous person'). As Indigenous woman Georgia Mantle has written: 'To me, my culture is not surprising . . . it is simply an intrinsic part of who I am. My Aboriginal identity is not represented through my pale skin, but rather through my very essence and being.'

PROJECT

Compare a map of Australia from 65,000 years ago to a map of Australia today to see how much the geography has changed. Consider the areas that were above sea level 65,000 years ago but aren't today, and how this might have affected how humans arrived in Australia.

PROJECT

Prepare an acknowledgement of country for the traditional owners of the land you live in that you might give at an event such as a school assembly. You can make a poster of your acknowledgement that shows distinctive features of the country you live on.

A Land of Cultural Diversity

IN THIS CHAPTER

- ✔ Taking in the special relationship that Indigenous people have with their lands
- ✔ Looking at the diversity of Indigenous nations across Australia
- ✔ Exploring the concepts of kinship
- ✔ Pondering Indigenous languages
- ✔ Examining trade and cultural connections
- ✔ Considering modern links to traditional country

The idea of land ownership didn't exist in traditional Indigenous societies in the same way as it did in European cultures. Aboriginal people and Torres Strait Islanders thought of their relationship to the land as being more like one of guardianship or custodianship. They believe they had — and continue to have — an obligation to their traditional land. To have the world's oldest living culture, surviving over 65,000 years, they must be doing a lot of things right!

This strong attachment to traditional country is a trait of Aboriginal and Torres Strait Islander cultures across Australia. But across the diverse landscapes of the continent were rich and varied nations. More than 500 different Aboriginal nations or language groups flourished. Their diversity of lifestyle was often shaped by the local environment. Aboriginal nations in coastal areas had a different way of surviving than those in the desert. Though they were spread out across the country, Indigenous groups still connected with each other. Through ceremonies and trade, they kept links with each other. These trade routes and songlines went across the whole country.

In this chapter, I explore those special relationships between Indigenous people and their country, and with each other. I look at the kinship systems that groups had. And I uncover some of the different languages and dialects that existed across the country — and which of them have survived.

REMEMBER

With over 500 different nations and language groups, a lot of diversity exists across Australia. In any general discussion about Aboriginal and Torres Strait Islander peoples, this diversity and nuance must be kept in mind.

Exploring the Indigenous Relationship to Land

Indigenous people have a strong attachment to their land. They had — and still have — a strong spiritual relationship with it. They also rely on it for their food, shelter and work. Indigenous societies didn't think of ownership like European cultures did. Their relationship to the land was more one of custodianship. In other words, the relationship of Indigenous people to their traditional land was based on their responsibilities to look after their country. They also had to hold certain ceremonies and to ensure that the ecosystems were kept in balance. And these responsibilities still exist today.

For Indigenous cultures across Australia, land means more than just something that's essential for physical survival. Spiritual life is strongly linked to land too. In this way, ancestral land had personal importance. Each person had to look after it. Other people's land had no meaning to someone who was a stranger to it. Conflicts over the boundaries of where one nation's land ended and another's began were rare. Some land was shared between different groups because of its spiritual or ecological importance. But, generally, a nation or clan had sole responsibility for each area of country.

CULTURAL PROTOCOLS

The relationship where Indigenous people believe they are guardians of their country is very different from European ideas of ownership of land. In the European concept, land can be bought and sold.

Oral title deeds

Indigenous cultures were oral. Attachment to the land was expressed through song, art, dance and painting. People 'inherited' stories and songs, and became their keepers. They passed them down to the following generations. Boundaries of tribal areas are fixed and are explained in these cultural stories. Through this storytelling, ancestral land was passed on to younger generations. The responsibility to care for this country was also passed on. Knowledge created an obligation to do the following:

- Protect the land

- Respect the past

- Not exploit the land's resources

- Take responsibility for passing the country on to future generations

- Keep the religious ceremonies that needed to be performed there

Accessing another's country

Entry onto the traditional land of another nation or clan was by ceremony and negotiation. A visiting group had to, in return, allow access to or through its lands. This rule is still seen today in the practice of acknowledging or welcoming outsiders onto country (refer to Chapter 2). These ceremonies symbolise Indigenous peoples' attachment to the land and their commitment to protect it. Special religious significance is attached to the resting places of great ancestors. These sacred sites have importance for women as well as men. In this way, the landscape was richly symbolic for the Indigenous people who lived on it.

Mythical stories noted appropriate behaviour and set standards. In this way, mythical beings were lawmakers. These standards were enforced by applying social pressure to ensure that everyone followed them. Children were taught acceptable behaviour through cultural stories and they were taught by example rather than by the strict discipline used to raise European children.

Celebrating Cultural Diversity

Aboriginal values and worldviews had similarities right across the country. But, as you may expect for such a large continent, there were regional differences between different clans and nations. Torres Strait Islander values and worldviews are like those of Aboriginal people on the mainland. But they are also influenced by interaction with other cultures such as the Papuans. Differences in language, art, cultural and religious practices, and social order occurred around the country. This happened especially between regions in different climates.

REMEMBER

Australia is a vast and mostly dry continent. Much of its interior is desert. But it's surrounded by coastline and has rivers and rainforest. Aboriginal people lived across the continent, in every corner and climate. They changed to survive in different environments. They did so by using different plants and food sources, and making the most of varying conditions. The Torres Strait Islands lie between the Cape York Peninsula and Papua New Guinea. The culture of the Torres Strait Islanders is defined by their heavy dependence on the sea.

CULTURAL
PROTOCOLS

An example of the different cultures throughout the country is that didgeridoos weren't played across Australia. These wind instruments were traditionally played only in the north of Australia, from Cape York in the east and Arnhem Land in the Top End of the Northern Territory, to the Kimberley in the north-west. And they were played only by men. The didgeridoo's first appearance in rock art is from a period about 2,000 years ago. This appearance led archaeologists and anthropologists to guess that this is when the instrument was first invented. The didgeridoo is now played by people across Australia — black and white. It appears in many modern musical forms, from country music to opera. (See Chapter 4 for more on didgeridoos. Flip to Chapter 13 for information about Indigenous music.)

CULTURAL
PROTOCOLS

The iconic dot painting style wasn't universally used across Australia. It was specific to the areas of the Central and Western Deserts in the middle of Australia. This style of painting is now blended into modern art by Indigenous artists across the country. See Chapter 12 for more on traditional art styles.

Clans and nations

Nations were large language groups. *Clans* were smaller extended family groups within a nation. Each clan had its own land and totems. Sometimes each clan had its own dialect of the common language of the nation. Although a clan had its own territory, members of one clan could live with another. Women who left their clan's country to live with their husband's clan kept their clan association with their father.

CULTURAL
PROTOCOLS

Nations share a common bond and language. Often, within that language the word for 'man' or 'person' is the word used for the nation. For example, in Arnhem Land, people are from the Yolngu nation and the name for 'man' in their language is *yolngu*.

More than 500 different nations

The British didn't know how big Australia was when they started the Sydney Cove colony. They thought some of the middle of the country might be filled with an inland sea. They also didn't really understand the governance structures within Indigenous communities and their relationships with each other. But the common estimate of the number of nations around Australia when the British arrived is between 500 and 600.

REMEMBER

An exact number of Indigenous clans and nations is difficult to arrive at. Why? Anthropologists often can't agree on whether a group was a clan or a nation. In some cases, identified clans that were classified as a subgroup of one nation now claim they're a separate nation, not a clan. The most commonly accepted and used map of the nations of Aboriginal Australia was developed by the Australian Institute of Aboriginal and Torres Strait Islander Studies (AIATSIS). Chapter 2 explains how to get a copy.

MYTH
BUSTER

The impact of colonisation on Aboriginal people was dramatic and their populations decreased quickly. By the early 1900s, many people thought that Aboriginal people would die out. In parts of Australia, some nations or clans were thought to have died out. For example, the last Aboriginal Tasmanian was long thought to have died in 1876. That was not the case, as Tasmanian traditional owners now say. (Refer to Chapter 2 for population statistics.) In many instances, Aboriginal people moved to other places to survive. They can today identify their nation or clan and its traditional lands and trace their heritage back to them.

CULTURAL PROTOCOLS

In the city of Sydney, local Aboriginal clans include the Gadigal and Dharug people of the Eora nation. In the city of Melbourne, the local Aboriginal clan is the Wurundjeri people of the Kulin nation.

Freshwater people and saltwater people

Another distinction exists among Indigenous nations. Even today, Aboriginal people sometimes call themselves either *freshwater* or *saltwater* people. In other words, they tell themselves apart by whether they live by the rivers inland or by the sea in coastal areas. Each group of people has a different style of living. Torres Strait Islanders, of course, are all saltwater people.

Aboriginal people on the coast were skilled at fishing. They used the sea and its animals to help themselves survive. Technology to build boats and nets, as well as spears for fishing, developed in these areas. Shells, fish bones and turtle shells were used to help make these tools. Turtles, dugongs, crocodiles and different fish all appear in the stories and ceremonies of the Aboriginal people and Torres Strait Islanders living off the sea.

Desert people

Aboriginal people living in the desert also learned how to live in their environment. For example, people had to remember carefully the location of sources of water. People also dug wells to access water. The locations of these watering spots were told through stories and songs. In many desert areas, few, if any, trees exist. Technology changed so that spears were made from the long roots of plants, rather than tree branches. Interestingly, the language of the Warlpiri people in the Northern Territory doesn't have any words for saltwater things such as ocean and waves. As desert people, the words in their language relate to their local area.

Kinship and Totemic Systems

Aboriginal people knew their relationships to others and the universe through their position in their group's kinship system. Then they used their identification with specific totems.

For many Aboriginal people, these kinship systems are still important. This is especially true for those in remote communities who still live by traditional laws and culture. Even in cities, relationships, and therefore roles and responsibilities, between people are crucial to social unity. Many educated and urban-dwelling Aboriginal people know their skin names and totems.

Moieties and skin names

Moieties are a form of kinship system where the people of a nation or clan were divided into two groups. (The term comes from a Latin word meaning *half*. It's definitely not an Aboriginal word!) Moieties can be decided by the mother's side (*matrilineal*), from the father's side (*patrilineal*) or can switch between each generation (*generational*). Each person belonged to one or the other moiety. This was important when it came to marriage. A person had to marry someone who was the other moiety to them. Otherwise, the partnership was considered a 'wrong-way' marriage.

TECHNICAL
STUFF

Often, the moieties were then divided into four to eight different kinship groups with a specific name for all members of each group — called kinship names or skin names. These names identified individuals as a member of that kinship group. Sometimes different names were used for male and female group members. Skin names are given at birth, according to the mother's skin name, along with other names. The subsections further identified different relationships within the clan or nation. Examples include mother to child, or uncle to nephew or niece, or potential marriage partners.

CULTURAL
PROTOCOLS

In Aboriginal cultures across Australia, social limits exist between some members of a group. For example, a man is banned from talking directly to his mother-in-law. Communication would take place through a third party. A mother-in-law would have a separate fire to her son-in-law and his spouse, with the daughter bringing over food. Some think this custom developed as a way to reduce friction in families!

Some clans or nations used both moieties and subsections. Some use just one or the other. Pitjantjatjara people, for example, only use moieties. These moieties and skin names give each person their totems (see the next section). Figure 3-1 shows the relationship between these elements.

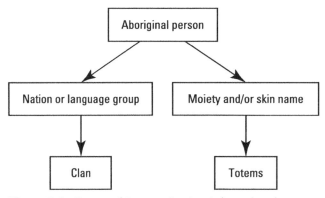

Figure 3-1: Geographic organisation is based on language groups, or nations. Social and spiritual organisation are based on a kinship system.

DHUWA DREAMING

The Yolngu people of north-eastern Arnhem Land are one of two moieties, Dhuwa and Yirritja. These moieties are then further divided into four skin names for each gender, making eight skin names in all. For people of the Dhuwa moiety, a particular Dreaming story is important. The story is about the Djang'kawu, who were the major creators of all things Dhuwa. Arriving from heaven in a canoe, the Djang'kawu sisters set off to walk across the land carrying digging sticks. When the sisters touched the ground with these sticks, they created the water, trees, animals and all other features of the Earth. The sisters were always pregnant and their children filled the Earth.

Totems

In addition to their place in the kinship system, Indigenous people have totems. A *totem* is an animal, plant or other object believed to be related to a person through their ancestors. People considered themselves to be descended from a totem. For example, they wouldn't eat the meat of any animal of their own totem. They would have to ensure that the animal's population was steady. A totem can also be represented in nature in the form of a large rock, tree, hill, river or other landform.

Indigenous people have three totems:

🖚 A clan totem that links a person to other people

🖚 A family or personal totem that links a person to the natural world

🖚 A spiritual totem that links a person to the universe

Through these totems, Indigenous people realised how they were connected with other people, their land and ancestors, and the universe. Figure 3-2 shows typical totems for an individual. Linking the natural and the spiritual world with people gave importance to totems as a source of Indigenous identity.

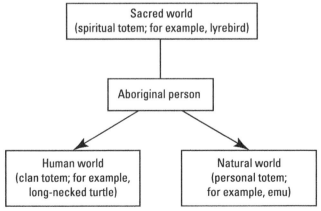

Figure 3-2: Specific totems link each individual with other people, the environment and the spiritual world.

CULTURAL
PROTOCOLS

Indigenous people believe they're related to their totems. For example, they believe that their ancestors were mythical beings who had the features of, or became, certain animals or trees.

REMEMBER

Much of Indigenous art is connected with the imagery of totems. Paintings tell stories of ancestral beings that may relate to a totem. Clans have a distinct pattern or marking that may appear in paintings as well. See Chapter 12 for more on Indigenous art.

Talking Languages

Many Indigenous people spoke at least two or three languages, and often five or more. Some languages were similar so learning a new language was easy. Others were different so they needed more skill to learn. Each nation had its own language and often clans would have a regional variation of it. Experts estimate that about 250 broad language groups were used when the Sydney Cove colony was started. Some of these language groups included more than one nation.

REMEMBER

Aboriginal and Torres Strait Islander cultures had an oral tradition, with nothing written down. This explains why different spellings of Indigenous words are common today, even for the names of Aboriginal nations.

Who speaks what now?

Australians speak more than 400 languages. In 2014, the second National Indigenous Languages Survey found that around 120 of the over 250 Australian Indigenous languages were still spoken. This number was down from 145 languages when the first survey was taken in 2004. Of the roughly 120 languages spoken in 2014, 100 are in major danger, and 13 were considered strong (still spoken by all age groups and passed down to children). During the period between the two surveys, 30 languages had seen an increase in levels of use. This showed a regrowth of Indigenous languages in some parts of Australia.

The 2016 Australian Census showed that 63,754, or around 10 per cent, of people who identified as Indigenous people reported speaking an Indigenous language at home. For some Indigenous people, English is their second or third language. The largest Indigenous language groups (not including the various hybrid languages, or *creoles*) are

- Djambarrpuyngu (4,264 speakers), north-east Arnhem Land

- Pitjantjatjara (3,054 speakers), northern South Australia and into Western Australia

- Warlpiri (2,276 speakers), north of Alice Springs

- Tiwi (2,020 speakers), Tiwi Islands

- Noongar/Nyungar (443), south-west Western Australia

- Wiradjuri (432), central New South Wales

- Ngarrindjeri (302), south-east of Adelaide

Here's the breakdown of Torres Strait Islander language speakers:

- Kalaw Kawaw Ya, also spelled Kala Lagaw Ya (1,216 speakers), central and western islands, with four dialects, including Mabuiag

- Meriam Mir (212 speakers), eastern islands

- Torres Strait Creole (5,800 speakers) across the islands

- Other Torres Strait languages (463 speakers)

BILINGUAL EDUCATION

Indigenous children who speak an Indigenous language as their first language can have trouble in English-only schools. They can fall behind in their learning compared with students who speak English as their first language. For this reason, some communities, particularly in the Northern Territory, have come up with bilingual educational models. (*Bilingual* means containing two languages, and in this case is used to mean English and Indigenous languages.) In this model, teachers learn the local languages and then use those languages to teach English. These bilingual educational models use a lot of resources and are not often supported by the government.

Vulnerability of languages

Sadly, many Indigenous languages have died out. More continue to be in danger. Of the 120 Indigenous languages spoken today, 100 are listed as 'critically endangered'. This figure has led to the creation of several programs to save languages. Indigenous publishing houses focus on printing materials that foster familiarity with Indigenous languages, such as teaching resources and bilingual books. (Check out Chapter 14 for details about Indigenous literature and publishing.)

Language centres have also been built to promote language in some Indigenous communities. Some of these projects include

- ✔ **Diwurruwurru-Jaru Aboriginal Corporation (Katherine Regional Aboriginal Language Centre**, www.kathlangcentre. org.au): The centre was started in 1992. It supports the needs of 32 language groups across 15 major communities in the middle of the Northern Territory.

- ✔ **Federation of Aboriginal and Torres Strait Islander Languages and Culture** (www.fatsilc.org.au): FATSILC is the national peak body for community-based language programs in Australia. It works to maintain, preserve and revive Aboriginal and Torres Strait Islander languages and culture.

- **Muurrbay Aboriginal Language and Culture Co-operative** (www.muurrbay.org.au): The Gumbaynggirr Elders of the Many Rivers area on the northern coast of New South Wales started this cooperative. Its goal is to revive and maintain language and culture in that area. The cooperative prints language dictionaries and teaching materials and supports the Many Rivers Language Centre, which helps those reviving languages from the Tweed to the Hawkesbury Rivers.

- **Yuwaalaraay gaay–Gamilaraay garay Language Project** (www.yuwaalaraay.org): This project focuses on recording, teaching and preserving Aboriginal languages in the north-west of New South Wales. The project has produced dictionaries and other resources. These resources include CDs and songbooks and online interactive teaching materials.

- **Bundjalung-Yugambeh Dictionary** (bundjalung.dalang.com.au/plugin_wiki/index.html): This project has been set up to revitalise the language of the Bundjalung community in northern New South Wales and southern Queensland. It includes a dictionary and teaching materials.

- **Wiradjuri Language** (www.wiradjuri-language.com): This site aims to help to revitalise the Wiradjuri language of central New South Wales. It has been led by the work of Elder Stan Grant Snr.

CULTURAL
PROTOCOLS

English as a second language for Indigenous people who speak their own language has always been difficult when they're in court. In the past, many Indigenous people have been convicted of offences when they couldn't understand what was going on, including the crime they were charged with. These days, courts are supposed to make sure that interpreters of Indigenous languages are available for Indigenous people charged with offences.

MIXING IT UP

Aboriginal English is a version of English that encompasses some regional Aboriginal words but also applies certain meaning to other English words. It's spoken across Australia because all Aboriginal communities have changed English words into their own everyday use.

Popular words in Aboriginal English include the following:

- Deadly: Great, good, awesome — as in, 'That's deadly!' or 'Too deadly!'
- Mob: Family, kin — as in, 'Who's your mob?'
- Shame: Embarrassed — as in, 'I was real shamed'.
- Gunjies: Police — as in, 'He was picked up by the gunjies'.
- Gubbas: A non-Aboriginal person — as in, 'I went to the part of town where the gubbas live'.

Coming Together

Indigenous nations and clans came together for large gatherings and ceremonies regularly. But no sense of a national identity grew out of these gatherings. That came after colonisation when Aboriginal peoples and Torres Strait Islanders joined together at a national level for a stronger political and cultural voice.

REMEMBER

Aboriginal nations and clans had strong networks with each other across the country. These networks were often based on trade. They were also a way in which kin relationships were strengthened. Cultural and spiritual practices also connected nations across the country. People came together to perform ceremonies and exchange stories and songs. A lot of contact also existed between Aboriginal nations of north Queensland and Torres Strait Islanders, as it does today.

Trade routes

Not surprisingly, Indigenous peoples traded with each other. Practices of exchange took place between clans and between nations. So trade routes developed around the country. Goods — stones, tools, ochres, shells and fish bones — could find their way from the north all the way to the south. Or goods could travel from the east coast across to the west. Trade also needed people of different clans and nations to respect each other's land boundaries. Trade links connected nations right across Australia.

Changes in sea levels sometimes led to new chances for trade. While Australia was an isolated continent, there is proof of contact, such as tools, whale bones and shells, between the Torres Strait Islanders and peoples of mainland Australia. There is also proof of contact between the peoples of the Torres Strait and Papua and Indonesia. Bones of animals from the northern parts of Australia were found in the southern parts. Shells from coastal areas were used in the desert. All of this is proof of trading across large areas of country and by many different nations.

Tasmania was cut off from mainland Australia by rising sea levels 11,000 years ago. The Aboriginal people living there lived without contact with the outside world.

Songlines

Tools and cultural items weren't the only things that travelled across the country. Ideas, songs and ceremonies were also exchanged. This happened in a network of routes that followed the relationships between different nations.

These routes are often called *songlines*. They would often track the journeys of ancestral beings (Dreaming tracks). They were recorded in traditional songs, painting and dance. A songline could span several nations or language groups.

CULTURAL
PROTOCOLS

Songlines are not easily translated into western concepts. A great way to find out more when travelling to different parts of Australia is to go on a cultural tour with a local Aboriginal or Torres Strait Islander guide.

Maintaining Links to Traditional Country

Today, Aboriginal peoples and Torres Strait Islanders keep their connection to the land in many ways, even if their traditional life-styles have disappeared or changed. They have kept this connection through groups such as land councils and through schemes to buy back control of land. Co-management of natural environments through agreements over national parks is another way. Here are just some of the ways these connections are kept alive:

- **Ranger programs:** Aboriginal and Torres Strait Islanders across the country care for their traditional country through ranger programs. They use a blend of cultural knowledge and modern technologies to keep the country, waterways and seas healthy. They help preserve the diversity of the ecosystem, plants and animals. They also do important *biosecurity* work, preventing the introduction and/or spread of disease to the plants or animals of a particular region.

- **Engaging in ecotourism:** Some Indigenous people run cultural centres, tour groups that focus on art (such as dance and storytelling performances) or bush tucker, and even fancy resorts at such places as Uluru and Kakadu. This is a way to provide an economic base for their communities.

- **Hunting, gathering and fishing:** Many Indigenous people add to their diet by hunting, fishing and collecting bush tucker (see Chapter 4 for details). Traditional land, waterways and seas, where Indigenous people have some form of land tenure, let Indigenous people hunt and fish certain species, for personal or community use, that are otherwise protected.

- **Maintaining obligations to care for country:** Some communities work with government to manage national parks. Many Indigenous people also work as rangers in national parks and reserves.

- **Practising ceremonies:** Many different ceremonies are still practised. These include welcomes to country (see Chapter 2), smoking and *sorry business* (funeral) ceremonies, and ceremonies on sacred sites.

Aboriginal land councils

In most states and territories, some pieces of land have been granted back to Aboriginal peoples or Torres Strait Islanders. Sometimes, these grants have limits on land use. But other times, Indigenous people can use the land as they wish. This use can be for cultural and ecological purposes (such as performing ceremonies), for hunting, gathering and fishing, or for preserving the environment. Other uses are economic or community-based. These include development, tourism, business, community centres and housing.

The return of land rights under legislation is usually done through Aboriginal land councils. These are groups through which Aboriginal people can hold, own and manage their interests in land. The largest land council in Australia is the New South Wales Aboriginal Land Council. It has more than 23,000 members. This body is statewide but has a network of more than 120 local Aboriginal land councils. With the council executive elected by the Aboriginal members, it's Australia's largest representative body of Aboriginal people.

Other key land councils are the Northern Land Council and Central Land Council in the Northern Territory, the Kimberley Land Council in the north of Western Australia, and Carpentaria Land Council and Cape York Land Council in north Queensland.

Indigenous Land and Sea Corporation

The Indigenous Land and Sea Corporation was started by the federal government to buy land and invest in projects that help with economic development in Aboriginal communities. The corporation was started in 1995 as part of the government's response to the Mabo native title case brought to the High Court by Torres Strait Islanders, including Eddie Mabo. The fund was set up to pay back Indigenous peoples who had been dispossessed so long ago that they could no longer claim native title.

Projects funded by the Indigenous Land and Sea Corporation have included the following:

✓ Working with the federal government, listing more than 38 Indigenous Protected Areas, covering more than 23 million hectares, where arrangements are in place to ensure Aboriginal involvement in protection of sacred sites, management decisions and job opportunities, particularly as rangers

✔ Jumbun Farm in Queensland, a 244-hectare property that supports a community of 130 Aboriginal people, 26 houses, a community store and a health centre

✔ Purchase of the National Black Theatre site in Redfern, Sydney, to be used by local Aboriginal radio and other community groups (see Chapter 15 for more on the Black Theatre)

✔ A commercial fishing venture to support the Ngarrindjeri owned Kuti Co in South Australia, to harvest small clams known as pipis

✔ The Kakadu Plum Project, which supports the Indigenous community to work with commercial harvesting of this unique, highly nutritious food

SHARING THE RICHES OF ULURU

In November 1983, the Hawke Government announced that the title for Uluru-Kata Tjuta National Park would be handed back to the traditional owners. (Uluru is also known as Ayers Rock but the park also includes Kata Tjuta, also known as the Olgas.) The official handover ceremony was held on 26 October 1985. The traditional owners then leased the land back to the Australian National Parks and Wildlife Service. This service is now the Australian Nature Conservation Agency (ANCA). The traditional owners work with ANCA on the planning and management of the park. This includes managing use of the park by Aboriginal people, protection of sites of cultural significance and nature conservation.

The Indigenous Land Corporation recently bought the Yulara resort near Uluru. The purchase included all the hotels, tourist and staff lodging, and the airport. The purchase meant the return of 104,000 hectares of culturally significant freehold land to the traditional owners, the Anangu. They play a continuing role in operating and managing the resort. The Anangu already co-manage the Uluru-Kata Tjuta National Park. This park has more than 300,000 visitors every year. The purchase of the Yulara resort by the Aboriginal community allows for a cultural and environmental tourism experience at Uluru-Kata Tjuta National Park. It will also provide jobs and training for Aboriginal people in the local area.

The relationship between the Aboriginal community and tourists hasn't always been easy. Climbing the rock was a popular tourist activity. But the traditional owners found this offensive and a desecration of a sacred site. They lobbied to have walking on the rock banned. On 26 October 2019, the 34th anniversary of the Uluru handback, the climb was officially closed.

National parks

Thousands of national parks and other conservation reserves exist in Australia. They protect many environments. They range from deserts to rainforests, and from coral reefs to eucalypt woodlands. Co-management plans often include

↙ Community involvement in decisions

↙ Jobs and training as rangers and guides

↙ Identification and preservation of sacred sites

Almost all national parks have an Indigenous program and Indigenous rangers. You can find out more about the local environment and its Indigenous history by taking a cultural tour.

CARING FOR COUNTRY, CARING FOR SEA

GhostNets Australia (www.ghostnets.com.au) is an alliance of 22 Aboriginal communities surrounding the Gulf of Carpentaria. They pull back fishing nets that have been thrown out at sea, largely from South-East Asia. These 'ghost nets' still trap fish and other marine life, destroying species and habitats. The program has recently spread across the northern coastline to the Kimberley. The project has removed over 14,000 nets across about 1,500 kilometres of coastline. It has saved some of the trapped marine life. Most animals trapped (52 per cent) are turtles. The rest are mostly sharks, as well as crocodiles, fish, sea snakes and dugongs. The Aboriginal communities involved see the program as just one way in which they can care for and meet their responsibilities to look after their coastal environment.

PROJECT

Look at one of the websites dedicated to strengthening the use of an Aboriginal language listed in the section 'Vulnerability of languages', earlier in this chapter. Learn to say a few phrases.

PROJECT

Go on an Indigenous cultural tour in your local area or a nearby national park.

Traditional Cultural Values and Practices

The relationship that Aboriginal peoples and Torres Strait Islanders had — and continue to have — with their land created particular worldviews and values. The need to survive in a hunter-gatherer lifestyle led to depending on nature and other members of the clan. This came with a strong belief in the importance of peace and connection.

Indigenous people became tuned in to the world around them. They became aware of where to find water, food and medicines in nature. They also became skilled at making tools to help with cooking, hunting, fishing and getting medicine.

In this chapter, I look at the sense of social unity that remains a great strength for Australia's Indigenous peoples. I describe traditional practices and how they led to both survival and harmony in Australia's sometimes challenging environment. I examine the amazing technologies that Indigenous people came up with. And I look at modern values in Indigenous cultures.

Going Back to the Dreamtime

The *Dreamtime* is sometimes also called the *Dreaming.* This name is given to the period when, according to Indigenous cultures, the world was created. The Dreamtime is really important to Indigenous worldviews and spirituality. Aboriginal people across the country and Torres Strait Islanders in the north share similar ideas. But some practices apply to one or the other.

Traditional belief was that the Earth and sky always existed and were home to supernatural beings. When the sun first shone, animal shapes came out in the form of humans. This is why, in many Dreamtime stories, people turn into animals and the creatures' features are explained. For example, the stingray was created, according to one story, by a man falling from a cliff onto rocks. This explains why the stingray is flat. His tail, this story explains, is supposed to be what's left of his spear.

As these beings moved around the Earth, they created the Earth's features and things such as stars and the moon. Their trips across the landscape are often called *Dreaming tracks.* Some landscapes are linked with the Dreaming of a particular animal. Examples are Honey Ant Dreaming or Kangaroo Dreaming. These Dreamings have special meaning to people conceived or born in that country. Indigenous people believe they came from these supernatural people and creatures. They trace their ancestry back to these people and creatures.

Many of these beings came back to the Earth. They often did so in important and sacred sites such as waterholes or caves. Others were turned into animals or physical features, such as mountains and rock formations. In this way, the landscape has rich meaning for Indigenous people. They can look out over their country and see reminders of the stories of their Dreaming.

REMEMBER

The Dreamtime refers to a period of creation. But it isn't seen as simply occurring a long time ago. Indigenous people have a different concept of time than Europeans do. They believe that the stories and characters of the Dreamtime are strongly linked to the present. They are even believed to help in determining the future.

TIP

Indigenous cultures have a lot in common. But they also have a lot of differences. It's important not to generalise. A good way to appreciate the distinctiveness of an Indigenous culture is to listen to local Elders. You can also take a cultural tour with an Indigenous guide.

Aboriginal leader and Yolngu Elder Silas Roberts described the Dreamtime in this way:

> *Aboriginals see themselves as part of nature. We see all things natural as part of us. All the things on Earth we see as part human. This is told through the ideas of Dreaming. By Dreaming we mean the belief that, long ago, these creatures started human society. These creatures, these great creatures, are just as much alive today as they were in the beginning. They are everlasting and will never die. They are always part of the land and nature, as we are. Our connection to all things natural is spiritual.*

MYTH
BUSTER

Dreamtime obviously isn't an Indigenous word. The term is traced back to anthropologist Baldwin Spencer. He noted that the Arrernte word *altyerre* means both 'time of creation' and 'dream'. So he came up with the word 'Dreamtime'. In most other Aboriginal languages, no similarity exists between the words for *dream* and *creation.*

How was the world made?

All Aboriginal and Torres Strait Islander groups had their own theories about how the world came into being and where people came from. There are similarities between these theories across the country. For example, everyone had a creation spirit. But there are some differences.

Indigenous peoples believe that the sky and Earth always existed but didn't have any features. In many places, the spirit of creation can be found in a snake that wove across the landscape creating its form. In other places, the spirit is a crocodile. In some places, this spirit is linked to the rainbow (and so called the *rainbow serpent*). And, in some places, the spirit was a female spirit.

The southern sky

The sky is also believed to be where ancestral beings live. In some Indigenous cultures, souls also go to the sky after death. Just as with creation stories, many different stories explain the placement of stars in the southern sky.

Different constellations are related to different myths. Many Indigenous groups believe that the Milky Way is a heavenly river or stream. In other parts of the country, the Milky Way is believed to be the sparks and fire from the campfires of ancestral beings that live in the sky.

REMEMBER

Indigenous people were as skilled at reading the sky as they were at reading the landscape. Both were used as important tools in travelling. Changes in the location and look of objects in the night sky showed seasonal changes. So did changes to plants and animal habits.

HOW THE ECHIDNA GOT ITS SPIKES . . .

In the Kamilaroi language, *biggi billa* is the word for echidna. The following story may sound like a simple account of how this creature got its spikes. But a bit more is going on:

Back in the Dreamtime, there was a terrible drought and the people were hungry. There was little food so, even when people had shared what they had managed to catch and find, they were still hungry. Everyone was getting thinner and thinner, except one old man. So one night, after they had shared some small fish that had been all the food they could find, the other men followed the old man back to his camp.

From the bushes, they could see the old man over his fire. And they could see, just as they smelt the sweet smell of cooking meat in the air, that the old man was eating a big piece of bundar (kangaroo) from one he had killed and kept to himself.

The men were mad and came to beat the old man who had broken the law with his selfishness. As he crawled away, his legs broken, the men threw spears at him. The old man crawled over the land, his spears turned to spikes, and his legs faced inwards because of the broken bones. You can see them in the footprints of the biggi billa, who is forever a reminder of the selfishness of the old man.

The story explains the important value of the need to share with others. It warns of the punishment and loneliness that can come from not working with the rest of the clan for survival. It also reminds people of the distinct tracks left by the echidna in the soil due to the positioning of its feet.

An oral tradition of storytelling

Aboriginal and Torres Strait Islander cultures were rich with storytelling. Dreamtime stories are often told today as though they're children's stories. But they were told with different levels of detail, depending on the maturity of the listener. Values, laws, responsibilities, history and cultural practices were all recorded in stories told orally. These stories were often told sitting around a campfire or in ceremonies.

Some stories told of how certain parts of the landscape were formed. Other stories told of how certain animals came to have their distinct traits. They could remind people where food or water supplies were. They could note important relationships with other clans and nations. They could record how ceremonies were to be held. The stories could also explain important values such as the need to share and the importance of respecting nature.

CULTURAL
PROTOCOLS

Dreamtime stories had important cultural value. That's why often strict rules were in place about who could tell and who could hear stories. Some stories could only be told by people of certain status within the clan. Others could only be heard by those who had been through certain stages of initiation. If the stories were about 'women's business' or 'men's business', they weren't to be told to people of the opposite sex. (See the later section 'Separating women's business from men's business'.)

Stories may have other purposes too. For example, there were scary tales about evil figures or dangerous creatures in a waterhole or hiding in the dark. These stories made sure that children stayed out of important water sources, so as not to get them dirty. They also made sure that children stayed near the campfire at night so they didn't wander off and get lost or hurt.

CULTURAL
PROTOCOLS

Indigenous peoples had no written language. So messengers were often sent off with a message stick. This stick was carved in a way that would help with memorising the message. The stick also proved that the person with the message was for real.

Indigenous Worldviews

To survive, Indigenous people's lives were closely linked with their natural environment. They were tuned in to what was happening in the world around them. They knew about the seasons, the paths of the stars, and the movement of fish, birds and animals.

Living closely with nature, and needing it for survival, led to certain values and worldviews. These values and worldviews showed the need to work closely with nature, and with each other. Common ideas included reciprocity (giving something in return for something else), respect for Elders, respect for the different roles of women and men, and, of course, respect for the environment.

Parts of Aboriginal and Torres Strait Islander worldviews can be understood from the values and beliefs that shaped traditional culture. They continue to shape those communities today.

Sharing based on reciprocity

A strong value within Aboriginal communities and Torres Strait Islander communities was that people should share their resources, tools and food. They should help each other when needed. In exchange, people could expect that others would give help when it was needed and share what they had. This is the idea of *reciprocity.*

Think about the size of clan groups and the need for families to work together to keep everyone fed and looked after. Given that, reciprocity being so important isn't surprising. This need also placed the key job on the healthiest to look after the more helpless within the group. These included the young, the old, and the sick. Even today, this idea that you help others in your family and community is strong.

**CULTURAL
PROTOCOLS**

Aboriginal people treat extended family the same as close family. In traditional culture, the term 'mother' was used for aunts as well as a child's birth mother. The term 'father' was used for uncles as well as the birth father. Quite distant relatives are called 'uncle', 'aunt' or 'cousin'. This latter practice is still used today. It makes for a huge family!

Respecting the wisdom of Elders

Older people are the custodians of Indigenous cultures. In traditional society, they were respected for their wisdom. Someone being old didn't mean that she had status as an Elder, though. The position came from respect for someone's cultural and moral knowledge. Elders had a strong role to play in the decision-making of the community. They were often asked for advice. Their role was important in determining cultural matters. One example is deciding whether certain people could marry each other or not.

**CULTURAL
PROTOCOLS**

Today, there is strong respect for the wisdom of Elders. They are the people who can do a 'welcome to country' (refer to Chapter 2). A proper 'acknowledgement of country' recognises Elders, past and present. At Aboriginal community events, careful thought is often given to Elders. For example, a special 'Elders' tent' may be set up where they can sit in comfort.

TIP

When people are revered by the community and given the status of Elder, they are called 'Aunty' or 'Uncle' as a sign of that respect.

Separating women's business from men's business

Indigenous cultures had certain roles for men, such as hunting, and for women, such as food gathering and raising children. Cultural stories and spiritual life were also split into matters for men only and for women only. Decisions around birth were for women. Initiation of boys was mostly the duty of men. Girls' initiation was the duty of women.

The roles of men and women are still called *men's business* and *women's business.* At large events, in many Aboriginal communities, the women are commonly seen in one area and the men in another.

REMEMBER

Male and female roles in Indigenous cultures were specific. But the idea behind the separation is not one of women being lower in rank than men. In Aboriginal society, female Elders can have as much impact — or even more — as male Elders. They take part in key decision-making processes of the community.

The role that women had in traditional Aboriginal culture was challenged by the colonisation of Australia. Their status was also challenged by the introduction of European values and views about the role of women. Today, some people think that Aboriginal culture always was okay with violence and other forms of oppression against women. Others say that the impact of European culture has worn down the power that Aboriginal women traditionally had in their communities.

Respect for the environment

Living so closely with nature over tens of thousands of years has created a deep feeling of being connected to the environment.

Indigenous people believe that you need to keep the ecosystems that provide the basics for life (food and shelter) healthy. Why? You need them to live. The air needs to be clean because you breathe it. Water needs to be clean because you drink it. Food and plant sources need to be strong and healthy because you eat them.

Indigenous people and their communities are becoming more involved with development on their lands. More Aboriginal people and Torres Strait Islanders live in cities. But a strong link still exists between people and land. Indigenous people are concerned about nature. They take part in activities that make sure it stays cared for and healthy.

A key part of Indigenous cultures gives respect to the land. This respect notes the role the land plays in creating and supporting life.

Living with Nature

Aboriginal people didn't farm or tend to the soil for crops in a large-scale way. They were mostly hunter-gatherers. They grew tubers such as yams, grain such as native millet, macadamia nuts, fruits and berries. But their farming has been called an activity, not a lifestyle. They did, however, know a lot about their ecosystems. They were careful to make sure those systems were in balance. They also used many things in their natural world to help with their survival.

Torres Strait Islanders did have forms of farming on their islands. Their land was clearly marked for different family groups.

Ecosystems across Australia are vastly different. Geography and climate have changed over time. Indigenous people have adapted to these changes. Around 20,000 years ago, the last Australian ice age reached its coldest peak. This peak lasted for about 5,000 years. Aboriginal people had to change their practices to survive. The world was colder and drier. Aboriginal people moved into all parts of Australia, including the mountains, made changes and lived.

In the drier areas, groups were smaller and went farther to find water. In colder places, the focus was more on building shelters and making warm clothes. On the coast, where the land was richer, the environment could support more people. They depended more heavily on the sea and waterways for food and for items such as shells that could be used for tools.

Indigenous peoples knew when to burn certain areas for new grass growth and to attract kangaroos. (See the later section 'Fire' for more on this.) They knew what parts of plants could be eaten safely and how to prepare food that may be unsafe to get rid of its poison. Knowing the medicinal purposes of plants was important. So was knowing how to use natural products — bark, wood, grass, seeds and leaves — and parts of animals — bones, tissues and fur — for tools, clothing and shelter.

MYTH BUSTER

Indigenous peoples built neither cities nor monuments. So some Europeans described their societies as 'primitive'. This view compares Indigenous cultures only with technology in other parts of the world. It fails to note that Aboriginal cultures have been around for more than 65,000 years. Over that period, they managed all the major issues in a society. These issues include social unity, environmental matters, and population growth. Given this, some would argue that Aboriginal cultures are 'advanced' and other modern cultures are 'developing'.

Hunting and gathering

About 25,000 years ago, the large animals (also called *mega fauna*) living in Australia became extinct (or died out). These giant marsupials, birds and reptiles disappeared just like the dinosaurs did. Scientists are still figuring out whether this extinction was caused by humans or major climate change. In any case, Indigenous people lived with the large animals for thousands of years before the mega fauna died out.

Around the same time, Aboriginal people began using grindstones to better use seeds and other plant products. Hunting and gathering required deep knowledge of the environment to survive. The ability to adapt as ecosystems changed was important. Watching for hawks as they hunted small animals during bushfires helped to find game. In the Northern Territory, people built small horseshoe-shaped hiding places to help in hunting. Camouflage and imitation were also used in hunting. Bushes, grass and animal skins were worn. Human scents were hidden by covering the skin with mud.

Even today, many Aboriginal and Torres Strait Islander people add to their modern, store-bought diets with *bush tucker* — plants and small animals gathered for food. They also add to their diets through hunting and fishing. In areas such as Arnhem Land, Cape York and the Torres Strait, between one-quarter and two-thirds of the population take part in hunting and gathering. In these areas, bush tucker also is a big part of people's health.

Bush food

Indigenous people living in Australia before it was colonised were healthier than they generally are today. They had a better diet and ate more nutritious foods.

Many traditional foods are still eaten today. Indigenous people use knowledge, techniques and skills that have developed over tens of thousands of years. Some foods, such as kangaroo, emu and crocodile, are on fine dining menus around the world. Edible fruits, vegetables, flowers and seeds can all be found in the Australian bush. Here are some of the foods in the diets of Aboriginal people and Torres Strait Islanders:

- **Crayfish, yabbies, shrimps, mussels:** Caught with nets and by hand. Cooked in holes in the ground covered in ashes.

- **Cycad fruit:** Must be leached, pounded and baked to make sure the poisons and toxins are taken out before eating. Provides an important staple source of carbohydrate.

- **Ducks and swans:** Hunted with nets and cooked in coals.

- **Emus:** Captured with nets, spears, woomeras and boomerangs. Their feathers were removed and they were gutted. Then they were cooked in coals or under the ground. Their eggs were a delicacy.

- **Fish:** Caught using lines, bone hooks, nets, stone traps and spears. They were cased in mud and then cooked in ashes.

- **Grass and acacia seeds:** Gathered by hand, sometimes ground into a paste, and cooked in ashes.

- **Honey ants:** Honey ants store honeydew in their abdomens. In Central Australia, Aboriginal women know where to dig to find their underground nests. In the Top End, a green ant, also with a sweet abdomen, nests in trees.

🗸 **Kangaroos:** Hunted with spears, woomeras, clubs and boomerangs. They were gutted and skinned and then cooked in coals or under the ground. The tail was thought to be one of the tastiest parts. It's now cooked in a variety of ways, including in honey and soy sauce. The skins were used for clothing and tools.

🗸 **Mallee fowls, brush turkeys, galahs, pigeons and other small birds:** Caught in nets and cooked in underground ovens.

🗸 **Nectars:** Flowers from plants such as the grevillea, banksia and bottlebrush have nectars that taste sweet. Putting the flowers in water creates a sweet drink. Blossoms of some plants are ground in a coolamon, with water added to make a drink. (See the later section 'Baskets, buckets and coolamons'.)

🗸 **Possums:** Caught in hollow trees. They were gutted, skinned and cooked in coals. Their skin and fur were prized and used for clothes and tools.

🗸 **Quandongs:** The quandong tree, found in arid areas, has a large round fruit that can be eaten fresh or dried. It has a tart but nice taste. The seeds of the fruit have a rough texture. They are often strung together and used as body ornaments. The nutritious and oil-rich kernels are sometimes eaten after roasting. They also can be ground into a paste and used to treat skin problems or as a skin and hair conditioner.

🗸 **Snakes, lizards and frogs:** Tracked, often dug out and cooked in coals.

🗸 **Turtles:** Caught with nets. They were cooked either in holes in the ground covered in ashes or cooked in coals. Their shells were used for tools and ornaments. Eggs were gathered and eaten raw or boiled.

🗸 **Yams, shoots and wild onions:** Dug out from the ground and eaten raw, boiled or cooked in ashes. Sometimes they were pounded until soft and cooked as a paste.

🗸 **Water ribbons and water lilies:** Gathered from fresh water. Water ribbons are tubers and sweet when steamed. Water lilies have pods and seeds that can be eaten.

- **Wild honey:** Bees were followed back to their nests high in the trees, which were usually chopped down. Whatever was in the hive was taken out and placed in a paperbark container. (This container was later sometimes known as a sugarbag.)

- **Witchetty grubs:** Dug out of red gum trees and cooked in ashes.

- **Wombats, water rats and small animals:** Caught in traps and nets. They were cooked in holes in the ground filled with ashes.

CULTURAL
PROTOCOLS

Mutton-birds and their eggs are a traditional source of food for Aboriginal people in Tasmania. Many of the surrounding islands that have mutton-bird colonies have been returned to Aboriginal ownership. So they are still an important source of food and cultural practice.

Bush medicine

Living as hunter-gatherers brought many dangers. Burns from fires, eye infections, upset stomachs, headaches, tooth decay, stings from jellyfish and snakebite were all dangers that lay in wait. People also had accidents or were hurt in fights or while hunting. Indigenous peoples also believed that serious illness and death could be caused by spirits or sorcery.

Over tens of thousands of years, Aboriginal people have found plants, minerals and other materials from nature to help them treat injuries and illnesses. These items also help with good health. The range of medicines used herbs, animal products, hot water, coals, mud and massages. Chants or spells and special trinkets were also thought to have healing powers.

People often thought that sorcery or spirits caused illness. So some Indigenous people were trained as spiritual doctors. They were trained from an early age on spiritual matters. Then they grew to have great power within their communities. They performed certain rites. They also were thought to be able to see events in other places and into the future. They would sometimes use herbal cures in ceremonies. But they didn't treat health problems that weren't seen as caused by spirits or sorcery.

Day-to-day health needs were taken care of by women who knew a lot about the healing items in the natural world around them.

Some women were noted as having a certain skill at healing. Healing would often take place in two stages. First, women in the community would apply their knowledge. Then, if that didn't work, a senior woman who specialised in medicine would be asked for help.

Here are some common remedies:

- **Eucalyptus bark:** Could be made into a drink that would stop diarrhoea.

- **Green plums:** Used to stop toothaches and soothe sore eyes.

- **Lemongrass:** Used to create a wash to treat fevers and to treat diarrhoea if drunk. Its root could also be used to help cure sore ears.

- **Maroon bush, prickly fan flower, currant bush:** Has been used to treat heart disease, intestinal trouble, and kidney problems, among others. Some people claim it can help treat cancer.

- **Tea-tree, or paperbark trees:** Leaves breathed in to treat colds. Put on the skin to stop stings. Crushed in water to treat fevers. The bark was also used as bandages.

REMEMBER

No doses existed. Medicine was mostly applied on the outside of the body. Ointments were made by mixing crushed leaves with animal fat. There was little chance of overdosing.

TIP

Some natural medicines vary in strength, depending on the season. Lemongrasses were picked when they were still green. Green plum leaves were thought to be stronger if used during the dry season.

Tools

Aboriginal people have been living in Australia for about 65,000 years. Archaeological proof suggests that technology stayed about the same until about 10,000 years ago. The tools found from before that time were usually simple. Stone tools were used to carve other tools from wood. The wooden tools don't survive today because they decayed. But some stone tools have been saved.

About 5,000 years ago, a major change occurred in the stone technology. Tools with delicate points and blades were made. Some think that this feature came about because spears with stone points took the place of spears with wooden points. A spear-thrower was also made.

MYTH
BUSTER

Certain beliefs about the way Aboriginal people lived thousands of years ago are based on what's left of stone tools and campfires. But other technology was widely used as well. Aboriginal people had to be smart to survive. They used many things in their natural world to help. For example, resins from trees and plants were used for glue and shells for spearheads. String and rope were made from various fibres and woven into bags, mats and other objects.

Spears, spear-throwers and shields

Spears were used for hunting, fishing and fighting. Some were carved from a single piece of wood. Others used attached spear-heads made from materials such as stone, shells or wood. The spears of different materials were more popular and found throughout Australia.

Spear-throwers increased the force of a spear. Several different types of spear-throwers were made. But a common feature was a hook or peg fixed at one end where the spear was placed. *Woomeras* were a type of spear-thrower. They could be used for hunting, chopping wood, cutting tree branches and chopping meat.

Shields were also carved from wood. They were used in hand-to-hand fights. They were also used for protection against spears thrown from a distance. Shields were usually highly decorated.

MYTH
BUSTER

Spears were far from being weak weapons, as some may think. Spears used with a spear-thrower were the fastest weapons in the world before the invention of the self-loading rifle.

Baskets, buckets and coolamons

Containers were made from different materials, such as wood and bark. They were used for carrying food and water. Baskets could be made in many ways. One way was from two sheets of paper-bark stitched together. Baskets were used mainly as containers for food and for personal items.

String bags were a special type of basket. They were made in many ways, such as weaving and plaiting. They used materials such as hair, bark, reeds, grass and palm leaves. They could be folded up and stretched wide. Bags could be used to carry babies and food. If they were finely woven, bags could be used to sift seeds.

Coolamons were a popular type of curved container. They were popular in desert areas and made from the burl of a tree. (A *burl* is a dome-shaped growth on the trunk of a tree.) Containers could also be made from shells, leaves, bamboo and animal skins. They could be made from any usable materials in the local environment.

Boomerangs

Boomerangs were tools used for hunting or as weapons. They were invented over 10,000 years ago. A boomerang could kill a small animal and knock down a larger one. Carved from wood, they were used across most of mainland Australia. But they were not used in the north or in some of the central desert areas (Pitjantjatjara lands) or in Tasmania. They came in lots of shapes.

People in desert areas used the heavy wood of the mulga tree to make boomerangs. These boomerangs helped in hunting kangaroos. On the New South Wales coast, lighter boomerangs were made from mangrove trees. These were used for duck hunting. The two main types were returning and non-returning. Most were of the non-returning kind. The type that returns only comes back if it fails to hit its target.

MYTH
BUSTER

Most people don't think of Indigenous people when it comes to modern scientific invention. But David Unaipon, an Aboriginal man from South Australia born in 1872, noted the principles of boomerang flight to back up the upcoming invention of the helicopter. (See Chapter 14 for more on this writer and inventor.)

Didgeridoos

The *didgeridoo*, also spelled *didjeridoo* (and sometimes even *didjeridu*), was a musical instrument made from a hollowed branch eaten out by termites. This instrument was used only in the northern parts of Australia, in Arnhem Land, the Kimberley and Pilbara regions. It also was played only by men. The inside is smoothed out. A resin or gum from trees or plants is added at the narrower end to make the mouthpiece. See Chapter 13 for more on musical instruments.

Canoes

Canoes were used to travel rivers and coastal areas. They helped in hunting and gathering fish, eels, plants, birds and bird eggs. *Canoe trees* are trees with a visible scar from where a canoe was carved out of the bark.

Looking to the Skies

Indigenous people were astronomers with a strong understanding of the skies. Many cultural stories contain knowledge about the skies. Indigenous people know the sky as well as they know the land. Stars, the sun and the moon were used to travel across not only water but also land. They were also used to figure out when the seasons were coming. Objects in the sky often stood for beings such as people and animals. (They weren't seen as constellations as in Western astronomy.) Cultural stories around objects in the sky ensure that knowledge is passed down from one generation to the next.

In Indigenous astronomy, the Dark Emu is a formation in the sky that is not made of stars but from the dark space between them. This is an important concept. Why? It means the space between the stars is not empty but full. This theory links in with recent theories on dark matter and the universe. The position of the emu in the night sky notes when the emus are nesting. It also notes the best time to collect emu eggs.

TIP

Interest in Indigenous astronomy is growing. Observatories with public programs often have lectures or tours by Indigenous astronomers so you can learn more. One example is Sydney Observatory.

Controlling the Environment

Aboriginal people and Torres Strait Islanders came to understand nature because they lived so closely with it. Being hunter-gatherers required understanding the cycles and patterns of plants and animals. They also needed to know the timing of the tides and the seasons' cycles and patterns. Indigenous people also found ways to work with nature, or to get it to work for them, to help with their survival.

Indigenous people came up with methods that helped to control their environment. For example, they placed rocks in rivers and tidal areas to create fish traps. They used fire to help keep the ecosystems in balance. They also changed the landscape to make food collection easier. Knowledge of animals' travel patterns also helped ensure a steady supply of food.

Fire

Bushfires happen naturally. They are usually caused by lightning strikes. But Aboriginal people came to use fire as a way of managing their environment. Fire was used across Australia to clear undergrowth. This encouraged regrowth to attract animals. Fire also flushed out game. It was used carefully and has been called *firestick farming*. Indigenous fire technology uses a 'cool fire'. This type of fire is easily controlled and burns slowly. It is different from the 'hot fire' of an out-of-control bushfire.

In the Arnhem Land region of the Northern Territory, fires are lit during the cooler parts of the year. This cuts down on huge fires in the dry months. This is a continuing custom. Some experts believe that this practice helps with lowering greenhouse gas emissions.

Fire was made by two methods:

⌐ **The friction method:** Friction is created by drilling, sawing or ploughing.

- *Drilling* is where a pit is made in a softwood stick and another stick — or drill — made of harder wood is fitted vertically into the pit. The drill is spun by hand at a quick rate. The wood powder created starts to smoulder from the heat made by the friction. The smouldering powder is then tipped onto tinder and blown gently, which ignites it.

- *Sawing* is where the edge of a hardwood stick is drawn rapidly back and forth across a cleft stick. This creates heat similar to drilling.

- *Ploughing* is where a hardwood stick is rubbed along a groove in a softwood stick. Ploughing wasn't as widely used as the other friction methods.

✔ **The percussion method:** In this method, a flint is hit hard against stone, creating a spark. It was a less common method, used only in the central and southern parts of Australia.

Harvesting

Although Indigenous people were hunter-gatherers, they came up with ways to make the most of seasonal and temporary abundance of food. Aboriginal people are thought to have scattered seeds on purpose as they walked across their country. That way, they could harvest the plants the next season.

Some food, such as nuts and kernels, were stored. Strips of kangaroo meat or whale meat were sometimes dried. But in most cases, food was hunted and gathered for immediate use. Seasonal times of plenty were usually times of increased social togetherness and ceremony. They involved a lot of people from the region. For example, every spring, the bogong moth migrates from the west and north of New South Wales to the Australian Alps. While the moths gathered in their thousands, people from as far away as the east coast would come to harvest them. The bunya nut (like a chestnut and just as tasty) was a traditional food of the Aboriginal people in the rainforests of south-eastern Queensland. Aboriginal people went long distances to feast on the nuts that ripened in the summer.

Fish traps

Large and complex fish traps have been built in different parts of Australia. These traps of stones or plant fibres were built in coastal areas or tidal streams where fish were seasonally plentiful. Fish traps are still present in some places. These include the Torres Strait Islands, the Gulf of Carpentaria and in Brewarrina, in the north-west of New South Wales. Stone traps also were used in parts of Victoria to catch eels.

Middens

Middens often show the proof of community life. These were places where tools were made, fish were killed, shell necklaces were woven and meals were cooked. In some parts of Australia, middens were mound-like structures built with the bones of fish, dugongs or other objects.

TIP

These middens are of major cultural importance. They provide a lot of information about the practices of Indigenous people over thousands of years.

Shelter

Indigenous people built a range of structures for shelter. Natural places of protection from the weather such as caves could be used. But many different housing structures were also built. These included lean-tos. They involve the weaving of plants, and the use of plants with materials such as spinifex to make shelter. In several places such as in Victoria and in the Pilbara, stones were used to make house-like structures. The shelters used depended on the climate and the materials available. They highlight the diversity of cultures across Australia.

Modern Cultural Values

Today, Indigenous people still live across Australia in many different circumstances. Close-knit communities thrive in cities. Communities have grown on the outskirts of towns where missions or reserves once were (see Chapter 7). Some Aboriginal people live in remote communities and on remote *outstations.* This is usually where a family group sets up camp separate from the broader community.

Indigenous people in remote and rural communities still often add traditional food to their diets. But even in the remotest areas, where many traditional practices form a part of everyday life, Indigenous people use modern technology. People wear clothes, travel by car and use mobile phones and satellite technology.

There have been changes in technology and living conditions. But key aspects of Indigenous life remain. The connection and networks among families and communities remain strong. So, too, does connection to land, spiritual beliefs, and cultural and artistic practices. Part 4 covers modern culture in detail.

CULTURAL PROTOCOLS

When Indigenous people meet each other, they usually ask, 'Where are you from?' or 'Who's your mob?' This is often a way to see how they may be connected through complex community and extended family relationships.

So, are modern Indigenous and non-Indigenous people really that much different from each other? Describing the differences between cultures without making generalisations is never easy. But Table 4-1 shows a few cultural values that Indigenous people have noted to show how their cultures are different from European cultures.

Table 4-1   Comparing Indigenous and European Cultural Values

Indigenous Cultural Values	European Cultural Values
People live in groups and are connected	People are focused more on the individual
Ask 'Where are you from?', 'Who's your mob?'	Ask 'How are you?', 'What do you do?'
Only certain people can know some things	Knowledge is something for everyone
Women have an equal place around the campfire	Women had to fight for equality
Keep culture alive with storytelling	Write it down!
People are connected to their environment	The environment often has to make way for progress

Caring for Country

Today, large areas of Australia are looked after through Aboriginal and Torres Strait Islander ranger programs. These programs are successful in making sure that Indigenous people keep a link to their traditional country. They help make sure that Indigenous people meet their cultural duties to care for their country. They also help create jobs and ensure that the deep knowledge local communities have of their country are used to best care for the land. They use a range of traditional methods and modern technology to track and preserve species. They also study the health of ecosystems, undertake fire burning and clean the waterways.

TIP

You can find out more about the many ranger programs across Australia at www.countryneedspeople.org.au.

PROJECT

Read a Dreamtime story and see if you can see what the lessons in it are.

PROJECT

Make a poster of different traditional plants used by Indigenous peoples and identify their health and nutritional benefits.

PROJECT

Make a poster about the benefits of traditional fire technology practised by Aboriginal people.

Part 2
Invasion

In This Part . . .

☐ Find out more about the passing contact
between Indigenous peoples and foreign
voyagers, both from Europe and from the
islands to the north.

☐ Examine how international law at the time
gave the British what they thought was
the right to take the land of Indigenous
people — and how Aboriginal people had a
very different view.

☐ Trace the spread of the British colony at
Sydney Cove, with new colonies established
around Australia, and the increasing conflict
between Aboriginal people and the colonists
as they battled for land, water and food.

☐ Understand the ideas behind policies that took
children from their families, and the tragic
effects of these policies.

First Contacts

James Cook claimed most of the east coast of Australia for the British in 1770. But he was not the first European to meet the Indigenous people of the country that became Australia.

The Dutch and the French had been interested in the great land to the south. But they hadn't pressed their claims over it the way the British wanted to do. Plenty of proof also exists of strong connections with nearer neighbours. These include the Macassans to the north, from what's now known as Sulawesi in Indonesia. They also include the Papuans, who still have close connections with the people of the Torres Strait Islands.

Indigenous people were curious about their visitors. But they also had an interest in developing trade relationships with them.

In this chapter, I go over some of these early visits and the British aims for the great southern land. They set the stage for what was to become a strong and independent multicultural nation, though not before great loss for the country's Indigenous people. I also look at what's known of Aboriginal people's responses to these first contacts.

Looking for the Unknown Southern Land: Contact before 1770

The British started the first colony in Australia. But they weren't the first to find their way to the Unknown Southern Land (*Terra Australis Incognita*). Aboriginal people for the most part lived in this land, and Torres Strait Islanders lived on the islands between Cape York and Papua.

Long before the British came, trade links existed with the Macassans and the Papuans. And, as Europeans started to colonise the globe, they found their way to Australia. Dutch sea-farers sailed and mapped parts of Australia. Historians also believe that explorer Luis Vaez de Torres, working for the Spanish Crown, saw Australia as he sailed through the Torres Strait in 1606. In the 18th century, after Cook's claim on Australia, several French explorers also visited various parts of the continent. They include Marc-Joseph Dufresne in 1772, Jean-Francois de Galaup (he added Lapérouse to his name) in 1788 and Bruni d'Entrecasteaux in 1792.

Such meetings saw curiosity from both sides, even if not all the encounters were peaceful.

MYTH
BUSTER

Portuguese sailors possibly knew of the Australian continent in the 1500s. Sixteenth-century Portuguese maps show a land mass like Australia called 'Java la Grande'. There is similar guessing about visits from the Chinese in the 15th century. This was sparked by the discovery in 1948 of a statuette from the Chinese Ming period (which ran from 1368 to 1644) near Darwin in the Northern Territory. But by 1878, the Chinese population was larger than the European population in the Northern Territory. In 1888, the Chinese population numbered 6,122. They worked on building railway lines and on the goldfields. So, the statuette may have been owned by one of these early workers rather than Chinese seafarers.

Meet the neighbours: The Macassans

The Macassans are indigenous people from what is now Indonesia. They were skilled at sailing and living off the sea. They routinely visited Australia as part of a trading cycle that depended on the seasonal monsoon winds. The Macassans collected items such as sea cucumbers, sea turtles and their shells, and trochus shells.

They sailed to Australia in boats called *praus* and then fished in dugout canoes. Some of these canoes were traded with Aboriginal people. Aboriginal men would sometimes sail with the Macassan fishermen. Tools such as knives and axes, pipes and fishhooks were also traded for tortoise shells and pearl shells. The Macassans collected plants and wood from Australia, especially to help fix their ships. Macassan words also became part of some Aboriginal dialects, such as words for the points of the compass, some words for tools and words for boat parts.

Remains of Macassan campsites on the northern shores of Australia have been dated back to over 800 years (see Figure 5-1). Tamarind trees still mark these spots, where Macassan fishermen dropped the seeds during their visits. Trade between Aboriginal people and the Macassans continued until it was stopped by the Australian government in 1906.

Figure 5-1: A Macassan fireplace at Bremar Island in the Northern Territory.

Aboriginal people and Torres Strait Islanders noted their contact with the Macassans by referring to them in ceremonies. They also showed the Macassans in rock paintings.

Papuan people regularly travelled to Arnhem Land, Cape York Peninsula and the Torres Strait. Papuan language and culture had an especially strong impact in the Torres Strait. Canoes, masks, spears and ornamental weapons were traded. The Torres Strait Islands Treaty, signed in 1978, made this relationship formal. (Refer to Chapter 2 for more on this treaty.)

The Dutch were here

The first recorded contact between Europeans and Aboriginal people and Torres Strait Islanders in Australia wasn't with the British. It was with the Dutch. The Dutch rose as a superpower and started the Dutch East India Company — based in Jakarta, Indonesia — in 1602. They sailed a lot between Europe and what was then known as the East Indies. In 1605, Willem Janszoon (also known as Jansz), on his ship *Duyfken,* reached the Gulf of Carpentaria in the north-east of the land the Dutch had named New Holland.

The first marked landing of a European was that of Captain Dirk Hartog in October 1616 at what is now called Cape Inscription on the west coast of Australia. He left an inscribed pewter plate that was found in 1697 by his countryman Willem de Vlamingh, who was on his way to the East Indies.

In 1623, Dutch explorer Jan Carstensz was sent to sail around the Gulf of Carpentaria. He and his crew clashed with Aboriginal people and didn't seem to have a high opinion of them. Carstensz wrote that the Aboriginal people were 'more miserable and insignificant than I have ever seen in my life'.

A trip sponsored by Antonie van Diemen and led by Abel Tasman set out in 1642 to explore the unknown land that lay to the south of the Dutch trading empire. His route took him first to Mauritius to make use of the prevailing winds. He then sailed towards the west coast of Australia. But, unknowingly, he went far to the south of the mainland. He found what he called Van Diemen's Land (after his patron), which is today known as Tasmania. Then he continued to New Zealand and north through the southern Pacific back to Batavia.

In ten months of exploring, Tasman had gone around the Australian mainland without ever seeing it. Not surprisingly, van Diemen was not impressed. But Tasman set sail again in 1644 and explored the Gulf of Carpentaria and Arnhem Land in the north of New Holland. Then he sailed some way down the west coast. He observed Aboriginal people as being, 'poor, naked people walking along beaches; without rice or many fruits, very poor and bad tempered people in many places'.

The Dutch didn't seek to start a colony in the country that would become known as Australia. This was perhaps because they found nothing that they thought was of value to them.

And then came the English . . .

William Dampier was the first British person to explore New Holland. He came to the north coast of Australia in 1688 and again in 1699. He was a famous English buccaneer (similar to a pirate) who had made a career sailing around the Americas and then the Pacific. He also gave a negative account of the Aboriginal people when he returned to Britain: 'The Inhabitants of this Country are the miserablest People in the World. Setting aside their Humane Shape, they differ little from Brutes'. These notes contain the assumption of white superiority and black inferiority that the British believed was the condition needed to make a claim over this country. Such notes were laced with the prejudices of the time.

William Dampier wrote that he found the landscape empty of any riches. But he took away about 40 samples of native plants. He published *A Voyage to New Holland* in 1703. This was the first printed account of what would later become known as Australia.

Landing in Australia: Cook's Arrival

The British made a claim over Australia in 1770, during the first Pacific trip of Lieutenant James Cook. (He earned the rank of Captain when he finished his second Pacific voyage in 1775.) His ship *Endeavour* sailed the coast of New Zealand, then turned west, sighting the southern coast of New South Wales on 19 April 1770.

He sailed north and, on 29 April 1770, planted the British flag in the soil of Kurnell at what he later named Botany Bay. The area is about 30 kilometres from what's now the city of Sydney. There, he also carved details recording his arrival into a tree.

The first member of Cook's crew to step foot on Australian soil was Isaac Smith. He was an 18-year-old midshipman who was also the cousin of Cook's wife, Elizabeth. A small brass plaque now marks the site on the beach.

The Aboriginal people of the area, the Dharawal, were hunting, gathering and fishing that day like usual. They thought the ship looked like a big white bird as it sailed into their cove. Wanting to keep their own food sources safe, they threw spears at the landing party. Cook fired a shot, wounding one man. This scattered the Aboriginal people and let Cook's party land.

Cook charted the Australian coast all the way north to the tip of Queensland. There, on what became known as Possession Island, just before sunset on Wednesday 22 August 1770, he declared the entire east coast a British possession. He later named it New South Wales. His log records:

> At six possession was taken of this country in his Majesty's name and under his colours, fired several volleys of small arms on the occasion and cheer'd three times, which was answer'd from the ship.

Cook recorded signs that the coast was populated during the voyage north. He noted the great number of fires on all the land and islands about them, 'a certain sign they are Inhabited'.

Cook returned to England in May 1771. His journal entries show that he tried to understand the world of the Aboriginal people he saw:

> These people may truly be said to be in the pure state of nature, and may appear to some to be the most wretched upon the earth; but in reality they are far happier than ... we Europeans.

Cook's instructions

Cook had been given instructions that laid out two courses of action for claiming the continent. The Secret Instructions were in the Letterbook carried on the *Endeavour.* They included the Additional Instructions that gave James Cook power to take possession of 'a Continent or Land of great extent' thought to exist in the south.

The letter given to Cook on 30 July 1768 stated that, should he find the land inhabited, he was to 'endeavour by all proper means to cultivate a friendship and alliance with them'. He was told 'with the Consent of the Natives to take the possession of convenient situations in the country in the name of the King of Great Britain'.

He was also told: 'If you find the Country uninhabited Take Possession for His Majesty by setting up Proper Marks and Inscriptions as first discoverers and possessors'.

TECHNICAL
STUFF

Cook planted a flag and carved a tree instead of seeking to engage in any activity that might amount to gaining consent from 'the Natives'. These actions indicate that he chose to make British claims over Australia by asserting *possession* rather than *conquest.* The British thought the country was theirs for the taking. But they needed to make their claim to it over other European colonising powers, so these displays of British possession were designed for them. The *Doctrine of Discovery* was a rule of (European designed) international law that gave a European country the right to take land if they discovered it. The land had to be *vacant* but that didn't mean *unpeopled.* It just meant not inhabited by Christians. If the indigenous people were thought to be heathens, they were deemed as not having rights to their own land and so it was 'vacant'.

Joseph Banks' observations

Joseph Banks was the naturalist who accompanied Cook on the voyage. (A *naturalist* is someone who studies or has an expert knowledge of natural history, especially animals or plants.) He noted: 'This immense tract of land, considerably larger than all of Europe, is thinly inhabited'. He and Cook had seen only a small part of the coast and none of the interior.

**MYTH
BUSTER**

Banks guessed that the interior would be uninhabited because not enough fish would be available and the 'produce of the land' didn't seem to be enough to support a population. He was, of course, wrong about this. The whole continent was filled with people. The pre-contact Aboriginal population may have been as high as a million people.

Banks recorded his general impressions of the Australian east coast. He noted plants, insects, molluscs, reptiles, birds, fish and animals. He also recorded the Aboriginal customs he saw. A lot of plant material was collected and sorted on the trip. The collected herbarium specimens had about 1,300 new species.

Banks noted: 'Collection of plants was . . . grown so immensely large that it was necessary that some extraordinary care should be taken of them least they should spoil . . .'

REMEMBER

Botany Bay got its name due to the richness and uniqueness of the plants that were found there. Cook, Banks and the rest of the crew spent a week there collecting specimens and studying the area's suitability for farming.

**MYTH
BUSTER**

Banks thought the Aboriginal people would run away and give up their rights to land. He and Cook were both wrong. Aboriginal people fought many battles, were killed and killed others during raids and ambushes in defence of their land.

The French floating around

The focus on Cook in Australia's recent history has papered over the presence of French explorers in the region at the time. They had a role in charting the mysterious southern land mass and studying its people, plants and animals. In 1785, King Louis XVI, after reading stories about Cook's voyage, hired Jean-François de Galaup, Comte de La Pérouse, to travel completely around the Pacific. He sailed to Chile, Alaska, California, East Asia, Japan and the South Pacific. Then the trip continued to Australia. By then, news had reached them of an English fleet setting out to start a penal colony in New South Wales.

La Pérouse sailed into Botany Bay on 26 January 1788, days after the British fleet came. After six weeks, his ships left for New Caledonia and were never seen again. Luckily, his journal and other papers were sent back to France before he disappeared.

Establishing a British Colony

On his return to England, Cook said that Australia didn't have a lot of people. Cook and his crew also thought that Aboriginal people in Australia were less technologically advanced than other indigenous groups that the British found when they were building their empire. They didn't wear clothes. They had small, basic huts and knew 'nothing of Cultivation'. From the accounts of Cook's voyage, Britain viewed Australia as almost empty. In a vast continent with a small, moving population, the land was available to take.

In 1783, James Matra, who had been a midshipman on Cook's voyage, was a leading supporter of starting a colony in New Holland. The idea became known as the *Matra proposal.* Matra's idea was that the new colony could be started using Americans who had remained loyal to the British during the War of Independence (1775–1783). This argument was shot down. But he later changed the proposal to include 'transportees' or convicts among the settlers to relieve Britain's overflowing prisons. He also argued that the land offered an environment for growing flax, trade with China and others, and the availability of timber for ships' masts. Sir Joseph Banks supported the proposal.

Seeing through Indigenous Eyes: Perspectives on the Arrival

Europeans who sailed the world would have been used to seeing cultural difference. They found people living in different lands and circumstances. Proof exists of some contact with Europeans who sailed past or went inland — either on purpose or because they were lost. But the cultural differences must have been striking for Indigenous people. The white skin, blond hair, clothing and new technology must have been strange curiosities.

'We thought they were ghosts'

Some Aboriginal people thought that white people were the ghosts of their ancestors returning from the spirit world.

CULTURAL
PROTOCOLS

In many Aboriginal languages, the same word used for 'ghost' was used for Europeans. In Gamillaroi, the word *wunda* means *ghost* and was used as a name for white people. In South Australia, the Ngarrindjeri used the word *grinkari* for white people, the same word used to describe a human corpse with its skin peeled off. In the south of Western Australia, the Noongar people used the word *djanga* for Europeans, the same word used to describe the spirits of dead people.

'Are they human?'

European clothing was mystifying to Indigenous people. They had never seen such fancy cloth. Upon meeting Europeans, some Aboriginal men would ask the newcomers to remove their clothes to prove that they were human.

CULTURAL
PROTOCOLS

Contact with Europeans was handled by the senior men of Aboriginal clans. The men avoided, where they could, placing women and children in a position where they would meet the visitors. When outsiders approached islands in the Torres Strait, the women were also hidden, with the men interacting with the visitors. Women weren't allowed to speak with them.

PROJECT

Write a short story about what it might have been like to be an Aboriginal person seeing a European person for the same time. What would seem strange to you? How would you feel about them?

The Brits' First Colony: 1788

The reports of Australia from Lieutenant James Cook and his crew planted a seed about the new territory. The occupation would grow the British Empire. It would create a base in the southern part of the world. It would also provide a place to send prisoners from England's overcrowded prisons. (This would form a *penal colony*.) These arguments led to Captain Arthur Phillip setting out on the long trip to Australia in 1787. He was in charge of 11 ships and 1,500 convicts, crew, marines and civilians. He had orders from the British government to start the colony.

The Aboriginal people were as unfamiliar to the British who came on this First Fleet as the landscape, animals and plants. The British found the environment tough to get used to. And the new arrivals were just as strange to the Aboriginal people. Relationships between Aboriginal people and the British quickly became strained. The Aboriginal people began to realise that the white people weren't going away.

In this chapter, I look at how the British fared as they started their new colony. I also look at how the relationship between Aboriginal people and the British unfolded.

Captain Phillip and the First Fleet

Britain had moved convicts from its overcrowded prisons to the Americas since the early 1600s. After the American Revolution (1775 to 1783), the United States stopped taking them. Britain then had to find somewhere new. It was also thought that a new southern colony would help in making claims over the land against other colonising powers, particularly the French. On 18 August 1786, the decision was made to send a fleet to Botany Bay.

REMEMBER

Captain Arthur Phillip was chosen to lead the First Fleet because he had transported slaves from Africa to America.

The First Fleet set sail from London on 13 May 1787 for Botany Bay. It was made up of:

- Eleven ships, including two naval escort ships, three supply ships and six convict ships

- Around 1,500 people, including more than 700 convicts (200 of them female convicts and their children), about 250 marines, up to 400 crew, around 50 civilian women and children (the families of the marines) and about 15 officials and passengers

The long trip over

The Fleet criss-crossed the Atlantic. It stopped for food, animals and other supplies in the Canary Islands (off the coast of north-western Africa) and Rio de Janeiro (in Brazil, on the east coast of South America). Then it sailed again, stopping at the Cape of Good Hope at the southern tip of Africa. There it took on board more supplies and livestock.

The trip was long and hard. It was more than 15,000 miles (24,000 kilometres) and took eight months. Conditions were cramped. Food was scarce. The smell of humans and animals in such close quarters was powerful. People became sick. But only 23 people, all of them convicts, died.

The ships variously arrived at Botany Bay between 18 and 20 January 1788. Concerns were quickly raised about the spot first chosen for the settlement. There was little fresh water. The soil was sandy and not rich enough for farming. Captain Phillip and a small number of his crew sailed north to search for a better spot. They found a protected cove in a harbour they named after the British Home Secretary, Lord Sydney. The Fleet landed at this spot on 26 January 1788. A British flag was planted in the ground. The British colony was declared.

TECHNICAL
STUFF

James Cook had claimed the east coast of Australia for Britain during his trip in 1770. Britain thought it owned a huge part of the country. Aboriginal people didn't fence or develop the land. So the British thought their control of the land was valid. But the area that became known as Sydney wasn't empty. It was the land of the Gadigal or Cadigal people of the Eora nation. Their interests weren't considered when their lands were claimed as part of the British Empire. In raising the British flag and claiming the land, the British also stated their control over the Aboriginal people. The British made them British subjects who were expected to obey British laws.

CELEBRATING SURVIVAL

Australia Day is marked as a national holiday on 26 January each year. Aboriginal people often refer to 26 January as *Invasion Day* or *Survival Day*. On that day, the National Australia Day Council announces the Australian of the Year. Indigenous people who have won this title include

- 1968 — Lionel Rose, boxer
- 1971 — Evonne Goolagong, tennis champion
- 1978 — Galarrwuy Yunupingu, Aboriginal leader
- 1979 — Neville Bonner, politician
- 1984 — Lowitja O'Donaghue, Indigenous rights advocate
- 1992 — Mandawuy Yunupingu, schoolteacher
- 1998 — Cathy Freeman, athlete
- 2009 — Mick Dodson, Indigenous rights advocate
- 2014 — Adam Goodes, AFL footballer, Indigenous rights advocate

The captain's orders

Phillip had been told to make friendly contact with the local Aboriginal people. He was to create peaceful relations with them. He also had to see if they could be useful in starting the colony. Before he set sail, Phillip got his instructions from King George III. They advised him about managing the convicts, granting and developing the land, and exploring the country. They also included instructions about how to deal with the Aboriginal people. The instructions stated that the Aboriginal people's lives and livelihoods were to be protected. They also stated that friendly relations with them were to be supported.

But the instructions made no mention of protecting or recognising Aboriginal lands. The British thought that the land was now theirs. The First Fleet was told to start the colony at Botany Bay. But Phillip was separately given power to choose any other appropriate neighbouring territory.

CULTURAL
PROTOCOLS

In his task of making friends with the Aboriginal people, Captain Phillip had an edge that he didn't realise: a missing front tooth. In Aboriginal culture, a missing front tooth was a symbol of status within society.

TECHNICAL
STUFF

By claiming Australia, Britain was working with the *doctrine of discovery*. This meant that a colonial power that first 'discovered' a land had a right to own it. The doctrine was an understanding between other colonial powers. It was not with the people of the land being claimed. British claims to Australia would later be justified on the basis that the country was *terra nullius* — vacant or without a government. Neither of those reasons was correct in fact. Aboriginal people were there and they did have a system of laws and government. This became known as a 'legal fiction' and stayed in Australian law until 1992.

Starting a Penal Colony

The day after the First Fleet arrived in Sydney Cove, male convicts were put to work. They cleared the land. They put up tents. They unloaded the stores. They penned the animals. They planted seeds and corn. They then began to build permanent structures.

Captain Phillip became the governor of the colony. He oversaw the construction of his own home, Government House. He also watched over the building of storehouses, a hospital, huts and a church. By November 1788, another settlement was started at Parramatta, 25 kilometres upstream to the west. The soil there was more fertile. To survive in the early years, the British needed the knowledge of the Aboriginal people in the area. They helped with identifying where water sources were, what plants and seeds could be eaten safely, and how to successfully hunt animals.

REMEMBER

The first conflict between Aboriginal people and the British occurred on 29 May 1788 in the area that's now Rushcutters Bay. Two convicts were killed after they tried to steal a canoe.

First impressions

Many of the white colonists' first impressions of Aboriginal people were not positive. They didn't understand or value the culture of the Aboriginal people. But the Aboriginal people's knowledge helped the colony to survive. Aboriginal people were called 'stupid', 'barbaric' and 'primitive'. Some of the white settlers were afraid of the Aboriginal people. They didn't want the Aboriginal people near the settlement.

Other people in this first colony understood that Aboriginal culture, while different from European culture, had its own benefits. They also understood that Aboriginal people were deeply attached to their land. They knew that the Aboriginal people were trying to fight the presence of the British.

One such person was Watkin Tench, an officer in the First Fleet. He studied the cultural practices and habits of the Aboriginal people. His diary notes the way Aboriginal people lived at the time of the start of the colony at Sydney:

> It does not appear that these poor creatures have any fixed Habitation; sometimes sleeping in a Cavern of Rock, which they make as warm as a Oven by lighting a Fire in the middle of it, they will take up their abode here, for one Night perhaps, then in another the next Night. At other times (and we believe mostly in Summer) they take up their lodgings for a Day or two in a Miserable Wigwam, which they made from Bark of a Tree. There are dispersed about the woods

near the water, 2, 3, 4 together; some Oyster, Cockle and Muscle [sic] Shells lie about the Entrance of them, but not in any Quantity to indicate they make these huts their constant Habitation. We met with some that seemed entirely deserted indeed it seems pretty evident that their Habitation, whether Caverns or Wigwams, are common to all, and Alternatively inhabited by different Tribes.

REMEMBER

When he arrived, Captain Phillip guessed that the population of Aboriginal people in the Sydney region was 1,500. But the total population of Aboriginal people in Australia at that time is thought to be between 750,000 and 1 million. This guess is according to the Australian Bureau of Statistics (ABS), based on anthropological minimum figures.

CROSSING CULTURES, BRIEFLY

The first Aboriginal person to be captured by the British was Arabanoo. He was taken in December 1788. The British thought forcing contact would be a way of learning the Aboriginal language of the area. They also thought it would improve relationships. Arabanoo was taken to the settlement, where a convict was told to guard him. Reports say that Arabanoo was at first pleased by a handcuff on his wrist. He thought it was an ornament. But then he became angry when he found its purpose. Over time he wore European clothes, learned to speak English and dined regularly with Governor Phillip. He didn't like all the European customs. He was horrified by the practice of publicly flogging (beating) people.

Smallpox broke out among the Aboriginal population in April 1789. Arabanoo helped to care for two children, Nabaree and Abaroo. Then he caught the disease and died in May. During his time among the British, he gave them information about the language and customs of his people.

Other Aboriginal people were captured by the early settlers. Those settlers also had goals of learning the language and culture, and forcing closer relationships with the Aboriginal people.

A tough start

The first years of the colony were hard. It almost didn't survive. The first harvest produced nothing. Governor Phillip then sent a ship to the Cape of Good Hope for more supplies. In June 1790, the Second Fleet, which had six ships, came. Its supplies were badly needed. But the new convicts were so ill, with many close to death, that they were more of a drain than a help. Of more than 1,000 convicts who came with the Second Fleet, 278 died on the voyage over. (This was compared with 23 of the 1,500 people on the First Fleet.) The Second Fleet got the nickname of 'the Death Fleet'.

The 11 ships of the Third Fleet carried some 2,000 convicts (with fewer than 200 dying on the trip). It landed in 1791. By 1800, another 20 convict ships had come. Deaths on board stayed pretty high on most trips until around 1804. That's when the figure dropped to a handful each trip. By 1817, Britain was sending more than ten ships per year until 1840. Each carried around 150 to 200 people. Another four arrived in 1849.

Food was still in short supply. But it's fair to say that the colony was stable by 1792. By this time, trading ships were regularly visiting Sydney. A whaling industry had been started. The sheep were producing wool. Released convicts were farming. But problems continued in the colony because of the gender imbalance. There were about four men to every woman.

Governor Phillip found it hard to start relationships with the local Aboriginal people. He and some others in his colony tried to reach across the cultural divide. But he was frustrated by the lack of results. He tried to make better contact. Aboriginal people seemed generally uninterested in European customs and ways. Phillip's frustrations grew when he was speared in the shoulder in May 1790 at Manly Cove. This was the traditional land of the Cammeraygal.

His patience with the local people was further strained when Aboriginal resistance fighter Pemulwuy speared a white colonist. This attack happened because the man had killed some Aboriginal people. Phillip wanted his own revenge. He ordered the troops to kill ten and capture two Aboriginal people. Fifty troops were sent into the bush. But they had no skill in the local environment. They gave early warnings of their presence to the Aboriginal people. The party failed to catch a single Aboriginal person.

REMEMBER

Conflict between Aboriginal people and the new arrivals occurred due to the pressures placed on the environment by the colony. Local resources, such as food, ran low. This meant some of the local clans were without enough food. This was especially true in the winter months. Some people took up offers from Phillip to move into town. They slept and ate in the settlers' homes.

Governor Phillip went back to London in 1792. By this time, the colony was stable. Between 1792 and 1794, the governance of the colony was the job of Major Francis Grose and then Captain William Paterson. Governor John Hunter took over in 1795.

Seeing How the Locals Dealt with the New Arrivals

The arrival of the British led to changes that couldn't be undone in the culture, lifestyle, health and spiritual life of Aboriginal people.

Aboriginal people along the east coast of Australia had had contact with white people before. Their ships would sail along the coast. Though they would stop sometimes, they would always move on.

Aboriginal people didn't seriously resist the new colony at first. They thought that the white people wouldn't stay. In Aboriginal culture, people had duty to their traditional country. Their spiritual life was wrapped up in the landscape around them. They thought that white people would have those jobs and worldview too. They thought that white people would have to return to their own land to look after it. The way the Europeans colonised other people's land was a strange concept to Aboriginal people.

When it became clear that the white people were going to stay, the attitudes of Aboriginal people began to harden. There were many violent acts of resistance. They took a stand against the takeover of their lands and the threats to their culture and way of life. They were worried about the spoiling of water sources and the impact on food supplies. European practices such as building houses and farming seemed to destroy the landscape. Conflict also rose over the treatment of Aboriginal women by British men and the destruction of sacred sites by the British.

Some Aboriginal people kept resisting — sometimes violently — the continual takeover of more Aboriginal land. Others worked with the new arrivals and took on some of their customs. They became well-known figures in the colony.

Bennelong

Governor Phillip believed that one way to improve his relationship with the Aboriginal people was through an interpreter of sorts. In November 1789, Bennelong and Colebee were captured and taken to the Governor. Colebee escaped. But Bennelong stayed in the colony. He took on some of the habits and customs of the British. He dressed in their clothes and learned their language. His portrait appears in Figure 6-1.

NOVEMBER.]   IN NEW SOUTH WALES.   439

Figure 6-1: Portrait of Bennelong by an unknown artist, around 1798.

Bennelong went back to his clan in May 1790. But he was seen again in September at the large gathering at Manly where Governor Phillip was speared. He wasn't involved in the incident, which resulted from a misunderstanding. But afterwards he often appeared at Sydney Cove to ask after the Governor's health. This contact continued. Bennelong was told that he wouldn't be detained. In 1791, a hut was built for him on the eastern point of Sydney Cove at a place now called Bennelong Point. It is the site of the Sydney Opera House. (See the following section for the different approach taken by Barangaroo, Bennelong's wife.)

When Governor Phillip went back to London in December 1792, Bennelong went with him, along with another Aboriginal man called Yemmerrawanne. They were presented to King George III. Yemmerrawanne died in Britain after battling a chest infection. Bennelong went back to Sydney with Governor Hunter in 1795. Reports at that time note his ill health due to cold, homesickness and the long delay in leaving for Australia. On his return, he seemed to find fitting in or being fully accepted by either his own people or the colonists hard. He began drinking heavily and died in 1813. He was buried at James Squire's orchard at Kissing Point on the Parramatta River.

MYTH
BUSTER

The British presence in Australia saw the population of the Aboriginal people dramatically drop. This wasn't due to frontier violence. The immune systems of Aboriginal people couldn't cope with the diseases that the British brought with them. Smallpox, colds and flu were deadly to Aboriginal people. The drop in population around Sydney Cove was so drastic that bodies were found in the water or on rocks. This was proof that the customary burial practices couldn't be carried out because not enough people were alive or well enough to carry them out.

Barangaroo

Barangaroo was an important senior Cammeraygal woman and famous fisherwoman. Women like her were the main providers of food in the community. She was a strong figure in the colony. Her husband, Bennelong, worked with the colonists (refer to the previous section).

Barangaroo was against her husband's relationship with the people who were settling themselves on Aboriginal land. She was encouraged to also drink wine and wear European clothes. But she wouldn't. She didn't take the trinkets that the colonists tried to tempt her with. This made her husband angry. All she ever wore was a slim bone through her nose, even when dining with the Governor.

Barangaroo kept fighting for her rights to her country. She is also recorded as taking a stand when a convict was being beaten. Horrified by the act, she threatened to flog the man giving out the punishment. A headland in Sydney Harbour, where the Aboriginal women used to gather, is now named after her.

CULTURAL
PROTOCOLS

To show goodwill, the colonists collected 4,000 fish in one day in 1790 as a gift to the Cammeraygal men. This showed both how plentiful the resource was and how little the colonists thought about resources. When Barangaroo found out, she was angry at the waste. But she also understood that the economic power of Aboriginal women was being weakened.

CULTURAL
PROTOCOLS

Barangaroo wanted to give birth at Government House. This was built on a site that was important to the local Aboriginal people. Their practice was to give birth in such places for cultural and spiritual reasons. Governor Phillip said no. Barangaroo didn't want to have her baby in the hospital. She viewed it as a place of death. Phillip got Bennelong to let him take her there. She died shortly after giving birth. (The child died as a baby.) Bennelong buried her ashes in the garden of Government House.

REMEMBER

Bennelong and Barangaroo stood for the two different approaches that Aboriginal people had to the invaders. Bennelong worked closely with them and tried to be like them. Barangaroo kept fighting their presence and the way European culture affected Aboriginal people.

Pemulwuy

Pemulwuy was a leader and warrior within the Aboriginal community. (See Figure 6-2 for the only known image of him.) He came from the Bidjigal clan of the Dharug nation to the south and west of Sydney Cove. This was around the Georges River and Parramatta area. The colonists found out about him when he speared Governor Phillip's gamekeeper, John McIntyre, in September 1790. Around this time, the colonists had started to take over more and more land. This led to the Hawkesbury and Nepean wars.

Figure 6-2: The only known image of Pemulwuy, by Samuel John Neele (1758–1824). This is from James Grant's *The Narrative of a Voyage of Discovery in HM Vessel Lady Nelson 1803–1804.*

Led by Pemulwuy and his son, Tedbury, Aboriginal people raided stations or killed sheep and cattle in these wars. They also used fire to burn buildings and destroy crops.

REMEMBER

The various clans made these raids for many reasons. Sometimes the purpose was to get food, particularly corn. Other times, the raids were in response for evil acts against Aboriginal people, particularly Aboriginal women. This guerrilla war of resistance continued until 1816.

In May 1801, Governor King gave orders that Aboriginal people near Parramatta, Georges River and Prospect could be shot on sight. In November a reward was offered for Pemulwuy's death or capture. Pemulwuy was twice shot seriously and survived. This led to the myth that he couldn't be killed by bullets. He did die from bullet wounds in June 1802 after being shot by two colonists. His son, Tedbury, kept up the fight.

REMEMBER

Pemulwuy's impact on the colonists in his resistance to their growing settlement is shown in the words of Governor King. He wrote that Pemulwuy was 'a terrible pest to the colony'. But he noted that 'he was a brave and independent character'.

CULTURAL
PROTOCOLS

Some of the local clan members who survived the impact of the diseases looked to move away from the settlement. But other clans came to the Sydney area. Some came to help with the resistance to the British presence. Some wanted to know more about the new settlement.

MYTH
BUSTER

Sydney Cove was the place of the first European colony in Australia. The arrival of the British affected the culture and practices of the Aboriginal people who lived there. But traces of Aboriginal presence in the area can still be found today. Shell middens and rock carvings can be found around the harbour, as well as the surrounding areas. Check out the carving shown in Figure 6-3 (from Bundeena, just south of Sydney). Cultural connections between people have also been kept up.

Patyegarang and Lieutenant Dawes

Patyegarang was a young woman, perhaps around 15 years old, at the time the colony was started. She has become a well-known figure today because she became friends with one of the engineers in the colony, Lieutenant Dawes. He was also an astronomer.

Figure 6-3: Rock art depicts a kangaroo, from Bundeena, Sydney.

Dawes set up a hut at what is now called Dawes Point on Sydney Harbour. He was curious about Aboriginal culture, particularly their understanding of the skies. Patyegarang was his key teacher. Dawes recorded the words of the Eora language that she taught him in his journals. That language is being revived today based on those journals. This is a lasting legacy.

Dawes left the colony after a disagreement with Governor Phillip. The governor wanted an expedition to punish the local Aboriginal people after his gamekeeper was speared. Dawes became heavily involved with the international anti-slavery movement.

REMEMBER

The relationship between Patyegarang and Lieutenant Dawes is notable. Unlike others who wrongly saw Indigenous people as primitive, Dawes was respectful and curious about the knowledge of the local Aboriginal community. He wanted to learn from them.

FIGHTING FOR A PROPER BURIAL

The skeletal remains of Indigenous people were treated as curiosities by the Europeans in the 18th century. Theories that certain races were inferior to Europeans were common at the time. These theories also created scientific interest in remains. Skeletons were collected from burial sites and sent back to universities, museums and private collections in Britain and Europe. Today, Indigenous people strongly support the return of those remains. When they are successful, they give those remains a proper burial.

PROJECT

Write a short story from the point of view of an Aboriginal person witnessing the growth of the British colony after the arrival of the First Fleet. How would this person feel once they realise the British were here to stay?

PROJECT

Write a short biography of one of the Aboriginal figures who was around at the time the colony was established in Sydney. Options include Bennelong, Barangaroo, Pemulwuy or Patyegarang.

The Loss of People and the Land

The penal colony in Sydney Cove was started in 1788. The colony was stable for some time before starting to grow. The British then began colonies across the country. They eventually took over all of Australia.

The colonisation of Australia wasn't peaceful. Indigenous people call it an invasion. But the Europeans carried something that had a greater impact on the Aboriginal people than firearms. They had diseases that Aboriginal people couldn't fight off.

The British colonists began to give Aboriginal land to settlers. They freed convicts so that they could farm. Europeans took Aboriginal land and destroyed the balance of nature. They ruined hunting grounds and ceremonial sites. They stopped access to waterholes. They used up resources for food and medicine. This led to conflict as Aboriginal people tried to defend their traditional lands and their way of life.

In this chapter, I look at the growth of the colonies and its effect on Aboriginal communities around the country. I also look at the legal effects of the way the British took over land.

Opening Up the Land: White Settlement Spreads

The Sydney colony spread out quickly to the north and south, and soon to the west. The Blue Mountains (part of the Great Dividing Range) stopped the growth for a short period. But the range was crossed in 1813. This opened up vast new country that the colonists thought could be used for farming. Penal colonies were started in Van Diemen's Land (Tasmania) in 1803 and at Moreton Bay in 1824. (The Moreton Bay settlement, later the city of Brisbane, was to become Queensland.) Free settlements started in Melbourne, Adelaide and Perth.

By the 1880s, the colonists had reached Central Australia and started pastoral stations. Even some of the most remote parts of the country were being settled. The colonies were each separately claimed over this period. They split off from New South Wales. Then they were united as separate states under the banner of the Commonwealth of Australia in 1901. See the later section 'Growing the British Colony' for more details.

In the beginning, Aboriginal people often met the colonists with friendliness. But when they realised that the colonists were not going to leave, attitudes began to change and conflict was certain.

As the colony grew, pressure increased for more land for the settlement. The British had always wanted to take over the land when they set up the colony in Sydney Cove. As the penal colony was established, more people — including freed convicts — wanted to try working on pastoral lands and gaining the wealth they promised. And the colony needed more food to support its growing population. Land grants were given for this purpose. The colony spread further across the lands of Aboriginal people.

Spreading Disease Far and Wide

Colonists tried to attract Aboriginal people to European customs and values. But they brought something that would destroy Aboriginal society more quickly than colonisation — their diseases.

Aboriginal people had lived for tens of thousands of years largely without contact with other people. They lived in a healthy and clean place. Their immune systems had not developed natural resistance to diseases that were common in Europe. For this reason, disease was the deadliest thing that the settlers brought with them. It was quite likely the greatest factor behind the huge population decrease among Aboriginal people during colonisation. Before contact with Europeans, the chief medical issues for Aboriginal society related to eye and skin problems.

REMEMBER

The diseases that swept through Aboriginal communities included the common cold, influenza, leprosy, measles, smallpox, tuberculosis and whooping cough. They often were deadly. Europeans could still die from these diseases in the 18th century. But for Aboriginal people with no immunity, the death rate was much higher.

The *frontier* was land that was in the process of being colonised. In some places there, disease killed most of the Aboriginal population before any contact with white people took place. Some areas reported that the spread of the diseases had killed all their children.

By 1850, disease had led to a big drop in Aboriginal numbers. This dramatically affected Aboriginal cultural life and society. Older people, as well as children, were likely to get sick from diseases. So Elders and medicine experts died, and with them went their knowledge. Kinship systems were badly affected by the loss of so many people so quickly. Links between generations were also impacted. The tradition of handing down oral knowledge to people was disrupted. Traditions, knowledge and languages were lost during this period. By the time Aboriginal people were physically defending their land, they were dealing with lowered numbers. They were also dealing with the loss of loved ones and basic changes to their culture and society.

Meeting Aboriginal Resistance

Europeans had thought that Aboriginal people would like the benefits of European culture. They believed that they had a better and more advanced civilisation. They thought that Aboriginal people were backward and savage. But Aboriginal people could see little point in many European practices when the colonists came. They didn't need to farm or keep domestic animals. They survived well with their hunter-gatherer ways. They also had their own worldviews and understandings of nature. They saw little need to take on European religions and beliefs.

REMEMBER

Many instances have been reported where Aboriginal people were, in fact, horrified by some British practices. They were especially alarmed seeing the public flogging (beating) of convicts as a punishment.

It seemed, at first, that the colonists had more to learn from Aboriginal culture. Aboriginal people showed them how to cut and treat the barks of Australian trees to build shelters. They showed how to use bark fibre to make ropes and the best timbers for making boats. They also proved to be excellent guides around the land. They often helped Europeans seeking to explore.

The knowledge Aboriginal people had of their environment helped the colony to survive. But some colonists said that Aboriginal people were naturally evil, untrustworthy and prone to violence. This was, of course, not true. Aboriginal people were generally peaceful. Fighting was usually on a small scale and often stopped when first blood was drawn. No wars over land or beliefs took place such as those that had taken place in Europe.

Aboriginal people didn't understand the way Europeans took others' land. They had a spiritual and cultural attachment to their own traditional land. They thought that the British would have the same connection with their own country. The idea that you would take over someone else's land was unknown to them.

TECHNICAL
STUFF

For the British, the issue around who owned the land was clear. They believed they had properly claimed the land and had the rights to it. Lieutenant Cook had claimed the east coast of Australia in 1770. The establishment of a colony in 1788 had further strengthened the British claim. (Refer to Chapters 5 and 6 for more on these issues.) With these actions, the British thought they had defeated the claims of all other colonial powers such as the French and the Dutch. They also thought that they now had power over Aboriginal people, who had now become British subjects. The British tried to explain this new legal setup to Aboriginal people. This challenge was made harder because they had to communicate across languages and cultures. They tried to put these ideas in pictures. The most famous example comes from what's known as Governor Thomas Davey's Proclamation to the Aborigines in 1816 in Van Diemen's Land, shown in Figure 7-1. (Note that some images used in the Proclamation are distressing.)

This position of power was clear to the British. But it wasn't so clear to Aboriginal people. They didn't understand British property law. They had their own Aboriginal laws that noted their custodianship of the land and their duty to it. They didn't understand they were subject to British law any more than they understood that they had become British subjects.

REMEMBER

Governor Lachlan Macquarie started an Aboriginal school at Parramatta in 1814. It was called the 'Native Institution'. Its aims were to 'civilise, educate and foster habits of industry and decency in the Aborigines'. Parents took their children out of the school after they saw that its aim was to distance the children from their culture and families. The school closed in 1820. Macquarie also started a farm that Aboriginal people could work on in Port Jackson. The aim was to put them into white society as farmhands and house servants. Like the school, the farm failed.

CULTURAL
PROTOCOLS

Governor Macquarie and the governors before him were frustrated that Aboriginal people didn't seem interested in learning the ways of Europeans. He came up with the idea to identify a 'king' or 'queen' in different Aboriginal clans. He thought this would lead to better relationships with them by having a person who could speak on behalf of others. This idea, of course, completely misunderstood how Aboriginal society worked. Decision-making in Aboriginal society was much more open than the strict structure of European cultures. The naming of a person as 'king' or 'queen' by the colonists didn't raise that person's power within the clan. Instead, the breastplates Aboriginal people were given to mark their position stood for attempts to weaken Aboriginal society and talk down to Aboriginal people.

Figure 7-1: Governor Davey's Proclamation to the Tasmanian Aborigines in 1816.

TECHNICAL
STUFF

Within European culture, strong views were held about the racial superiority of white people and the inferiority of all other races. This meant that the British who came to Australia thought Aboriginal people were naturally inferior to the British. Some colonists wanted to 'civilise' the Aboriginal people so they would live more like Europeans. Others thought Aboriginal people would die out because they wouldn't be able to handle European colonisation.

BUNGAREE, ABORIGINAL DIPLOMAT

Aboriginal people and colonists had different ways of dealing with each other. One Aboriginal figure who became famous in the Sydney colony was Bungaree.

Bungaree was originally from the Broken Bay area north of Sydney. He moved to Sydney and walked between the two worlds. Bungaree was smart and curious, with a strong sense of humour. He imitated the governors and other local figures. He became friends with Governor Macquarie, who built huts for him and his family. He also sailed with Matthew Flinders as he went around Australia from 1801 to 1803. He was a popular figure in the new colony. News of him was regularly in the newspapers. He was often drawn and painted by artists. He also helped the colonists in tracking escaped convicts. Governor Macquarie gave him the title of King and he became known as King of Broken Bay. But he also made an impact in his own community. He looked after his family by selling or trading fish. Like a diplomat, he worked with the colonists and his own people.

Like several other Aboriginal figures around Sydney Cove, Bungaree had a wife who was also a colourful local character. Her name was Cora Gooseberry. She became known as the Queen of Sydney to South Head. She was often shown wrapped in a government-issued blanket, with a scarf on her head and smoking a pipe. When she died in 1852, at the age of 75, she was thought by the colonists to have been the last member of the Kuring-gai clan. But historians later found that descendants of her clan had joined the last members of other groups to ensure their survival.

Growing the British Colony

As the colony started to grow, demand for land grew too. Between 1788 and 1868 about 150,000 convicts came from the United Kingdom. Free settlers started coming in 1793. Colonists and eventually freed convicts wanted to try to work in the growing sheep and cattle industries. Sometimes people were given land grants by the colonial government. Other times they simply took the land. These people became known as *squatters.* They took their sheep and settled in the spacious lands around the Macquarie and Lachlan Rivers. These lands were thought to work well as pastures. By 1804, colonists lived on most of the Cumberland Plain west of Sydney.

Settlement spread to the north and south of Sydney, and out to the west to the base of the Blue Mountains. Other sites were explored. Over the next 100 years, new *penal colonies* (areas developed using convict labour, as well as providing places of imprisonment) were established. There were also *free settlements* (those built without convicts). Some include the following:

- **1788:** Penal colony at Port Jackson (Sydney Cove) started.

- **1803:** Penal colony at Van Diemen's Land started at Risdon Cove and then Hobart Town in 1804. (Prisons were open on the west coast at Sarah Island and Macquarie Harbour, 1822 to 1833 and 1846 to 1847, and on the east coast at Port Arthur, 1833 to 1877.) Proclaimed as separate colony in 1825. Name changed to Tasmania 1856.

- **1813:** Blaxland, Wentworth and Lawson crossed the Blue Mountains.

- **1824:** Penal colony at Moreton Bay (Redcliffe Point) started. Moved to current site of Brisbane in 1825. Queensland proclaimed 1859.

- **1824 to 1838:** Military settlements started along the coast of the Northern Territory (all abandoned by 1849). Western border of New South Wales shifted west to include them.

- **1826:** Military settlement started at King George Sound (later site of Albany, Western Australia). Extended the British claim to the whole of Australia.

- **1829:** Free settlement started at Perth and western half of Australia named Swan River Colony. Western Australia proclaimed 1839.

- **1831:** Free settlement of Port Phillip (Melbourne) started. Colony of Victoria founded 1851.

- **1836:** Colony of South Australia proclaimed and free settlement of Adelaide started.

- **1863:** Northern Territory added to South Australia. Darwin established 1869.

- **1871:** London Missionary Society arrives on Erub (Darnley Island) in the Torres Strait. Torres Strait Islands added to Queensland 1879.

REMEMBER

When the Torres Strait Islands became part of Queensland in 1879, the traditional owners were under the control of the Queensland government and covered by its laws. The Queensland government passed the first complete legislation dealing with Indigenous people that meant Torres Strait Islanders had to follow the same policies of protection and segregation that Aboriginal people were. (This legislation was called the *Aboriginal Protection and Restriction of the Sale of Opium Act 1897*.) They also lost their legal status as British citizens. They became, in effect, wards of the state.

Figure 7-2 shows the spread of development during the 19th century. In the following sections, I focus on the following:

- The settlement of the Bathurst region in New South Wales.

- The Port Arthur and Moreton Bay penal colonies.

- The free settlement of South Australia. This free settlement was intended as a model settlement.

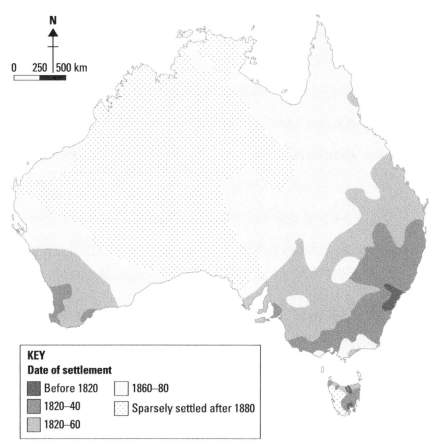

Figure 7-2: Development quickly spread from the British Colony of New South Wales during the 19th century.

Over the mountains

Gregory Blaxland, William Wentworth and William Lawson crossed the Blue Mountains in 1813. This step was important for the colony. This mountain range had been seen as a barrier to growth of the colony. The land between the sea and the mountains was limited and had quickly been taken up by colonists wanting farm land. At this time, 250,000 sheep were in the colony. Finding a way through the Blue Mountains gave entry to the fertile plains to the west. In 1815, a government settlement was started as the site of the town of Bathurst. It was at the end of a narrow convict-built road across the mountains. Exploration parties set out from there. Free settlers soon followed.

The growth past the mountains also affected the Aboriginal people living in that area — the land of the Wiradjuri. Conflict grew stronger there in 1824.

After a period of guerrilla warfare, Governor Brisbane declared martial law in the region. Soldiers moved through the area and killed any Aboriginal men they saw. At one camp, 30 Aboriginal men, women and children were killed. Another 30 were forced to jump off a cliff. In revenge, a group of Wiradjuri men, including a warrior called Windradyne, attacked several pastoral properties. Military patrols then killed even more Aboriginal people. The conflict only ended when many of the Wiradjuri leaders surrendered to the governor.

MYTH
BUSTER

Europeans going into parts of Australia where white people hadn't been before were often said to be 'discovering' them. This term suggested that this was the first time these places had been seen by people. But, of course, Aboriginal people had lived in those areas for tens of thousands of years. Some memorials to European explorers now note that they were the first white visitors to arrive in a certain area. This recognises the fact that Aboriginal people were there all along.

WINDRADYNE: A NOTABLE LEADER

Windradyne was a leader of the Aboriginal resistance to white settlement in the upper Macquarie River region of the central-western area of New South Wales around Bathurst.

Violent clashes between Aboriginal people and settlers resulted in the deaths of convict stockmen and Aboriginal women and children. Governor Brisbane placed the district under martial law in August 1824.

Windradyne's part in incidents that had led to the death of white settlers resulted in a reward being offered for his capture. The reward was 500 acres, just over 200 hectares, of land. Windradyne remained at large. But martial law was ended in December 1824. Two weeks later, in an apparent move to make a deal with Governor Brisbane, Windradyne and many of his

(continued)

(continued)

people crossed the mountains into Parramatta. They aimed to go to the governor's annual feast. There he was formally pardoned by Brisbane. Windradyne was a major figure in the resistance of the spread of white settlement. He died on 21 March 1829 from wounds suffered in a tribal fight.

To Van Diemen's Land

The colony in Van Diemen's Land was started as a penal colony in 1803. (This land became known as Tasmania in 1856.) Lieutenant John Bowen landed at Risdon Cove on the Derwent River with about 50 settlers, crew, soldiers and convicts. Hobart Town was started the next year. A colony in the area was thought to be a good idea for several reasons. One was making sure the British claim to Australia was further secured against other colonial powers such as the French. The colony also was a place for more punishment of convicts in the Sydney colony. Government officials thought that they could be used as free labour to help build this new colony.

Sealers had started working in the area in 1798. By 1810, the industry had overworked the area. But it had, in the meantime, created angry relations with local Aboriginal people due to the practice of kidnapping Aboriginal women.

In 1804, a group of 50 peaceful Aboriginal people were murdered just outside of the colony at Risdon Cove. This set off a cycle of killings of blacks by whites and then whites by blacks. Settlers were given permission to kill Aboriginal people even if they were unarmed. Freed convicts and sealers were violent towards the Aboriginal people. They kidnapped Aboriginal women, causing more clashes of revenge. Some colonists wanted to simply kill off all the Aboriginal people on the island. Governor George Arthur tried other ways to control the situation. But these didn't work because Aboriginal resistance was strong. In the end, he declared martial law. He banned Aboriginal people from being in any area settled by whites.

REMEMBER

In 1830, the colony started a forceful military drive known as the Black Line. More than two thousand troops swept through the whole island. The purpose was pushing Aboriginal people into one part of the island. The operation didn't work. Only two Aboriginal people were captured. It was an example of how Aboriginal people were better able to survive in the landscape they had lived in for tens of thousands of years. The newcomers had trouble dealing with the new environment. After this failed attempt, the new governor, George Robinson, worked with the remaining clans to move onto Flinders Island in Bass Strait. There they would be kept safe from further frontier violence. They were later moved to Cape Barren Island.

Life on Flinders and Cape Barren Islands was tough and cruel. Often, food was scarce and people starved to death. Disease also wrecked the population. Many mourned for their traditional land and their spiritual life. They struggled with European language, culture and religion. By 1850, few had survived. See Chapter 9 for more on Flinders Island.

MYTH
BUSTER

The Tasmanian Aboriginal population, the Palawa nation, was commonly believed to have died out with the death of Truganini in 1876. This wasn't the case. The population of Aboriginal people in Tasmania today is about 16,900. This is about 3.5 per cent of the total Tasmanian population. After Truganini's death, and against her wishes, her bones were shown in a museum. A century later, the Tasmanian Aboriginal community cremated them and scattered them into the water.

Into Moreton Bay

Moreton Bay, on the Redcliffe Peninsula, lands of the Kabi Kabi people, was started as a penal colony in 1824. (It is about 40 kilometres from what's now Brisbane.) Now in Queensland, at the time the colony was started it was still part of New South Wales. The Aboriginal name for Moreton Bay was Quandamooka. It was home to the Nooghie, Noonuccal and Goenpil clans.

The colony moved up the Brisbane River in 1825 to a site called Mean-jin by the Turrbal people whose land it was. This site is now the central business district of Brisbane. Squatters began arriving from the south in the late 1830s. The first immigrant ship from England came in 1848. This began a period of immigration that built up the colony further.

The region had very fertile lands sought by the colonists. It witnessed some violent clashes between Aboriginal people and the settlers. By the 1840s, the settlers had begun moving into the Darling Downs, which offered valuable farming lands. This caused growing conflict with Aboriginal people, the Wacca-burra and the Goonnee-burra. Aboriginal people were killed. They were often also poisoned, using flour laced with arsenic or other poisons. As the 19th century progressed, settlement spread north and west into the Hervey Bay region, and central and northern Queensland. The conflict between the colonists and Aboriginal people spread with it.

The Adelaide experiment

The colony of Adelaide was started in 1836 in South Australia. It was the first in the country that wasn't started as a penal colony. For this reason, the colonial powers hoped it would be different from those with more brutal beginnings. South Australia hoped to give greater protection to Aboriginal people. It also hoped to give them the benefits of European civilisation and Christian religion. (See the later section 'Refuge at a cost: Missions and reserves' for details.) But the impact of the colony was devastating on the Kaurna people. Their numbers quickly shrank. Those surviving felt little benefit from the attempts by missionaries to look after the wellbeing of Aboriginal people.

Adelaide didn't become a model colony. It had the same problems as other colonies. Tensions built between Aboriginal people and settlers over land. This conflict sometimes became violent. The idea of protecting Aboriginal people gave way to the idea of protecting white settlers and their lands.

REMEMBER

A British Select Committee studied the treatment of Indigenous people in all British colonies. But Australia came in for special criticism. The report recommended that Protectors of Aborigines be appointed. (See Chapter 8 for more on these roles.) It also noted that Aboriginal people had a 'plain and sacred right' to their lands.

Dealing with Frontier Conflict

The British believed they had taken control of the land in Australia. But Aboriginal people were serious about keeping it. Aboriginal people didn't accept the presence of the British. They fought back actively — and sometimes violently. They took part in guerrilla warfare. Small groups of Aboriginal men raided settlers' farms, killed stock, burned buildings and killed people. And the British punished them forcefully.

The fierceness and length of conflict on the frontier was different from place to place. It often depended on the landscape (whether it was flat or mountainous), the speed of settlement, the number of Aboriginal people in the area and the number of colonists.

REMEMBER

Aboriginal people were losing their ability to survive. They were also losing their connection to country — their culture and their spiritual life. All of this affected their wellbeing.

A wealth of misunderstanding

Traditional food-sharing practices meant that Aboriginal people took only what they needed. This included cattle on their traditional hunting grounds. They didn't understand that this was thought to be stealing.

The British considered Aboriginal people to be under the protection of British law. But this protection was of little or no use on the frontier in the face of conflict. The law was far better at protecting the property rights of the colonists than it was at protecting the lives of the Aboriginal people. The Aboriginal people were struggling to keep their lands, their culture and their livelihood.

On the edges of the spreading colony, there was little government or military presence. White settlers often took matters into their own hands. They didn't seem to understand or worry that their move onto Aboriginal lands had taken away food, water and the ability to survive. Aboriginal people were shot and their waterholes were poisoned. They were sometimes given poisoned food. This wasn't just an economic conflict. Settlers had little, if any, understanding of Aboriginal spiritual practices. Their activities often destroyed or took over sacred sites. The anger this created in Aboriginal people wasn't understood either.

Many white settlers claimed they didn't believe that Aboriginal people had an attachment to the land and so they believed that Aboriginal people couldn't be dispossessed. Aboriginal people didn't put fences around their land. They didn't farm it (at least not the way Europeans farmed). They didn't even stay in one place. But others understood that Aboriginal people had deep attachment to their lands. Others knew that the loss of their land was a key reason Aboriginal people were so actively fighting white people trying to set up farms.

Colonial governments had no good solutions for controlling either violence by the settlers or the violent payback of Aboriginal people. In this battle, Aboriginal people were at a disadvantage. They had mostly been peaceful and didn't fight with other Aboriginal nations. Their tools were made for hunting and killing animals, not people. They were no match for the firepower that the settlers had with their guns. This was especially true with their shrinking numbers already weakened by European diseases.

REMEMBER

The exact number of people killed in frontier wars is still a guessing game. But one estimate puts the total killed in frontier conflict at 20,000, with 2,000 being white settlers and the other 18,000 Aboriginal people. Exact numbers are hard to come by. Most times numbers weren't recorded and oral histories were depended on. When they were recorded in police reports or settlers' diaries, unofficial figures often differed from official figures. These oral histories and records were also challenged or denied by settlers as quickly as one generation later. So historians had a lot to argue about!

TECHNICAL
STUFF

Debates between historians about the number of Indigenous people killed by frontier violence happened alongside other fierce debates. These were about what Australian history should include and how it should talk about the experiences and treatment of Indigenous people. These debates are known as the *culture wars*, or *history wars*.

THE WILD WEST

The colony in Perth was set up in 1829. This is the land of the Noongar, or Nyoongar, people. Their resistance to the colonists was led by a warrior named Yagan until he was killed in 1833. Some of his remains were sent to England. He's a great hero to Aboriginal people. So his failure to be buried in his traditional land made them upset and angry. They actively asked for the return of his remains from England. His skull was finally brought back to Australia in 1997. In 2010 it was buried in a traditional Noongar ceremony in the Swan Valley.

Conflict in the area continued after Yagan's death. In 1834, Governor Stirling led a party down the Swan River to attack local Aboriginal clans. This conflict became known as the Battle of Pinjarra. Official reports say a single colonist and 14 Aboriginal people were killed. But unofficial reports say that a whole clan (maybe up to 300 people) was wiped out.

The colony was started by free settlers. But it became a penal colony in 1850. Convict labour was used to help build structures such as Fremantle Prison and Government House. Over 9,000 convicts were sent to the Perth colony.

Official responses

By the late 1790s, the Sydney colony had spread to the Hawkesbury and Parramatta regions. This was also met with resistance from Aboriginal people.

Governor King took control of the colony in 1800. He started a policy that let settlers fire on Aboriginal people. He ordered that Aboriginal people gathering around Parramatta, Georges River and Prospect Hill be driven back from the settlers' areas by firing at them. This was a form of martial law. It made visiting the colony dangerous for Aboriginal people.

By 1810, most of the Cumberland Plains, west of Sydney, was settled by colonists. The Aboriginal people in the Sydney basin were completely dispossessed of their land. Along the Hawkesbury and

Nepean Rivers, Pemulwuy and his son, Tedbury, led the resistance (refer to Chapter 6). Aboriginal people raided cattle and sheep stations as they were set up. They also used fire to destroy buildings and crops.

In 1815, farms were attacked on the edges of the Sydney settlement. Governor Macquarie sent a party to arrest the attackers. This ended in an attack on an Aboriginal camp at Appin. In the attack, 14 Aboriginal people were killed. None of them was known to have been involved in the initial incident.

By the following year, Macquarie had set up regulations to control the movement of Aboriginal people. None was to be armed within a mile of any colonial settlement. They couldn't meet in groups of more than six. He then issued passports or certificates to Aboriginal people who were thought to 'conduct themselves in a suitable manner'. This meant a manner that was fine with Europeans.

The guerrilla warfare in these areas continued until 1816. It set the pattern and style of resistance that would occur across the country as Aboriginal people tried to defend their lands.

Increased violence

Violence grew against Aboriginal people in the 1830s around the colonies.

REMEMBER

The Port Phillip District Wars raged in what is now Victoria from 1830 until 1850. At the time, the area was considered part of New South Wales.

In 1838, conflict occurred on the Liverpool Plains in north-central New South Wales around present-day Tamworth. Mounted police led by Major Nunn then killed 60 to 70 Aboriginal people at Vinegar Hill, at a place called Slaughterhouse Creek.

On 10 June 1838, the infamous Myall Creek Massacre occurred in northern New South Wales. A group of 28 local Aboriginal people — mostly old people, women and children — were bound together and shot. They had been accused of stealing sheep. But they were later found to be innocent. They were tied together with rope and taken to a place where they were killed. Their bodies were then burned.

The station owner, William Hobbs, was away when the massacre happened. He reported it to authorities when he returned. This case was unusual because the seven white station hands responsible were charged with murder. After two trials, they were convicted and hanged. Many people in the colony were angered that white people could be charged and hanged for the deaths of blacks.

REMEMBER

The Myall Creek massacre was recognised by the local community. They placed a memorial near the site on 10 June 2000. Both the memorial and the site were given national heritage listing on 7 June 2008.

Over a period of almost one hundred years, many massacres took place. Here's a list of some of the most infamous:

- **1838:** An entire community of Aboriginal people is killed at Long Lagoon in Queensland.

- **1840:** At Rufus River, in New South Wales, 30 Aboriginal people are killed.

- **1861:** More than 170 Aboriginal people are killed at Emerald, Queensland.

- **1868:** More than 150 Aboriginal people are killed in the Kimberley, Western Australia, for 'resisting arrest'.

- **1870 to 1890:** More than 900 Aboriginal people of the Kalkadoon nation are killed in the Kalkadoon Wars in Queensland.

- **1883:** A massacre of Aboriginal people takes place at the McKinley River in the Northern Territory.

- **1916:** Nine Aboriginal men are chained together, shot and thrown off a cliff at Mowla Bluff, Western Australia.

✏ **1928:** A massacre at Coniston Station in the Northern Territory lasts for several days. Official reports put the number of men, women and children killed at 31. But historians believe it was closer to 170.

An interactive map of known massacre sites has been developed. This map is based on research by the University of Newcastle Colonial Frontier Massacres Project team. The team is led by historian Lyndell Ryan. It can be found at the website c21ch. newcastle.edu.au/colonialmassacres/map.php.

REMEMBER

When looking at any online sources, keep in mind that dates aren't always consistent between information sources.

In the Northern Territory, conflict was no different from elsewhere. But it occurred in the later stages of colonisation. It grew stronger around the 1920s and 1930s. Land was less fertile but was used for grazing cattle. John McDouall Stuart started exploring vast areas in this part of northern Australia in the early 1860s. Conflict increased greatly between Aboriginal people and settlers. Administrators tried to calm the situation. But matters relating to Aboriginal people were left to those seeking to take the land and start large pastoral properties. Many of these people thought they had the right to use violence to achieve their aims.

CULTURAL
PROTOCOLS

Massacre sites have been rebuilt using a mix of historical archive, oral history and archaeological proof. Dates and numbers are often not exact because the killings were covered up. Talking about this history is seen by many Indigenous people as an important part of the process of truth telling about the past.

MYTH
BUSTER

Not all regions of Australia fell to the settlers completely. In some places, such as in parts of the Kimberley and Arnhem Land, Aboriginal people stopped the frontier from spreading. The number of Aboriginal people killed on the frontier was far greater than colonists killed. But the mere presence of Aboriginal people created great anxiety among colonists. This caused some of them to abandon their farms. In the west Kimberley, the great warrior Jandamarra, a member of the Bunuba nation, led a resistance effort that stopped settlement for six years. This effort used methods such as attacks on introduced crops and livestock. Jandamarra was shot in 1897 along with 19 other Aboriginal men who were fighting beside him.

Refuge at a cost: Missions and reserves

In some places, Aboriginal people were offered refuge on missions. Here, they could trade their physical safety for their cultural practices. They were expected to learn European habits and language. Governments also started reserves as safe havens for Aboriginal people. Some reserve communities started farms. But conditions on the reserves were generally poor. The food provided was unhealthy and limited. Housing and health conditions added to the poor standard of living of Aboriginal people in these areas.

In other areas, Aboriginal people started relationships with the pastoralists who now farmed their traditional land. They could live on the property and work in return for food and other items.

THRELKELD: ONE MAN'S PASSION

One early missionary was Lancelot Threlkeld. He was asked by the London Missionary Society (LMS) to set up a mission at Lake Macquarie, near present-day Newcastle, in about 1826. The LMS took away their support for the mission in 1828. But Threlkeld got private funds and a grant of land from Governor Darling on the other side of the lake to start his mission. It was open until 1841.

Threlkeld's system was thought to be progressive. It was to 'first obtain the language, then preach the gospel, then urge them from gospel motives to be industrious at the same time being a servant to them to win them to that which is right'. In fact, Threlkeld spent much of his life studying the Awabakal language of the region. He published a grammar of the language in 1834. His role as an interpreter was often valuable in representing Aboriginal people who couldn't defend themselves under white law.

(continued)

(continued)

Threlkeld's intent had a problem, though. By the time he had learned the language, few Aboriginal people were left in the area. The population had either been killed or moved on. Failure of the early missions was common.

The missions

Missionaries were active in colonies around the world in the 18th and 19 centuries. Australia was no exception. At first, these missions aimed to improve the moral standards of the colonists. But some of the early missionaries also wanted 'to preach the Gospel to the Australian Aborigines'. These missionaries included Samuel Marsden, who became assistant chaplain to the Sydney colony in 1794. The idea soon formed that Australia would become a base for missionary activity in the Pacific. Marsden put most of his work into missions in New Zealand.

The missionaries believed that Indigenous people were heathens because they didn't believe in God. They sought to take their religious beliefs to 'the natives' so they could become Christians and saved. The missionaries also believed that they could provide the benefits of their culture — such as proper clothing and education — to Indigenous people. They started missions across Australia and in the Torres Strait. The missions were sometimes called 'the coming of the light' in the Torres Strait. Indigenous people were often drawn to these missions out of curiosity. They also wanted protection from the violence on the frontier.

Missionaries went to the south-eastern colonies and to remote areas of Australia. The following list is by no means complete. But it outlines the chronological order in which they did so:

- **1825:** The Church Missionary Society was started in Sydney. It ran the Wellington Valley Mission in New South Wales from 1830 to 1842.

- **1836:** The first mission in Victoria was started by the Wesleyan Missionary Society at Buntingdale, near Geelong.

🖊 **1838:** German Lutheran missionaries set up at Zion Hill in bushland that's now the Brisbane suburb of Nundah. The mission didn't get converts. It closed in 1846.

🖊 **1859:** The Moravian Church was made up of evangelical Protestants also known as the Bohemian Brethren. It started Ebenezer Mission at Lake Hindmarsh, Victoria. It closed in 1904.

🖊 **1871:** The London Missionary Society began a mission on Erub (Darnley Island) in the Torres Strait.

🖊 **1877:** The Australian Lutheran Church and the Hermannsburg Mission Society of Germany set up the Hermannsburg Mission on the Finke River in Central Australia.

🖊 **1882:** A group of Jesuits started St Joseph's, at what is now the Darwin suburb of Rapid Creek, in 1882. It closed in 1899. The Jesuits were also active in the Daly River area of the Northern Territory from 1886 to 1891.

🖊 **1890:** Trapist monks arrived at Beagle Bay, north-west of Broome. The Pallottine order set up at nearby Lombardina in 1910.

🖊 **1913:** The Seventh Day Adventist mission at Mona, near Kuranda in north Queensland, began. It was open until 1962.

🖊 **1925:** The Church of England started a mission at Oenpelli in western Arnhem Land in the Northern Territory.

🖊 **1935:** The Methodists began a mission at Yirrkala on the Territory's Gove Peninsula.

🖊 **1937:** The Presbyterian Church started a mission at Ernabella in the Musgrave Ranges just over the border in South Australia.

Dozens of missions were open throughout Australia during the 1800s and into the 1900s. Some had good relations with the Aboriginal people and gave some protection from the frontier. Some have been accused of their own terrible treatment of

Aboriginal people. In many cases, Aboriginal people from different nations were unhappily grouped together.

Today many Indigenous communities are on areas that were once missions.

BETWEEN THE CHURCH AND THE GOVERNMENT

In 1861, the Victorian colonial government set aside 3,500 acres (about 1,400 hectares) of land near Warrnambool, in western Victoria, as an Aboriginal reserve. In 1865, the Framlingham Aboriginal Reserve was started there by the Church of England as a mission station. But it soon handed over the reserve to the Central Board Appointed to Watch Over the Interests of Aborigines.

Control of the settlement shifted between the Board and the missionaries. The government tried to close the reserve several times. It was met with great resistance by the residents. In 1970, the land was handed over by the government. This was, along with Lake Tyers (Bung Yarnda) in Gippsland, the first Aboriginal land rights victory in Australia.

Another Aboriginal settlement that began as a mission is Hopevale in north Queensland. In 1885, a Lutheran missionary started the Elim Aboriginal Mission at Cape Bedford. This land had been set aside as an Aboriginal reserve in 1881. He left the mission in 1887. He gave the job of running the mission to George Schwartz. Schwartz stayed at the mission, later called Hope Valley, for more than 50 years. When World War II broke out, the German missionary was sent to an internment camp.

In May 1942, 254 Aboriginal people were sent away from the mission without warning. The majority were removed to Woorabinda. The mission was taken over by the Australian Army, the RAAF, the United States Army and the Civil Construction Corps. Many people died at Woorabinda. Those who lived weren't allowed to go back to the mission until 1949.

A new site was started on land previously owned by the Cooktown Plantations Company. It was about 25 kilometres from the old mission.

The new mission site was set aside as an Aboriginal reserve in September 1952. In 1955, the Hope Vale Mission Board made a complaint about the move of a cattle company onto land belonging to the mission. Eventually this land was cut from the reserved land. In 1986, a deed of grant in trust was issued to the Hope Vale community for 110,000 hectares of land.

Government reserves

Governments also started reserves. They had a similar goal to the missions of creating small communities of Indigenous people who could be protected but also controlled. Some communities became politically active. They tried to have the control of the reserve and the ownership of the land given to the Indigenous community. See Chapter 9 for details.

Some reserves were given to their communities through land grants. But many governments sold off land that had been set aside for Indigenous reserves to raise money.

What happened to the remaining Aboriginal people?

Often, with their traditional way of life destroyed, those Aboriginal people who didn't end up in reserves or missions lived on the edge of European settlements. They begged and took up the worst European habits. These habits included drinking too much alcohol. This behaviour wasn't always viewed with sympathy. Some white people saw this decline of Aboriginal people as natural because they believed that they were a backward people with a savage nature.

The population of Aboriginal people had dropped a lot by the end of the 19th century. Disease was still widespread. Food supplies were scarce. Water supplies were polluted or taken over. Conflict continued. All of this played a part in reducing the numbers. This decline in numbers also meant that cultural practices were disturbed. Beliefs, customs and languages were weakened. Initiation ceremonies and other rites weren't performed. Oral traditions couldn't be handed down. In particular, 'right way' marriages weren't possible.

By the end of the 1800s, Australia was moving towards becoming its own nation. It was believed that Aboriginal people were a dying race.

Ignoring Prior Ownership: No Treaties

Why were no treaties made between the British and the Aboriginal people? The British made treaties with indigenous people in other parts of the world. These areas include the United States, Canada and New Zealand. But no attempt to make a formal agreement with Aboriginal people was made when their lands were being colonised. The exception was John Batman at Port Phillip Bay (see the nearby sidebar 'Batman's attempt at a treaty').

A lot of proof shows that colonists knew Aboriginal people had an attachment to their land. Colonists knew Aboriginal people should rightly keep some interest in it. One possible reason no treaties were struck in Australia is that they weren't needed to secure territory. Force was used instead.

The number of Aboriginal people dropped across much of the country. Conflict and frontier violence occurred almost routinely. Over time, the colonists settled themselves in different parts of the country without getting the agreement of Aboriginal people. Consent was never part of dealing with Aboriginal people in the colony.

This failure to enter into agreements meant that Australian law wouldn't recognise the laws of Aboriginal people or their governance structures and sovereignty. And it wouldn't recognise their rights to their lands under common law until 1992. But land rights legislation in some areas would give some rights to land before that. The issue of a treaty between Indigenous people and the Australian state is still an important part of the political agenda today. Several states, including Victoria and Queensland, have started modern treaty-making processes.

BATMAN'S ATTEMPT AT A TREATY

In 1835, an ambitious pastoralist from Van Diemen's Land, John Batman, sailed to Port Phillip Bay in what is now Victoria. He wanted to secure good grazing land along the Yarra River. This was the land of the Wurundjeri people of the Kulin nation. He bargained with the local Aboriginal people for the land. On 6 June, he negotiated for 240,000 hectares — most of the land of the Kulin nation. But the treaty wasn't as honest as it seemed.

Aboriginal people had no idea about legal contracts. They were a strange concept to them at the time. Batman thought he was negotiating with 'chiefs' when he was speaking with Elders. The Elders weren't in a position to sell their people's land, even if they'd wanted to. In fact, the act of selling land was unknown to Aboriginal people.

It was later believed that the Wurundjeri thought Batman was offering them gifts for safe passage through their lands. Some historians have also asked whether the signatures of the Aboriginal Elders on the treaty were real. The markings matched some found in Batman's journals.

The New South Wales governor declared this private treaty to be illegal. It was clear that the government held all the territory and only it could grant, sell or distribute land. A settlement of Europeans began in the area in what's now Melbourne. Aboriginal people began to find their land taken and their way of life threatened. The colony appointed people to protect the Aboriginal people. But the population declined.

PROJECT

Write a short biography of an Aboriginal resistance fighter. Options mentioned in this chapter include Windradyne, Pemulwuy and his son Tedbury, Jandamarra and Yagan. Or search online to find other Aboriginal warriors from the 18th and 19th centuries.

Taking the Children

Aboriginal populations went down dramatically because of the impacts of colonisation. This led to the idea that Aboriginal people were a dying race. Some people believed that Aboriginal children could be saved if they were assimilated into (or made part of) white culture and society. A key way of putting the policy in place was the forcible removal of Aboriginal children from their families. Torres Strait Islanders had more contact with white settlements on the mainland. The policy affected them too. Queensland took over the islands in 1879 and had control over the Torres Strait Islanders. This chapter looks at the rules passed that gave governments the power to take Indigenous children from their families.

This policy was common practice for more than 60 years. It affected generations of Indigenous children and their families. Indigenous children were fostered or adopted out. Some were placed in institutions. Many suffered neglect and abuse under the control of the state. Most white Australians didn't know how common the practice of removing Indigenous children was. They also didn't know how badly many children were treated. The generations of children removed from their families because of these government policies became known as the *Stolen Generations*.

This chapter also looks at the impacts of these practices on the lives of children removed from their families. It also looks at the effects on the parents who had children taken from them. These effects were covered in the report *Bringing Them Home*, published in 1997. It was the result of a major inquiry. Among its key advice was the need for a national apology and a national compensation (or payment) scheme. A national apology was delivered to the Stolen Generations in February 2008. But the issues of compensation are still not solved.

Examining the Ideology of Assimilation

From the time Sydney Cove began as a colony, the British tried to put their own values, customs and beliefs on Aboriginal people. They thought that their culture and worldviews were better. From the 1850s onward, a bigger effort was made by colonial governments to get rid of Aboriginal cultural practices. Aboriginal people were moved onto reserves. On these reserves, they couldn't use their Aboriginal names. They were steered away from speaking their languages. They were not allowed to perform their cultural practices. They were expected to leave their old ways behind.

Life on the reserves was heavily controlled and cruel. But Indigenous people moving to cities and towns to find work found it hard too. Racism and discrimination were so common in the broader community. Instead of being assimilated, they were often avoided or ignored. They were not given services. They were forced to live on the edges of the community without jobs and in poverty. In towns, they were often barred from swimming pools. They could only attend the cinemas at certain times and sit in certain places.

At first, the policy of removing Aboriginal children from their families was sparked by the belief that they were part of a dying race and so needed to be protected. This thought and the accepted ideas of white superiority and black inferiority were common in the 19th and early 20th centuries. These ideas led to the common view that Aboriginal people should be left to die out or, where possible, become part of the white community.

TECHNICAL
STUFF

Assimilation had existed in practice long before the 20th century. But it became an official government policy in the 1950s. In 1951, federal Minister for the Territories Paul Hasluck was a strong voice for assimilation. He believed that Aboriginal people would improve how they were treated and their living conditions if they behaved more like white people. But assimilation didn't work. Indigenous people were told to aspire to be white. But they were never accepted as equal in a community that still thought of them as an inferior race.

REMEMBER

The idea that white races were better than black races wasn't just related to Australia's Indigenous peoples. From the early 1900s, the White Australia immigration policy actively sent back Chinese immigrants who had lived and worked in Australia since the 1850s. It limited moves by all non–British people until the 1940s. But its main aim was to stop Asian and African migration into Australia. By the late 1940s, 97 per cent of the Australian population was Australian or British born. People from elsewhere, especially Asia, found moving to Australia hard. Anyone coming from abroad was expected to fit into this culture. The policy wasn't officially stopped until 1973. For more on the White Australia policy, check out *Australian Politics For Dummies.* It's written by Nick Economou and Zareh Ghazarian (John Wiley & Sons Australia).

Some people believed that if Indigenous people could be 'more like white people' they would have better lives. Others thought that it was too late to change or assimilate older Indigenous people so it was best to 'focus on the children'. Many believed that actions such as removing children from their families to bring them up like white people were 'for their own good'.

COLONIAL CONTROL

Britain, like other colonial powers, had strict control over the people they colonised. British penal colonies, such as Australia, had an extra layer of control designed to limit the convict population. This included brutal punishments, the regulation of marriage and servitude. It was part of the colonial culture that people who were considered less than human could be treated that way.

'Making them white'

The idea that Aboriginal people were dying out also produced the thinking that Aboriginal people who weren't 'full-blood' should become assimilated into the broader society. It was believed that Aboriginal people should take on European habits, customs, life-styles and values. Much attention was paid to 'half-caste' and light-skinned Aboriginal children. They were often removed from their families as young as possible. Lighter-skinned Aboriginal children were more likely to be considered for adoption into white families. Those with darker skin were more likely to be sent to institutions or to work.

The policy also focused on the marriages of 'half-caste' Aboriginal women. In some areas, a 'half-caste' Aboriginal person couldn't marry anyone other than an Aboriginal or 'half-caste' without the approval of the Protector of Aborigines. (This was a powerful position created in the late 1830s and used in some regions of Australia.) In practice, no permission was given for white or 'half-caste' males to marry 'full-blood' Aboriginal women. But they could marry 'half-caste' women. The idea behind this policy was that 'half-castes' could survive. 'Full-bloods' should be left to die out as quickly as possible to get rid of Indigenous culture. (Refer to Chapter 2 for definitions of these terms.)

'Focus on the children': Forget about the oldies

The main aim of forcibly removing Indigenous babies and children from their families was to absorb them into the broader community. The goal was to make their cultural values and identities disappear. Adults, it was feared, were too connected to their Indigenous cultures. They were harder to assimilate. The Chief Protector of Aborigines in Western Australia, A O Neville, gave the goals behind this policy in a speech in April 1937:

> ... the native population is increasing ... Are we going to have a population of 1,000,000 blacks in the Commonwealth or are we going to merge them into our white community and forget that there ever were any Aborigines in Australia? ...

To achieve this end, however, we must have charge of the children at the age of six years; it is useless to wait until they are twelve or thirteen years of age. In Western Australia we have the power under the Act to take any child from its mother at any stage of its life, no matter whether the mother be legally married or not.

Children were taken from their Indigenous parents so they could be brought up as white people. They could be taught to reject their heritage. They could not be exposed to their own cultures. Their names were changed. They weren't allowed to speak their traditional languages. Some were never told they were Indigenous. They were never told anything about the families they'd been removed from. Indigenous children were placed in institutions and schools. They were trained to be labourers or domestic servants for white families and employers on their release. This path meant that little attention was given to the education that Indigenous children in these institutions received. The people in power thought that Indigenous children would not complete school or hope to do anything other than manual work.

After the 1950s, Indigenous children, especially those with lighter skin, were adopted into white families. The theory behind this was that Indigenous people with lighter skin would be more easily assimilated into the white community.

EARLY ATTEMPTS AT ASSIMILATION

In 1814, Governor Macquarie opened the Native Institution, a school for Aboriginal children, at Parramatta. The purpose was 'to civilise, educate and foster habits of industry and decency in the Aborigine'. The parents of the Aboriginal children who started at the school, over time, saw that its aim was to distance them from their families and cultures. They then withdrew the children from the school. The school closed in 1820. In 1837, the Catholic Church began its missionary work through the creation of schools for Aboriginal children. (Refer to Chapter 7 for more on the missionaries.)

'For their own good'

Many people involved in the forced removal of Indigenous children from their families thought they were doing the right thing. They thought that Indigenous culture was primitive. They believed that Indigenous children faced harsh lives if they stayed with their Indigenous families. These views were affected by racist ideas that Indigenous people were bad parents who didn't care for their children.

Removal from Indigenous families was forced in many cases. Parents who could and wanted to look after their children were cruelly denied the chance to care for them. They had few, if any, ways to fight to have their children returned. Some were told their children had died when, in fact, they had been fostered or adopted to white families. Others said they had been made to sign adoption forms. Some said they had been misled about what they were signing.

Many Indigenous children taken away from their parents didn't have better lives than if they'd stayed with their families. They were often at risk, exposed to abuse, and not given the love and affection they would've had from their natural parents. Their natural parents never wanted to give them up in the first place.

Rules for the Removal Policy

Every Australian state and territory passed legislation that made the policy of forcibly removing Indigenous children from their families official. These laws gave Chief Protectors or Protection Boards many powers over Indigenous people. Some early legislation said that only neglected children should be removed. But in practice being Indigenous was often enough. Later, all legislation allowed for the removal of Indigenous children from their families based on their race alone.

The positions of Protector of Aborigines were the result of a report from the Select Committee of the House of Commons on Aborigines in 1838. The committee thought that people in this role would learn the language of Indigenous people under their control. The committee thought people in this role would watch over the Indigenous people. The position was supposed to make sure Indigenous people were not treated cruelly or unjustly. But many have said that the role was one of social control. State governments passed laws to create the following positions that were supposed to 'protect' Aboriginal people:

✓ **Victoria**, *Aborigines Protection Act 1869*: The Port Phillip Protectorate was started in 1839. It had several Protectors of Aborigines. The later Act started the Victorian Board for the Protection of Aborigines. This board could take Aboriginal children from their families and house them in dormitories.

✓ **Queensland**, *Aboriginal Protection and Restriction of the Sale of Opium Act 1897*: This Act gave superintendents powers over Aboriginal people. This included directing where they should live. Its inclusion with rules about the sale of opium shows the way in which laws were used to control the lives of non-white people. Opium was thought to be of danger to Indigenous people. But a lot of Europeans also used the drug. It was freely available until 1906. Queensland created positions of Protector of Aborigines from 1898 to 1904. It did so again from 1963 to 1986. This legislation also applied to the Torres Strait Islands.

✓ **Western Australia**, *Aborigines Act 1905*: In 1915, Western Australia created the position of Chief Protector of Aborigines. This position had vast powers.

✓ **New South Wales**, *Aborigines Protection Act 1909*: The first Protector of Aborigines was appointed in 1882. The Aborigines Protection Board was started in 1883. But changes to the legislation in 1909 allowed the board to take Aboriginal children from their families without parents' consent or court order. The board was changed to the Aborigines Welfare Board in 1940. But its powers still focused on the removal of Aboriginal children from their families.

✓ **South Australia**, *Aborigines Act 1911*: South Australia had a Protector of Aborigines from 1837. The 1911 Act was like the powers of the Northern Territory Ordinance.

🖊 **Northern Territory,** *Northern Territory Ordinance 1911*:
Changes in 1918 made the Chief Protector the legal guardian
of every Aboriginal and 'half-caste' person under 18 years
of age. Before 1911, the Northern Territory was part of South
Australia. So a Protector of Aborigines had existed since
1837. Baldwin Spencer became the first Northern Territory
Protector of Aborigines in 1911.

🖊 **Tasmania,** *Infants Welfare Act 1935*: This Act wasn't specifically for the removal of Aboriginal children. But it was used
to carry out an assimilation policy in the same way other
states did. In 1830, Tasmania appointed its first Protector of
Aborigines, George Robinson. He later headed the Port Phillip
Protectorate in Victoria.

Note: All states and territories ended child removal legislation
by 1969.

The impact on Indigenous children

Many Indigenous children removed from their families were
abused after being placed in state care, fostered or adopted out, or
sent out to work. Aboriginal children placed in institutions were
steered away from having contact with their parents. Some were
told that their parents had died or had left them. The institutions
aimed to turn children away from their culture and force them to
follow 'white ways'. This often gave children bad feelings about
their culture and background. It made them ashamed of their
Indigenous heritage. The living conditions in the institutions
were harsh. Children were often hungry and cold. Little affection
was provided. But there was plenty of physical punishment.
Children were whipped, beaten, placed in dark places or tied up.
Psychiatrists have noted that depression, anxiety, low self-
esteem, post-traumatic stress and suicide are common among
the Stolen Generations.

REMEMBER

Some Indigenous people who were removed under the policy
don't know where they were taken from. They haven't been able
to find information about their removal. Sometimes papers have
been lost or destroyed.

In New South Wales, Aboriginal girls taken from their families were placed in the Cootamundra Domestic Training Home for Aboriginal Girls. The boys were placed in the Aboriginal Boys' Training Home at Kinchela. Here's a little about each of those places:

- **Cootamundra Domestic Training Home for Aboriginal Girls:** Aboriginal girls placed here were trained to become domestic servants in the homes of middle-class white people. The Home was open from 1911 to 1986. Girls forcibly taken from their families weren't allowed to contact their parents. Letters from family were often not passed on. So many girls wrongly believed they were unwanted, left or forgotten. Proof later showed that girls were harshly punished and sometimes beaten.

- **Kinchela Aboriginal Boys' Training Home:** The home was started in 1924 near Kempsey. It was known for being poorly managed and mentally isolating for the boys. It did not fulfil the agreement to train its charges. In 1935, a report into the home caused the Aborigines Protection Board to 'strongly advise' the manager 'to give up intoxicating liquor entirely', particularly when in the company of the boys.

  Later proof noted the brutal physical punishment and abuse suffered by boys placed there. Reform of the Home didn't take place until after World War II. It finally closed in 1970. By that time it had housed up to 600 boys. In 1976 the Home became a drug and alcohol rehabilitation centre — 'Bennelong's Haven' — for the local Aboriginal community. It closed in 2018.

The impact on Indigenous families

A lot of attention has been given to the impact on children of removal from their Indigenous families. But less attention has been given to the trauma faced by parents who had children taken from them. The loss was harmful to many parents. They never got over the grief of having their children taken from them. Some died from their heartbreak. Others used alcohol to numb their pain. Many parents fought to get their children back. They went to authorities. They even tried legal action to have their children returned to them. Letters written to children in state care were usually not delivered. Legal action rarely worked. Families were further broken when more than one child was removed. In many instances, all the children were removed. Siblings who were removed were often separated from each other on purpose and grew up apart.

REMEMBER

The removal of children over several generations meant a severe disruption to the Indigenous oral culture. Much cultural knowledge was lost as a result.

TIP

Link-Up is a group started by the Indigenous community in New South Wales in 1980. It helps Indigenous people who were removed from their families. Link-Up helps with finding a family, provides counselling services and support to family members and sets up reunions. It helps to find suitable Indigenous foster care families when needed. It also helps in finding kin or family members who can help Indigenous children being taken into state care. Similar Link-Up services now operate in Queensland, Victoria and South Australia.

Acknowledging the Stolen Generations

The policy of forcibly removing Indigenous children was devastating for those who were taken away and the families who were left behind. The trauma hurt people. Many had trouble getting over their abuse. Others were angry when they found out that parents who they had been told were dead were alive and had fought hard to get them back.

The Going Home conference took place in Darwin in 1994. Over 600 Aboriginal people and Torres Strait Islanders from across Australia attended, all of whom had been removed from their families. They called for an inquiry into the policy of forced child removal and its legacies. In 1995, an inquiry began. It worked with the broad community. Then it delivered a report that told what had happened to the people who were beginning to call themselves the Stolen Generations.

REMEMBER

Many books and movies deal with the child removal policy and its legacies. See Chapters 14 and 15 for more about Indigenous literature and movies on this topic.

The report of the inquiry into the Stolen Generations

On 11 May 1995, federal Attorney-General Michael Lavarch issued the terms of reference to the Human Rights and Equal Opportunity Commission to undertake an inquiry. It would become the National Inquiry into the Separation of Aboriginal and Torres Strait Islander Children from Their Families.

The terms of reference were to 'trace the past laws, practices and policies which resulted in the separation of Aboriginal and Torres Strait Islander children from their families by compulsion, duress or undue influence, and the effects of those laws, practices and policies'. The inquiry was also to suggest ways to correct the impacts of the policy. This included consideration of compensation (or repayment for the suffering caused).

The inquiry held hearings around Australia between December 1995 and October 1996. It received 777 submissions, 69 per cent from Indigenous people. The *Bringing Them Home* report was tabled in parliament on 26 May 1997. The report estimated that between 10 per cent and 33 per cent of Indigenous children were removed from their families between 1910 and 1970. The report was careful to evaluate past actions in the light of the values and standards in place at the time. But it still found that the policy of forcible removal violated fundamental human rights. These included:

- Doing away with parental rights by taking children and taking custody and control over them

- Abuses of power in the removal processes

- Breaches of guardianship duties by governments and 'carers'

- Loss of liberty by holding children and confining them to institutions

Children suffered many abuses in the institutions and workplaces they were sent to. Sometimes they suffered abuse in the families they were adopted into. The report showed how these childhood traumas hurt people in their adult lives. These traumas often made it hard for them to get used to family life and parenthood. A quarter of the witnesses who had been fostered or adopted reported physical abuse. Almost one in five who had been raised in institutions reported physical abuse. One in ten reported sexual abuse. The report also showed that many Indigenous children who were sent out to work weren't paid wages. (See the later sidebar 'Where have all the wages gone?' for more about this issue.)

The report noted the practice of sending children born to Torres Strait Islander mothers and non-Islander fathers to mission dormitories on islands or to mainland institutions. This practice continued up until 1970. Church representatives in the Torres Strait would notify the Department of Native Affairs of pregnancies and of any mixed parentage. The department would plan for girls born of those unions to be placed in the Catholic Convent dormitory on Thursday Island. Boys were sent to mainland institutions or adopted out to Islander families.

Many Australians knew of the practice of removing Indigenous children from their families. But they often didn't know just how common the practice was. They didn't know how much Indigenous children who were removed suffered until the release of the *Bringing Them Home* report.

REMEMBER

The day on which the *Bringing Them Home* report was tabled in federal parliament, 26 May, has been marked as *National Sorry Day* since 1998.

MYTH
BUSTER

Some people have said that many of the Indigenous children taken from their families were removed for their own good. Conditions in Indigenous communities could be dreadful due to neglect by government agencies. Many Indigenous families were poor. But the *Bringing Them Home* report found that Indigenous children separated from their families 'fared no better than those not separated when assessed on social indicators such as education, employment and income'. It also stated: 'Those removed were twice as likely to have been arrested . . . and they suffer more health problems'.

A TRAGIC CYCLE

Many Indigenous people believe that the policy of removing Indigenous children from their families still has impacts today. People who were put in institutions or brought up in places where they were abused can find it hard to get used to family life. They've never seen good parenting. So, in some cases, parenting skills aren't learned and children are neglected. These circumstances have set up a tragic cycle in some Indigenous families. Generations grow up in state care.

Laws specifically designed to remove Indigenous children from their families have been repealed. But Indigenous children are still at greater risk of removal from their families. Factors found to have added to this include cultural bias against Indigenous ways of parenting and poor services for Indigenous families. Indigenous juveniles also face discriminatory treatment within the criminal justice system. See Chapter 16 for more on these issues.

The official response

The Keating Labor government had asked for the *Bringing Them Home* report (refer to the previous section). But it was received by a Liberal government, that of John Howard.

The Howard government had concerns about the report. It rejected its statement that the removal of Indigenous children was a form of genocide (or destruction of a race of people). It said that the number of children taken away was only one in ten. It said that many had been removed for their own benefit. It also wondered whether people were 'stolen' or if they could be considered a 'generation'. It did not even note the several generations that were affected by the assimilation practices.

Howard rejected two recommendations of the report strongly. He rejected both the need for a national apology to the Stolen Generations and the creation of a compensation scheme for victims of the policies. Howard believed an apology wasn't a proper response. He believed strongly that a current generation should-n't be made to feel guilty or sorry about things done by previous generations, especially if what had been done was with good intentions. Others opposed a national apology because it would 'open the floodgates' for compensation claims. Aboriginal Affairs Minister Senator John Herron said that stories of widespread removal of Indigenous children from their families were exaggerated. He said that, where children were taken, it was for lawful reasons.

The Howard government fought the findings of the *Bringing Them Home* report and rejected recommendations. But it did provide money for other services and initiatives suggested by the report. Financial support was granted for

- Counselling services

- Networks to link up family members

- Programs to make stored material more easily available

- Programs to record the oral histories of people removed by the policy

- Indigenous family support and parenting services

On 4 April 2000, the Howard government stated that it was 'concerned that there is no reliable basis for what appears to be a generally accepted conclusion as to the supposed dimensions of the "stolen generation"'. It went on to add, 'At most, it might be inferred that up to 10 per cent of children were separated for a variety of reasons, both protective and otherwise, some forcibly and some not. This does not constitute a "generation" of "stolen" children. The phrase "stolen generation" is rhetorical'. The statement was made in a submission to a Senate inquiry on compensation for children forcibly removed.

MYTH BUSTER

The *Bringing Them Home* report found that the aim of the policy of removing Indigenous children from their families was to 'breed out' Aboriginal and Torres Strait Islander peoples and their cultures. Some people believed this amounted to 'cultural genocide'. Under international law, policies and practices designed to destroy a race of people are known as *genocide.* They are forbidden under the 1948 Convention on the Prevention and Punishment of the Crime of Genocide. Policies and laws can be genocidal even if they aren't fuelled by hatred. People thinking the policy is for the good of the members of a race doesn't matter when it comes to whether the action amounts to genocide. But the use of the word 'genocide' in this context has caused deep debate and disagreement.

WHERE HAVE ALL THE WAGES GONE?

The practice of placing a large part of the wages of Indigenous workers in government trust accounts was common. It wasn't only used for Indigenous children sent out to work but also other Indigenous workers. Most Aboriginal workers were given some pocket money. But they were not told where most of their earnings were going. They were not told that they had rights to the earnings. They never saw the wages again. This meant they were effectively treated as slave labour. Not being able to access good wages locked Aboriginal people into a cycle of poverty.

Historians think that the state of Queensland alone owes around $500,000,000 to Indigenous people for these 'stolen wages'. In New South Wales, the amount is thought to be $70,000,000. Indigenous people have tried to get back some of these wages in recent years. But many records of the trust accounts were destroyed or lost. This made it hard for people to prove that they had their wages stolen or to specify the amount.

Governments have fought claims for compensation for stolen wages. Many of the claimants are old, poor and of weak health. Many have passed away while waiting for their claims to be heard. New South Wales set up an Aboriginal Trust Fund Repayment Scheme to repay stolen wages. It offered to pay

(continued)

(continued)

> $3,521 for every $100 owed in stolen wages. But by March 2008 only 24 per cent of the 1,177 claims from direct claimants had been successful. The scheme finished processing claims at the end of 2011.
>
> In 2019, the Queensland state government settled a historic class action. It agreed to pay out $190 million. Nearly 2,000 former workers signed up as parties to the action. The funds will be divided between more than 11,000 Indigenous workers who had their wages stolen, or their relatives.

Unfinished Business: Reparations and Compensation

The *Bringing Them Home* report made recommendations about the reparations (or ways to repair the wrongs) that could be made to the Stolen Generations and their families. The report took a broad view about what these reparations should consist of. (The view followed international law.) It also made specific suggestions. These include

✔ Acknowledgement of the truth and an apology — specifically that apologies should be issued to the Stolen Generations and their families

✔ Guarantees that the human rights abuses wouldn't occur again, with a specific recommendation that public education about the removal policy and its impact be provided

✔ Returning what had been lost (restitution), as much as possible, specifically in helping people who were removed to find their families

✔ Rehabilitation, including recording oral histories of those removed

✔ Compensation, with a specific recommendation to start a national compensation fund

Only 3 of the 54 recommendations of the report have been put into place. They are an oral history collection program at the National Library of Australia, starting a National Sorry Day and the issuing of formal apologies by all parliaments, state and federal. But because of the report, resources have been put into collecting more oral histories. Resources have also been put towards counselling and other support services for the Stolen Generations. The one area where governments have been slow to follow recommendations has been in giving compensation packages to the Stolen Generations.

Saying sorry

State and territory governments were generally quick to offer apologies to the Stolen Generations:

- **Western Australia:** Delivered 27 May 1997 by Leader of the Opposition Geoff Gallop (motion supported by Premier Richard Court)

- **South Australia:** Delivered 28 May 1997 by Minister for Aboriginal Affairs Dean Brown

- **Australian Capital Territory:** Delivered 17 June 1997 by Chief Minister Kate Carnell

- **New South Wales:** Delivered 18 June 1997 by Premier Bob Carr

- **Tasmania:** Delivered 13 August 1997 by Premier Tony Rundle

- **Victoria:** Delivered 17 September 1997 by Premier Jeff Kennett

- **Queensland:** Delivered 26 May 1999 by Premier Peter Beattie

- **Northern Territory:** Delivered 24 October 2001 by Chief Minister Clare Martin

Prime Minister John Howard stayed steady in his belief that an apology from the federal government to the Stolen Generations wasn't necessary. But, on 26 August 1999, the federal government issued a statement of 'deep and sincere regret that Indigenous Australians suffered injustices under the practices of past generations, and for the hurt and trauma that many Indigenous people continue to feel as a consequence of those actions'.

REMEMBER

This 'statement of regret' was seen by many to fall short of an apology. The issue remained a difficult matter. Many Australians urged Howard to change his mind. Actions that tried to get the government to issue an apology include:

- **26 January 1998:** Australians for Native Title and Reconciliation (ANTaR) launched the Sorry Books campaign. The books invited Australians to write something in response to the federal government's refusal to make a formal apology. Many Australians signed these books.

- **28 May 2000:** A crowd thought to be close to 250,000 walked across Sydney Harbour Bridge to call for an apology to the Stolen Generations by the federal government. They were in support of reconciliation between Indigenous peoples and other Australians. The day before, Howard had once again ruled out an apology to the Stolen Generations.

- **22 November 2001:** Pope John Paul II issued a formal apology on behalf of the Vatican to the Indigenous Australians affected by the actions of any Catholic authorities in connection with the policy of removing children from their families.

- **26 May 2004:** A memorial to the Stolen Generations was created at Reconciliation Place in Canberra.

A Labor government was elected in November 2007. The party had earlier promised to make an official apology to the Stolen Generations if it won government. On 13 February 2008, Prime Minister Kevin Rudd gave an apology from the federal government to members of the Stolen Generations on the first sitting day of the new parliament. Here's a part of that apology:

> *We apologise for the laws and policies of successive Parliaments and governments that have inflicted profound grief, suffering and loss on these our fellow Australians.*

We apologise especially for the removal of Aboriginal and Torres Strait Islander children from their families, their communities and their country.

For the pain, suffering and hurt of these Stolen Generations, their descendants and for their families left behind, we say sorry.

And for the indignity and degradation thus inflicted on a proud people and a proud culture, we say sorry.

We the Parliament of Australia respectfully request that this apology be received in the spirit in which it is offered as part of the healing of the nation.

The day before the Prime Minister delivered the speech, Minister for Indigenous Affairs Jenny Macklin issued a statement. It noted that financial compensation wouldn't be paid to the Stolen Generations. But it also noted the Rudd government's commitment to improve the lives of Indigenous people to match those of other Australians.

REMEMBER

In 2000, Australia went before the United Nations Committee on the Elimination of Racial Discrimination. The committee criticised the Australian government's failure to adequately respond to the recommendations of the *Bringing Them Home* report.

Seeking legal justice

Indigenous people tried to get compensation through the courts for the harms they suffered in state care. Some of these cases failed because government action in taking Indigenous children was legal at the time. Some failed because there was not enough proof for the case. Later cases had more success. These cases focused on the harms suffered in state care. They didn't focus on challenging whether the removal was legal in the first place.

Kruger and others versus the Commonwealth

In 1997, the High Court of Australia heard a case brought by Aboriginal people from the Northern Territory who had been removed from their families when they were young under the Northern Territory Ordinance. Among them was Alec Kruger. Also included was a parent who lost a child under the same laws. They claimed the policy had breached their human rights. These rights included due process before the law, equality before the law and freedom of movement. The High Court found against them. The court said that, although those rights may have been breached, they're not rights protected by Australian law. So no legal remedy is available for their infringement.

Peter Gunner and Lorna Cubillo

In 2000, Peter Gunner and Lorna Cubillo claimed they'd been wrongly taken as children. The Federal Court stressed that it wasn't denying that the Stolen Generations existed. It believed that Mr Gunner and Ms Cubillo had suffered greatly since being removed from their families. But it said it had to find, on the legal matter, that no proof suggested that the removal from their families was done in an unlawful manner. The case was lost.

Valerie Linlow

In 2002, Valerie Linlow, a member of the Stolen Generations, got an award of compensation of $35,000 from the New South Wales Victim's Compensation Tribunal. The compensation was for sexual assault and other injuries suffered after she had been removed from her Aboriginal family by authorities. She was placed, at the age of 16, as a domestic servant for a white family. She said: 'It's not the money that's important to me. It is the knowledge and recognition that this happened to Aboriginal people. No-one could pay any amount for what happened to us because we lost a lot'.

Bruce Trevorrow

On 1 August 2007, Bruce Trevorrow, a member of the Stolen Generations, was awarded $525,000 by Justice Thomas Gray of the South Australian Supreme Court. The payment was to compensate for the sorrow and pain he had suffered after being taken from his mother, in 1957, at the age of 13 months. This happened while he was being treated in Adelaide Children's Hospital for gastroenteritis. Six months after he was taken, his mother wrote to the Aboriginal Protection Board asking for her son back. But the board lied to her. The board said he was making good progress but doctors needed to keep him for treatment. Instead, he was fostered into a white family. He grew up unaware of his

Aboriginality. He did see his mother again. But by that time he was already troubled and couldn't adjust to either culture. He found himself going in and out of prison and other institutions. He had poor health. He suffered from alcoholism and depression.

The court, in its judgement, found that the circumstances in which Mr Trevorrow was removed were wrongful imprisonment. It was a breach of the state's duty of care. It was also able to compare the problems faced by Mr Trevorrow with those of his brother, who hadn't been removed. Upon hearing the judgement, Mr Trevorrow said: 'At the end of the day, you can't put a dollar value on what happened to me'. The South Australian government appealed. But the decision of the court and the award of compensation were upheld in 2010. Unfortunately, Mr Trevorrow died in 2008, before the appeal was dismissed and the decision in his favour was confirmed.

The realities of litigation and compensation

Litigation (or lawsuits) is a hard way to get justice. The claims take a long time to move through the courts. The Stolen Generations are likely to have low levels of education, few resources and poor health, including mental health issues. This mix makes the process long and tough for them. For this reason, ideas have been given for a national compensation scheme that could be run through a type of court called a tribunal. This would make the process simpler. It would make bringing a claim cost less money. It would also be more flexible about the rules of evidence.

Federal Labor and Liberal governments continue to oppose a national compensation scheme. They say that the states, territories and churches were legally responsible. So those bodies should create compensation measures. The federal government says it's giving resources to community actions. These include counselling and the recording of oral histories. It says it would rather do this than pay individuals. Others have argued that, even if legal responsibility lies elsewhere, the federal government should take leadership and start a fair national compensation scheme. People have also pointed out that the federal government had responsibility for Aboriginal people in the Northern Territory when the policy of removing Aboriginal children was at its height. So the federal government should at least consider a compensation scheme for them.

Some states did follow with compensation schemes. In 2006, the Tasmanian government passed the *Stolen Generations of Aboriginal Children Act 2006* (Tas). It placed $5 million into the compensation scheme to be split among Aboriginal people who qualified. This process showed that it was possible to start a reparations process to compensate members of the Stolen Generations. New South Wales, Victoria, Western Australia and South Australia all introduced schemes.

TECHNICAL
STUFF

On 2 April 2009, the United Nations Human Rights Committee released a report on Australia. It suggested that the Australian government 'adopt a comprehensive national mechanism to ensure that adequate reparation, including compensation, is provided to the victims of the Stolen Generations'. Federal Attorney-General Robert McClelland advised that the Rudd government wouldn't follow that recommendation. He said the government was instead focusing on improving the lives of Indigenous people and starting a 'Healing Foundation'.

The Aboriginal and Torres Strait Islander Healing Foundation was started on 30 October 2009. It is an Indigenous-controlled not-for-profit organisation. It funds community-based healing programs that 'seek to address the traumatic legacy of colonisation, forced removals and other past government policies'. The Healing Foundation has focused on programs to deal with trauma. But it has also helped to raise awareness about the idea of intergenerational trauma. This is the idea that, if someone has not recovered from their own trauma, they may, through their behaviour, pass it down to their children. In this way, the impact of the child removal policy flows down to the next generation. (For more on the Healing Foundation, go to healingfoundation. org.au.)

MYTH
BUSTER

The claim is often made that child removal policies are a thing of the past. The formal policy had ended in all states and territories by the end of the 1960s. But the experiences of many living survivors of the policy show the impact is not in the past. Research shows the extent of intergenerational trauma among the children of the Stolen Generations. It is further proof that people are still living with the impact of the policy today.

CULTURAL
PROTOCOLS

The strongest support for the members of the Stolen Generations has come from the community groups formed by the survivors of the child removal policy. Groups such as Link-Up NSW help people who were affected by the removal policy to find their families again (see www.linkupnsw.org.au; similar Link-Up services are available in Queensland, Victoria and South Australia). Groups such as the Kinchela Boys Home Aboriginal Corporation provide support and a sense of community for survivors of the trauma of the child removal policy (see kinchelaboyshome.org.au).

MYTH
BUSTER

The Australian government has been slow to look at a national compensation scheme for members of the Stolen Generations. Canada had a similar policy of forcibly removing Indigenous children from their families. It announced a compensation scheme in 2005. Aboriginal children in Canada were taken from their families and placed in institutions called Residential Schools. The Canadian government set aside $1.9 billion for the compensation package. The money created an Aboriginal Healing Foundation and a Truth and Reconciliation Program. But it also provided for individual compensation payments. This Common Experience Payment is $10,000 for the first year spent in a Residential School and $3,000 for each following year.

PROJECT

Carefully read the excerpt of the National Apology to the Stolen Generations delivered by Kevin Rudd in 2008. (Refer to the section 'Saying sorry', earlier in this chapter.) List five things included in the apology that you think are important.

PROJECT

Watch the film **Rabbit Proof Fence** *(which looks at the topic of Aboriginal children forcibly removed from their families) and write a short review of it.*

Part 3
Indigenous Activism

In This Part . . .

☐ Follow the struggle of Indigenous peoples, which, up until the 1960s, had a big focus on the claim to be equal with other Australians, and to be treated the same as other Australian citizens.

☐ See the significant change that occurred in 1967, when a constitutional referendum gave the federal government the power to make laws for Indigenous people.

☐ Understand the more recent strategies federal governments have implemented to work with Indigenous people, including a national apology for past wrongs and an intervention.

Citizenship Rights and a Referendum

By the late 1880s, colonisation had been going on for more than 100 years in the south-eastern part of Australia. Aboriginal people across the country were making their way around their new environment. But they stayed firm in their fight against the claims made by the British over their land. They fought against the control colonial governments tried to exercise over their lives. Aboriginal people made — through letters and petitions — their claims to equal rights as citizens and their claims to land. In this chapter, I provide several examples of Aboriginal people on reserves using their literacy skills to fight for better conditions. Later, this advocacy led to the creation of Indigenous groups that worked on political reform for the Indigenous communities.

The Australian Constitution came into force in 1901. But Indigenous people had been left out of the process of drafting it. The Constitution left power over the lives of Indigenous people with the states. The states continued an approach of 'protection'. This saw the creation of government bodies that controlled the lives of Indigenous people. Here, I look at the ways laws failed Indigenous people and kept them from having basic rights. Laws placed controls over where they could live, who they could marry and who they could be with. They weren't allowed to control their own money. They had no power to stop the removal of their children.

Indigenous people made a lot of contributions during World War I and World War II. They did so both at home and overseas. But after serving their country, Indigenous people didn't return to enjoy the same rights as other Australians. In this chapter, I look at how the treatment of the black diggers was a symbol of the difficulty Indigenous people faced. This sparked a citizenship rights movement to fight against the deep discrimination that filled the lives of Indigenous people across the country.

Early Claims to Better Treatment

Colonial governments began moving Aboriginal people onto pockets of land for their own protection. Aboriginal reserves were first created to keep them safe from violence and other hardships on the frontier. Then they became places where government bodies had great control over the lives of Indigenous people. This 'protection' quickly became treatment that was different from — and lesser than — the rights of other Australians. Indigenous people began to focus on the need for recognition of their citizenship rights. They wanted to break free from discrimination and take control over their own lives.

Equal access to education, work and the economy was seen as the key to improving the situation of Indigenous people. Aboriginal leaders came up, such as William Cooper and Fred Maynard. They had both worked on pastoral stations that they were stopped from owning. They were self-taught men. They wanted Aboriginal people to have the same chances as other Australians. They wanted Aboriginal people to make key decisions about their communities, their families and their lives. Then they'd be able to solve their own problems. This idea of access and opportunity was the basis for the desire for citizenship rights. Along with the claim for land and the desire for self-determination, it created the key pieces of the Indigenous political program. (See Chapter 17 for more on self-determination.)

Many people still believed that Indigenous people were inferior and, as such, the colonists had a duty to colonise and civilise them. Many also knew that Aboriginal people had been stripped of their lands through a brutal process of colonisation. Aboriginal people had lost their traditional means of support. Colonists believed the best approach for surviving Aboriginal populations was to place them on parcels of land. There they could be watched by missionaries or government officials who could 'civilise' them.

REMEMBER

From the 1830s, Aboriginal communities that had fought the attacks on their lands began to organise politically in a different way. The focus for their struggle was still their land. They often fought to be granted or to keep reserve lands. But Aboriginal people also worked to be treated fairly. They fought against the discriminatory and strict rules used by colonial governments to control their lives. They constantly fought to be treated fairly and to have a greater say over their own lives. This political activity often focused on petitioning the British monarchy. These appeals to the Crown tried to show that the British had a duty to look after Aboriginal people. They also showed a lack of trust in the colonial government to really 'protect' Aboriginal people or to have their best interests at heart.

Flinders Island

Aboriginal people in Van Diemen's Land bitterly fought against the colonisation by the British that began in the 1820s. (This land is now Tasmania.) Between 1831 and 1834, Aboriginal people were forced to leave the main island and move to Flinders Island. Flinders Island is the largest island of the Furneaux Group in Bass Strait (between Tasmania and mainland Australia). Here, the government promised that Aboriginal people would enjoy safety from frontier violence. They would also have the benefits of civilisation and Christianity.

It became clear these promises were empty. Food was hard to find. The living conditions were poor. Many of the Tasmanian survivors who were sent to Flinders Island died. Others suffered from poor nutrition and disease. Life on the island was heavily controlled. Strict rules focused on sticking to Christian standards. Those in charge of running the island and watching over Aboriginal people were often not very kind to them.

This situation caused many older Aboriginal people to worry. But the younger men and women used their new literacy skills to fight against their poor treatment. From 1836 to 1837 they had their own newspaper — the *Flinders Island Chronicle* or *Flinders Island Weekly Chronicle*. The protest leaders used the rules of Christianity to stand up for themselves. They were also affected by the anti-slavery movement that was growing in Australia.

Political protest on Flinders Island reached a peak in the mid-1840s. It included a petition to Queen Victoria that claimed the colonial government had broken promises to them. The petition of 17 February 1846 pleads that its former superintendent, Dr Henry Jeanneret, not be sent back the island. It also gives a view into the treatment of Aboriginal people on the reserve. The petition states in part:

> *Our houses were let fall down & they were never cleaned but were covered in vermin & not white-washed. We were often without Clothes except a very little one & Dr. Jeanneret did not care to mind us when we were sick until we were very bad. Eleven of us died when he was here. He kept us from our Rations when he pleased & sometimes gave us Bad Rations of Tea & Tobacco. He shot some of our dogs before our eyes & sent all the other dogs of ours to an Island & when we told him that they would starve he told us they might eat each other . . . We were never taught to read or to write or to sing to God by the Doctor. He taught us a little upon the Sundays & his Prisoner Servant also taught us & his Prisoner Servant also took us plenty of times to Jail by his orders.*

The Aboriginal people of Flinders Island clearly understood that they should be treated fairly and with dignity. Jeanneret did return to Flinders Island. But the settlement was ordered to be closed in 1847 by the Tasmanian governor. The remaining 40 or so Aboriginal people were taken to Oyster Cove, a former convict settlement south of Hobart.

FIGHTING SLAVERY

The anti-slavery movement was focused on ending the slave trade. It was influential among evangelical (a Christian movement) and humanitarian groups. In Britain, the anti-slavery movement was the first large philanthropic mass movement. It affected anti-slavery movements in other countries. It planted the seeds for other social changes such as voting rights, the rights of women and workers' rights. It also affected people's thinking about Indigenous people. They saw Indigenous people as entitled to the same rights as white people. They actively worked for the better treatment of Indigenous people in the colonies, including Australia.

Coranderrk

Aboriginal people living in the Port Phillip District had been affected by diseases, loss of their lands and frontier violence. All of these had caused their population to drop to only a few thousand by the 1850s. (The Port Phillip District became the colony of Victoria in 1851.) During this period, gold rushes also added to the demand for land and pressures on the Aboriginal community. Reserves, such as the one at Coranderrk, were started for the shrinking Aboriginal population.

Coranderrk was an area of almost ten square kilometres. It was set aside as a reserve in 1863 after about 40 Wurundjeri people settled at a traditional campsite near Healesville. The Wurundjeri people asked for its ownership. The settlement ran well for many years as an Aboriginal enterprise. It grew wheat and hops that were sold in Melbourne. In the 1870s, the reserve was threatened with closure by the Aboriginal Protection Board. The people of the Coranderrk reserve began a long protest. They were strong voices for their own abilities to take care of their affairs. They were critical of the control the managers of the reserve had over their lives. They wrote letters to the newspapers and to government ministers. They asked for the support of humanitarians. Their actions forced the Victorian government to hold two major inquiries. In 1877, they inquired generally into policies relating to Aboriginal people. In 1881, they specifically inquired into conditions at Coranderrk.

The Aborigines Protection Bill came before the Victorian Parliament in 1886. It gave the Board for the Protection of Aborigines many powers over the lives of Aboriginal people. The people who lived at Coranderrk wrote in protest to the newspapers:

> We wish to ask for our wishes, that is, could we get our freedom to go away shearing and harvesting, and to come home when we wish, and also to go for the good of our health when we need it; and we aboriginals all wish and hope to have freedom, not to be bound down by the protection of the Board, as it says in the Bill, But we should be free like the white population. There is only a few blacks now remaining in Victoria. We are all dying away now, and we blacks of Aboriginal blood wish to have our freedom for all our life time, for the population is small, and the increase is slow. For why does the Board seek in these latter days more stronger authority over us aborigines than it has yet been. For there is only 21 aborigines on the station Coranderrk including men and women.

But the 1886 legislation forced Aboriginal people of mixed heritage under the age of 34 off the reserve and into the general community. With only a few healthy people left to work the farm, Coranderrk became useless. Almost half the land was resumed in 1893. The reserve was ordered closed in 1924. But a handful of people wouldn't move and were allowed to live out their days there. In 1995, part of the reserve was handed back to the Wurundjeri Tribe Land Compensation and Cultural Heritage Council. This was when the Indigenous Land Corporation bought almost one square kilometre.

Cummeragunja reserve

Maloga mission was founded on the New South Wales side of the Murray River near Echuca in 1874. Aboriginal people of the Yorta Yorta and Bangerang nations soon asked for their own independent reserve on their traditional lands. In this, they were supported by Aboriginal people from the Coranderrk reserve in Victoria (refer to the previous section).

By 1881, land had been reserved about five kilometres from Maloga mission. This became the Cummeragunja reserve in 1883. But Aboriginal people began stating their desire to own their own blocks of land. They asked the governor in 1887 to be allowed to do so. Like the people of Coranderrk, they believed that they could provide for themselves if they were given the chance to tend their own land. This would allow them to take care of themselves and to no longer depend on the government.

They also appealed to the Queen's authority. One of these men was William Cooper. Decades later, he became the leader of one of the first major Indigenous political groups in Australia, the Australian Aborigines' League. He also was involved with other key political groups such as the Aborigines Progressive Association. (See the later section 'Indigenous people organise' for more on these groups.) Cummeragunja became famous for the activism of its residents. As well as William Cooper, Pastor Doug Nicholls also came from there. The reserve was closed by the Aborigines Protection Board in 1953 because the number of residents was low.

REMEMBER

This spirit of activism continues today. Members of the community were involved with the first native title claim made in Victoria, in 1994. They lost the claim in 1998. But the Yorta Yorta worked out an agreement to co-manage part of the lands with the Victorian government in 2004.

British Subjects, but Not Quite . . .

Colonial governments confidently stated that the British legal system applied all over Australia. They said that Indigenous laws no longer applied. In theory, Australia's Indigenous peoples became British subjects. But in practice, they were treated differently.

REMEMBER

British law failed Indigenous people on several fronts. In the early years of colonisation, specific laws let settlers shoot Aboriginal people under certain circumstances. 'Protection' acts allowed the removal of children. Discrimination against Indigenous people living within the wider community was everywhere. No laws provided real protection. This section talks about a range of those circumstances.

Denying basic rights

Indigenous legal systems weren't recognised by the British. This meant that Indigenous rights to land were also ignored. No payment was given for the loss of property. But the legal system discriminated against Indigenous people in other ways, too. They couldn't press charges or appear as witnesses. They were sometimes punished as a group for the crimes of other Indigenous people. Ideas such as due process before the law and equality before the law didn't always apply. In fact, the colonial laws that were supposed to apply equally to all British subjects targeted Indigenous people in some big ways. Here are just a few of them:

- **1816:** Martial law was declared in New South Wales against Aboriginal people. They could be shot if they were armed or within a certain distance of colonial settlements.

- **1824:** Tasmanian colonists were allowed to shoot Aboriginal people.

- **1869:** A Board for the Protection of Aborigines was started in Victoria. It could order the removal of any child to a reform or industrial school.

- **1890:** The Aborigines Protection Board in New South Wales could forcibly take children off reserves to resocialise them.

TECHNICAL
STUFF

A *citizen* is someone who shares both in ruling and being ruled. The right to vote and the duty to obey the law are central to ideas of citizenship. Today, ideas of citizenship are also linked to some basic human rights. These include

- Civil rights needed for freedom (such as freedom of speech)

- Political rights to take part in the political process (right to vote, right to stand for election)

- Social rights needed to take part in society (right to education, right to adequate standards of living)

Many of these rights weren't respected when it came to Indigenous people. That's why the struggle was ongoing to gain *citizenship rights.*

TECHNICAL
STUFF

The 2020 High Court decision in *Love v Commonwealth; Thoms v Commonwealth* held by a majority that an Aboriginal person is not 'an alien'. Section 51(xix) gives the Federal Government the power to make laws about 'naturalization and aliens'. The case involved men who had not been born in Australia and had not become citizens under the law. But they were Aboriginal. The court ruled that if they could prove they were Aboriginal, they could not be subject to an order to leave the country. Proof of being Aboriginal requires having Aboriginal descent, identifying as Aboriginal and being recognised by the Aboriginal community as Aboriginal.

For their own 'protection'

All the colonies passed laws that set up specific government bodies with powers to control the lives of Indigenous people, particularly their children (refer to Chapter 8). They usually had the words 'Aborigines Protection' or 'Aborigines Welfare' in their titles. These laws made Indigenous people *wards of the state.* The laws placed Indigenous people in a legal position where they had fewer rights than citizens. The laws gave these bodies almost complete control over the lives of Indigenous people:

- 1869, **Victoria:** The Aborigines Protection Act created the Victorian Board for the Protection of Aborigines.

- 1883, **New South Wales:** The Aborigines Protection Act created the Aborigines Protection Board. The 1909 Act gave extra powers to the board over the lives of Aboriginal people and their children. It was changed to the Aborigines Welfare Board in 1940.

- 1897, **Queensland:** The Aboriginal Protection and Restriction of the Sale of Opium Act gave Superintendents powers over Aboriginal people. These powers included directing where they should live.

- ↙ **1905, Western Australia:** The Aborigines Act created a Chief Protector of Aborigines who had huge powers over their lives.

- ↙ **1911, Northern Territory:** The Northern Territory Ordinance gave powers to the Chief Protector. Changes in 1918 made him the legal guardian of every Aboriginal and 'half-caste' person under 18 years of age.

- ↙ **1911, South Australia:** The Aborigines Act grew the powers of the Protector of Aborigines. This was a position South Australia had from 1836.

The Protection Boards and Chief Protectors in each state or territory had huge powers over Indigenous people. Laws gave them control over who could live on government land or reserves, who could work and who could marry. They also had control over whether children would be removed from their families to be sent to institutions or out to work.

NEVILLE'S ROLE

One Chief Protector of Aborigines in Western Australia was A O Neville. He held the office from 1915 until 1936. He then took the position of Commissioner for Native Affairs until his retirement in 1940. He was responsible for rules that gave the government more power over the lives of Aboriginal people, particularly children.

Neville's belief was that 'full-blood' Aboriginal people should be segregated (or separated). He also believed that those of mixed descent might be temporarily segregated and trained. But then they should be part of white society as domestics and farm workers. He believed they should eventually blend with the white population through marriage. He took an interest in record-keeping. He often inspected reserves and institutions.

The realities of assimilation

Away from the reserves, Indigenous people became part of the broader community with different degrees of success. Some married white people and had families. Some worked, often for less money or for food. They didn't have full and equal rights with other Australians just because they lived within the broader community.

REMEMBER

Indigenous people faced discrimination in their everyday lives. This was through the conditions of their work, their housing and the medical attention they got. Aboriginal people weren't allowed to live in rentals, especially in country towns. This meant they often had to live on the edges, in poorer housing, sometimes in nothing more than a lean-to. Rural hospitals didn't allow Aboriginal people inside. They would treat them on the verandahs. This discrimination pushed Indigenous people further to the edges of mainstream society. It meant they were more likely to be in poverty and have poor health.

TECHNICAL STUFF

Between 1856 and 1900, all the states had given Aboriginal men the right to vote. But this right was limited in Western Australia and Queensland. There was a property ownership requirement that few could meet. South Australia (which at the time included the Northern Territory) gave women, including Indigenous women, the right to vote in 1895.

Leaving Indigenous People Out of the Constitution

The Australian Constitution came into effect in 1901. It was an Act of the British Parliament. But it created the legal system in Australia. At the time the Constitution was drafted (in the 1880s and 1890s), the Aboriginal population had been destroyed. It was living away from mainstream society — on reserves, in pockets within cities and on the edges of towns.

Several common ideas within Australian society influenced the role and place that Indigenous peoples were given through the document. Australian society had a powerful culture that thought the white races were better than other races, and so were natural leaders. (This was the same as in many other parts of the world that had been colonised.) Many people thought that the Indigenous peoples would die out. They thought that the kindest thing to do for Indigenous peoples was to place them in areas such as reserves. There they could live out their days with some dignity.

The states set up their powers

Indigenous people were left out of the drafting of any parts of the Constitution. Matters about Indigenous people would be the duty of the states. The federal government had responsibility for only those Indigenous people who were living in the territories, such as the Northern Territory. (The referendum to change this section of the Constitution is covered later in this chapter.) But ideas of white racial superiority ran more deeply in the Constitution than simply leaving out Indigenous people from talks about this document.

TECHNICAL
STUFF

The Australian Constitution created the Australian courts, including the High Court. It set up the two houses of federal parliament — the House of Representatives (the lower house) and the Senate (the upper house). And it divided power between the courts, the executive (the public service) and the federal parliament. It also divided power between the federal and state governments. Any power not specifically given to the federal government in the Constitution was left with the states. (These are known as *residual powers*.) For example, the area of industrial relations is the responsibility of the federal government. Criminal law is the responsibility of the states.

From the 1850s, the Australian colonies governed themselves. Most of them soon let male British subjects vote. This happened in South Australia from 1856, Victoria from 1857, New South Wales from 1858 and Tasmania from 1896. But in these states, Indigenous people weren't encouraged to enrol to vote. Most stayed off the rolls. In 1885, Queensland specifically left out Indigenous people from voting. Western Australia did the same in 1893.

After 1901, some Commonwealth legislation did affect Indigenous people and their right to vote. For example, the federal *Electoral*

Act 1902 gave women the right to vote in federal elections. But that right wasn't given to Indigenous women who weren't already enrolled to vote in state elections. The federal government extended the rights of Australians to the minimum wage in 1907, age and invalid pensions in 1909 and maternity benefits in 1912. But these benefits weren't given to Indigenous people. Discriminatory laws and practices were just as common under state laws.

Allowing Racial Discrimination

The framers of the Australian Constitution believed that the parliament should decide on rights protections. These included which rights are recognised and the extent to which they're protected. They looked at the French and American constitutions. They talked about the inclusion of rights within the Constitution itself (similar to the Bill of Rights included in the US Constitution). They rejected this option, though. They wanted instead to leave Australia's founding document silent on these matters. A non-discrimination clause talked about during the process of drafting the Constitution stated in part:

> *nor shall a state deprive any person of life, liberty, or property without due process of law, or deny to any person within its jurisdiction the equal protection of its laws.*

This clause was rejected for two reasons. Many people argued that protection for rights were unnecessary. And they thought it was a good idea to ensure that the states had the power to continue to pass laws that discriminated against people based on their race.

REMEMBER

The drafters of the Constitution never wanted it to protect against racial discrimination. As a result, even today, the Australian government — and the governments of states and self-governing territories — are allowed to pass legislation that discriminates based on race. This is allowed if they suspend any conflicting parts in the Racial Discrimination Act or similar legislation. This has been done several times in recent years.

In 1936, the Torres Strait Islanders held a four-month All Island Maritime Strike. They fought against the poor working conditions of pearl divers. They also demanded the rights to control their wages and their own affairs. As a result, in 1939, the Queensland government passed legislation for elected community councils in the Torres Strait.

War Heroes: Frontier Wars and Beyond

Aboriginal people often say they fought a 'frontier war' against the British in some parts of Australia. Many long conflicts were referred to as wars:

- Hawkesbury and Nepean Wars (1790 to 1816)

- Black Wars in Tasmania (1803 to 1830)

- Port Phillip District Wars in Victoria (1830 to 1850)

- Kalkadoon Wars in Queensland (1870 to 1890)

- Western Australian Conflict (1890 to 1898)

Indigenous people have fought in all the main wars Australia has entered since the Boer Wars (in 1880 to 1881 and 1899 to 1902). These include World War I, World War II, and the Vietnam, Korean, Gulf, Iraqi and Afghanistan Wars. They have also worked as peacekeepers in places such as East Timor. Today, more than 1,000 Indigenous people are in the armed services — about 1.4 per cent of the workforce.

The black diggers

About 500 Aboriginal people and Torres Strait Islanders fought for Australia in World War I. About 5,000 fought in World War II. Accurate numbers can't be counted, though. Many Aboriginal people didn't identify themselves as such. If they had, they may not have been allowed to join. Some pretended they were Indian or Maori. When World War I broke out in 1914, many Indigenous people who tried to enlist were rejected. But some managed to sign up. By the end of 1917, recruits were harder to find. The military then allowed for 'half-castes' to enlist, 'provided that the examining Medical Officers are satisfied that one of the parents is of European origin'.

At the start of World War II, Indigenous people could enlist. But in 1940, the Defence Committee decided that the enlistment of Indigenous people was 'neither necessary nor desirable'. This was partly because they thought white Australians wouldn't want to serve beside them. When Japan entered the war, the need for recruits grew. Rules were loosened. Indigenous people enlisted as soldiers or worked in the labour corps. Many said that racial slurs and discrimination were part of their everyday life when they were civilians. But once they were in the trenches, racial differences were gone. Everyone was treated equally and included in the community.

Back home, Aboriginal people worked in the cattle industry that was feeding the soldiers and in factories. But they weren't paid equal wages. Aboriginal women helped in hospitals.

When Japan entered the war, the army decided that Indigenous people in the north of Australia were an important labour source. Indigenous people were then put into labour settlements. Some struggle occurred between governments and the army about who controlled the Indigenous people in these camps. But the army-run camps often had better housing and conditions than Indigenous people had been given before.

REMEMBER

Many Indigenous women enlisted in the women's services or worked in the war industries during World War II. In the north, they worked hard to support RAAF outposts. Aboriginal poet Kath Walker joined the Australian Women's Army Service in 1942. She served as a signaller in Brisbane. She later changed her name to Oodgeroo Noonuccal.

REMEMBER

Many local Aboriginal men in Port Hedland, Western Australia, were members of the Volunteer Defence Corps (VDC). They ran coastal defences, anti-aircraft batteries and searchlights. They also moved people to air-raid shelters when military planes were overhead. Some received military training. They made sure that people on pastoral properties followed blackout rules.

In 1941, anthropologist Donald Thomson started the Northern Territory Special Reconnaissance Unit. It was an irregular army with 51 Aboriginal people, five white people and some Pacific and Torres Strait Islanders. They used their traditional knowledge of the bush to watch over the coastal waters. They had fighting skills and traditional weapons. They were expected to fight a guerrilla war with the Japanese if they landed ashore. The unit was broken up after the Japanese no longer posed a threat. The Indigenous people in the unit got no pay. They were finally paid back for lost wages in 1992. Medals were awarded to them.

Most Indigenous people enlisted in the Australian Imperial Force (AIF). This was a special army of volunteers for overseas service formed during both wars. But some enlisted in the other services.

The Royal Australian Air Force (RAAF)

The RAAF was less restrictive in its recruiting than the army. But according to Australian War Memorial historians, not much is known of Indigenous aircrew. Leonard Waters was an Aboriginal man who joined the RAAF in 1942. He was, after long and competitive training, selected as a pilot. He was stationed in Dutch New Guinea and then in Borneo. His squadron flew Kittyhawk fighters. Waters named his 'Black Magic'. He flew in 95 military operations. After the war, he hoped for a career in civilian flying. But bureaucratic delays forced him to return to shearing. He found that civilian life in Australia didn't let him use the skills he had gained and used in the war. (This was the same as other Indigenous people in the armed services.)

The Royal Australian Navy (RAN)

As with the RAAF, little is known as to how many Indigenous people enlisted in the navy. But the RAN also hired Indigenous people in informal units. One notable member of the RAN was John Gribble. He had, during the war, formed a group of 36 Aboriginal men who joined him in patrolling the coast and the islands of the Northern Territory. This was a large area. But the men who did this valuable work weren't enlisted. They were promised that they would be paid for this work. But they never were.

Labour units

During World War II, the army and the RAAF depended on Indigenous labour in northern Australia. They drove trucks. They built construction sites. They worked on the army farms and in butcheries. They also handled cargo. The RAAF placed its airfields near Aboriginal reserves to make use of their labour.

Indigenous people at first worked in the war effort on much the same terms as they worked in the pastoral industry and as domestic servants. There were long hours, hard labour, poor-quality food and housing, and low pay. As the war went on and the army took over control of Indigenous communities, conditions improved. For the first time, Indigenous people were given decent housing and fixed working hours. They got proper rations and access to proper health care at army hospitals. But pay rates stayed low. The army tried to raise the wages of Indigenous people. But pressure from civilians, particularly pastoralists, kept the rates low.

TORRES STRAIT ISLANDERS DEFENDING THE NORTH

In 1941, the Torres Strait Light Infantry Battalion was formed to defend the Torres Strait area. Other units were also created that specialised in important matters such as water transport. Although they never took part in conflict, they patrolled an important strategic area. This included areas of Japanese-controlled Dutch New Guinea. By 1944, almost every male Torres Strait Islander who was eligible had signed up. But they were paid much less than their white counterparts. At first, wages were only a third of what was paid to their non-Indigenous counterparts. That rose to two-thirds in December 1943. Other aspects of the war were particularly hard on Torres Strait Islanders. The pearl luggers that provided most of the local income were taken away to make sure that they didn't fall into Japanese hands.

(continued)

(continued)

The United States Navy recruited about 20 Torres Strait Islanders as crewmen on its ships around the Torres Strait Islands and Papua New Guinea. One Islander, Kamuel Abednego, was given the rank of lieutenant within the US Navy. This was at a time when no Indigenous person served as a commissioned officer in the Australian services.

The Torres Strait Islander community is a small section of the Australian community. If the number of people in that community who played a part in the war effort in World War II is considered, it can be argued that no other community in Australia gave as much to the war effort.

Returned soldiers and racism

When they came back to Australia, Indigenous diggers found they were treated in the same discriminatory manner as they had been before they fought for their country. Many didn't get recognition for their part in the war. Even worse, many had their names left off war memorials. They weren't allowed entry to the Returned Services League clubs that all the other diggers got access to. They couldn't get the veterans' benefits such as pensions. Schemes were set up to grant land to returned soldiers. But Indigenous diggers weren't allowed. In fact, Aboriginal reserve land was taken away to provide land for this 'soldier settlement' scheme.

Many diggers had to return to the reserves. Government officials controlled their lives there. The Department of Veterans' Affairs provides plaques for the graves of returned soldiers. But this wasn't done for many Indigenous diggers when they died. Some steps have been taken to make up for this neglect today. Over the years, other efforts have tried to give Indigenous diggers the recognition they deserve. In 1949, the Commonwealth Electoral Act gave the vote to Indigenous people who had been or were members of the defence forces. Eventually, they were given membership in Returned Services League clubs. They were also acknowledged on Anzac Day for their contribution to Australia's war effort.

CULTURAL PROTOCOLS

On Anzac Day in 2007 — 25 April — a parade of Aboriginal people and Torres Strait Islanders marched through Redfern in Sydney. This parade included Indigenous veterans and their families. This was the first of what has become a yearly event to mark the contribution of Aboriginal and Torres Strait Islander people in the armed services. The Indigenous community celebrates the 'black diggers' with a special ceremony. It shows honour and respect to members of their community who made sacrifices during the war.

REMEMBER

The Australian War Memorial has significantly increased its focus on the contribution of Aboriginal and Torres Strait Islanders to the war effort. It has included more stories of Indigenous people through their main displays and has a special dedicated gallery. Many community-based projects have also tried to collect the stories of Indigenous contributions to the war effort. You can check some out by going to redfernoralhistory.org. Click on Organisations and select Coloured Diggers from the drop-down list.

Still Denied Equality

The treatment of returned veterans became a symbol of the tough situation faced by Australia's Indigenous peoples. They were denied basic equal rights and made wards of the state for their own protection. But even when they participated fully within the broader community, they were never treated as equal. Not even military service to their country was enough commitment to ensure basic human rights.

Dispossession grows

In the period between the world wars, particularly in the 1930s, changes were made to protection legislation. The changes effectively took away many basic rights from Australia's Indigenous peoples. These included where they could travel, where they could live, who they could be with and whether they could own property. Legislation forced savings of wages that were often never paid. During the 1930s, powers to remove children were increased and the practice grew. This period between the wars was also a period of more dispossession (losing of land). Governments began to lease or sell land that had been held as reserves for Indigenous people. In Victoria, all reserve land except for one was sold. Half of the reserves in New South Wales that had existed in 1911 had been sold by 1924.

No money was given to Indigenous people for the loss of this land or their homes. Families were often forced into worse situations. They had no savings and no resources. They had few job opportunities and no money for rent. Many built makeshift homes on the edges of towns. There was no decent housing and no water or sewerage services. So authorities found it easy to claim that Indigenous children were not properly cared for or neglected.

After World War II, limits remained on Indigenous people and their rights. Protection boards and their legislation kept strict control over the lives of Indigenous people. The removal of Indigenous children increased.

A piece of paper to say you're white

From the 1940s, state governments gave citizenship rights to Indigenous people in certain situations. They had to give up their traditional ways. They could not be with other Indigenous people. They had to live among white Australians. These rights could be cancelled or suspended for bad behaviour or violating conditions.

Citizenship Certificates (in Western Australia) or Exemption Certificates (in New South Wales and Queensland) were issued to some Indigenous people. These certificates allowed them to vote, go to hotels and let their children go to school. The certificates meant they were free from the protection laws. Legally, the certificates also meant they were no longer Indigenous. You couldn't be an Indigenous person and a citizen.

Indigenous people called these certificates 'dog licences' or 'dog tags'. This name highlights the level of resentment Indigenous people had for them and the system that issued them. Around 14,000 people were eligible for the certificate in New South Wales. But only 1,500 applied for one. People who did so were treated with suspicion or ridicule by their friends and family. But given the difficult circumstances Indigenous people were forced to live under, some thought it was a better way to live.

Not Taking It Lying Down

The invasions that colonial and Australian governments made into the lives of Indigenous people in the name of 'protection' were strongly fought against. Indigenous people began building their own political groups that stood up for citizenship rights, rights to land and rights to political participation. These political rights included voting and being represented in parliament. This activism peaked in important political statements. One example was the Day of Mourning held on Australia Day in 1938 to mark the sesquicentenary — the 150-year anniversary — of the founding of the colony of Sydney Cove.

Indigenous people organise

Indigenous people took part in many forms of activism. They also formed many groups to help in achieving their political goals. Some of the key ones formed before 1967 are listed here. I also provide some brief information about their founders.

The Australian Aboriginal Progressive Association (AAPA)

The AAPA was started in 1924 in Sydney. A key figure in the group was well-known Indigenous rights activist Fred Maynard. The AAPA called on the government to return traditional lands. It also called on the government to return children and to stop the practice of removing them from their families. It complained about the treatment of Aboriginal women while they were under the care of the Aborigines Protection Board. They also petitioned to have the board shut down.

REMEMBER

Fred Maynard was born in 1879 in Hinton, New South Wales. He was a member of the Worimi people. But he was raised in a strict Protestant household in Maitland after his mother died. He first worked as a bullock driver, drover and photographer. In 1914, he began working on the wharves and joined the Waterside Workers' Federation. He spoke publicly about matters affecting Indigenous people, especially workers. He died in 1946.

The Australian Aborigines League (AAL)

The AAL was formed by William Cooper and others in 1932. It fought to end discriminatory practices against Indigenous people. It focused on gaining full citizenship rights, particularly to work and education. It wanted to end the Protection Board's ability to take children and to kick people off reserves. Its national work focused on Indigenous representation in parliament. It stood up for a federal department for Indigenous affairs that would manage the state agencies. And it focused on the need to include Indigenous representatives in such federal agencies.

REMEMBER

William Cooper was a great Aboriginal leader from the Yorta Yorta people, also known as the Joti-jota people. He was thought to have been born around 1861. He had lived on the Cummeragunja reserve. He was a well-spoken and literate man who took part in many political activities. These included writing letters and getting petitions signed. He was also a member of the Australian Workers' Union. Cooper believed that, as British citizens, Indigenous people had the right to petition King George V for better conditions and representation in parliament. He presented the petition to the Australian government in 1937. But the government didn't forward it to the king (George VI, by this time). It was stated that since it was constitutionally impossible for an Indigenous person to be a member of parliament, no point could be found in sending the petition. Cooper died in 1941.

The Aborigines Progressive Association (APA)

The APA operated in New South Wales. Bill Ferguson and Pearl Gibbs represented the western communities. Jack Patten represented the coastal communities. It focused on ending discrimination in employment and access to social security benefits. In 1937, the APA fought against the Aborigines Protection Board. This work led to an inquiry into the board and its practices. The board was eventually shut down. It was replaced with the Aborigines Welfare Board. In 1943, it elected two members. One was Bill Ferguson.

REMEMBER

William 'Bill' Ferguson was born in 1882 at Darlington Point in New South Wales. He had a brief education at the Warangesda mission school. Then he began working in shearing sheds. He later became an organiser for the Australian Workers' Union. He worked around New South Wales in different jobs. He started the APA in Dubbo in 1937. He worked with William Cooper and Jack Patten to hold the Day of Mourning protest in 1938. He sat on the Aborigines Welfare Board from 1944 to 1949. There he advocated for inquiries into the poor conditions on Aboriginal reserves. In 1949, he became vice-president of the AAL. He died in 1950.

REMEMBER

Pearl Gibbs was born in 1901 at La Perouse in Sydney. She had fair skin. But the racial discrimination she and her family faced caused her to strongly identify as Aboriginal. She worked at the APA in 1937. Then she was their secretary from 1938 to 1939. She was one of the few Aboriginal women speaking publicly at the time. She raised awareness about issues facing Indigenous women and children, especially about the abuse facing girls working as domestic servants. Gibbs was a member of the Union of Australian Women. She became a link between the white women's movement and the Indigenous rights movement. She became secretary of the Dubbo branch of the AAL in 1950. She worked nationally and locally at Dubbo on Indigenous issues until she died in 1983.

REMEMBER

Jack Patten was born in New South Wales in 1905. He was educated on the Cummeragunja reserve. He became president of the APA in 1937. With Bill Ferguson, he co-authored material exposing the huge powers of — and abuse of them by — the Aborigines Protection Board. He gathered support for the Day of Mourning protest in 1938. Patten toured north coast reserves to speak with and engage other Indigenous people in the campaign. He enlisted to fight in World War II in 1940. But he was discharged due to injury in 1942. He settled in Melbourne after the war and became involved with the AAL. He died in 1957.

The 1938 Day of Mourning

On Australia Day in 1938, a group of Aboriginal people protested in front of Australia Hall in Sydney. (They had been moved off the Sydney Town Hall steps.) This small protest was the result of decades of activism by Indigenous communities and their leaders in the south-east of Australia. These leaders included William Cooper, Bill Ferguson and Jack Patten. They had fought for the same rights as all other Australians, especially in relation to owning land and getting jobs, education and health services.

The protest was also the beginning of the Indigenous rights movement. It was the start of the long road to the search for equality under the legal system. The focus on citizenship rights was a key part of the activism of leaders such as Cooper and Maynard. It affected future generations.

Steps towards Equality

In the second half of the 20th century, some big steps were taken to try to give Indigenous people the same rights as other Australians. The *Nationality and Citizenship Act 1948* (Cwlth) made Indigenous people citizens in theory because they were born in Australia. But this didn't automatically guarantee equal rights.

In 1959, the federal Social Services Act was changed to give age pensions and maternity benefits to Indigenous Australians. But these benefits didn't go to Indigenous people who were 'nomadic' or 'primitive'. Benefits were paid into trust accounts of Indigenous people who lived on reserves. But many didn't receive this money.

The Commonwealth Electoral Act was changed in 1949. It gave the vote to Indigenous people who had been or were members of the defence forces. It was further changed in 1962. It gave Indigenous people the right to vote in Commonwealth elections. But it wasn't required for them to enrol or to vote.

REMEMBER

The changes over time to electoral and welfare legislation didn't stop Indigenous people from being discriminated against. Many felt that what was needed was a change to the Australian Constitution. A change was needed that would let the federal government make laws more specifically for the betterment of Indigenous people.

The Freedom Ride

A group of University of Sydney students had formed a body called Student Action for Aborigines (SAFA) in 1964. In February

THE RIGHT TO VOTE

When the colonies began their own parliaments, from 1850, men aged over 21 could vote. This included Indigenous men. But they weren't encouraged to enrol, so few did. Queensland passed legislation in 1885 and Western Australia in 1893 that denied Indigenous people the right to vote. But South Australia gave all adults, including women, the right to vote in 1895. This included Indigenous men and women.

At Federation, Section 41 of the Constitution seemed to decree that Indigenous people could vote in Commonwealth elections if they could vote in state elections. But in 1902, the Commonwealth Franchise Act specifically left out any people Indigenous to Australia, Asia, Africa or the Pacific Islands from voting. An exception was made if they were on the roll before 1901. This legislation created a lot of confusion about who could and couldn't vote!

In 1949, the Commonwealth Electoral Act was changed. People who had completed military service and those who already had the right to vote in state elections were given the right to vote in federal elections. A step back was taken in 1957. That's when the federal government said that Aboriginal people in the Northern Territory were wards of the state. They didn't have the vote unless they were exempted from guardianship. By 1962, the Electoral Act was changed to allow Indigenous people to enrol. But it wasn't compulsory. Western Australia lifted its ban and let Indigenous people vote in state elections. Queensland did the same in 1965. From that time, all Indigenous Australians had the same voting rights as non-Indigenous Australians in both state and federal elections.

1965, they put together a bus tour of western and coastal towns in New South Wales. Their goals on the trip were to

- Draw public attention to the poor state of Aboriginal health, housing and education

- Point out and hopefully lessen the social divisions in the towns and highlight the discrimination against Aboriginal people

- Encourage and support Aboriginal people to fight against discrimination

The students were inspired by protests against racial segregation in the United States. They decided to draw attention to similar issues in Australia. The *Freedom Ride*, as it became known, was headed by Charles Perkins. He was an Aboriginal student in his third year of an Arts degree. (See Figure 9-1 and the sidebar 'Charles Perkins: Fighting the good fight' for more.) The group included students Jim Spigelman and Ann Curthoys. Spigelman later became Chief Justice of the New South Wales Supreme Court until May 2011. Curthoys became a historian and wrote a book about the trip, using her diaries from the time.

The Freedom Riders brought attention to the crude and racist conditions in places such as Walgett, Gulargambone, Kempsey, Bowraville, Brewarrina and Moree. The trip showed segregation in towns. Aboriginal people were barred from clubs, swimming pools and cafes. They frequently didn't get service in shops and hotels. The Freedom Riders held protests outside the Moree Baths, the Kempsey Baths, the Bowraville Picture Theatre and the Walgett Returned Services League. The protesters recorded their journey and the reaction of townspeople. This made news around the country.

REMEMBER

In 2011, 30 high school students followed the original route of the Freedom Ride to celebrate its importance and impact.

Figure 9-1: Charles Perkins returning home after studying at Sydney University, circa 1963.

CHARLES PERKINS: FIGHTING THE GOOD FIGHT

Charles Perkins was an Arrernte man born at the Alice Springs Telegraph Station Aboriginal Reserve in the Northern Territory in 1936. He was a gifted soccer player. He played professionally, first in England in 1957 and then in Australia (see Chapter 11). He went to the first FCAA conference in Brisbane in 1961. Four years later, he and his fellow students went on the Freedom Ride.

(continued)

(continued)

Perkins was the first Aboriginal person to graduate with a degree from a university. He graduated with a Bachelor of Arts in May 1966. After his years of student activism, he became an important administrator and public servant. In 1965, he became the manager of the Foundation for Aboriginal Affairs in Sydney. In 1969, he moved to Canberra to begin work in the Office of Aboriginal Affairs. By 1984, Perkins was Secretary of the Department of Aboriginal Affairs. He was the first Aboriginal Australian to have such a position in the government.

Perkins was a central figure in Indigenous affairs even after retiring from the public service. He played key roles on the boards of Aboriginal arts, sport and media groups. He was elected to the Aboriginal and Torres Straits Islander Commission (ATSIC) in 1993. He then served as Deputy Chairman in 1994 to 1995. Perkins was also a member of the Arrernte Council of Central Australia. When he passed away in October 2000, he was given a state funeral.

The Referendum Is Announced

Prime Minister Harold Holt took over from Robert Menzies in 1966. On 23 February 1967, his government decided to hold a referendum later that year. On 2 March, Holt introduced legislation for a referendum to be held on 27 May. Both the government and the opposition parties supported the referendum question. In fact, neither party even put a case for a no vote. The referendum question asked was:

Do you approve the proposed law for the alteration of the Constitution entitled 'An Act to alter the Constitution so as to omit certain words relating to the people of the Aboriginal race in any State so that Aboriginals are to be counted in reckoning the population'?

This question related to two sections of the Constitution. It covered two main issues:

✔ Should Indigenous people be counted in the Australian census?

✔ Should the Commonwealth government be given the power to make laws for Indigenous people?

TECHNICAL STUFF

A constitutional change in Australia can be made only by a referendum. The majority of people in the majority of states (known as a *double majority*) have to vote yes for the change to occur.

REMEMBER

Australians hesitate to vote for changes to the Constitution. At the time of the 1967 referendum, only 5 out of 26 referendum questions put to the Australian public had been successful. Today, out of a total of 44 referendums put to Australians, only 8 have been passed. Another question was asked in the 1967 referendum. It was related to the make-up of parliament. It was rejected by the Australian people.

Getting to 'yes': The constitutional campaign

FCAATSI planned for a group to go to Canberra in April 1967 to lobby politicians. (FCAATSI stands for the Federal Council for the Advancement of Aborigines and Torres Strait Islanders, founded in 1958.) They wanted to make sure that the general public understood the issues involved in the referendum. The churches were supportive of the 'yes' campaign. So were the trade unions. Both gave information to their members. Both encouraged them to vote in favour of the changes.

Those fighting passionately for the changes believed that they would lead to better conditions for Indigenous people. Their view was that, if the federal government could legislate for Indigenous people, it would act in their best interests. Another strong argument for the changes was that they would ensure the same laws for Indigenous people across Australia. At the time of the referendum, laws were different from state to state. Major examples of these differences include

✔ Indigenous people could vote in state elections in all states except Western Australia and Queensland.

✔ They could own property in New South Wales and South Australia but not in other states.

✔ They could receive award wages in New South Wales but not in other states.

Not everyone supported all the changes. In 1965, Prime Minister Robert Menzies argued against changing the Constitution to give the federal government the power to make laws for Indigenous people. He warned the change could lead to a 'separate body of industrial, social, criminal and other laws relating exclusively to Aborigines'. But he did support the changes to include Indigenous people in the census.

TECHNICAL
STUFF

Why weren't Indigenous people counted in the Australian population? One reason was that politicians worried that their inclusion could affect the quota that decided the number of seats a state could hold in parliament. The greater the number of Indigenous people in the state, the greater the number of seats the state was entitled to. Including Indigenous people in the population count gave more seats to states with larger populations. It was feared that Western Australia and Queensland could lose seats. This fear seems odd. The white Australian population at the time of the referendum was 3.7 million. The Indigenous population was thought to be 60,000. Also, Indigenous people weren't included in the population count by the federal government for the purposes of allocating money to the states.

Australia decides

Of the total population eligible to vote in the referendum, 90.77 per cent voted for the proposed changes. This was the biggest yes vote ever in a referendum in Australia. Table 9-1 gives the Australian Electoral Commission's breakdown of the vote by state.

Table 9-1 **The Yes Vote by State**

State	Number of Votes	Percentage of Eligible Voters
New South Wales	1,949,038	91.46%
Victoria	1,525,026	94.68%
Queensland	748,612	89.21%
South Australia	473,440	86.26%
Western Australia	319,823	80.95%
Tasmania	167,176	90.21%
Total	**5,183,113**	**90.77%**

Source: Parliamentary Handbook of the Commonwealth of Australia, 32nd Edition.

TECHNICAL
STUFF

At the time of the 1967 referendum, only people in states were able to vote in referendums. People in the Northern Territory and the Australian Capital Territory couldn't vote in the referendum. This included between 3,000 and 4,000 Indigenous people in the Northern Territory.

REMEMBER

Historian Marilyn Lake, in her biography of Faith Bandler, explains why the constitutional change focused in part on including Indigenous people in the census. It was thought that their inclusion would help Australians think of Indigenous people as part of the Australian community. As such, it would be a nation-building exercise. It would be a symbolic coming together.

The referendum made two changes to the Constitution:

✔ **Section 127, the census:** Before the referendum, this section of the Constitution stated:

In reckoning the numbers of the people of the Commonwealth, or of a state or other part of the Commonwealth, aboriginal natives shall not be counted.

When the population was counted, Indigenous people weren't included in the count. After the referendum, this section was repealed. It is no longer part of the text of the Constitution. This change made sure that Indigenous people would be included in the census.

✎ **Section 51(xxiv), the 'races power':** Before the referendum, this section of the Constitution stated:

The Parliament shall, subject to this Constitution, have power to make laws for the peace, order, and good government of the Commonwealth with respect to — the people of any race, other than the aboriginal race in any State, for whom it is deemed necessary to make special laws.

The federal government could make laws for anyone in Australia, *except* Indigenous people living in any of the Australian states. But they could make laws for those living in the Northern Territory and the Australian Capital Territory. After the referendum, this section was changed to read:

The Parliament shall, subject to this Constitution, have power to make laws for the peace, order, and good government of the Commonwealth with respect to — the people of any race for whom it is deemed necessary to make special laws.

PROJECT

Write a short biography of William Cooper, Fred Maynard, Pearl Gibbs or Charles Perkins – or another person who fought for Indigenous rights in Australia during the 20th century.

PROJECT

Draw a map of the places the 1965 Freedom Ride visited.

PROJECT

Make a pamphlet to promote the 'Yes' case in the 1967 Referendum.

From Apology to Uluru

Through the 1970s, 1980s and 1990s, Indigenous people took some big steps towards gaining better land rights and recognition of citizen rights. In the early 1990s, the Keating Labor government developed a strategy for dealing with Indigenous native title rights following the 1992 Mabo case. However, the election of John Howard's Liberal government in 1996 then marked a large change in the direction of Indigenous affairs in Australia. Howard was of the view that the pendulum had swung too far in favour of Indigenous rights.

The federal election of November 2007 saw John Howard's Liberal government was voted out and Kevin Rudd's Labor government voted in. Rudd said that on election, he would recognise the Stolen Generations. He would give the apology that Howard didn't think was needed. Rudd's government also made another important move. It would support the Declaration on the Rights of Indigenous Peoples. This was an international document for the protection of Indigenous rights.

In this chapter, I look at these positive steps. But I also look at the way the Rudd government continued many parts of the Northern Territory Emergency Response. When Julia Gillard took over as leader of the Labor government in 2010, little changed. Australian law has few human rights benchmarks. International instruments such as the Declaration on the Rights of Indigenous People must be a guide to proper human rights standards.

Indigenous people are still focused on big issues such as a treaty, a new representative body and constitutional change. This chapter looks at how Indigenous people are facing these issues now and into the future.

A New Government — A New Era?

Prime Minister John Howard believed that an apology to the Stolen Generations was not needed (refer to Chapter 8). This refusal became a symbol for his views on Indigenous peoples and their rights. It was also an example of his beliefs about Australian history and reconciliation.

When Kevin Rudd became prime minister, he showed that he had a different view. He gave a national apology. His government also endorsed the Declaration on the Rights of Indigenous People.

The apology

Kevin Rudd had said he would give the apology to the Stolen Generations on the first sitting day of the new parliament. And he was true to his word. On 13 February 2008, Rudd tabled an apology to Indigenous people. This was particularly for the Stolen Generations and their families. The apology was broadcast across Australia. It played in public spaces such as Martin Place in Sydney and Federation Square in Melbourne. Some polls showed that before the apology, a third to a half of Australians supported the idea. After the apology was given, polls showed that two-thirds of Australians thought it had been a good thing for the country. (Refer to Chapter 8 for more on the Stolen Generations.)

REMEMBER

After the apology, the federal government made clear that it wouldn't bring up the issue of compensation for members of the Stolen Generation. This means giving a money amount to make amends to those people who were removed from their families and suffered harm in the care of the state.

REMEMBER

In 2009, Prime Minister Rudd said that he thought it was time that Australia moved on from the 'history wars'. He said that we should celebrate 'reformers, renegades and revolutionaries, thus neglecting or even deriding the great stories of our explorers, of our pioneers and of our entrepreneurs'. He believed that we should also no longer refuse to face hard truths about our history. He said, 'In a liberal democratic society, we can agree that events happened while we agree to differ in how we interpret them'. The issues of whether Indigenous children had been 'stolen' and whether they were removed 'for their own good' were argued over as part of these history wars.

CULTURAL
PROTOCOLS

The anniversary of the National Apology is often marked as 13 February. National Sorry Day or the National Day of Healing is 26 May. This is a day to remember and think about past injustices as a part of reconciliation. This day was first observed in 1998. This was a year after the *Bringing Them Home* report was tabled in Parliament.

The Declaration on the Rights of Indigenous Peoples

The Declaration on the Rights of Indigenous Peoples was adopted by the United Nations General Assembly on 13 September 2007. Australia was one of four countries that voted against its adoption. That position changed when the Rudd government endorsed the declaration on 3 April 2009. But the government gave no sign as to *how* it would use the document.

The declaration is the broadest statement of the rights of Indigenous peoples ever created. It gives attention to collective rights to a degree unseen in international human rights law. The adoption of this declaration is the clearest sign yet that the world wants to protect the individual and collective rights of Indigenous peoples.

REMEMBER

The four countries that voted against the Declaration on the Rights of Indigenous People in the General Assembly of the United Nations in 2007 were Australia, Canada, New Zealand and the United States. These countries didn't sign the declaration on that day. So they can't become signatories. They can, as Australia has done, endorse the declaration.

Some of the central ideas in the declaration are about

- Non-discrimination and basic rights
- Self-determination (see Chapter 17)
- Cultural integrity
- Rights to lands, territories and natural resources
- Other rights relating to social and economic welfare

But applying these ideas is not always easy.

Self-determination

One key idea in the declaration is something for which Indigenous peoples have always fought. Article 3 deals with the collective right to self-determination — that is, for indigenous people around the world to decide for themselves the actions taken in areas concerning them. Self-determination is found in both major international human rights covenants. These are the International Covenant on Civil and Political Rights and the International Covenant on Economic, Social and Cultural Rights. The Declaration on the Rights of Indigenous People mirrors their language. Article 3 applies the language specifically to Indigenous peoples.

TECHNICAL STUFF

A *covenant* is different from a *declaration* under international law. Covenants create standards that are binding on signatories. (They are valid and legal.) Declarations are aspirational documents only. (They describe goals.)

There are major debates at the international level over what self-determination needs in any given situation. This is true especially over how the right to self-determination works with another basic principle: state sovereignty. Sovereignty is shown through the protection of a state's land and political unity.

REMEMBER

In a nutshell, the declaration recognises the right to self-determination. But this right can't override the rights of a state or sovereign nation.

Self-government

Article 4 states that Indigenous peoples have 'the right to autonomy or self-government in matters relating to their internal and local affairs, as well as ways and means for financing their autonomous functions'. Indigenous peoples 'have the right to maintain and strengthen their distinct political, legal, economic, social and cultural institutions'. But they also have 'their right to participate fully, if they so choose, in the political, economic, social and cultural life of the State'.

TECHNICAL
STUFF

In the Declaration on the Rights of Indigenous People, Indigenous peoples have the right to take part in decision-making in matters that would affect their rights. They do so through their chosen representatives (Article 18). Law-makers and policy-makers must, in good faith, work with Indigenous peoples. The aim is getting their 'free, prior and informed consent before adopting and implementing legislative or administrative measures that may affect them' (Article 19). Indigenous peoples can be 'actively involved in developing and determining health, housing and other economic and social programmes affecting them and, as far as possible, to administer such programmes through their own institutions' (Article 23). Article 33(2) says that Indigenous peoples are able to 'determine the structures and to select the membership of their institutions in accordance with their own procedures'.

The effect of these ideas of autonomy is that:

- ✓ Governments must work with Indigenous people on policies, laws and programs that affect them. Governments must get consent before putting them in place.

- ✓ Indigenous people should be actively involved in creating programs that affect them. They should, if possible, run those programs through their own groups and representatives.

- ✓ The structure and membership of Indigenous groups should be decided by Indigenous people.

↗ Indigenous people should have access to ways of funding these autonomous duties.

↗ Indigenous people should keep their right to take part in mainstream political, economic and cultural institutions.

Basic rights and principles

The rights noted in the declaration are meant to be a minimum for the 'survival, dignity and well-being' of Indigenous peoples (Article 43). Also, nothing in the declaration may be taken as decreasing the rights Indigenous peoples already have now or may get in the future (Article 45). Article 46 says that the declaration must be read in agreement with the ideas of justice, democracy, respect for human rights, equality and non-discrimination. It must also be read in agreement with the ideas in the UN Charter. But any limits placed on the declaration rights must be 'strictly necessary' for securing respect for the rights and freedoms of others. They must also be needed for meeting the 'most compelling requirements of a democratic society'.

States must, in working with Indigenous peoples, take proper measures (including national legislation) to meet the goals of the declaration. They must also give Indigenous peoples access to financial and technical help for the enjoyment of the rights contained in it (Articles 38 to 39).

REMEMBER

Basically, the declaration aims to provide for fundamental rights and principles. These can only be limited by the situation where the rights themselves violate the rights of others. Also, governments must make sure that Indigenous people have access to financial and technical help to carry out the work outlined in the declaration.

The Intervention Continues

The Rudd government was different from the Howard government. It used gestures such as the apology and the endorsement of the Declaration on the Rights of Indigenous People. But on the ground, many policies stayed the same.

The Howard government's policies for the Northern Territory Emergency Response (NTER or the intervention) are an example. Key policies used as part of the intervention from the new Labor government were

- Income management, where 50 per cent of welfare payments to Indigenous people were set aside and could only be used in certain shops

- The condition that Indigenous people lease their land back to the government before they could get housing and infra-structure funding

REMEMBER

The Northern Territory Emergency Response was introduced in the lead-up to the 2007 election. The Howard government had no time to study how well the intervention worked before it was voted out. The Rudd government promised a review. When that review was finally done, it suggested changes to the key policies. It also noted concerns about the intervention's impact on the lives of the Indigenous people affected by it. The government used the Stronger Futures legislation in 2013. It claimed that it repealed the NTER in full, but that is not correct. It did restart the Racial Discrimination Act. But it kept in place the controversial parts of welfare reform. These pieces set apart income and linked school attendance with welfare payments.

Studying the Northern Territory intervention

One of the key purposes of the intervention was to respond to the *Little Children are Sacred* report. This report found broad abuse, neglect and different factors leading to disadvantage within the Northern Territory. In June 2007, the Howard government announced the intervention. Six months after it was put into place, no new charges had been laid for abuse. No new community-based programs had been started. The BasicsCard, which supported the policy of income management for those Indigenous people on welfare payments, had cost $88 million.

A year after the Rudd government came to power, it asked for the Northern Territory Emergency Response Review. The review committee gave its findings on 13 October 2008. Chief among its recommendations was stopping the policy of required income management. It said that there was a place for targeted income management. But it shouldn't be applied to people in a blanket way. And it shouldn't be limited to the Indigenous community. The review noted that many Indigenous people had found the policies 'punitive, coercive and racist'. Despite the suggestions, the government decided to keep the policies unchanged.

The federal government said it supported most of the recommendations of the review. These included better resourcing of legal services, more policing, and more resources for education and child protection. It didn't agree to end required income management. But it did agree that management should be open to review by outside groups.

REMEMBER

Two years after the Northern Territory Emergency Response was introduced, anaemia rates in children were up. Malnutrition rates in the Indigenous community had risen. Indigenous community-owned housing was moved to the Northern Territory. Rents had gone up. At the same time, complaints that houses weren't being maintained were widespread. The number of Indigenous people being charged with driving offences grew. School attendance rates for Indigenous children were slightly lower. No houses had been built under the $600 million housing program (though some were built later). Violent offences were up. Substance abuse had increased. The coalition, now in opposition, stated that the intervention was failing. The current government hadn't used it properly and should have made the measures tougher.

Ten years after the NTER in 2017, its impact was studied further by Dr Paddy Gibson. He found the following:

- Rates of Aboriginal children being removed from their families had grown.

- School attendance rates had not improved.

- Suicide and self-harm had increased.

- Houses were still overcrowded.

✔ Income quarantining made life harder for families and was discriminatory.

✔ Unemployment had grown.

✔ Rates of family violence had not grown.

✔ The number of Aboriginal people in custody had grown a lot.

REMEMBER

In 2016, a Royal Commission into the Protection and Detention of Children in the Northern Territory was held. It made its report in 2017. Its several findings included that youth detention centres were not fit for housing, let alone reforming, children and young people. It confirmed children were subject to verbal abuse, physical control and humiliation. Many children in juvenile detention were in out-of-home care. The Royal Commission also found that the Northern Territory Government failed to meet the requirements that all children in out-of-home care have care plans.

International criticism

In August 2010, a report of the Committee on the Elimination of Racial Discrimination raised concerns about Australia's policies regarding Indigenous people. The report noted the apology, the signing of the Declaration on the Rights of Indigenous People and the commitment to 'closing the gap'. (This term refers to the wide difference in many social, economic, health and educational factors between Indigenous people and the rest of Australia. It also refers to the need to greatly reduce that difference.) The report also noted that these were only first steps towards genuinely strengthening relationships between Indigenous peoples and non-Indigenous people. Its main criticisms were focused on the Northern Territory Emergency Response (the intervention). The use of income management was seen as discriminatory and not working well. Required leasing back of land was also targeted. And the committee raised concerns about the large number of Indigenous people in the criminal justice system.

In September that year, the United Nations Human Rights Committee issued a report. It named parts of the Northern Territory Emergency Response as policies that breached Australia's duties under international human rights documents. That same year, the UN's Special Rapporteur on the rights of indigenous peoples, S James Anaya, visited Australia. He went to the Northern Territory and other parts of Australia. Then he made similar notes about the negative impact of the measures in the Northern Territory. He suggested that the government remove the 'overtly' racially discriminatory aspects of the intervention. He said that proof that some parts of the intervention were working was 'ambiguous' (or unclear) at best. The hardship caused by compulsory income management was clear.

The Rudd government announced it would make sure that its policies followed the principles of the Racial Discrimination Act. The government changed the policy of income management so it could also be used with people receiving welfare in non-Indigenous communities. This made it no longer racially discriminatory. But most people who were subjected to this change were still Indigenous. Other parts of the policy — such as compulsory leasing of land — were argued to be 'special measures'. So, it was argued that they were exceptions to the Racial Discrimination Act. Indigenous people affected by the policies pointed out that the government changes were only technical. The way that these policies were applied to them hadn't changed. Others have pointed out that the spirit of the Racial Discrimination Act has not been respected. The act is supposed to keep people from being subjected to racial discrimination.

REMEMBER

Policies such as income management — where a percentage of a welfare payment can only be spent in certain shops — were part of the Northern Territory Emergency Response. But they were rolled out into other Indigenous communities around Australia. The income arrangement now can apply to both black and white Australians. But still most people subject to the policy are Indigenous. Also, the requirement that land be leased back before housing money could be accessed was also rolled out into Indigenous communities around the country.

Finding a National Voice

A new national Indigenous representative body — the National Congress of Australia's First Peoples — was announced in November 2009. It was supported by the Rudd and Gillard governments. This body was the first nationally elected representative body for Indigenous people since the end of ATSIC (the Aboriginal and Torres Strait Islander Commission) was announced in 2004. But it would go on to end too.

In 2017, the Uluru Statement from the Heart was delivered. It set a path forward for Voice, Truth and Treaty.

Finally, debates continue around whether current policy approaches in Indigenous affairs are fair and working well. International human rights benchmarks still play an active role in these debates.

Another representative body

When the Rudd government was elected in 2007, it had a policy to start a new representative body for Indigenous people. In December that year, the terms of the people on the National Indigenous Council ended. New Minister for Indigenous Affairs Jenny Macklin didn't renew their appointments. (This council had effectively replaced ATSIC.)

The Rudd government said that the new body it started wouldn't be another ATSIC. It would, at the first chance, work with Aboriginal people and Torres Strait Islanders about what such a body should look like. Aboriginal people and Torres Strait Islanders had already done quite a bit of work on what they would like a new body to look like.

REMEMBER

ATSIC was officially shut down in 2005. Then a large national meeting was held in Adelaide. This began an informal work process among Aboriginal peoples and Torres Strait Islanders about the kind of replacement body they wanted. Over time, the Australian Human Rights Commission took over this process. This led to the recommendation of the creation of the National Congress of Australia's First Peoples. Throughout consultation for the new body, two factors seemed important. First, unlike

ATSIC, the new group should have the main roles of developing policies and watching government performance. Second, the new body should be apart from government. That way, unlike ATSIC, it couldn't be ended by the government suddenly.

A new model included a process of electing representatives. It created an ethics council to watch behaviour and manage conflicts of interest. Of the 120 delegates that would make up the National Congress of Australia's First Peoples, half had to be women. Representatives would be elected through three chambers, 40 coming from each. One chamber was formed from national Aboriginal and Torres Strait Islander peak bodies and organisations. Another was all other Aboriginal and Torres Strait Islander groups. The last one was all Aboriginal people and Torres Strait Islanders 18 years and over.

The National Congress of Australia's First Peoples was founded in 2010. It had its first elections in 2011. The new body was started as a company. But it depended on ongoing federal government funding.

REMEMBER

The original model asked that the Congress be given a large one-off grant. This grant would allow it to run on the interest earned by that money. This set-up would limit its need for government resources. This part of the model wasn't followed. It still depended on government funding. That funding ended in 2013 and its financial reserves were used up by 2019. The national representative body went into voluntary administration and closed.

Constitutional change

The 2010 election saw the issue of constitutional recognition put back on the table. It was considered in different ways. They included the following:

- **An Expert Panel:** An Expert Panel on Constitutional Recognition of Indigenous Australians was started in 2011. It recommended the repeal of section 25 (which gives state governments the power to pass legislation to prevent certain people, based on their race, from voting) and section 51 (xxvi) (the 'races power'). The panel instead proposed a new rule. It would recognise Aboriginal and Torres Strait Islander peoples. It would give the federal government the power to make laws for Indigenous people in line with that recognition. It suggested adding a rule that banned racial discrimination. It also suggested a rule that recognised Indigenous languages. To make these changes, the panel suggested a single referendum question. It suggested that the referendum only proceed when it had the support of all major political parties and most state governments. It also recommended the funding of a public information campaign.

- **A Joint Select Committee:** The Joint Select Committee on Constitutional Recognition of Aboriginal and Torres Strait Islander Peoples was started in federal parliament in 2013. Its report was handed down in 2015. This report recommended that a referendum on constitutional recognition be held when it has the highest chance of success. It recommended the repeal of sections 25 and 51 (xxvi). It suggested that a new section keep the ability for the federal government to make laws for the benefit of Aboriginal and Torres Strait Islander peoples. The new section should recognise Aboriginal and Torres Strait Islander peoples in the Constitution. It also suggested a ban on racial discrimination.

- **Recognise:** In 2012, a new movement grew to speed up change that would include Aboriginal and Torres Strait Islander peoples in the Constitution. That's when the Recognise campaign was launched. It was sponsored by Reconciliation Australia. The campaign ran to 2017 and focused on gaining acceptance for the general idea that Aboriginal and Torres Strait Islander peoples should be included in the Constitution. But it didn't put forward a specific model. During that time, a poll run by the ABC showed that 72 per cent of Australians surveyed supported a change that recognised Indigenous people and their culture.

- **A Referendum Council:** The Referendum Council was started in 2015. It gave its report in 2017. The council built on the work of the Expert Panel and the Joint Select Committee. It recommended a referendum to include a representative body in the Constitution. This body would give Aboriginal and Torres Strait Islanders a voice to the Commonwealth Parliament. This would recognise Aboriginal and Torres

Strait Islander peoples as Australia's first peoples. It also recommended a Declaration of Recognition. This declaration would be enacted by legislation and passed by all Australian Parliaments.

The Joint Select Committee on Constitutional Recognition of Aboriginal and Torres Strait Islander Peoples made another report in 2018. It gave several recommendations about an Indigenous voice to parliament. These included suggesting further considerations about its form and constitutional recognition.

TECHNICAL
STUFF

A question of whether to add a preamble to the Constitution was put to the Australian people in 1999. The proposed introduction had phrases such as 'honouring Aborigines and Torres Strait Islanders, the nation's first people, for their deep kinship with their lands and for their ancient and continuing cultures which enrich the life of our country'. Another phrase was 'recognising the nation-building contribution of generations of immigrants'. In the referendum, 39.34 per cent of Australians voted yes to the change. But 60.66 per cent voted no.

The hope for constitutional change is still on the agenda. But focus moved from constitutional recognition to the Uluru Statement from the Heart when it was released in 2017. This statement calls for a 'voice to parliament' to be placed in the Constitution as a priority.

The Uluru Statement

In 2017, 250 Aboriginal and Torres Strait Islander delegates met. They released a 'statement from the heart'. Among other things, this statement set a roadmap for Indigenous reform that includes

✔ A First Nations Voice in the Constitution

✔ A Makarrata Commission to supervise a process of agreement making and truth telling about Australia's history

The Statement reads:

We, gathered at the 2017 National Constitutional Convention, coming from all points of the southern sky, make this statement from the heart:

Our Aboriginal and Torres Strait Islander tribes were the first sovereign Nations of the Australian continent and its adjacent islands, and possessed it under our own laws and customs. This our ancestors did, according to the reckoning of our culture, from the Creation, according to the common law from 'time immemorial', and according to science more than 60,000 years ago.

This sovereignty is a spiritual notion: the ancestral tie between the land, or 'mother nature', and the Aboriginal and Torres Strait Islander peoples who were born therefrom, remain attached thereto, and must one day return thither to be united with our ancestors. This link is the basis of the ownership of the soil, or better, of sovereignty. It has never been ceded or extinguished, and co-exists with the sovereignty of the Crown.

How could it be otherwise? That peoples possessed a land for sixty millennia and this sacred link disappears from world history in merely the last two hundred years?

With substantive constitutional change and structural reform, we believe this ancient sovereignty can shine through as a fuller expression of Australia's nationhood.

Proportionally, we are the most incarcerated people on the planet. We are not an innately criminal people. Our children are aliened from their families at unprecedented rates. This cannot be because we have no love for them. And our youth languish in detention in obscene numbers. They should be our hope for the future.

These dimensions of our crisis tell plainly the structural nature of our problem. This is the torment of our powerlessness.

We seek constitutional reforms to empower our people and take a rightful place in our own country. When we have power over our destiny our children will flourish. They will walk in two worlds and their culture will be a gift to their country.

We call for the establishment of a First Nations Voice enshrined in the Constitution.

Makarrata is the culmination of our agenda: the coming together after a struggle. It captures our aspirations for a fair and truthful relationship with the people of Australia and a better future for our children based on justice and self-determination.

We seek a Makarrata Commission to supervise a process of agreement-making between governments and First Nations and truth-telling about our history.

In 1967 we were counted, in 2017 we seek to be heard. We leave base camp and start our trek across this vast country. We invite you to walk with us in a movement of the Australian people for a better future.

In short: Voice, Treaty, Truth.

REMEMBER

The Uluru Statement from the Heart pulls together several strands of the long-standing Indigenous reform agenda. These are a representative voice, constitutional recognition (refer to Chapter 9), treaty and a truth telling about Australian history.

At the time the statement was released, Prime Minister Malcolm Turnbull said that his cabinet rejected the idea of an Indigenous voice to Parliament. He said it wasn't 'desirable or capable of winning acceptance at referendum'. Turnbull argued it would be seen as 'a third chamber of parliament'.

In 2020, Minister for Indigenous Australians Ken Wyatt began a process that worked with Indigenous experts in coming up with a model that could give advice to government. It was not meant to be put into the Constitution. But whatever the model decided upon would be created through legislation.

PROJECT

Read the UN's Declaration on the Rights of Indigenous People (available online; an 'adolescent friendly' version is also available on the UN's website page). What areas seem to be the most important for the rights of Indigenous People? Summarise these in point form.

PROJECT

Create a poster that reflects the themes of the Uluru Statement from the Heart.

Part 4

Contemporary Indigenous Cultures

In This Part . . .

☐ Get to know how modern expressions of Aboriginal and Torres Strait Islander cultures don't just keep Indigenous communities alive and strong but also make a significant contribution to Australian cultural life.

☐ Look at the contribution of Indigenous people to many different forms of sport in Australia, often displaying amazing skill.

☐ See Indigenous peoples' traditional and recent expression of culture through fine art, music and dance.

☐ Understand how Indigenous storytelling traditions have been kept alive through poetry, books, films and broadcasting.

Indigenous People and Sport

IN THIS CHAPTER

- ✔ Looking at sporting traditions and traditional sports
- ✔ Competing in the mainstream
- ✔ Claiming a first in cricket whites
- ✔ Boxing above their weight
- ✔ Excelling in all kinds of football
- ✔ Succeeding in every sporting sphere

Indigenous peoples were left out of many parts of Australian life. But sportspeople overcame those barriers to achieve in their chosen fields. In some areas, they're underrepresented, such as cricket and golf. But in others — such as football and boxing — they almost dominate the scene.

The revival of traditional Indigenous games is a strong sign that Indigenous cultures can survive. In this way, traditional games are helping Indigenous people stay fit. They're also a way of keeping culture strong.

Indigenous people have had a high profile in all kinds of Australian sport. From boxing legends to Olympian runners and stars across all codes of football, Indigenous people have made an impact on the sporting field.

In this chapter, I look at both traditional and modern sports. You also meet Indigenous sportspeople who have made, and are making, their mark today.

A (Traditional) Sporting Life

Indigenous people, as hunters and gatherers, lived active lives. Everyday activities such as spearing and digging needed physical fitness. People would travel across their country walking great distances all the time.

Recreation in traditional life was focused on games that included friendly competition. They strengthened ideas of teamwork and loyalty. Games also encouraged a show of skill, strength and staying power. They improved skills such as spear throwing and hand–eye coordination. Traditional games include a range of ball games, bat-and-ball games, wrestling games, water games, games where a target had to be hit, tag games and hide-and-seek games. One well-known traditional sport is *marngrook*, a type of football. Another is *coreeda*, a game that combines wrestling and dance. Many of these games disappeared during the colonisation of Australia. At that point, traditional recreational activities were replaced by other sports.

Marngrook

Marngrook means 'game ball'. It is credited by many as providing some of the rules for what's now known as Australian Rules Football, or Aussie Rules. It was a traditional game played by Aboriginal people of regions across Victoria and The Riverina in south-west New South Wales. The game was played with a ball about the size of an orange. This ball was made from possum skin stuffed with pounded charcoal and/or grass. The ball was kicked and caught. But it wasn't supposed to touch the ground. Teams were made up of many players. Membership was based on a player's totem. (The Warlpiri nation, north-west of Alice Springs, had a similar game. They called it *pultja*.) The *Marngrook Footy Show* took its name from the game and aired on NITV, ABC2 and SBS. It also focused on Indigenous participation in Australian Rules Football.

REMEMBER

In 2002, the Australian Football League (AFL) teams of the Sydney Swans and Essendon Football Clubs started to compete for the Marn Grook Trophy.

Coreeda

Coreeda is often described as a wrestling game. But it includes elements of traditional dance as well as combat. It's played as a team sport. It combines three segments of dance with a fourth of fighting. It replaced traditional spearing punishments in parts of New South Wales. The dance is said to be based on the movements of the kangaroo when it fights.

Competitors can only touch the ground with their hands and feet. They must stay within a circle. The third dance segment sees the competitors trying to push each other outside of the circle. They can also try to make each other touch the ground with a part of their body other than their hands or feet. The winner of this dance stage can choose the position he starts in for the fourth combat segment. In the combat stage, one person is inside the circle. His opponent is outside it. The person within the circle is the defender. The person on the outside is the attacker. The attacker tries to force the defender outside the circle by pushing him. The defender tries to fight off the attacker from within the circle. Competitors then change positions.

Today, the game is played in quarters and with time limits. Competitors get points in each quarter. The game is played in teams. Individual scores are added together. Teams are made up of six competitors of different weight divisions. These divisions are named after species of kangaroos or wallabies. Teams are then further divided into two moieties, black and red. The revival of coreeda is still relatively new. Indigenous wrestlers Shane Parker and Stephan Jaeggi have been ambassadors for the game.

Other traditional Indigenous games

In 2008, the Australian Sports Commission produced a resource called *Yulunga: Traditional Indigenous Games*. This resource details the rules of many traditional Indigenous games. *Yulunga* means 'playing' in the Gamillaroi language. Today, some schools and Indigenous community groups, such as land councils, run programs to teach children how to play traditional Indigenous games.

Apart from marngrook and coreeda, other games focused on skills such as spear throwing, boomerang throwing and diving. Here's a sample of some of those games:

- **Battendi** was played in South Australia by the Kaurna people. It was a spear-throwing game that tested accuracy and distance.

- **Boomerang games** tested skill with boomerang throwing. Boomerangs used for hunting weren't always designed to come back. But returning boomerangs were often used for entertainment and sport.

- **Buroinjin** was played by the Kabi Kabi people of southern Queensland. It was said to be like basketball. But the ball is made of kangaroo skin and filled with grass.

- **Kalq** was played in the Cape York region. Men use a woomera to project a spear towards the next player in a circle. That player used a woomera to deflect the spear from the first player. Younger men used spears with blunted ends until their skill levels improved!

- **Keentan** is a game where two teams try to keep a ball between their own players. They try to take it off the players of the other team. The ball was made from possum, wallaby or kangaroo hide and tied with twine. The game has been compared to basketball. It was played in parts of Queensland. Keentan means 'play' in the Wik-Mungkan language.

- **Koolchee** used small balls of about 10 centimetres diameter and made of sandstone, mud or gypsum. Players rolled the ball on the ground between two teams. The aim was to hit the balls of the other team. The game has been compared to lawn bowls.

- **Murrumbidgee** is played by throwing stones into the water and then diving to catch them before they reach the bottom.

- **Parndo** was played in South Australia by the Kaurna nation. It was a kicking and passing game played with a ball made of possum skin. In Kaurna, parndo means 'ball to play with'.

- **Taktyerrain** is a combat game in which players throw toy spears. It was a way for children to practise for adult life. The spears were made from light sticks or grass. This word means 'to fight' in the Wemba Wemba language of Victoria.

- **Tarnambai** was played on the Tiwi Islands. Children tossed the seed heads of spinifex grass and then tried to catch them as the wind blew them along the beach. Tarnambai means 'running'.

- **Walle ngan werrup** was a game of hide and seek played by children. They pretended to be on a kangaroo or emu hunt.

- **Wana** was played by the Noongar people of north-west Western Australia. A stick was placed in the ground. A player had to defend it with her digging stick (a wana) as other players tried to hit it. The game has been compared to French cricket.

- **Yiri** was played in the Ulladulla area on the southern coast of New South Wales. It involved throwing a spear at a moving target such as bark placed in running water. Yiri means 'to throw'.

Torres Strait Islanders also used games for skills development and recreation. Here are a few of them:

- **Kai** was played by having players standing in a circle singing the 'kai wed' song as they hit a 'ball'. They tried to keep it in the air by using the palm of one hand. The thick, roundish red fruit of the kai tree was used as a ball. It was quite light when it was dry.

- **Kokan** used a small ball (a kokan). The ball was probably made from reeds and long leaves. The game was played on the beach. The aim was to hit the kokan with a bat or club made from bamboo. It has been described as a kind of hockey.

- **Kolap** was an object-throwing game that used beans of the Kolap tree.

Playing Them at Their Own Games

Indigenous people are often thought to be natural sportsmen and sportswomen. No proof suggests Indigenous people are genetically inclined to be better skilled at sport. But plenty of proof does exist that they're good athletes and they like playing sport.

From the first Indigenous cricket team that toured England in 1868, Indigenous people have shown they can excel at sports in the national and international arena. The later sections of this chapter detail the specific sports and athletes. Many of these athletes have been leaders in the development of younger Indigenous players in the sport.

Getting in and having a go

In 2017, Michael Dockery and Sean Gorman released a report that looked at participation in sport, particularly the AFL. They found a strong link between playing sport and well-being. Here are some of their findings:

- For Aboriginal and Torres Strait Islander children, 46.6 per cent had played sport in the last 12 months.

- Around 65,000 Indigenous Australians took part in sport, other than as a player.

- Mental health is thought to be higher among Indigenous men and women who participate in organised sport.

- The most popular sports played by Indigenous boys are Australian Rules Football (17 per cent), rugby league (16 per cent) and soccer (11 per cent).

- The most popular sports played by Indigenous girls are netball (13 per cent), swimming (7 per cent) and basketball (7 per cent).

Because of the known health benefits of participation in sport, physical activity is encouraged among Indigenous people. (They have poorer health levels than other Australians.) Participation in sport can bring Indigenous and non-Indigenous people together.

It also builds confidence and self-esteem among Indigenous young people.

Teaching through sport

Some sporting programs have given boosts to young Indigenous people to stay in school and to let them meet good role models. For example, the Clontarf Academies for boys and the Role Models and Leaders Academy for girls use sport to encourage Indigenous students to stay at school. The first Clontarf Academy was set up at Perth's Clontarf Aboriginal College in 2000. By 2021, 131 Clontarf Academies had been set up within 141 schools across Western Australia, Northern Territory, Victoria, New South Wales, Queensland and South Australia.

Strong role models — often footballers who have had successful careers on the field — work in the programs. The programs focus on growing the interest young people have in sport. But they also aim to teach students about the importance of learning, leadership, healthy lifestyles and making good life choices.

The National Aboriginal Sporting Chance Academy (NASCA) was founded in 1995. It mentors young Indigenous people in sport. It offers school and health programs and helps to send famous Indigenous athletes to Indigenous communities. It also promotes healthy lifestyles and gives additional training in various sports. These sports include rugby league, Aussie Rules, cricket and basketball.

READY, SET, GO

The GO Foundation was started by AFL stars Adam Goodes and Michael O'Loughlin. It focuses on education and provides opportunities for Indigenous children from kindergarten to university. These include cultural mentoring, homework support, leadership training, STEM training and job opportunities. Scholarships support a range of student needs. These include providing laptops, internet access, sporting equipment and trips. To find out more about the good work the foundation does, GO to www.gofoundation.org.au.

Slipping on the Whites: Cricket

From the early 1860s, cricket matches had been played between Indigenous people and Europeans in western Victoria. An all-Aboriginal cricket team was the first Indigenous sports team to tour internationally. Later, rules on movement limited the chance of Indigenous people to play representative cricket. But Indigenous people continued to play the sport.

These racial barriers kept talented Indigenous cricketers from playing representative cricket up until the end of the 20th century. Despite the skills of players such as Eddie Gilbert and Vince Copley, it wasn't until 1996 that an Indigenous cricketer — Jason Gillespie — was selected for the Australian test team. Today, Indigenous players at the highest levels of the game are more common.

The first Indigenous cricket team

An all-Aboriginal team was put together and played a match at the Melbourne Cricket Ground on Boxing Day in 1866. They came from the western districts of Victoria. The team then played matches in Sydney and Brisbane. The idea of touring the team to England took shape. But raising the money for the tour took some time.

The team of 13 that arrived in London in May 1868 was coached and managed by Charles Lawrence. As a sign of the time, the men on the team had English nicknames and traditional names. A crowd of 20,000 people turned out to watch the first match. Over the course of the six-month tour, the team played 47 matches. The results surprised many who thought the team would be worse than the English stars of the game. They won 14 matches, lost 14 and drew 19. The most outstanding player was all-rounder Johnny Mullagh. He scored 1,698 runs and took 245 wickets.

The members of the team also put on shows of boomerang and spear throwing at the end of the game. One player, Dick-a-Dick, held a narrow shield and fought off cricket balls that he invited the crowd to throw at him. Sadly, King Cole died of tuberculosis early in the tour. Sundown and Jim Crow went back to Australia before the tour was finished due to ill health.

The team went back to Sydney in February 1869. They played a match against a military team and then the team broke up. Many players weren't heard of again. Mullagh went on to play for the Melbourne Cricket Club. He represented Victoria against a visiting English team in 1879. Johnny Cuzens also played for Melbourne as a professional. Then he went bush in 1870. He is believed to have died the following year. The only other player to appear again in representative cricket was Twopenny. He played for New South Wales against Victoria in 1870.

Participation in cricket by Indigenous people was ended by a change of law in 1869 in Victoria. The law made it illegal for Indigenous people to travel out of Victoria without approval from the government minister.

A TRIBUTE TO THE 1868 CRICKET TOUR

Several Indigenous cricket teams have followed that first team's tour to England. In 2001, an Indigenous cricket team calling themselves the Downunders played nine one-day games in England. Four of the games specifically honoured the 1868 tour.

In 2009, 14 Aboriginal players aged 16 to 26 left Brisbane, Queensland, on 20 June. They followed in the footsteps of the 1868 tour. They played 11 matches within a month. Some were on the same grounds where the earlier tour had been played. This tour was a success, too. The team won 8, lost 3 and drew 1 of their 12 games.

In 2018, to commemorate the 150th anniversary of the tour, Cricket Australia sent a men's team and a women's team to England. They played a series of matches during the first two weeks of June. Four of these matches were played at the same places used 150 years ago.

Indigenous male cricketers today

The segregation of Indigenous people on reserves, as well as other social barriers in Australian society for most of the 20th century, kept Indigenous people from playing representative cricket. Cricketers such as Jack Marsh, Eddie Gilbert and Vince Copley, who had great skills, found themselves left out of the sport on a national level. But Gilbert did play at state level. Bernie Lamont, Jeff Cook and Dan Christian also played at state level. Dan Christian, known as a natural all-rounder, became the first Indigenous person to play for Australia in Twenty20 cricket. He was selected in 2010.

To date, the most successful Indigenous male cricket player is Jason Gillespie. In 1996, he played for the Australian cricket team. He was the first male Indigenous player to play at that level. (The first Australian test team played in 1877. It took well over 100 years for an Indigenous person to be selected for the national team. This highlights the barriers Indigenous players faced in the game.) Gillespie played 71 test games for Australia. He retired in 2008 after playing at international level for 14 years. He took 259 wickets.

Women cricketers

Indigenous women have also played cricket. Faith Thomas (her maiden name was Choulthard) played test cricket for Australia in 1958. The first Indigenous man wasn't selected for the Australian team until 1996. So Thomas was a real groundbreaker in the game. She was the first Indigenous woman to earn national honours. Female cricketers Edna Crouch and Mabel Campbell were both inducted into Queensland's Indigenous Hall of Fame.

Today, a new generation of Indigenous women are playing the game. The most successful female Indigenous player to date is Ashleigh Gardner. At the age of 18, she captained the National Indigenous women's squad on a tour to India. She soon after became the second Aboriginal woman to play test cricket for Australia. She has played for Australia in international test, one-day and Twenty20 competitions. She made her test debut playing against England in 2019. In 2020 she was part of the winning Australian team in the T20 Women's World Cup. This team chose to wear a uniform designed by Indigenous artists.

SHOWING UP BRADMAN: EDDIE GILBERT

In 1931, Indigenous cricketer Eddie Gilbert made cricket history. He famously became the only bowler to knock the bat out of Sir Donald Bradman's hands. He bowled Bradman out for a *duck* — a score of zero. Bradman said later that the six deliveries he faced from Gilbert in that match were the fastest he'd seen in his career.

Gilbert was born in Queensland. He was taken from his family at the age of three to Barambah Aboriginal Reserve, now known as Cherbourg. He took up cricket at a young age and became an exceptionally talented fast bowler. Gilbert said the skill in his flexible wrist was developed from boomerang throwing. He played for Queensland from 1931. In the 23 matches he played at representative level, he took 87 wickets. Because of the laws of the day, Gilbert had to get written permission from the government to travel from his Indigenous reserve each time he played a representative match. He retired in 1936 and went back to his community. He died in 1978, aged 72, after years of battling alcoholism and substance abuse. Gilbert is a member of Queensland's Indigenous Hall of Fame.

REMEMBER

Ashleigh (Ash) Barty is better known for her success on the tennis court. But she played cricket in the Women's National Cricket League. She also played for the Brisbane Heat in the inaugural Women's Big Bash League.

Stepping Up in the Boxing Ring

Boxing was a popular sport in Australia from the 1920s to the 1960s. During this period, tent boxing was a common form of entertainment throughout rural Australia. Travelling troupes of professional boxers travelled the outback. They followed the agricultural fairs and carnivals. They built large tents and the professional boxers took on anyone who wanted to enter the ring.

Indigenous boxers had the chance to become stars. Many Indigenous boxers got their first shot in the boxing tents. But others also took to boxing through more traditional means. They were some of Australia's finest title fighters.

The boxing tents

Roy Bell, Jimmy Sharman and Fred Brophy ran the boxing tents. Jimmy Sharman Senior started the Sharman tent in 1911. His son, Jimmy Sharman Junior, took over the business in 1955 and ran it until 1971. That's when the sport was heavily regulated due to safety concerns. The tent visited 45 to 50 different locations every year. Fred Brophy's boxing tent is the last surviving tent boxing troupe in the world. It returned in 2021 after a break due to COVID-19.

The tents — and the sport of boxing — offered a chance for money and moving up in the world. They were a small victory over powerlessness. Boxing also offered a chance for dignity and collective pride as Aboriginal people cheered for their heroes. But exploitation of black boxers also existed. Managers took major percentages. In some places, they were still treated differently from other Australians. Their movement and wages were limited. These tents included many Indigenous boxers. One was Dave Sands — a leading contender for the world middleweight title before dying in a car accident at the age of 26. In a career lasting only eight years, Sands had 110 fights. He won 97 (63 by knock-out), lost 10 and had 1 draw.

Title fighters

Boxing has been popular for Indigenous athletes, both professional and amateur. The first Aboriginal person to become a national boxing champion was Queensland middleweight Jerry Jerome, in 1913. In 1968, Lionel Rose achieved hero status for both black and white Australians. That's when he won the world bantamweight title in Tokyo against Fighter Harada. More than 250,000 people lined Melbourne streets to welcome him back from Japan. Another of the best-known Indigenous boxers was Tony Mundine. He competed in four different weight divisions. His son Anthony is also a champion boxer. (See the sidebar 'The Mundines' for more details.)

And the interest in boxing goes beyond the gloves. Chris Collard was the first Indigenous person to win a world kickboxing title. In 1999, he won the world middleweight kickboxing title.

Here are just a few Indigenous people who've made a name in the boxing ring:

- **George Bracken** was born on Palm Island in 1935. He won the Australian lightweight title in 1955. He was arrested on a fake charge in Innisfail in 1957 and was beaten by police for an hour. Bracken was an outspoken voice for the rights of Indigenous people. He spoke out against the conditions on reserves, racial prejudice, the lack of educational opportunities, and for an insurance scheme for black athletes.

- **Wally 'Wait-awhile-Wal' Carr** fought 101 matches between 1971 and 1986 in a range of divisions. In 2010, he was inducted into the Australian National Boxing Hall of Fame.

- **Chris Collard** was also known as 'the Aboriginal Warrior'. He spent his 18th birthday in prison. Five years later, he became the World Kick Boxing Champion. He was the first Indigenous person to claim the title. Now that's turning your life around!

- **Jeff 'Mitta' Dynevor** was one of the first two Indigenous people (along with high-jumper Percy Hobson) to win a Commonwealth Games gold medal. In 1962, he won in the bantamweight division.

- **Bradley Hore** represented Australia in two Olympic and two Commonwealth Games. He retired from boxing in 2016. Then he started the charity Keep Your Hands to Yourself.

- **Damien Hooper** represented Australia in the 2012 Olympics. He caused a stir when he stepped into the ring with a T-shirt that had the Aboriginal flag on it. The Australian Olympic Committee demanded an apology. Hooper replied: 'I'm representing my culture, not only my country'.

- **Jamie Pittman** turned professional after representing Australia at the 2004 Summer Olympics. He has a record of 25 bouts (22 victories, 11 knockouts, 3 losses). He has turned his talents to coaching. In 2019 he was named National Futures Coach for Boxing Australia.

- ✓ **Ranold (Ron) Richards** won three Australian titles (middleweight, light heavyweight and heavyweight) and a British Empire (middleweight) title. He retired from boxing in 1945 with a career of 142 fights and more than 60 knockout victories. By 1946, Richards was broke. He was charged with vagrancy in 1947. Richards was inducted into the Australian National Boxing Hall of Fame in 2003. He joined the Queensland Indigenous Sporting Hall of Fame in 2010.

- ✓ **Frank Roberts**, at the age of 21, was one of Australia's first Indigenous Olympians. He competed as a welterweight at the Tokyo Olympic Games in 1964.

- ✓ **Lionel Rose** was the first Indigenous Australian to win a world title in boxing. He became the world bantamweight champion in 1968. By that time, he already had several Australian bantamweight titles under his belt. Rose was born in Gippsland into poverty. His father, Roy, was a regular of the boxing tents. He looked after his early training. He won the Australian amateur flyweight title at 15.

  Rose was Australian of the Year in 1968 and appointed a Member of the Order of the British Empire (MBE) in the same year. He wouldn't travel to South Africa when invited in 1970. Due to the apartheid system there, he would have had to travel as an 'honorary white', which he refused to do. He retired from boxing that year. But he remained a strong voice for Indigenous rights throughout his life. After his career in the ring, he started a singing career.

- ✓ **Hector Thompson** was born in Kempsey, New South Wales. He won 73 fights (including 27 knockouts). He lost 12 fights and drew 2.

- ✓ **Dave Sands** had 97 wins and only 10 losses and 1 draw. He was killed at the age of 26 in an accident. He's still considered one of the most talented Indigenous boxers even with his life tragically cut short.

THE MUNDINES

Tony Mundine was born in Baryulgil in New South Wales. He won 20 of his first 21 bouts, including the Australian middleweight title. He won eight straight knockouts, winning the Australian heavyweight title in 1972. He added the Commonwealth light heavyweight title in 1975. In 1981, he won the Australian heavyweight, cruiser and light heavyweight titles. He retired in 1984 with a record of 80 wins (64 knockouts), 15 losses and one draw. He is the only Australian boxer to fight in four separate weight divisions! Mundine was awarded the Order of Australia (OAM) in 1986.

His son is one of Australia's most charismatic boxers and a superb athlete. Anthony Mundine — affectionately known as 'The Man' — is a two-time champion. He has won both the World Boxing Association super middleweight and the International Boxing Organization middleweight divisions. He also played rugby league for the St George Dragons and represented New South Wales in the State of Origin. When other representative opportunities didn't happen in rugby league, he raised racism as a possible explanation. This theory is shared by some and contested by others.

Anthony left football in 2000 and entered the world of competitive boxing. Trained by his father, Mundine fought his first professional boxing match in July 2000 at the age of 25. He fought his first world title after only ten professional bouts. Mundine went on to claim the title of World Boxing Association super middleweight champion in 2003. Mundine was named Aboriginal and Torres Strait Islander Person of the Year in 2000. He won the Deadly Award for Male Sportsperson of the Year in 2003, 2006 and 2007. After his last fight in 2021, he had a record of 48 wins (28 by knockout) and 11 losses.

We Love Our Footy!

Indigenous sportsmen have been famous across all codes of football in Australia — Australian Rules, rugby league, rugby union and soccer. Codes have been keen to develop younger Indigenous players. They have also wanted to use high-profile Indigenous players as role models for Indigenous young people. Many Indigenous people see football as a community sport. Crowds gather to watch their team. Football games and carnivals become important social and cultural events.

REMEMBER

The skill shown by Indigenous players means they play with non-Indigenous players and for non-Indigenous fans. So they are seen as breaking down racial barriers. But, at the same time, they can be subjected to racist abuse from crowds and other players. Sometimes they're stereotyped as natural athletes. Other times they thought to be high risk, because they're thought to be more prone to antisocial behaviour. Breaking down these stereotypes is another task that falls to high-profile football players.

Australian Rules Football

Australian Rules Football started in south-eastern Australia but is played all over Australia. It's a popular sport in Indigenous communities across Australia. In 2020, of the total AFL player base, 10 per cent identified as Indigenous.

Research by Michael Dockery and Sean Gorman in 2017 showed that almost 50 per cent of Indigenous men aged 15 to 19 living in AFL states (Victoria, South Australia, Western Australia, Tasmania and the Northern Territory) played the game. Its popularity is even greater away from major cities. The study found that children who played football were less likely to have learning difficulties due to poor health. It also found that boys living in remote areas who played AFL had 20 per cent lower truancy rates.

One of Australia's most successful football clubs is St Marys Football Club. It was created in 1952 in Darwin, Northern Territory, to give Indigenous people a place to play football and socialise. At the time, Indigenous people were banned from being in the city after 6 pm. One of the club's records is a winning streak of 50 consecutive games, beginning in 1994. By 2020, the club had won 903 out of 1,254 games. It only collected their first 'wooden spoon' (finishing on the bottom of the ladder) in 2019. That's a 72 per cent winning ratio!

REMEMBER

On Elcho Island (off the coast of Arnhem Land), over 800 people play the game. This is about a third of the population. It's the place with the highest AFL participation rate in Australia.

Each year, one round (or more) of the AFL is the Indigenous Round. This is meant to acknowledge and celebrate Indigenous footy players. This round traditionally ends with the 'Dreamtime at the 'G' clash at the Melbourne Cricket Ground. It's always played between the Richmond and Essendon football clubs. In 2020, round 13 saw the first-ever 'Dreaming in Darwin' game. That was still played between Richmond and Essendon. In 2021, two rounds (rounds 11 and 12) celebrated Indigenous players.

Here's a list of some of the best-known Indigenous Aussie Rules players:

- **Eddie Betts** joined Carlton in 2004. He played for Adelaide between 2014 and 2019 before going back to Carlton in 2020. In his time at Adelaide, he was the leading goalkicker in 2014, 2015, 2016 and 2017. He had the goal of the year in 2015, 2016 and 2019.

- **Shaun Burgoyne** was with Port Adelaide from 2002 to 2009. Then he moved to Hawthorn in 2010. In 2017, he was named captain of the Australian International Rules football team. He has been a strong supporter of other Indigenous players. He was an inaugural member of the Indigenous Players Advisory Board when it was started in 2011. He became its chair in 2016.

- **Barry Cable** played and coached in the Western Australian Football League and Victorian Football League. He also coached in both competitions. He debuted with Perth Football Club in 1962. He ended his playing career in 1979 at East Perth. During that time, he played 383 games and scored 508 goals. He was named in the Indigenous Team of the Century. He also is named in the Sport Australia Hall of Fame and the Australian Football Hall of Fame — Legend. Legend indeed!

- **Troy Cook** played 301 games between 1993 and 2010. He played 108 games for the Perth Demons, 43 for the Sydney Swans and 150 for the Fremantle Dockers. He also represented Western Australia.

- **Graham 'Polly' Farmer** played a key role in the 1963 Geelong Cats premiership win. He played 392 games and was selected in the AFL Team of the Century. He was also selected as the vice-captain of the West Australian Team of the Century and the captain of the Indigenous Team of the Century. He went on to coach Geelong, West Perth and Western Australia's first State of Origin team. In 1971, he became the first footballer to receive an MBE.

- **Lance 'Buddy' Franklin** played with Hawthorn from 2005 to 2013. Then he moved to the Sydney Swans in 2014. He was a six times leading goal kicker during his time at Hawthorn. He was the leading goal kicker his first five years at the Swans. He scored the AFL goal of the year in 2010 and 2013. He was consistently named in the All-Australian team.

- **Adam Goodes** played with the Sydney Swans and won two Brownlow Medals (2003 and 2006). He is a four-time All-Australian team member and a member of the Indigenous Team of the Century. He has represented Australia internationally. He played his 250th game in 2009. He retired in 2015, having played 372 games.

- **Joe Johnson** is thought to be the first Indigenous Australian to play in the Victorian and Australian Football Leagues. He played for the Fitzroy Football Club in 1904 and Brunswick Football Club in 1907.

- **Michael Long** began his football career with the famous St Marys Football Club in Darwin. In 1989, he started playing for Essendon, playing 190 games for the club. He was inducted into the AFL Hall of Fame in 2007. He has been a strong voice on Indigenous issues and rights.

- **Andrew McLeod** played a record 340 games in the AFL competition before retiring in 2010, and was the first player to win back to back Norm Smith Medals. He captained the 2008 Dream Team.

- **Peter Matera** played over 253 games for the West Coast Eagles in the 1990s. He was often admired by commentators of the game for his skills. He had seven siblings, and two of his brothers — Wally and Phillip — also played in the AFL.

- **Stephen Michael** played for South Fremantle from 1975 to 1984, kicking 231 goals. He won the Sandover Medal twice (1980 and 1981). He represented Western Australia on 17 occasions. Despite large offers from the Victorian competition, he always said no and didn't leave his home state.

- **Michael O'Loughlin** was selected for the Indigenous Team of the Century and twice represented Australia. He was only the third Indigenous person in the AFL to play 300 games.

- **Maurice Rioli** played 118 games for the Richmond Tigers between 1982 and 1987. He was a three-time All-Australian and won a Norm Smith Medal in 1982. He later moved from the football field into the political arena. In 1992, he won a seat in the Northern Territory Legislative Assembly. Sadly, Rioli passed away in December 2010, aged just 53.

- **Gavin Wanganeen** was nicknamed the 'Indian Rubber Man' because he was so flexible. In 1990, aged just 17, he began his AFL career playing for Essendon. He played 127 games for that club, and went on to play 173 for Port Adelaide and 8 for South Australia. This track record made him the first Indigenous player to reach 300 AFL games. In June 2010, he was inducted into the Australian Football League Hall of Fame.

- **Neil 'Nicky' Winmar** became a symbol of Indigenous pride with his powerful reaction to racist taunts. In 1993, after a match-winning performance for St Kilda against

Collingwood, hardcore Magpies fans were yelling racist comments at him. (They had done so for the whole game.) Winmar famously lifted his jumper and pointed to his black skin. This became an iconic moment for the Aboriginal community.

✔ **David Wirrpanda** made his debut at the age of 16 years for the West Coast Eagles. He played 227 games for the club before retiring in 2009. He represented Australia in international matches against Ireland. He was awarded the inaugural AFL Community Leadership Award in 2003. He started the David Wirrpanda Foundation to help underprivileged young people.

REMEMBER

Adam Goodes called out a young spectator for racial abuse in 2013. He was then subjected to ongoing and relentless abuse from crowds, particularly in 2015. Some have pointed out a link between Adam Goodes speaking out about Indigenous issues and becoming more of a role model for Indigenous Australians, and the abuse from crowds. This shameful episode in AFL history was explored in the documentaries *The Final Quarter* (2019) and *The Australian Dream* (2019). In April 2019, on the eve of the premiere of *The Final Quarter*, the AFL and all of its 18 clubs issued an unreserved apology for the sustained racism and events that drove Goodes out of the game. They also apologised for their failure to call it out.

REMEMBER

In 1995, the AFL introduced *Rule 30: A Rule to Combat Racial and Religious Vilification*. This was the first rule of its kind in Australian sport. It was brought in because of the use of racial abuse as an on-field tactic used against Indigenous players.

REMEMBER

AFL Women's is the league for female players. It is enjoying growing popularity and has expanded from eight teams in 2017 to 14 teams in 2020. Of the 2017 AFL Women's players, 4 per cent were Indigenous, a lower percentage than in the men's league (10 per cent). But the numbers are growing, with talented players such as Madison Prespakis (Carlton, winner of the 2020 AFL Women's best and fairest award), Ally Anderson (Brisbane), Cassie Davidson (West Coast) and Aliesha Newman (Collingwood).

HAVING A KRAK

Jim Krakouer played for Claremont in 1977 before moving to North Melbourne in 1982 and then St Kilda in 1990. By the time he retired in 1991, he had played 235 games and scored 450 goals. His son, Andrew Krakouer, was also a talented player who played for Richmond and Collingwood. He won the Sandover and Simpson Medals in 2010. Jim's brother, Phil Krakouer, was also an outstanding footballer who played for Claremont (1978–1981), North Melbourne (1982–1990) and Footscray (1990–1991). During this time, he kicked 423 goals across 238 games.

Rugby league

Rugby league was introduced to Australia in 1907. There is strong proof that it was first played just a year later in 1908 in Cherbourg, a small Aboriginal mission in Queensland. Today, Indigenous people continue to excel in the sport. In the National Rugby League (NRL), 12 per cent of the players are of Indigenous heritage. Here are some key events in Indigenous rugby league:

- **1908:** George Green was thought to be the first Indigenous footballer to play in competition. He played for the Eastern Suburbs and North Sydney teams between 1908 and 1922. His true heritage was never established. It's hard to know for sure, but more Indigenous rugby league players were probably involved in the game in the early years. Many hid their heritage for fear of facing prejudice and racism.

- **1930:** Indigenous communities started their own league clubs. The Tweed Heads All Blacks and the Redfern All Blacks became more than just sporting groups. They played political, social and cultural roles in their local communities.

- **1960:** Lionel Morgan was the first Indigenous person to play rugby league for Australia. He often faced racist abuse from the crowds, who also threw objects at him while he was on the field.

✔ **1973:** Arthur Beetson became the first Indigenous player to captain an Australian rugby league team. That same year, the first Indigenous side toured internationally, to New Zealand.

✔ **2008:** Australia's national rugby league team had five Indigenous players on their team of 13.

✔ **2020:** Josh Addo-Carr lifted his shirt before the Indigenous All-Stars match against the Maori All-Stars. This followed the classic display of pride shown by AFL legend Nicky Winmar. It reminded audiences of the importance of standing up to racism.

Here are just some of the famous Indigenous rugby league players:

✔ **Arthur 'Big Artie' Beetson** was a rugby league player for Queensland. He played representative football from 1964 until 1981. In 1973, when he captained the Kangaroos (the national rugby league team), he became the first Indigenous player to captain Australia in any major sport. He also captained Australia in 1974, 1975 and 1977. He went on to coach Australia, Queensland, Eastern Suburbs (Brisbane), the Redcliffe Dolphins (Brisbane) and the Cronulla-Sutherland Sharks (Sydney). Beetson was inducted into the Australian Rugby League Hall of Fame in 2003. He passed away in 2011 and his life was celebrated with a state funeral.

✔ **Preston Campbell** played for Cronulla, Penrith and the Gold Coast between 1999 and 2011. In 2001, he was awarded the Daly M medal. In 2008 he won the Ken Stephen Medal for his work with Indigenous communities, on and off the field.

✔ **Larry Corowa** played league for Balmain in the 1970s and continued his career into the 1990s. He was an Australian international and New South Wales interstate representative.

✔ **Laurie Daley** played mainly in the 1990s. He represented Australia in rugby league on 31 occasions and captained the team once. He was named in the list of Australia's 100 Greatest Rugby League Players (1908 to 2007). He was chosen for the first rugby league Indigenous Team of the Century in 2008.

- **Justin Hodges** started playing for the Brisbane Broncos in 2000 before moving to the Sydney Roosters in 2002. He went back to the Broncos in 2005 and played with them until he retired in 2015. He captained the team during his last year. He played for Queensland and Australia, and in the Indigenous All-Stars team.

- **Greg Inglis** played for the Melbourne Storm before joining the South Sydney Rabbitohs in 2011. He was awarded the Golden Boot in 2009 by *Rugby League World* magazine as the world's best player that year. Inglis played representative matches for Queensland and Australia.

- **Cliff 'God' Lyons** played for Manly during the 1980s and 1990s and played more than 300 first-grade games. He won a Clive Churchill Medal in 1987, when Manly won the final. He went on to also win two Dally M Medals in 1990 and 1994. Lyons made his State of Origin debut in 1987. In 1990, he played his first game for Australia in international tests.

- **Latrell Mitchell** was selected for the Australian Schoolboys team in 2014. He played for the Sydney Roosters from 2016 to 2019 before moving to South Sydney in 2020. He played in the Indigenous All-Stars and for Australia in 2018 and 2019.

- **David Peachey** played 255 NRL games — for the Cronulla Sharks, Widnes Vikings (in the English Super League) and South Sydney Rabbitohs. He retired from elite rugby league in 2007. During his career, he scored 468 points, including 117 tries. He was awarded Sportsman of the Year in 2002. He also played State of Origin and represented Australia.

- **Steve Renouf** played for the Brisbane Broncos from 1988 to 1999. Then he played two seasons in England with the Wigan Warriors. Over his career, he scored over 185 tries over 242 games. He played representative football for Queensland and was named in the Australian team each year from 1992 to 1998. He was named in the Indigenous Team of the Century.

- **Eric Robinson** played for the South Sydney Rabbitohs in the 1960s. But he left a legacy to the game that went beyond his own career. One of his sons, Ricky Walford, played first grade for St George. Three of his grandsons — Travis Robinson (Cronulla Sharks), Reece Robinson (Brisbane Broncos) and Nathan Merritt (South Sydney Rabbitohs) — also played in the NRL.

- **Wendell Sailor** is a Torres Strait Islander who debuted in 1993 and played a total of 222 games of league for Brisbane, the Dragons and St George Illawarra. He also represented the Queensland Reds in rugby union. He represented Australia in both codes, playing 14 rugby league and 37 rugby union representative matches. After playing rugby union from 2001 to 2006, Sailor returned to rugby league in May 2008.

- **Dale Shearer** played rugby league in the 1980s and 1990s. He is remembered for his record of being the top try-scorer in State of Origin history (12 tries and 6 goals). He also represented Australia in international test matches (scoring 12 tries and 9 goals).

- **Eric Simms** played rugby league for South Sydney in the 1960s and 1970s. He won four premierships while playing for South Sydney. He was the top point scorer for four consecutive seasons. He played 206 first-grade games, scoring a total of 1,841 career points. Even though he retired from the field decades ago, some of his club records still stand. They include most number of goals in a season (112 goals and 19 field goals), most career field goals (86) and most field goals in a game (5).

- **Gorden 'Raging Bull' Tallis** played rugby league from 1992 to 2004 for St George Dragons and the Brisbane Broncos. He captained Australia, Queensland and the Brisbane Broncos (with whom he won three premierships).

- **Sam Thaiday** played 308 games for the Brisbane Broncos between 2003 and 2018. He played representative football for Queensland and Australia. He was also named in the Indigenous All-Stars team from 2010 to 2016. He was awarded Daly M Second Rower of the Year in 2010 and 2011 and the Ken Stephen Memorial Award in 2011.

✔ **Johnathan Thurston** started his career with the Canterbury Bulldogs in 2001. Then he moved to the North Queensland Cowboys in 2005. Thurston won two Dally M Medals for best player in 2005 and 2007, and in those same years won the Dally M Medal for best halfback (which he also won in 2009). Not surprisingly, he was named as halfback in the Indigenous Team of the Century in 2008.

✔ **Ricky Walford** played most of his career for St George Illawarra Dragons. He played representative football for New South Wales in the State of Origin and in the Aboriginal side that toured Tonga in 1990. After retirement, Walford became the Indigenous Development Manager at the Australian Rugby League.

REMEMBER

The NRL Women's Premiership features the best female players. Four clubs fielded teams in the inaugural 2018 season: Brisbane Broncos, Sydney Roosters, St George Illawarra Dragons and New Zealand Warriors. Indigenous players for these teams included Taleena Simon (Sydney Roosters), Amber Pilley (Broncos) and Shakiah Tungai (Dragons).

REMEMBER

In November 2009, the NRL announced its first Indigenous All Star team. The team played against the NRL All-Stars on 13 February 2010. This marked the two-year anniversary of the federal government's apology to the Stolen Generations. The Indigenous All-Stars won 16–12. A women's game was first played in 2011 between Indigenous players and a side made up of Australian representatives and rising talents. The All Star's (men and women) continue to play a match every year at the start of the season, now playing an All Star Maori team.

An Indigenous Team of the Century was named in 2008. It included many well-known players such as Arthur Beetson, Laurie Daley, Greg Inglis and Sam Thaiday. In 2020, A Dream Team of the past 20 years was named: Greg Inglis, Nathan Blacklock, Latrell Mitchell, Justin Hodges, Laurie Daley, Johnathan Thurston, Andrew Fifita, Nathan Peats, Caral Webb, Gordon Tallis, Sam Thaiday and Greg Bird.

RUGBY IN REDFERN

Redfern is well known for its Indigenous community. Many rugby league initiatives have come from, or connected themselves to, this area of Sydney.

The Redfern All Blacks is the oldest Aboriginal rugby league football club in Australia. It was officially founded in 1944. But the origins of the club can be traced back to the 1930s. The club was started by Aboriginal players because they weren't accepted to play with other clubs in the local south Sydney area. Over the years, many players for the Redfern All Blacks came from around Sydney and from small country towns with large Aboriginal populations such as Walgett, Kempsey and Cowra.

The Redfern All Blacks are a feeder club for the South Sydney Rabbitohs, who are based in Redfern. They have a strong connection to the Indigenous community.

The South Sydney Rabbitohs formed in 1908 as one of the founding members of the New South Wales Rugby Football League. The Rabbitohs and the Sydney Roosters are the only foundation clubs still in the league. Souths has produced Indigenous players such as Eric Simms and Nathan Merritt. It continued to be home to some of the best Indigenous players in the game including Greg Inglis, Latrell Mitchell and Cody Walker.

Rugby union

Indigenous players have made their mark on the game of rugby union, as well as other rugby codes. But union hasn't had the same popularity as rugby league and Australian Rules within the Indigenous community.

Frank Ivory was the first Indigenous person to play representative rugby union. He played for Queensland in 1893–94. Lloyd McDermott was the first to play for Australia when he was selected for the national team in 1962. Other Indigenous players who have represented Australia include Lloyd McDermott, Mark Ella, Glen Ella, Gary Ella, Lloyd Walker, Andrew Walker, James

Williams, Wendell Sailor and talented twins Anthony Fainga'a and Saia Fainga'a.

Lloyd McDermott ('Mullenjaiwakka') was a rugby union player for the Wallabies in the 1960s. Born in Queensland, his father battled to give him an education. McDermott studied law at Queensland University. He played two Australian tests against New Zealand in 1962. During the 'apartheid era' in South Africa, he withdrew from playing for the Australian team rather than play as an 'honorary white'. In 1972, he joined the New South Wales Bar as a barrister. He was named a Queensland Great in 2016. He passed away in 2019. But the foundation he started, the Lloyd McDermott Rugby Development Team, continues his legacy of promoting rugby union and Indigenous rights.

SPORTING GREATNESS: THE ELLA FAMILY

The Ella family (Mark, Gary and Glen) has left a great mark on rugby union. All three played test matches for Australia and Glen's twin brother, Mark, played for Australia in 25 tests, captaining 9 of them. Despite his exceptional skills as a player and being offered large sums of money to continue playing, he retired in 1984, aged 25.

The Ella brothers occasionally faced racial abuse from crowds. Some speculation remains that Mark lost the captaincy of the Australian team because he was Indigenous. But Mark's abilities were admired by many. He was inducted into the International Rugby Hall of Fame in 1997 and the Australian Rugby Union Hall of Fame when it was started in 2005.

But the sporting accolades for the Ella family don't end there. The boys weren't the only talents in the Ella family. Their sister, Marcia Ella-Duncan, had sporting success in her own right. She played netball for Australia in the 1986 tour of England and then at the Tri Nations with New Zealand and Jamaica. She also played for the Australian team in the World Tournament in Glasgow, 1987.

Soccer

Soccer has produced a few Indigenous stars over the years. But its popularity among Indigenous communities has begun to grow only recently. Here are a few Indigenous soccer stars of note. They have all enjoyed successful careers outside of soccer:

- ✔ **John Moriarty** graduated from Flinders University a few years after his cousin Charles Perkins. He played for South Australia and was chosen for the Australian team to Asia in 1961. (This tour never went ahead, though. Australia was banned from international matches by FIFA, the Federation Internationale du Football.)

- ✔ **Charles Perkins** is perhaps the most famous Indigenous soccer star. At the age of 21 he was one of the most highly paid soccer players in Australia. Then he left to play in the English league. While there, he decided he would study at university. Football provided him with the means of paying for tuition. Perkins became vice-president of the Australian Soccer Federation in 1987. For more on Perkins' political career, see Chapter 9.

- ✔ **Harry Williams** was the first Indigenous person to play for Australia at the international level. He was chosen for the national team in 1970. He played 17 internationals and 26 other representative games between 1970 and 1978. This included 6 World Cup games in 1977.

REMEMBER

Indigenous people who've played soccer have noted that they faced much less discrimination against them than in other football codes, particularly among immigrants from European countries. But fewer players flocked to this code of football. They tended to prefer the 'glamour game' of Aussie Rules. Charles Perkins once said that he wasn't welcomed by Australian society but was more welcomed by ethnic groups and found the Aboriginal–ethnic relationship in soccer to be a good one. In 2016, the Football Federation Australia launched the National Indigenous Football Championships.

Indigenous Australians continue to have a presence in the game:

- **Travis Dodd** played 137 matches for Adelaide United before moving to Perth Glory in 2011. When he played his 100th match in 2009, he became the second Aboriginal person to reach this milestone. In 2006, Dodd became the first Aboriginal soccer player to score a goal for Australia.

- **Jade North** joined the Brisbane Strikers in 1998 at the age of just 16. He represented Australia at the 2004 and 2008 Olympics. By June 2011 he had represented Australia 34 times.

- **Kyah Simon** played for Sydney FC in the W-League. She joined the team in 2009 after a year playing for Melbourne Victory. In 2011, she was named Player of the Year, Young Player of the Year and Player's Player of the Year. She has also played in the United States and for Australia in the FIFA Women's World Cup. In the 2015 World Cup, the women's team became the first Australian team, male or female, to win a knockout stage match at a World Cup. They defeated Brazil by a score of 1–0 — with Simon scoring that winning goal.

- **Lydia Williams** played for Canberra United FC in the W-League. She joined the team in 2008. Since then, she has played in the United States and represented Australia. She now plays for Arsenal in England. In 2019 she published a children's book called *Saved!!!*

TIP

Indigenous historian and sports enthusiast John Maynard released an updated second edition of his book *The Aboriginal Soccer Tribe* in 2019. It's a thorough account of the Indigenous contribution to the game.

IT'S A KNOCKOUT!

The New South Wales Annual Aboriginal Rugby League Knockout began in 1971. Also known as the NSW Koori Knockout, it has grown over the years into a three-day event, held in later September or October. It is one of the biggest social events on the calendar for the Aboriginal community in New South Wales. Although originally held in Sydney, it became the custom, after Kempsey won in 1975, that the winning team would host the competition the following year. This tradition has seen the Knockout held around the state. The founders of the competition — including former St George Dragon's player Bob Morgan — saw it as a chance to showcase the talent in the Aboriginal community, especially in more remote country towns. These towns may have been overlooked by the talent scouts for the large Sydney-based clubs. In 2007 and 2008, and then every year since 2012, the event has also included a women's Knockout.

Track and Field

Indigenous people have traditionally excelled as athletes, so it's not surprising that many of Australia's track and field events have been won by Indigenous people. Here are some of the Australia's Indigenous Olympians and world champions:

- **Cathy Freeman** won gold in the 400-metre sprint at the Sydney Olympics in 2000. She'd won the silver medal four years earlier. Cathy won 400-metre medals at the 1997 and 1999 world championships. She also won four Commonwealth Games titles in the 200-metre and 400-metre events (in 1994), and in the 100-metre and 400-metre relays (in 1990 and 2002).

- **Benn Harradine** holds the Australian and Oceania records for discus throwing. He was the first Indigenous field athlete to represent Australia at the Olympic Games. He was selected in 2008.

- **Percy Hobson**, a high-jumper, was the only Indigenous track and field athlete to win a gold medal in the Commonwealth Games. He took the honours at the 1962 Perth games. He remained so until Cathy Freeman won the gold at the 1990 Commonwealth Games (she was on the relay team).

- **Patrick Johnson** is a sprinter who, in 2003, became the first Australian to break ten seconds (9.93) for the 100-metre sprint. At the time, this made him the 17th fastest man in history. He also won the men's 100-metre open at the 2006 Telstra A-Series.

- **Nova Peris-Kneebone** represented Australia on the women's hockey team at the 1996 Olympics. There, she became the first Aboriginal Australian to win an Olympic gold medal. At the 1998 Commonwealth Games in Kuala Lumpur, she won the 200-metre sprint and was a member of the 100-metre winning relay team. Nova Peris, as she later became known, was the first Indigenous woman to sit in Federal Parliament. She was brought in to fill a Senate vacancy for the Australian Labor Party.

- **Joshua Ross** won the Stawell Gift (a 100-metre race) in 2003. As a sign of his talent as an athlete, it took less than a year of participating in competitive athletics before he was ranked number six on the all-time-greatest list. When Ross retired in 2009, he was ranked as the third-fastest Australian of all time over 100 metres. He had run it in 10.08 seconds. He represented Australia at the 2004 Olympic Games, at the World Championships in Athletics in 2005 and 2009, and at the Commonwealth Games in 2006.

- **Kyle Vander-Kuyp** set the Oceania record for 110-metre hurdles in 1995. He competed at the 1996 and 2000 Olympic Games, and the 1994 and 1998 Commonwealth Games.

REMEMBER

After her career as an elite athlete, Cathy Freeman started a foundation to work with Indigenous children in remote Aboriginal communities. Focused on education and excellence, the foundation works with Indigenous children to strengthen academic skills, build self-esteem and develop other activities that promote well-being and success. To find out more about Cathy's good works, you can visit www.cathyfreemanfoundation.org.au.

Championing Other Sports

Like every community around the world, the Indigenous community enjoys, takes part in and excels at a range of sports. Across Australia, Indigenous communities play sports as diverse as basketball, netball, hockey, golf and surfing. Within these sports, the Indigenous community has produced some notable champions. Some of these have achieved elite international success, such as tennis player Evonne Goolagong-Cawley. Other sports have a growing following among Indigenous people, including golf and surfing.

All-rounders at basketball

Basketball is an increasingly popular sport in Australia, and Indigenous people have excelled in it. Here are some of the notable players:

- **Michael Ah Mat** represented the Northern Territory at the 1959 Australian championships. He played 588 games over 20 seasons. In 1964, he became the first Indigenous person to represent Australia at the Olympic games — and the first Northern Territorian to do it, too! In 1979, he retired from basketball. He died of a heart attack aged 41 in 1984. He was inducted into the Australian Basketball Hall of Fame in 2010.

- **Rohanee Cox** played in the Women's National Basketball League (WNBL). She won the Eddie Gilbert Medal in 2008 and was a member of the silver-winning Australian women's team at the 2008 Olympic Games. She holds the impressive record of having represented Australia more than 100 times.

- **Tyson Demos** grew up in Wollongong and played in the National Basketball League for the Wollongong Hawks.

- **Nathan 'Baby Shaq' Jawai** was part of the 2009 Australian men's basketball squad. He was the first Indigenous Australian to be selected into the NBA, in 2008, by Indiana Pacers. But he was traded to the Toronto Raptors that same year. In 2011, he played for the Serbian team KK Partizan, going on to play for Spanish and Turkish teams. In 2016, he went back to playing in Australia (and the club he began his career with).

✏ **Danny Morseu** was the first Torres Strait Islander to represent Australia. He qualified for the national team in the 1980 Olympics in Moscow. He also played with the Australian team in the 1984 Olympics in Los Angeles. He was the first Indigenous person inducted into the NBL Hall of Fame in 2002.

✏ **Patrick Mills** represented Australia at the 2008 Olympics. He was selected by the Portland Trailblazers in the 2009 NBA draft. In 2012, he signed with the San Antonio Spurs, and was still playing with them in 2021.

Excelling at netball

In 1987, Marcia Ella-Duncan became the first Indigenous person to represent Australia internationally in netball. She continued to be involved with the sport as a coach and administrator for the Randwick team. She trained them for the State Championships. She also helped found the Pearlers Netball Club in 2004. The club is based in the inner western suburbs of Sydney. It focuses on getting women from disadvantaged backgrounds into the sport and specifically targets involvement from Indigenous girls.

Several programs have been developed to promote the sport to younger Indigenous women. For example, an Australian Indigenous Schoolgirls Netball team, the Budgies, have been competing in the Trans-Tasman International Challenge since 2009. The New South Wales Echidna's Indigenous Schoolgirls Netball team has been competing in national selections since 2005.

Indigenous players have made their mark on the game, including Nicole Cusack, Bianca Giteau (nee Franklin) and Stacey Campton who, after a successful playing career, went on to umpire.

REMEMBER

Rose Damaso has represented the Northern Territory in softball, hockey, netball and basketball. This one athlete represented her state 36 times across four different sports, an astonishing record!

A few out of the box

Here's just a sample of some Indigenous people who have achieved outstanding success at their chosen sport:

- **Beach volleyball:** Taliqua Clancy represented Australia in the 2016 Olympics. She was the first Indigenous Australian to represent Australia at that level in the sport. As a show of her pride, she painted the flag on her fingernails for the Olympic matches. She won silver in the sport in the 2018 Commonwealth games.

- **Golf:** May Chalker won the Western Australian women's golf championship and was the captain of the state team in 1982. She represented her state six times during her career.

  Scott Gardner became the first Indigenous person to earn a PGA Tour card. He had played the European Tour in 2001 to 2003. He then played the Nationwide Tour for nine years. He won the Chattanooga Classic in 2010 and played in the US PGA tour in 2013.

- **Hockey:** Des Abbott played more than 80 times for Australia. This included his selection for the Australian men's hockey squad in the 2010 Commonwealth Games in Delhi. His cousin, Joel Carroll, also represented Australia internationally in hockey.

- **Motocross:** Chad Reed excelled in the sport of motocross. He was born and raised in Kurri Kurri in the Hunter Valley, New South Wales. He won two Supercross championships before racing overseas. He moved to the United States in 2002 and won the 2004 AMA Supercross championship. He was runner-up in the same competition in 2005 and 2006. Reed retired from racing in 2020.

- **Softball:** Stacey Porter was first selected for the national softball team in 2002. She captained the Australian women's team in 2010 at the International Softball Federation's world championships in Venezuela. At the 2004 Olympics, the team won silver and followed this performance with a bronze medal at the 2008 Olympics.

🗸 **Surfing:** Indigenous surf carnivals are becoming more popular. The numbers attracted to the sport have been helped by
initiatives such as the Indigenous Surfing Programs run by
Surfing New South Wales and Surfing Victoria. These programs promote the sport and the importance of education
and a healthy lifestyle. Here are a few noted Indigenous
surfers:

- **Ginava Henare** won the women's championship at the 2010
  Indigenous Classic.

- **Russell Molony** won his seventh Indigenous Classic in 2011.
  As a result, he was ranked in the world's top 225.

- **Dale Richards** won the Quicksilver Pro in 2007 and joined
  the world's top 45 professional surfers.

- **Mark 'Sanga' Sainesbury**, an Aboriginal man from New
  South Wales, surfed on the professional tour in the 1980s.
  He died of an aneurysm in the early 1990s while surfing.

Other notable Indigenous surfers include Andrew Ferguson
(Coffs Harbour), Barry Chanel (La Perouse), Dean McLeod,
Eric Mercy (also Coffs Harbour), Gus Ardler, Joel Slabb
(Fingal), John Ardler, John and Gary Brown, Kenny Dann
(Western Australia), Lara Haddon, Steven Williams and Todd
Roberts (Wreck Bay).

🗸 **Tennis:** Evonne Goolagong-Cawley is not only a famous
Indigenous Australian sportsperson, but also one of
Australia's most famous sportspeople! A world-class athlete,
she won a total of 14 Grand Slam titles — four Australian
Open, two Wimbledon and one French Open, six in women's
doubles and one in mixed doubles.

During the 1950s and 1960s, when Goolagong-Cawley was a
child, Aboriginal people still lived in harsh conditions and
faced discrimination. In this climate, it is remarkable that
Goolagong-Cawley became such a success. She was able to
play tennis because a white man, Bill Hurtzman, saw her
peering through the fence at the local courts and encouraged
her to come in and play. Things really changed for her in
1967. The proprietor of a tennis school in Sydney travelled to

Goolagong-Cawley's home town of Barellan after being told about her skills. He was impressed and convinced her parents to allow her to move to Sydney. There, she went to school and continued to train. She was named Australian of the Year in 1971, awarded an MBE in 1972 and made an Officer of the Order of Australia (AO) in 1982.

Ashleigh ('Ash') Barty is the second Indigenous Australian to reach the No.1 women's singles ranking. After winning the US Open doubles title in 2018, she won the singles title in the 2019 French Open. She serves as a National Indigenous Tennis Ambassador for Tennis Australia. Her down-to-earth attitude has made her a fan favourite. She played professional cricket during a hiatus from tennis between 2014 and 2016. She was named Young Australian of the Year in 2020.

✔ **Volleyball:** Dalma Smith was one of Australia's talented volleyball players. She was selected for the senior team to represent Australia in 1985, including at the World Championships Qualifying Tournament in Melbourne.

CELEBRATING SPORT THROUGH FESTIVALS

Many Indigenous sportsmen and sportswomen haven't just excelled at their sport but have also sought to increase the number of Indigenous people — especially young people — who play. One way to do that is through sports carnivals or festivals. In 2008, the Australian Indigenous Games Foundation was started. Its purpose was hosting a national Indigenous games event.

Here's a list of popular festivals from around Australia that celebrate culture and sport:

✔ **The Aboriginal Power Cup** was created in April 2008. Indigenous students must attend at least 80 per cent of their classes to participate in the cup, so the festival is used as an incentive!

- The **Barunga Festival** is named after its host town, about 80 kilometres south-east of Katherine. It is the largest annual festival in the Northern Territory. It is held over the Queen's Birthday long weekend in June. The local Jawoyn community uses the festival to celebrate their culture. Throughout the festival, sports competitions and events such as spear making and spear throwing are held.

- The **Ella 7s Rugby Union Carnival** is an annual event held in Coffs Harbour, New South Wales, and started in 2009. It was named after the Ella brothers and is aimed at promoting rugby union to Indigenous players. The tournament includes men's and women's games.

- The **Foley Shield** was started in 1948 and is held in far north Queensland with teams from the Torres Strait and Cape York. It is supported by the Queensland Rugby League. After a period of 'hibernation' in the mid-2010s, the competition was brought back in 2017.

- The **Generation Cup,** for netball, softball and football, has been held in Launceston, Tasmania since 1995. It is hosted by the Tasmanian Aboriginal Centre.

- The **Indigenous Reconciliation Rugby League Carnival** started in 2009 in Rockhampton, Queensland, and now involves 24 rugby league teams.

- The **Island of Origin Series Rugby League Carnival** is held on Badu Island and has been going since 1985. Many players and supporters travel by small boat to get there. The unpredictable seas and tides can prevent people from getting to the carnival — or delay their leaving!

- The **Newcastle Koori Netball Tournament** began in 1999 and aims to increase participation by Indigenous women in the sport. The competition attracts players and teams from across New South Wales.

(continued)

(continued)

> ✓ **The New South Wales Aboriginal Rugby League Knockout Carnival** was first held in 1971 in St Peters, Sydney, with eight participating teams. Teams represent Indigenous communities across New South Wales. The carnival has grown to be one of the biggest Indigenous social, cultural and sporting events in Australia, with its family-friendly feel and rules about being alcohol-free. The winning team gains the right to hold the next Knockout, so the tournament has been held in various locations across the state.

PROJECT

Write a short biography of an Indigenous athlete mentioned in this chapter.

PROJECT

*Watch a documentary on an Indigenous sports hero, such as **The Final Quarter, The Australian Dream** or **FREEMAN**. Write a summary of the main points or themes that emerge.*

More Than Rocks and Dots: Indigenous Art

IN THIS CHAPTER

- ✔ Seeing the spirituality and symbolism of Indigenous art
- ✔ Looking at the different styles of Indigenous art and crafts
- ✔ Diving into the art of the Torres Strait
- ✔ Taking stock of urban art
- ✔ Showing Indigenous art to the world

For Australia's Indigenous peoples, art is a living and changing tradition. It is important to the identity and cultural survival of Indigenous communities across the country. The oldest Aboriginal art that survives are the rock paintings seen in rock shelters, especially in northern Australia. From the early 20th century, artists began moving traditional artistic practices. There were images that were painted on bark shelters, symbols painted on the body and patterns made in the sand during ceremonies. They began to appear on bark, canvas, textiles and pottery. New forms of art have evolved.

In this chapter, I look at the types of Indigenous art that have arisen. They reflect the diversity of Indigenous cultures. I note some of the respected artists whose names have become linked with Australia's Indigenous art. I also look at the highly political art from urban areas. It is strongly linked to traditional country, values and practices.

Understanding the Role of Art in Indigenous Cultures

Indigenous art has become an important means of creative expression and economic self-support. But it's also a way of communicating with non-Indigenous people about things of importance. These things include sovereignty, self-determination and land rights.

Aboriginal art and art of the Torres Strait Islands has symbols as a record of Indigenous experience and history. Its existence is a political statement. Indigenous art is strikingly beautiful, vibrant and visually pleasing. But it also has strong spiritual and political messages.

Connecting to the spirit through art

Art is closely connected to the spiritual realm. It plays an important role in the religious life of Indigenous peoples. Works of art showing the actions of ancestors, and the right to produce their designs, are inherited by birth or initiation. They are, still today, produced during rituals.

Such ceremonies are often a mix of song, dance, sculpture and painting. Each part is an aspect of the actions of ancestors and the fulfilment of religious duty. The parts often make up only a small part of a much larger ceremony. Performance of the rites was needed to meet obligations to the ancestors and the land. The right to produce a story, an image or clan symbols belonged to the group. They were handed down and reproduced faithfully. (See the following section for more information.)

REMEMBER

The reproduction of artwork is part of the performance of the cultural obligation. (Artwork includes the patterns, artefacts and symbols.) Producing the art allows the artist to keep a connection with the ancestors in the spirit world.

To read more about what the patterns and symbols mean, see the later section 'Reading between the dots: Knowing what the symbols mean'.

Using art to inform

In the past, the process of creating art was a group activity and a way of communicating with and honouring ancestors. The result was often thrown away or destroyed. The art was made with non-permanent mediums — such as sand, in the case of the original dot paintings. The end products weren't kept for beauty or valued as property.

The process of creating an artwork is often educational. It instructs others how to proceed in a ceremony. Or it teaches them laws, obligations, duties and rights. People aren't allowed to steal or paint the wrong way. There are strict rules for reproduction. Artworks made in this way and for these purposes weren't produced for visual value. They weren't for the general public. They were certainly not for the collector of fine art.

CULTURAL
PROTOCOLS

Under traditional Aboriginal practice, knowledge of the artwork's content, the creation of the artwork, and even viewing of an artwork are carefully guarded. They are controlled by those who are the proper recipients of the knowledge, rights and duties. Unauthorised reproduction is a serious breach of law. It is even today met with punishment. Other people of different kinship groups within the same language group, as well as members of other Aboriginal groups who don't have rights to a particular Dreaming, aren't allowed to paint, create or otherwise represent the specific mix of images related to that Dreaming.

Aboriginal paintings are often maps of traditional land. Some artworks can be read as a map where features of the landscape are symbolically represented. But proportions may be skewed and distances may not be to scale. There may be no conventional compass orientation. Sometimes, these artworks map spiritual importance rather than landscape features.

Painting can also reflect the relationship with the sky. Aboriginal and Torres Strait Islanders were astronomers. They studied the movement of the skies. They used the skies for navigation and tracking the seasons. Cultural stories about the sky inspire artists.

TIP

If you are flying over large parts of the Australian country, look out the window. See how the land below looks like Aboriginal paintings. It is a great reminder of how well Aboriginal artists know their country. It shows how much their paintings reflect the features of their land.

REMEMBER

Art proves connection and duty to land. Indigenous peoples view artworks like legal documents — a chain of title. These 'legal rights' are traced back to the Dreaming. They reflect stories and obligations that define the relationship with the land.

Reading between the dots: Knowing what the symbols mean

An artwork may have multiple points of view. Trees may be viewed vertically on the same painting that shows waterholes from an aerial view. Several geographic locations may be in the painting. Often, there is a different idea of space. The same painting can show people both from above and face on.

Pictorial symbols can carry many meanings. Much art is representational. The art uses symbols, dots, aerial views (views from above) and x-ray (internal) views to tell of events and journeys. In most places, figures and geometric symbols work together to create representations.

TECHNICAL
STUFF

In the Central and Western Deserts, each design has a particular meaning. Symbols such as the following are used to tell stories:

- A half-circle like a crescent moon could represent a person. Several grouped around a circle could mean people meeting.

- A series of concentric circles (that all have the same centre) might stand for a campsite or a waterhole.

- Concentric circles linked by lines could mean waterholes connected by running water.

Aboriginal artworks may also map kin or communal relationships, just as they map landscape. They express the relationships between land and people. Clans have their own particular markings. They highlight both connection and difference. Paintings show the clan links.

TIP

Aboriginal and Torres Strait Islander art is so connected to culture and cultural stories. Artworks often come with an artist's statement that will let you better understand the deeper meanings of the work.

NGURRARA: THE GREAT SANDY DESERT PAINTING

The *Ngurrara Canvas* is an example of how painting is a practice of legal obligations and rights. The canvas is the largest example of Western Desert art. It was painted by over 60 artists from the southern Kimberley region at Pirnini. This area is at the northern edge of the Great Sandy Desert.

It makes sense that *Ngurrara* means 'home', the place that people have attachment to. In 1997, the canvas was presented to the National Native Title Tribunal as proof of ancestral, social, economic and personal connections to land. The *Ngurrara Canvas* communicated across the cultural divide. It brought the spirit of Aboriginal law to the court for consideration by the dominant legal system. The Ngurrara native title determination was the largest claim in the Kimberley region. It recognised exclusive possession native title over about 76,000 square kilometres of land. The determination was also handed down at Pirnini, where the *Ngurrara Canvas* had been painted. The canvas has been shown in galleries around Australia, including the National Museum of Australia. It is shown in the following figure being unrolled for a temporary exhibition at the South Australian Museum.

The canvas measures eight by ten metres. It is made of ten colourful harmonised patchworks. Each one shows a different story, a different place, a different piece of proof of connection

(continued)

(continued)

and attachment to land. The waterholes, trees, salt lakes and people are visible. It shows the path of serpents and ancestors. It tells a story of ceremonies being performed, creation stories, of spirits, and even of snoring fathers.

Looking at Indigenous Art around Australia

Indigenous artists have always been inspired by the world around them and the culture they know. They created artworks of deep spiritual importance with the materials that were most readily available to them. The earliest remaining art is in the Pilbara and dates from around 40,000 years ago. It is rock art painted on the walls of shelters. Paintings were also created on the bark that was used to build shelters.

Rock art

Rock art has left a lasting legacy that has survived. Existing rock art and ochre pieces prove human existence in Australia for over 65,000 years. (Refer to Chapter 2 for more details). Rock art gives insights into how people lived and how they saw their world. One piece of rock art could be linked in meaning to other pieces in the area. This art often appears at places that were important meeting places.

Artists made different types of rock art:

- Figures were carved into sandstone. These carvings were re-carved on the rock over time. This ensured survival of the artwork over so many thousands of years.

- Ochre was used to paint on the rock surface. Art was created as paintings or by using stencils. In stencil art, a hand was placed on the rock. Ochre was sprayed from the mouth to leave an outline of the hand on the rock surface. The ochre created a chemical reaction with the rock, sinking into it. These were usually made on rock surfaces that were safe from the elements in caves or overhangs. Examples of these ochre paintings are in south-eastern Australia and in central Queensland. There are also better known sites in Arnhem Land in the Northern Territory and the Kimberley in the north of Western Australia.

Today in Australia, proof of rock art exists across the country in cities — around Sydney Harbour and at Bondi and Kuring-gai National Park in Sydney. There is also proof in rural areas and remote areas. These include in Western Australia, the site of the oldest evidence of rock art at Carpenter's Gap, near Windjana National Park in the Kimberley, and the oldest surviving paintings on the Burrup Peninsula.

Sadly, many sites have been destroyed through the creation of urban centres, mining activities, vandalism and graffiti, and by environmental pollution. Governments keep giving approval for the destruction of sites. Wrongful destruction of sites leads to a fine. But this is of little reward to the communities. They could never put a price on the spiritual and cultural importance of rock art sites.

CULTURAL
PROTOCOLS

In the Kimberley, one of the most common images, especially in rock art, is that of the Wandjina, a creation being of great spiritual significance. These figures have large circular faces, though no mouth, and a headdress.

REMEMBER

Some early European visitors to Aboriginal communities didn't believe that Aboriginal people could have made the rock art they had seen. The paintings were thought too mature to have been done by people who (some) Europeans thought 'savage' and 'primitive'.

REMEMBER

In 2020, mining company Rio Tinto faced strong criticism after it destroyed a significant site of rock art in the Pilbara. The caves had engraved rock art and proof of human habitation dating back 47,000 years in one and 60,000 years in another. The company said the destruction was a 'misunderstanding'. But public outcry over the destruction led to the CEO and two other senior leaders of the mining company quitting.

Bark painting

Traditionally, painting was done on the bark used to build shelters. Today, bark is used as a canvas. The bark is cut from the stringybark tree right after the wet season, when it's still moist. (This tree is a type of eucalyptus.) The bark has to be in good condition. It must be free from splits and knots and not eaten by termites. Bark is cut off in rectangular pieces and then flattened.

TECHNICAL
STUFF

The bark is prepared by placing a wet sheet on the heat of hot coals (without directly touching them). Then the bark is pressed flat, with the rough side, not the side to be painted, having contact with the heat. This process also gets rid of the moisture from the bark. Weights are then placed on the bark for several days to flatten it further. To keep the bark from warping, sticks are tied to the ends of the bark with string.

Bark painting uses four basic colours that come from the soils — red, yellow, white and black. These colours are sometimes mixed to produce grey, orange or pink. The red and yellow come from iron oxide ochres. White comes from gypsum. Black comes from charcoal or manganese ore. The pigments were traditionally mixed with water and fixed with resins from trees. Today, artists also paint with acrylics.

Bark painting has been practised in parts of Australia for thousands of years:

- In south-eastern Australia, paintings were often done on shelters made with bark. In these areas, figures were either scratched into bark that had been blackened by smoke or drawn in charcoal.

- In the Kimberley region, painting on bark was of the same artistic style as the rock art, including images of the Wandjina. The painting was often quite distinctive, using bold blocks of colour. Artists of the Kimberley now sometimes paint on boards rather than bark.

- In the Arnhem Land region, bark paintings showed the same patterns used on important ceremonial objects. They could represent landscapes and their important features, ancestors or creation spirits. In western Arnhem Land, a distinctive x-ray style was popular. This style showed the internal organs and workings of animals that represented creation spirits. Bark paintings from central and eastern Arnhem Land mirrored the patterns that were used in ceremonial body painting.

- In the Tiwi Islands, a cross-hatching style was popular. Different patterns and designs had different meanings. They most often identified particular clans.

- Bark paintings from Groote Eylandt (an island in the Gulf of Carpentaria) also have a distinctive style. Figures are painted against a black background.

Macassan sailors visited northern parts of Australia. The artwork from those areas reflects these exchanges. Bark paintings show the Macassan boats. There are interesting similarities in style between the art of the Macassans and of the Groote Eylandters.

REMEMBER

From the early 20th century, Indigenous people, particularly in the Arnhem Land region, started using pieces of bark as a canvas. They copied the same designs they used before on the bark shelters. By the 1930s, bark paintings were offered for sale by Indigenous artists.

Today, bark painting is an important industry, particularly for artists from the Kimberley, among the Tiwi and in Arnhem Land.

REMEMBER

Here are a number of internationally renowned artists who paint on bark:

- **Wandjuk Marika** was a senior leader of his clan in the Yolngu community. He was a talented artist and active in protecting and promoting Indigenous art. He was a founding member of the Aboriginal Arts Board and went on to become its chair. He was awarded an OBE in 1979 for his contribution to Aboriginal arts in Australia. He passed away in 1987.

- **John Mawurndjul** is an artist from the Kuninjku nation of western Arnhem Land. He is well known for his bark painting. He uses a style of intricate cross-hatching that is then filled in. This particular style is called *rarrk*. His work has been shown around the world, including at the Hermitage Museum in St Petersburg, Russia. His work is in major collections in Australia. These include Sydney's Museum of Contemporary Art and the National Gallery of Australia in Canberra.

- **Narritjin Maymuru** was a Yolngu artist and a dancer. In the 1960s, he became one of the most prolific Indigenous artists. His highly symbolic work was known around the world. He saw his painting as an important way of keeping the Yolngu culture vibrant and alive. He died in 1982.

- **Lofty Bardayal Nadjamerrek** was taught to paint by his father, who instructed him in rock art. He was from western Arnhem Land. He moved rock art designs to both paper and bark. Some of his work uses traditional cross-hatching. But he also grew his artistic style. A major show of his work was held at the Museum of Contemporary Art, Sydney, in 2011. He passed away in 2009.

Dot, dot, dot . . . art

Central and Western Desert art is known best for its use of dots in paintings. They can be used to express many things, from the night sky to the landscape. (Refer to the earlier section 'Reading between the dots: Knowing what the symbols mean' for more information.)

In the 1970s, Aboriginal artist Johnny Warangkula used dots to create the background for his paintings. The effects were so beautiful that others soon followed. Artists could disguise the symbolism in their painting so that it could be hidden from people who weren't initiated. So dots were used as a way of hiding the true meanings of paintings. Artists from Papunya, then Yuendumu and other Central Desert communities also started to paint in this style.

This growth in Indigenous art led to huge Indigenous economic changes. Indigenous people began to set up their own companies to protect their artwork. One of the first Indigenous communities to set up their own art company was Papunya. This was a settlement about 240 kilometres north-west of Alice Springs created to support the Pintupi and Luritja people.

In 1971, schoolteacher Geoffrey Bardon encouraged some men of the community to paint on a school wall. This sparked an interest in painting across the community. The style of art from the school was inspired by the patterns and symbols used in body painting and sand painting, which was a big part of their ceremonies. But the artists have always been careful to take out the sacred symbols from their public art. The art from this group is in high demand. The group includes artists such as Clifford Possum Tjapaltjarri and Johnny Warangkula Tjuppurulla. (The group was started by men. But women artists in Papunya also became famous in the 1980s.)

REMEMBER

In 1972, the artists formed their own company, the Papunya Tula Artists, to help advance the sale of their work. The idea behind starting the company was to bring attention to the work of the artists. They wanted to make sure that financial benefits flowed to the artists from the sale of their work and they weren't ripped off. The company also ensures that cultural heritage is kept strong through the promotion of creating art. The group company is now owned by the Aboriginal people of the area. It represents about 120 artists.

The arrangement became an inspiration to other communities of artists who then started their own collectives, especially in the Central and Western Deserts. Artists worked more with the production of art as a creative outlet but also as a chance for sale and income. Many Aboriginal communities and outstations have now been formed with a group of actively working artists. These include Utopia and Hermannsburg in the Northern Territory, Ernabella in South Australia and Warmun (Turkey Creek) in Western Australia. Forming these groups is seen as an important cultural practice and a means of economic support for the community. Many of these communities have joined artists' collectives to make sure that they get the proper royalties for their work.

Here are some of the best-known artists of the dot style:

- **Paddy Bedford** was born in the East Kimberly in 1922 and faced the harsh racism of the times. He worked as a stockman for rations. He was laid off when the law changed in 1969 requiring wages to be paid. He was familiar with traditional body painting and began painting on canvas in 1998. He became one of Australia's most respected artists. He was the subject of a show at the Museum of Contemporary Art that opened in 2006. Bedford died in 2007.

- **Emily Kngwarreye** was born in 1910. In the 1990s, she became one of Australia's most successful painters. She was a skilled artist who painted landscapes and other themes inspired by nature on large canvases. She lived in Utopia (an Aboriginal community in the Northern Territory). In 1977 she became a founding member of the Utopia Women's Batik Group. They made their art collectively with no individual artist being singled out. The techniques and skills that Kngwarreye developed while producing batik shaped her work when she moved to painting on canvas. As her work became more popular, she continued to distribute her income across her large extended family. Kngwarreye passed away in 1996.

- **Rover Thomas** was born in 1926 in the Great Sandy Desert in Western Australia. His family moved to the Kimberley when he was a child. As he grew into adulthood, he began working as a stockman. He later moved to Warmun (Turkey Creek). His uncle, Paddy Jaminji, had painted storyboards used for a ceremony — the Krill Krill (see Chapter 13). These boards inspired Thomas to paint and he developed his own unique style. He became active, along with fellow artist Trevor Nickolls, at continuing and evolving the Krill Krill ceremony, which is primarily music and dance. Thomas won art prizes for his pieces. His work was shown in galleries around the world. He had a solo exhibition in 1994 at the National Gallery of Australia. Thomas died in 1998.

✔ **Clifford Possum Tjapaltjarri** was one of Australia's most influential Indigenous artists. He was born in 1933 at Napperby Station, north-west of Alice Springs, on his traditional country, the land of the Anmatyerre people. With no formal education, he grew up in the bush and worked as a stockman. He was already known as a talented woodcarver when he started painting in the 1970s. Then he became one of the most gifted artists of his community of Papunya with his large and complex paintings. He was chair of the Papunya Tula Artists — the community artists' collective — from the late 1970s until the mid-1980s. In 2004, one of his pieces, *Warlugulong*, sold at an auction by Sotheby's for $2.4 million. He had originally sold it for $1,200. He passed away in 2002.

✔ **Johnny Warangkula Tjuppurulla** was born in the mid-1920s, of the Luritja and Pintupi people in the Papunya area. He was raised traditionally, never receiving European education. He became a leading artist in the Papunya movement in the 1980s. He developed a distinctive style where he used several layers of dots in his works — a technique known as *over-dotting*. This created powerful optical illusions. In 1997, his painting *Water Dreaming at Kalpinypa* was sold at Sotheby's for $206,000. He had received just $150 for it when he sold it 25 years earlier.

Indigenous crafts

Skilled Aboriginal and Torres Strait Islander craftspeople have made everyday objects that are also of great works of art. From woven bags to carved spears, great skill was needed to make these artefacts.

Today, the artefacts are collected, not just as cultural curiosities, but because they are beautiful. Aboriginal artists now make objects, such as woven bags and possum coats, specifically to create a work of art. They don't intend for the piece to be put to practical use. Also, objects that once may have had spiritual importance are now made in versions as art pieces for display and sale. These include the morning star poles used in funerals (see the sidebar 'Morning star poles') and the headdresses used in ceremonies in the Torres Strait (see the following section).

Indigenous people have grown their arts and crafts practices into areas such as fabric design and batik, rug making, pottery, jewellery design and making, possum cloak making and papermaking.

TECHNICAL
STUFF

String bags are made by techniques using knots, loops and twists. Basket making also uses many techniques. Some are made with a weaving technique and others with a coil technique. In one method, the youngest branches of leaves of a palm tree are stripped of their prickly edges by hand. Then they are stripped into several fibres then left to dry. They are decorated with ochres or bush dyes or left with their natural colour before being used for weaving.

REMEMBER

Elizabeth Djuttara was a notable weaver from Arnhem Land, born near Ramingining in 1942. She won the Victoria Health National Craft Award for a richly coloured woven floor pandanus mat in 1992.

REMEMBER

The Tjanpi Desert Weavers is a social enterprise of the Ngaanyatjarra Pitjantjatjara Yankunytjatjara (NPY) Women's Council. They represent women of the Central and Western desert. They also produce beginner's kits so you can learn how to weave. See https://tjanpi.com.au/ for more information.

MORNING STAR POLES

Morning star poles were used in burial ceremonies. But today they are also made as beautiful works of art. The poles are painted and decorated with objects such as feathers and shells. They are works of art in themselves. But they are often shown standing in groups like soldiers, as seen in the following figure.

Also known as *larrakitj*, nine of these memorial poles by artist Dhambit Munungurr featured at the National Gallery of Victoria's Triennial in early 2021.

Examining Torres Strait Islander Art

The Torres Strait Islanders were active traders with the people of Cape York Peninsula and other islands off the mainland of New Guinea. Not surprisingly then, their culture and art are influenced by both its Melanesian and Australian neighbours. Torres Strait Islander art, as with its music and dance, pays strong tribute to the sea as well as to the seasons, rain and the distinctive winds.

A lot of the materials used in Torres Strait Islander art also come from the sea. Turtle shells and pearl shells are highly prized and used to beautiful effect. Shells and bones are also used in making ceremonial objects, jewellery and art. Wood, hair and fibre string were also used in making art and other objects.

Torres Strait Islander art was recognised early on for its uniqueness, beauty and craftsmanship. The Spanish explorer after whom the island chain got its European name (Luis de Torres) noted in his journals the beauty of the turtle shell masks worn in ceremonies.

Modern Torres Strait Islander art has stayed true to its traditions. It uses traditional materials. It is inspired by cultural stories, totemic systems and ceremonies. But some artists have experimented with evolving art practices.

REMEMBER

Torres Strait Islander artists produce work about their political situation. (See the later section 'Thinking about Urban Indigenous Art' for more details.) The 1991 legal case that found that Indigenous people have native title over their traditional land in certain circumstances — the Mabo case — was over land in the Torres Strait. Torres Strait Islander artists have taken up the theme of native title and the effects of the Mabo case in their work.

Today, a new generation of Torres Strait Islander artists are continuing the tradition of creating art pieces inspired by traditional dress and ceremony. They are also making art inspired by their view of the world, their spiritual life and totemic systems and their relationship with the sea. But they have also gone into new territory. They use non-traditional materials. Some Torres Strait Islander artists (for example, Alik Tipoti and Brian Robinson) have tried their hand at printmaking.

Some notable Torres Strait Islander artists include:

- **Destiny Deacon** is a photographer and artist. Her photography and video work contrasts European culture against Aboriginal and Torres Strait Islander identity and experience. She introduced the word 'blak' as a term to refer to modern art history and culture. The National Gallery of Victoria featured her work in a large solo show in 2021.

- **Ellen Jose** was an artist who was a painter, printmaker, photographer and sculptor. She explored issues of identity, the impact of colonisation and the strength of her people. She was interested in the way tradition blends with the modern world. Her work is in major galleries around Australia.

- **Dennis Nona** began his career as a traditional woodcarver. Nona then used his skills to create linocuts, etchings and sculptures that show important stories and legends of the Torres Strait. His work is in major galleries around Australia. He's thought of as one of the most important artists of the Torres Strait.

- **George Nona** is a craftsman specialising in headdresses (Dhoeri). Nona uses natural materials such as seeds, feathers, bones and shells to make headdresses that are pieces of art. Nona builds each piece based on advice and knowledge from Elders and from archival records and photographs. Some of his pieces are in the National Museum and the National Gallery of Australia.

- **Ken Thaiday** was born on Darnley Island in the Torres Strait. He began to paint while he went to ceremonies with his father, who was an important dancer in their community. Thaiday also performed as a dancer. He made the masks that were used in the performances. From there, he began to make them as pieces of art. He experimented with different shapes and materials to create sculptures inspired by his heritage. The masks are works of art more like sculpture than headdresses.

REMEMBER

Torres Strait Islanders have made ghost nets, sculptures made from discarded fishing nets and other materials that are polluting the seas. Their sculptures, made from this recycled material, reflect the importance of our relationship to the oceans and the need to keep them pollution free.

Thinking about Urban Indigenous Art

Urban Indigenous art became a strong art movement in the 1960s and 1970s. It included modern forms such as installation pieces and photography as well as painting and sculpture. It reflected the strong politics and the political struggles that Indigenous communities faced at the time. (For more information, refer to Chapter 9.) Modern Indigenous art is largely related to the important social and political issues facing Indigenous people today.

Many urban artists have used a range of mediums, including acrylic, oils and sculpture. Some artists have used strong imagery in their paintings that make comments about racism in Australian society and the legacy of colonisation. Artists such as Destiny Deacon, Brenda L Croft, Judy Watson, Bronwyn Bancroft and Fiona Foley explore issues of modern Indigenous identity. As women artists, they also explore the combination of race and gender politics.

REMEMBER

In 1987, a group of Aboriginal urban artists formed the Boomalli Aboriginal Artists Co-operative. (*Boomalli* means 'to make a mark' or 'to strike' in three prominent New South Wales languages: Bandjalung, Gamilaraay and Wiradjuri.) These artists were Bronwyn Bancroft, Euphemia Bostock, Brenda L Croft, Fiona Foley, Fernanda Martins, Arone Raymond Meeks, Tracey Moffatt, Avril Quaill, Michael Riley and Jeffrey Samuels. The cooperative provided a supportive and creative environment for artists, as well as an exhibition space. Several went on to enjoy international success. Brenda L Croft, who has also become a curator and academic, still practises her art. She uses it to explore Aboriginal family life, especially the connection between mother and child that was once so mocked by the policy of removing Indigenous children. Funding cuts have threatened the gallery. But it continues to survive.

Here are some notable urban artists:

- **Vernon Ah Kee** is known for his bold artistic statements, sometimes using text. He explores modern issues such as deaths in custody and challenging the historical treatment of Aboriginal people. His vibrant, painted surfboards are further proof of his broad range and intellectual and creative strength.

🖊 **Tony Albert** is an artist who uses eclectic mediums to explore issues of identity, racism and Indigenous experience. In 2014 he won both the Basil Sellers Art Prize and the Telstra National Aboriginal and Torres Strait Islander Art Prize. His large sculpture *Yininmadyemi Thou didst let fall* is in Sydney's Hyde Park and is a tribute to the black diggers. It is based on his grandfather's experience in the war.

🖊 **Bronwyn Bancroft** is an accomplished Bundjalung artist and illustrator. She started her career as a fashion designer. She was a founding member of the Boomalli Aboriginal Artists Co-operative. She has been a key driver in making sure the gallery has stayed open during tough financial periods. Bancroft's work uses rich contrasts of colours and detailed symbols that are eye-catching yet also deeply meaningful. A range of themes, from Indigenous identity to modern health issues, has inspired her artworks. She has also illustrated over 20 children's picture books.

🖊 **Richard Bell** won the Telstra Aboriginal Art Prize in 2003. His work is focused on challenging colonial stereotypes. He also challenges the prejudices of the mainstream art world. He set up his own event at the 2019 Venice Biennale. His solo show at the Tate Modern was the first solo exhibition of an Indigenous artist to be held there.

🖊 **Gordon Bennett** was an Aboriginal artist who worked in vibrant styles. He made bold statements about the place of Indigenous people in Australian society. He also focused on the historical treatment of Indigenous peoples. His work has been compared with Jackson Pollock's. It included responses to artists such as Jean-Michel Basquiat (an American multi-media artist).

🖊 **Daniel Boyd** reinterprets colonial narratives in ways that also speak to the ongoing modern legacy. He uses a unique and creative reinterpretation of dot-focused art to create visually stunning video pieces. His *Captain No Beard* shows Cook with a parrot and eye patch.

🖊 **Karla Dickens** is a Wiradjuri artist who works in installations and multimedia. They make powerful statements about her identity, gender and sexuality. She explores the historical impacts of colonisation and breaks down modern experiences and perspectives.

- **Blak Douglas (Adam Hill)** is an accomplished painter whose style is influenced by his background as a graphic designer. He has staged over 25 solo shows. His distinctive work is often used on posters and book covers. He is known for his use of stylised landscapes in which he uses symbols that critique the dominance of white culture in Australia. He is also known for his cheeky installations and plays on words. For example, in one installation he used stolen milk crates to spell out the word 'Stolen'. This is a reference to the Stolen Generations (refer to Chapter 8).

- **Fiona Foley** is a Badtjala artist who uses a variety of mediums in her creative practice. These include photography, painting, sculpture and installation. She makes sharp critiques in her work about identity, dispossession, historical narrative and racism. Her works include self-portraits representing colonial photographs of Indigenous women. They also include installations of clan-style outfits in vibrant African designs.

- **Jonathan Jones** is a Wiradjuri artist who puts traditional cultural practices and knowledge into his art. He often uses language in a soundscape for his installations. His installation in 2016, *barrangal dyara (skin and bones)*, part of the Kaldor Public Art Project, saw him use ceramic shields to recreate the outline of the Garden Palace exhibition building in Sydney. When the building burnt down in 1882, a large number of important Aboriginal artefacts were destroyed.

- **Tracey Moffatt** is an artist who takes photographs of highly stylised and posed panoramas. Her recent work retains its surreal quality. Her 2004 *Adventure* series is a set of images of what appear to be overacted scenes from a soap opera. The scenes are set on a tropical island, populated by doctors, nurses and pilots. In 2017 she represented Australia at the 57th Venice Biennale with her solo exhibition, 'My Horizon'. However, Moffatt has refused to be categorised as a photographer and she does delve deeply into other mediums, such as film (her films are described in Chapter 15).

✓ **Lin Onus** was a Wiradjuri artist whose works included sculptures of animals such as dingoes and bats. In one famous piece, now held by Art Gallery NSW, painted wooden fruit bats hang on a Hills Hoist, like washing on a line. Onus was active in Aboriginal rights issues, particularly on the campaign for a yes vote in the 1967 referendum. He was a founder of the Aboriginal Advancement League in Victoria.

✓ **Gordon Syron** is a Biripi man, born on the mid-north coast of New South Wales in the town of Minimbah. He was an amateur boxer and an electrical tradesman. He was given a life sentence in 1972 for the murder of a white man in a fight over his family's land. He started painting in prison and was released in 1982. Syron is famous for his vibrant landscapes of colourful wildflowers. They are a testament to what his traditional country looked like before it was mined. His other famous work, *Judgement by His Peers*, was painted while he was in prison. It shows a white defendant in a courtroom where the judge and jury are all Aboriginal.

✓ **Judy Watson** has had her work described as contemplative and original. It works to uncover hidden histories. She uses bold colour that is strongly connected to place and history. She works across print making, painting, video and installation. Her sculpture *Fire and Water* is in Reconciliation Place in Canberra.

✓ **Jason Wing** is a talented artist who has a graphic design background. He uses stencilling, a method used in traditional rock art painting. Of Aboriginal–Chinese heritage, he explores issues of dual identity in his work. He often paints on metal and also places his stencil art around urban landscapes. His work looks at the social problems facing Indigenous Australians. One installation had a bed of nails made up of syringes as an evocation of the problems of substance abuse in the community.

REMEMBER

proppaNOW is an important Queensland-based art collective started in 2003. It includes Richard Bell, Gordon Hookey, Jennifer Herd and Vernon Ah Kee.

TIP

Two excellent TV series about Aboriginal and Torres Strait Islander art were *Colour Theory with Richard Bell* (screened on NITV and SBS between 2013 and 2017) and *Art + Soul* (screened on ABC between 2010 and 2014) hosted by Hetti Perkins. While no longer readily available, these are definitely worth checking out if you see past episodes. Another option is the 2019 six-part *This Place Artist Series* by the ABC. This series looks at six Indigenous artists as they share stories about their work, their country, and their communities. Artists featured include Vernon Ah Kee and Ken Thaiday.

Indigenous Art as a Means to an Economic End

Before the 1940s, Indigenous art — rock paintings and the x-ray style bark paintings with their cross-hatching — were seen as cultural artefacts, not art. Museum collections gathered these items. They were thought to be the relics of a 'stone age' people, objects from 'past worlds'.

REMEMBER

Some anthropologists, such as A P Elkin, believed that collecting Indigenous art would create respect and compassion for Indigenous people. Nicholas Thomas notes that Elkin thought 'the prestige the art acquired would bolster indigenous pride in a fairly pater-nalistic way: it would be something that "we" could do for "them"'.

Indigenous people were encouraged on missions, such as those in the Warburton Ranges and at Ernabella, to make wood carvings for sale to the mission shops in the cities. In this way, missions promoted the production of Indigenous art to foster economic self-support and develop a Protestant work ethic. Missionaries traded these pieces as curios for collectors. This saw paintings and sculptures that were made outside of the ritual creation pro-cess. Ironically, these pieces often referred to the religious, cere-monial and cultural events and beliefs that the missionaries were trying to get rid of. Such artworks may have had 'traditional' stories as their base. But they still reflected the current experi-ences and issues in the artists' lives, including their connection to land.

For example, the Aboriginal mission at Hermannsburg has been a major producer of Indigenous art for many years. It is 125 kilometres west of Alice Springs. Founded in 1877 by Lutheran missionaries, Hermannsburg is the traditional land of the Western Arrernte people. The mission gave rise to one of the first distinctive Aboriginal art movements. It was identified by the deep watercolours used to paint outback landscapes of the Western Arrernte's traditional country in a European style. The community has continued with its artistic tradition. But that has changed over the years. Today, the area is best known for its pottery, mostly made by Aboriginal women. Hermannsburg also produced one of Australia's best-known artists: Albert Namatjira.

Albert Namatjira was the first Indigenous painter to have national and international success. He painted rich, colourful landscapes of his home country. He did over 2,000 paintings during his lifetime. His work had a European look. Namatjira was an Arrernte man, born in 1902 at the Hermannsburg Lutheran Mission. He learned to paint in 1936 when he was a guide for Australian painter Rex Batterbee. Fans of his work included Queen Elizabeth II, whom he met in 1954. His fame meant that he was the first Aboriginal person to be exempted from the legislation that made Aboriginal people wards of the state in the Northern Territory. This gave him the right to vote. He became an Elder of his clan and supported many of his extended family. But he lost his money and eventually lived in a camp. He was imprisoned for two months for providing alcohol to Aboriginal people. He was never the same after his time in prison. He died in 1959.

Commissions by collectors and others also created a change in Indigenous art. For example, bark paintings, once found only on the insides of shelters, became a way of cross-cultural communication. This was helped by bark paintings' resemblance of the rectangular works of the European art tradition.

REMEMBER

Indigenous art expert Wally Caruna tells how in Yuendumu in 1984 a group of older women switched from decorating objects such as carrying dishes and digging sticks for sale to painting small canvases. This was to raise money for a vehicle that would allow them better and easier access to their distant ceremonial grounds. His story shows the economic reason that boosted the creation of Aboriginal art.

Indigenous art changed from the 1950s in the following ways:

- **1950s:** Art galleries, such as the Art Gallery of New South Wales, began to collect Indigenous art for their major collections. It was no longer seen as just something for museums.

- **1960s:** Indigenous art was given a lot of mainstream recognition. The recognition of Indigenous art as not simply cultural artefacts meant Europeans rethought these objects as art. Aboriginal people were encouraged to put their fragile artwork into permanent forms, such as on canvas, board and bark (where it was not traditionally done). They were also encouraged to use watercolours and acrylics.

REMEMBER

This mirrored the process of changing the mediums for Aboriginal artists. Some examples are turning sand paintings into acrylic paintings, placing body paint onto canvas and thinking of functional pieces (such as baskets, boomerangs and shields) as sculpture. These new mediums were an extension of the traditional motifs, symbols and representations. They remained fundamentally Indigenous. Indigenous artists were making and selling a whole new genre of art that was specially created to communicate with the outside world.

- **Late 1970s and early 1980s:** Other Australian art galleries followed the early example set by the Art Gallery of New South Wales in the 1950s. (But it did not make a major purchase for 30 years after its initial purchase of Aboriginal art.) It was around this time that the Aboriginal Arts Board was created.

Corporations and public groups also began to buy Indigenous art for the walls of their offices and in their advertising. This was meant to highlight their Australian identity. By the mid-1980s, art galleries were working quickly to develop collections of Indigenous art.

- **1990s:** Aboriginal art had become big business. Collectors and collecting institutions internationally were looking for it. This continues to be true today.

REMEMBER

In 2013, the Musee du Quai Branly in Paris put an enlarged version of an artwork by Indigenous artist Lena Nyadbi on their roof. They wanted it to be seen by millions of people a year from the Eiffel Tower. It was a symbol that Indigenous art was well and truly making its mark on the art world internationally.

As Indigenous artists became more famous, the number of Indigenous curators at major galleries also grew. (This is just as Aboriginal people and Torres Strait Islanders are increasingly represented in Australian professional life.) Here are some of these curators and the galleries they have variously worked in:

- Brenda Croft at the Art Gallery of Western Australia and the National Gallery of Australia

- Djon Mundine at the Art Gallery of New South Wales, the Museum of Contemporary Art, the National Museum of Australia and the Queensland Art Gallery

- Keith Munro at the Museum of Contemporary Art

- Margo Neale at Art Gallery NSW, the Queensland Art Gallery and the National Museum of Australia

- Hetti Perkins at the Art Gallery of New South Wales

- James Wilson Miller at the Powerhouse Museum

REMEMBER

In 2020, Wiradjuri artist Brook Andrew became the first Indigenous person appointed to be Artistic Director of the Biennale of Sydney.

REMEMBER

The first Indigenous artist to win the prestigious Archibald Prize was Vincent Namatjira. He won for his portrait of footballer Adam Goodes in 2020. That same year, actor and writer Meyne Wyatt became the first Indigenous person to win the Archibald's Packing Room Prize with a self-portrait. It was the first painting he'd done in over ten years.

TIP

Most Australian art galleries have an Indigenous collection or gallery. These are usually accompanied by talks programs so you can find out more about the artworks.

CULTURAL PROTOCOLS

The Australia Council has made rules for working with Indigenous artists and their art. These rules are aimed at improving the respect for both. They include respect; Indigenous control; using communication, consultation and consent; ensuring proper attribution and copyright protection; and proper returns and royalties. You can find the protocols on their website (`www.australiacouncil.gov.au/ aboriginal-and-torres-strait-islander-arts`).

TIP

Buying art from community art centres and reputable art fairs are good ways to make sure you are buying real Indigenous art. Doing so also makes sure that the monies from the sale go back to the artist and the community. Many community art centres are now online so you can learn more about the artists and their art.

REMEMBER

A sale of art doesn't automatically pass on the copyright. Artists in Australia can have Viscopy, a non-profit, artist-owned copyright collecting agency, manage their interests. Of the 6,000 members of Viscopy, 4,000 are Indigenous.

PROJECT

Find a piece of Indigenous art that appeals to you and write a short review on what it means and why you like it.

PROJECT

Write a short biography of an Indigenous artist mentioned in this chapter.

PROJECT

Watch a documentary on an Indigenous artist or about Indigenous art, such as **Colour Theory, Art + Soul** *or the* **This Place Artist Series**. *Write some summary points about the artist or type of art featured.*

Singing and Dancing

CHAPTER 13

IN THIS CHAPTER

- ✔ Noting the importance of music and dance
- ✔ Putting a modern twist on Indigenous music
- ✔ Dancing across a cultural divide

Music and dance were a central and powerful part of traditional Indigenous cultural and spiritual life. But they were also a part of everyday life. Traditional music and dance are still practised and performed widely around Australia.

Music had both a spiritual and educational role. It was performed in ceremony. But it was also used to teach younger people about their duties and their clans. Songs were played with simple wood instruments. In some places these instruments included the didgeridoo. This is one of the world's oldest musical instruments.

Today, Indigenous people continue to use music for expression and storytelling. Genres of music such as country and, more recently, hip-hop have attracted Indigenous people. They use their songwriting to describe life experiences.

Modern Indigenous dance has grown steadily over the last few decades. Groups such as the Bangarra Dance Theatre are praised for their creative and artistic expression. They are also known for bringing a spiritual and political message to their audiences.

In this chapter, I look at both traditional and modern Indigenous performing arts, focusing on music and dance.

Traditional Expression through Music and Dance

Music has a central role in traditional Aboriginal societies and cultures. Music is often linked with ceremonies. It is important to ancestry and kinship, the landscape and connection to country, the totemic systems and the animals of the area. Music is also connected with important events such as changes of season, water and rain, healing and triumph over enemies. Aboriginal music is handed down from generation to generation through performance. Songs can sometimes be built upon and changed over time. They could be of sacred importance or for entertainment.

Dance also can tell a story through movement. Stories can be about the land, relationships between people, the journeys and lives of ancestors, and other culturally important information. Ceremonies that focus on dance are often called *corroborees*. Clan groups would gather together for these important cultural and spiritual events.

Indigenous cultures across Australia have created a lot of music and instruments. But most music is rhythmic and accompanied by handclaps, body slaps and instruments. These are usually percussion instruments played by banging the instruments together, or sometimes the didgeridoo.

Music for different times

Traditionally, certain music is meant for specific types of ceremony. But some music is open to anyone. The different ways music is performed is as follows:

- Sacred and secret music is only performed for sacred and secret ceremonies. These sometimes take place in a particular place or for a special purpose. Some songs can be performed and heard only by men. Other songs can be sung and heard only by women.

- Semi-sacred music is performed in full only at an appointed ceremonial ground. It seems to have been sung by men while women danced.

↙ Non-sacred music can be performed by anyone at any time and any place. It's often performed at large gatherings or corroborees. It is often sung by women while men dance.

Banging out a rhythm

Indigenous people made instruments from the materials that were around them, most often wood. Percussion instruments were the most common. They were used to create rhythms to go with singing and a beat for dancing. (The didgeridoo is an exception. It depends on rhythmic breathing to create its sound.) Many of the following instruments are used in modern music and dance. They have also been adopted by non-Indigenous performers:

↙ **Bullroarer:** A simple wooden slat on a piece of cord is spun and whirled to make a low-pitched roar. The sound was sometimes used to call people to ceremonies. But the instrument is more usually used at boys' initiation ceremonies.

↙ **Clapsticks:** Two sticks of wood are banged together to create a rhythmic beat. The paired sticks can vary a lot in shape. Usually one long and slightly flattened stick is grasped in the middle and held flat. The other stick is more rounded, held towards the end and is used to beat the other.

↙ **Didgeridoo:** The most famous instrument used in Indigenous music is the didgeridoo. (It is also called the *yidaki* in eastern Arnhem Land.) It is one of the oldest musical instruments in the world. The instrument is made from a hollow branch of a tree. It is further carved by termites nesting in the wood. These branches are cut to length — about 1.5 metres long — making sure both ends are hollow. The mouthpiece is moulded with beeswax or tree gum. Didgeridoos were only played by men. They were only used in the north of Australia, from Cape York to Arnhem Land and the Kimberley.

The didgeridoo's unique and melodic sound is made by blowing into the instrument with vibrating lips. A technique of *circular breathing* — breathing in through the nose while blowing out through the lips at the same time — achieves a continuous sound. Performers also use techniques for creating harmonic, energetic and rhythmic patterns. During ceremonies, didgeridoos were used to create a constant hum in a deep note with rhythmic patterns. Accents were created by using the tongue and cheeks. Playing the didgeridoo requires skill and strength. The sound is sustained through-out the songs in the ceremony.

↙ **Gum leaves:** A tree leaf (often of the eucalypt) is held against the lips and blown. The technique was usually used to imi-tate bird calls. But in more recent times it has also been used as an instrument to create a tune.

↙ **Rasp:** A notched stick is scraped by a second smaller stick. This is different from clapsticks. The rhythmic sound is cre-ated by scraping rather than hitting the two pieces of wood together.

↙ **Rattle:** Bunches of seed pods are shaken and used to make a rhythmic sound. This technique is found in Cape York.

↙ **Skin drum:** A drum was a rare instrument in Indigenous communities. An hour-glass shaped drum is made from liz-ard or goanna skin. It is used in ceremonies and dance in areas of Cape York.

Traditional songs

In Indigenous culture, songs were a main part of ceremonies. They were an important way of maintaining spiritual life. Songs were about mythical figures, the creation of the landscape, the journeys of ancestors, and other themes related to nature and the supernatural. Songs are made up of many short verses that may tell a story of a place or event. They may have a strong educa-tional value. Songs were a way to teach about Indigenous culture and the environment, and a person's place in them.

Young children learned songs about everyday tasks they had to perform. When they reached puberty, they were taught what are known as *karma songs*. These songs are about the totems of the clan and the history and mythology of the group. Each clan's songs have unique melodic formulas that distinguish them from the songs of other groups. Some songs are performed just as entertainment. But the karma songs are of central importance to the cultural traditions of the group.

CULTURAL PROTOCOLS

When a man marries and takes on more duties for family and clan, the karma songs are a big part of his education. They are believed to be his source of spiritual strength. His maturity can be measured in the knowledge he has picked up through songs and ceremonies.

Cultural dance

Traditional dancing is energetic and usually done for ceremonial purposes. It was closely linked to song. The performances were associated with specific places. Dance grounds were often sacred places. Body decoration and gestures related to kin and other relationships all added to the ceremony and the performance. Different communities have different dances and they tell different stories. The people who are the custodians of a particular story are the only ones allowed to perform those dances. Permission is needed before someone else can perform them. Dances have been passed on for centuries and generations. They remain important to Indigenous people today. Generally, dances, through movement, tell of particular stories or tasks. These include mimicking kangaroos or sharks, hunting with spears, paddling a canoe, or natural phenomena such as waves.

EVOLVING CEREMONY: THE KRILL KRILL

The Krill Krill ceremony is performed in the east Kimberley. It has an interesting beginning. Aboriginal artist Rover Thomas (c. 1926 to 1998) lived in the Warmun community near Turkey Creek from the 1970s. The spirit of a woman he had a spiritual connection with showed him the songs and story that are the basis of the ceremony. It related to significant religious sites around the area. Thomas told the stories over several years. Then they became a ceremony of song and dance.

Thomas's uncle, Paddy Jaminji, painted the storyboards that are used in the ceremony. These inspired Thomas and other

(continued)

(continued)

community members to paint in a form that wasn't like traditional art on canvas. They experimented with landscapes painted on dismantled tea-chests. The number and combination of songs in the ceremony depends on where they are performed and who the audience is. But the order of the movement across the landscape stays the same each time. The ceremony is an example of the continuation of an oral tradition of storytelling in changing and creative ways.

Carrying a Tune: Contemporary Indigenous Music

Songwriting is a form of storytelling. Many Indigenous people use music to continue a strong storytelling tradition from within their culture. Songs written by modern Indigenous songwriters reflect different issues. These include the struggle for land rights and a treaty, Christianity, homelands, animals and Dreaming. Their songs often include traditional language words. But they are also often about love. These themes are common to many songwriters.

Today, Indigenous musicians and performers have adopted many musical styles. They sometimes mix traditional instruments into their modern music. Modern Indigenous music is a mix of many styles of music. Rock and country music are two of the most popular. Younger Indigenous people are also attracted to urban street music such as rap and hip-hop to express their experiences and hopes.

Singers in the mainstream

A number of Indigenous Australians have achieved mainstream recognition in the music industry. Singers such as Jimmy Little, Archie Roach, Kev Carmody, Jessica Mauboy and country music star Troy Cassar-Daley are some of the most successful. Particularly through the 1970s and 1980s, Aboriginal bands such as No Fixed Address, the Warumpi Band and Us Mob mixed their experience with disadvantage and the politics of the era into their music. This music was a blend of different influences from rock, country and reggae. A new generation of Indigenous singers and songwriters have taken up the genres of heavy metal, hip-hop and rap. Of this same generation, some musical talents have risen through song contests such as *Australian Idol*. They have gone on to enjoy success.

The Torres Strait Islands also have a strong music tradition. Songs focus on the relationship with the islands and the sea. Torres Strait Islander musicians such as the Mills Sisters, Henry 'Seaman' Dan and Christine Anu have been popular with big audiences.

The strong storytelling theme in the lyrics of many Indigenous songs provides not just education and entertainment. Some Indigenous people talk about music as a way of healing from the harder parts of their lives. Aboriginal singer–songwriter Archie Roach once said, 'I'm blessed that I have music. Some people don't have any outlet whatever for life's knocks and they're the people my heart goes out to. Music — to me — is a medicine'.

A BIG CAREER: JIMMY LITTLE

Jimmy Little's musical career spanned six decades. A Yorta Yorta man, he grew up on Cummeragunja Reserve on the Murray River. (Refer to Chapter 9 for more about this reserve.) He left there in 1955 at the age of 18 to pursue his music career. His single 'Royal Telephone' reached the top of the Australian music charts in 1963. By then Little had already released 17 previous singles. He continued to release hit music until 1974, with his song 'Baby Blue'. Little then tried acting, teaching and community work. He was NAIDOC Person of the Year in 1989.

In 2004, he released his 34th album, *Life's What You Make It*. This was a collection of modern songs by songwriters such as Elvis Costello and Bruce Springsteen that he uniquely interpreted. In 2004, Little had kidney failure and received a life-saving kidney transplant. This led him to establish the

(continued)

(continued)

Jimmy Little Foundation to help other Indigenous Australians who suffer from kidney disease. Not surprisingly, Little was named a Living National Treasure and awarded the Order of Australia in 2004. Little retired from performing in 2010 and passed away in 2012.

Talent runs in Little's family. His daughter Frances Peters-Little is a singer-songwriter, an historian and a filmmaker. Grandson James Henry is also a singer-songwriter who sometimes performed with Little. And Jimmy's niece is famous Indigenous opera singer, composer and playwright Deborah Cheetham.

Going Country

Many musical genres have influenced Indigenous Australians. But country music has been a natural home for Indigenous musicians. The themes of connection to country, hardship in living off the land, rural poverty, the loneliness of heartbreak and the healing power of love all have meaning for Indigenous storytellers. Indigenous country stars such as Dougie Young, Jimmy Little, Col Hardy, Vic Simms, Gus Williams, Bob Randall, Warren H. Williams and Troy Cassar-Daley aren't just loved because their music is entertaining. Indigenous people also relate to the stories their songs tell. These artists, through their music, educate many people about Indigenous culture and experience.

Clinton Walker's book, *Buried Country: The Story of Aboriginal Country Music*, is based on a documentary of the same name. It provides an account of six decades of Indigenous country music. It explains how, even though songs in this genre seem simple, they express complex emotions and worldviews.

TIP

For a great range of Indigenous artists, check out CAAMA Music. The label has been working with Indigenous artists for over 40 years. It has developed talent from Central Australia and beyond. See https://caamamusic.com.au/ for more information.

THE TALENTED YUNUPINGUS

Yothu Yindi is a band with Indigenous and non-Indigenous members. It was formed in 1986. The founding Indigenous members were Yolngu men from near Yirrkala on the Gove Peninsula in the Northern Territory. Yothu Yindi means 'child and mother' in the Yolngu language. The band combines traditional Indigenous songs with pop and rock songs. It blends guitars and drums with traditional instruments. The group was led by singer and guitarist Mandawuy Yunupingu. He was not only a respected musician, but also the first Indigenous person to become principal of a school. (He left this position to pursue his musical career.) He was Australian of the Year in 1992. Now known as M Yunupingu, he passed away in 2013.

In 1991, Yothu Yindi achieved mainstream musical success with their song 'Treaty' and the album *Tribal Voice.* The group helped start the Yothu Yindi Foundation in 1990 to promote Yolngu cultural development. It produced the annual Garma Festival of traditional cultures. M Yunupingu's older brother, Galarrwuy Yunupingu, is chairman of the Yothu Yindi Foundation. He was named Australian of the Year himself in 1978 and sometimes joined Yothu Yindi, playing the guitar.

Another member of Yothu Yindi was Geoffrey Gurrumul Yunupingu. He was an exceptionally gifted musician. He played guitar, drums, keyboards and didjeridoo. But it was the clarity and strength of his singing voice that was his most famous talent. Born on Elcho Island in 1971, he taught himself how to play the piano and accordion at four. He took up the guitar the following year. Starting out in Yothu Yindi in 1989, he left in 1995 to start Saltwater Band. His first solo album, *Gurrumul*, was released in 2008. It won Best World Music Album at the ARIAs. He released three more albums, *Rrakala* (2011), *The Gospel Album* (2015) and *Djarimirri (Children of the Rainbow)* (2018). He was known after his

(continued)

(continued)

death in 2017 as Dr G Yunupingu. At the time of his passing he was the most commercially successful Aboriginal Australian musician. That Geoffrey was also blind, hadn't learned Braille and didn't use a cane or guide dog made his achievements all the more extraordinary.

Rock and pop

Jimmy Little hit the number-one spot on the Australian music charts with his single 'Royal Telephone' in 1963. He was hailed as the first Indigenous pop star. He paved the way for Indigenous performers. In the 1970s and 1980s, Aboriginal rock bands such as the Warumpi Band, Coloured Stone, No Fixed Address and Us Mob started to hit the mainstream. They attracted audiences through their tough lyrics. They spoke about fighting racism and overcoming disadvantage.

Many singers and songwriters have found country music the genre that attracts them. But performers such as Archie Roach, the late Ruby Hunter, Bobby McLeod, Dan Sultan, Vic Simms and Kev Carmody have played many genres, including rock and pop music. They gave voice to Indigenous experiences and viewpoints through their music and lyrics.

Aboriginal bands such as the Pigram Brothers from Broome and the Donovans from Sydney have appeal across Australia. Many bands mix traditional music with modern rock sounds. These bands include Yothu Yindi from Arnhem Land, Blekbala Mujik from Barunga and Nabarlek from the Manmoyi outstation in western Arnhem Land. Some mix their lyrics, using traditional language and English. Frank Yamma sings in English and Pitjantjatjara. And Saltwater — which included sometimes-solo performer Geoffrey Gurrumul Yunupingu — performed in a mixture of Yolngu Matha and English. David Hudson, an accomplished didgeridoo player, combines the traditional instrument with musical genres from classical to dance music.

Indigenous women have also used music to express themselves. Emma Donovan, Leah Flanagan, Kerrianne Cox, Marlene Cummins, Mo'Ju, Ursula Yovich, Thelma Plum and the late Ruby Hunter have all enjoyed success. Audiences relate to the powerful story-telling in their music. Indigenous all-female bands have enjoyed a popular following. Tiddas (*tidda* is Indigenous slang for 'sister') was a trio of Indigenous women from Victoria — Sally Dastey, Amy Saunders and Lou Bennett. They performed together in the 1990s and were loved for their rich harmonies. The Stiff Gins — Nardi Simpson and Kaleena Briggs, and previously Emma Donovan — hail from New South Wales. Miiesha, winner of the 2020 ARIA for Best Soul/R&B Release, mixes the sounds of R&B, gospel and soul with spoken word poetry.

Indigenous artists once found themselves on the outside of the mainstream music industry due to the colour of their skin. But today they not only have conquered every form of popular music genre but are also running the show. Gadigal Music Label was a record label started by the Gadigal Information Service. It also runs Koori Radio and offers a recording studio for hire. So not only do they help record Indigenous music, but they can also put it on the air. Similarly, CAAMA Music Label is connected with CAAMA Radio. They provide a place to record and spread the music of Aboriginal and Torres Strait Islander people.

REMEMBER

The Black Arm Band was a group of Australian musicians — Indigenous and non-Indigenous. They performed together in the 'spirit and action of reconciliation'. The make-up of the band changed over time. But it was popular at festivals, when touring to remote and regional areas, performing and running community workshops. Indigenous musicians who played with the Black Arm Band include Lou Bennett, Emma Donovan, Kutcha Edwards, Leah Flanagan, Jimmy Little, Amy Saunders, Dan Sultan, Bart Willoughby, Ursula Yovich, Geoffrey Gurrumul Yunupingu, Archie Roach and the late Ruby Hunter. Many non-Indigenous musicians also performed with the band. Special guest artists included Jimmy Barnes and Paul Kelly. The band won Band of the Year in the 2008 Deadlys.

COUNTRY'S GOLDEN BOY: TROY CASSAR-DALEY

Troy Cassar-Daley grew up in Grafton, New South Wales. He is an award-winning country musician. His first single, 'Dream Out Loud', was released in 1994 and reached the top position on the Australian country music charts. He released an album the following year and won the 1995 ARIA Award for Best Country Record. (He won again in 2000, 2006 and 2009.) He won Best Male Vocalist at the 1996 Country Music Awards in Tamworth. (He won again in 1998, 2000, 2003, 2006, 2008, 2010, 2013 and 2016!) Cassar-Daley has won a total of 37 Golden Guitars at the Tamworth Country Music Awards, the APRA Country Song of the Year in 2008 and 2010, and 9 Deadly Awards. His albums include *Beyond the Dancing, True Believer, Big River, Long Way Home, Almost Home* and *I Love This Place.* In 2016, Troy released an autobiography and accompanying album, *Things I Carry Around.* In 2020, he signed a new record deal with Sony Music and released the album *The World Today*, which debuted at number 3 on the Australian charts.

Just a few of the best

Many Indigenous bands have a strong following in the Indigenous community and on the country music, folk music and world music circuits. But some recent chart toppers have risen. These include Casey Donovan (see the sidebar 'All in the family: The Donovans') as well as the following:

⌐ **Jessica Mauboy:** Hailing from Darwin, Mauboy was the runner-up on *Australian Idol* contest in 2006. But she has gone on to be the highest-selling female contestant from the show. Her music career since then has gone from strength to strength. She released her debut live album, *The Journey*, in 2007. It reached number four on the charts. To date she has released six top-10 albums and nine top-10 singles. Mauboy made her acting debut in the movie *Bran Nue Dae* in 2010. (See Chapter 15 for more on this film.) She went on to star in *The Secret Daughter* in 2015. She competed for Australia in

Eurovision in 2018. In 2019 she released her fourth studio album, *Hilda*. It debuted at number one.

- **Dan Sultan:** Sultan's music has been described as 'an electrifying romp through rockabilly, blues, country, soul and rock 'n' roll'. His 2009 album *Get Out While You Can* was one of the highest independent country music releases in Australia. He won two Deadly Awards in 2010 and ARIA Awards for Best Independent Artist, Best Blues and Roots Album and Male Artist of the Year. His 2014 album, *Blackbird*, won the ARIA award for Best Rock Album of the year. Dan appeared alongside Jessica Mauboy in the 2010 film *Bran Nue Dae* as Lester. His album *Killer*, released in 2017, was nominated for three ARIA awards. Sultan grew up in Williamstown, Melbourne. He is descended from the Arrernte and Gurindji people. Sultan started playing guitar when he was four years old. He wrote his first song at the age of ten.

- **Archie Roach and Ruby Hunter:** Partners in life and in music, Roach and Hunter were a major duo. Archie Roach was born near Shepparton, in central Victoria, in 1956. But he was taken from his family at the age of about four. He walked out of his foster home at the age of 15. He spent many years on the streets and searching for his family. He recorded his first album, *Charcoal Lane*, in 1990 to great acclaim. Roach writes songs about some of the difficult issues that face Indigenous people. He is a strong voice against excessive drinking and domestic violence. His song 'Took the Children Away' is about the moment he was taken away from his family. It has become an anthem for members of the Stolen Generations. Archie released his biography, *Tell Me Why: The Story of My Life and Music*, in 2019.

Ruby Hunter met Roach when she was just 16 and they were both homeless. Ruby was a Ngarrindjeri woman and a respected singer and songwriter in her own right. Her albums included *Thoughts Within* released in 1995 and *Feeling Good* in 2000. She won Deadly Awards for Female Artist of the Year in 2000 and Outstanding Contribution to Aboriginal and Torres Strait Islander Music in 2003. She was deeply mourned when she passed away in 2010.

ALL IN THE FAMILY: THE DONOVANS

The Donovans is an Indigenous country band made up mostly of brothers Michael, Ashley and Merv, with Troy Russell on drums. The family also includes Casey Donovan, daughter of Merv Donovan. In 2004 at the age of 16, Casey became the youngest winner of the second *Australian Idol* competition. She has since released solo albums and singles, and starred in theatre, musicals and TV.

Singer-songwriter Emma Donovan is also a member of this famous musical family. She sang with the Donovans at the age of seven. In 2000, she started Indigenous all-female band The Stiff Gins. She left them in 2003 to have a solo career. Since 2013, Donovan has been performing as Emma Donovan & The PutBacks. They released an album in November 2014 and another in November 2020.

Hip-hop, rap and metal: Young people have their say

Hip-hop and rap are musical forms that spring from African-American performers from the United States. Their punchy, raw expression has attracted a fan base among younger Indigenous Australians. They relate to messages about disempowerment and reassertion of identity as a form of resistance. Young Indigenous performers are using these musical genres to give their views on the issues facing Indigenous young people, particularly in urban areas. They often focus on identity, urban poverty, and empowerment and disempowerment as themes. Groups working with young people often include hip-hop and rapping as a way to grow confidence and self-esteem.

Wire MC is a well-known hip-hop and rap pioneer from the Gumbaynggirr nation in north-eastern New South Wales. He has said that the MC stands for 'my cousin'. He sees his music as a way of communicating: 'Hip-hop is the voice of the community, of the area. It helps you represent where you're from. It teaches you self-knowledge and self-awareness'. He sees this new form of musical expression as an extension of an older tradition:

'Hip-hop is the new clapsticks, hip-hop is the new corroboree'. His son, Tasmin Keith, has followed in his father's footsteps, and they sometimes perform together.

Another important first wave hip-hop and rap group was The Last Kinection. It formed in 2006 in Newcastle, north of Sydney. Its members were Jacob Turier (who also performs as DJ Jaytee) and siblings Joel Wenitong (who used to be in another hip-hop and rap band, Local Knowledge) and Naomi Wenitong (who enjoyed some chart success as part of a female rock duo performing as Shakaya). The trio said they were inspired to form the band after the death of four of their Elders (hence the word 'kin' in their name). They used their music to express their pride.

Other well-known Indigenous hip-hop and rap performers include Mau Power, South West Syndicate, Urthboy, Baker Boy, Nooky, Jimblah, Ebony Williams, Morganics, Brothablack, Munkimuk (also known as Munki Mark) and Birdz.

TIP

To find out more about the strong voices in Indigenous hip-hop, check out an anthology edited by Ellen van Neerven. It's called *Homeland Calling: Words from a new generation of Aboriginal and Torres Strait Islander voices* (2020).

ALWAYS BLACK: A B ORIGINAL

A B Original is a hip-hop duo that brings together Briggs (Adam Briggs) and Trials (Daniel Rankine). Standing for Always Black Original, their music is feisty, political and passionate. Their single, *January 26*, featured Dan Sultan. It gave an honest view about having the day that the first colony was started as a national holiday. A multi-award winning album, *Reclaim Australia*, was released in 2016. They were awarded Songwriter of the Year at the 2018 APRA Music Awards.

Briggs, who also refers to himself as Senator Briggs, is well known as a solo rapper, actor and television writer. He is known also for his witty and insightful critiques of the issues facing Indigenous people in Australia. He has released three studio albums: *Blacklist* (2010), *Sheplife* (2014) and *Briggs for PM* (scheduled for 2021).

Heavy metal is another form of expression through music. NoKTuRNL is a metal band led by Craig Tilmouth and Damian Young from Alice Springs. Their music has appeared in the movies *Radiance* and *Yolngu Boy.* Their album *Time Flies* was released in 2003.

FROM THE TORRES STRAIT

Music in the Torres Strait was a central part of spiritual and cultural life. Songs were a part of ceremonies and a key way of passing down cultural stories. But many songs are unique to the Torres Strait. Many relate to the relationship to the sea and its main place as a source of food and life. Today, over two-thirds of Torres Strait Islanders live on the Australian mainland. Music is an important way for them to maintain their connection to country. Torres Strait Islanders also use modern song for storytelling and entertainment. Well-known Torres Strait Islander performers include

- Christine Anu, whose song 'My Island Home' has become an unofficial anthem for the Torres Strait Islands. 'Sunshine on a Rainy Day' was also a chart success. Her first album, *Styling Up*, went platinum. Anu also appeared in the movie *Moulin Rouge!*
- Henry 'Seaman' Dan, whose songs are a fusion of traditional Torres Strait Islander and pearling songs blended with jazz, hula and blues. Born in 1929, he continues to be a much-loved performer. His song, 'TI Blues' is a sentimental favourite in the Torres Strait.
- The Mills Sisters — Rita (guitar), Cessa (ukulele) and Ina (tambourine) — started singing in the 1950s. In the 1980s they started to tour outside the Torres Strait.
- Mau Power is a hip-hop artist from Thursday Island. During a period in prison in 2001, he decided to focus on music. In 2019 he released his third studio album, *Blue Lotus Awakening*.

Jumping into Modern Indigenous Dance

Many Indigenous dance groups in Australia perform to keep culture alive. They pass on dances and the stories they represent to younger generations. They teach non-Indigenous people about the diversity of Indigenous Australia. Dance is an important way in which non-Indigenous people can learn about and experience Indigenous culture. In recent years, the focus on modern dance by Indigenous performers and choreographers has grown. In particular, this focus has seen the creation of a dance academy, the National Aboriginal and Islander Skills Development Association (NAISDA). And national dance company the Bangarra Dance Theatre is known around the world.

Indigenous dance companies

Indigenous dance is popular around Australia. Indigenous dance companies give audiences an Indigenous cultural experience.

TIP

BlakDance is the peak body for Indigenous dance in Australia. It supports independent artists and small and growing companies. It embraces a philosophy of self-determination. (Go to www.blakdance.org.au to find out more.)

Some of the better known Indigenous dance companies are

- **Karul Projects** was started by Thomas Kelly and Taree Sansbury in 2017 in Queensland. *Karul* is a Yugambeh word that means 'everything'. The company uses dance and choreography to tell Indigenous stories and knowledge, and explore Indigenous people's relevance and responsibility in modern Australia. Their performance [MIS]CONCEIVE won the Best Dance Award at the 2020 Adelaide Fringe Festival.

- **NT Dance Company**, created by Larrakia man, choreographer and dancer Gary Lang, has professional dancers with Aboriginal, Filipino, Torres Straits Islander, African and Anglo heritage. The company uses dance performance to reflect the diverse cultures of Darwin. It also offers workshops, dance classes and school programs.

» **Nunukul Yuggera Aboriginal Dancers** from south-east Queensland perform dances from the Nunukul (also spelled Noonuccal), Yuggera (also Jagera), Yugimbir and Nugi clans. The company also has a strong focus on education. It aims to improve the understanding of its audiences about the culture of the area. It also wants to educate younger generations of Indigenous people about their cultural heritage.

» **Wagana Aboriginal Dancers** are inspired by the Blue Mountains and Central NSW West country. *Wagana* means 'dancing now' in Wiradjuri language, and the company honours the Darug, Gundungurra and Wiradjuri peoples of the lands they dance and create in.

REMEMBER

Indigenous dance companies are dedicated to continuing cultural traditions and educating the community about Indigenous culture. They provide job opportunities for Indigenous people as dancers, musicians, set and costume designers, and arts administrators. They also develop good role models for younger Indigenous people.

A NATIONAL DANCE ACADEMY

The National Aboriginal and Islander Skills Development Association (NAISDA) was started in 1975 to train Indigenous dancers. One of the driving forces was African-American dancer Carole Johnson. NAISDA grew the first Indigenous dance company — the Aboriginal Islander Dance Theatre (AIDT). AIDT broke up in 1998 when artistic director Raymond Blanco left the company. NAISDA is now based in Gosford in New South Wales. It produces graduates in all aspects of dance practice and performance, including arts management, music and film.

The Bangarra Dance Theatre

The Bangarra Dance Theatre (www.bangarra.com.au) is one of Australia's leading performing arts organisations. (The word *Bangarra* is from the Wiradjuri language and means 'to make fire'.) It was started in 1989 under the guidance of Carole Johnson. Stephen Page became its artistic director in 1991. They have been performing creative and commercially successful programs nationally and internationally ever since. The group performs to over 50,000 people each year.

Bangarra's works combine traditional Aboriginal and Torres Strait Islander history and culture with modern dance styles. The company works with traditional dancers around Australia. It makes sure cultural rules are followed when learning works from traditional dance. It also ensures the dancers return to country to show the finished production to the local community that helped foster it.

Stories are diverse and come from all over the country, including the Torres Strait Islands. *Bush* (2004) traced the journey of an older woman's spirit as she travels across her country. *Mathinna* (2008) is the story of an Aboriginal girl adopted into a white family. She then finds herself caught between two cultures. 'ID', part of the 2011 *Belong* performance, was an exploration of the issues surrounding modern Indigenous identity. *Patyegarang* (2014) and *Bennelong* (2017) explored the lives of two important Aboriginal figures in the first years of the Sydney colony. *Dark Emu* (2019) explored the richness of Aboriginal and Torres Strait Islander knowledges.

REMEMBER

Some of Indigenous Australia's finest dancers have worked with the company. They include the late Russell Page, Elma Kris, Yolande Brown, Jasmin Sheppard, Patrick Thaiday, Beau Dean Riley, Waangenga Blanco and Sidney Saltner. Senior Indigenous dancers from around Australia, including Kathy Marika and Djakapurra Munyarryun, mentor and work with dancers in the company. Alongside Stephen Page, Bangarra has seen the rise of Indigenous choreographers Frances Rings, Daniel Riley and Elma Kris. Also, the company has fostered talent in other parts of dance production. This talent includes musical director David Page and set designer Jacob Nash.

Bangarra works with other Australian performing arts companies such as the Australian Ballet and Sydney Theatre Company. They showcase Australian dance talent and perform at important international events. These events include the opening and closing ceremonies at the 2000 Sydney Olympic Games and the 2018 Commonwealth Games. Bangarra dancer Lillian Banks also was in the 2020 ABC documentary *FREEMAN*, which was co-directed by Stephen Page.

THE PAGE BOYS

Stephen, David and Russell Page were born into a family of 12 children. They were born in Brisbane and are descended from the Nunukul (also spelled Noonuccal) people. The three brothers became key artistic forces within the Bangarra Dance Theatre. They have worked more broadly in the Australian performing arts.

Stephen Page has been artistic director of the Bangarra Dance Theatre since 1991. He graduated from NAISDA in 1983. Stephen then danced for the Sydney Dance Company and in 1991 worked in choreography for the Sydney Dance Company, Sydney Theatre Company and the Australian Opera. He has been a driving cultural force within Bangarra. But he also continues to work with other performing arts companies such as the Sydney Theatre Company and the Australian Ballet. He won a Helpmann Award in 2016. He was named New South Wales Australian of the Year in 2008. He was presented the NAIDOC Lifetime Achievement Award in 2016. His son, Hunter Page-Lochard, has danced with Bangarra and has a successful career as an actor.

David Page wrote the musical scores for Bangarra's major works. He created the soundscapes that helped make the Bangarra Dance Theatre a unique cultural experience. He studied at the Centre for Aboriginal Studies in Music at Adelaide University before joining his brothers in Sydney in 1989. David's music has been used in important ceremonial events such as the opening ceremony for the 2000 Sydney Olympic Games. David contributed music to television and worked with Indigenous filmmakers. He also received an award for his performance in the play *Page 8*. This was a coming-of-age story about his own life, told through spoken word, dance, home movies and music. He continued to perform to critical acclaim onstage. He was an Artist in Residence at the Bangarra Dance Theatre. His body of work made him one of the busiest composers in Australia until his death in 2016.

Russell Page was the lead male dancer for the Bangarra Dance Theatre from 1991 until his death in 2002 at age 34. Russell was also a talented rugby league player. He became famous as a dancer due to his charismatic stage presence. He performed at the opening ceremony of the Sydney Olympic Games in 2000. He also had roles in film and television productions.

Torres Strait Islander dance

Torres Strait Islanders have a distinctive dance tradition. Their ceremonies include dances that reflect central aspects of Torres Strait Islander life. Costumes are also an important part of the cultural practice of dances of the Torres Strait. They often honour the people's relationship with the sea. Sometimes they include fishing tools or headdresses with shark motifs. The feather headdresses of the Saibai Islanders are also dramatic and unique. They add to the festive feeling of the dance. Two-thirds of Torres Strait Islanders now live on the mainland. So the tradition of dance is taught in some mainland schools with larger Torres Strait Islander student populations. These schools include Djarragun College in Gordonvale, near Cairns in Far North Queensland.

**CULTURAL
PROTOCOLS**

The different islands have their own dances. Mer, also known as Murray Island, in the eastern Torres Strait, has a unique shark dance known as the 'Baizam'. It has a distinct style of dance known as Kab Kar and costumes particular to their island, including the dhari headdress. This headdress is shown on the Torres Strait Islander flag (refer to Chapter 2).

The closeness of the Saibai Islands to Papua New Guinea has affected cultural practices there. This is seen in the use of long drums that are sometimes covered with sharkskin. These islands have distinctive dances. They include the 'Maumatang', a warrior dance performed with bows and arrows, and the 'Eagle Dance', where dancers use wooden wings and large headdresses and perform with rapid head movements.

SHOWCASING INDIGENOUS MUSIC AND DANCE

Indigenous music and dance is often showcased in festivals — sort of modern-day corroborees. Many festivals in Australia include a strong program of Indigenous performers. For example, WOMADelaide is a festival dedicated to a 'World of Music, Art and Dance'. Several festivals focus on Indigenous culture. Key festivals include

- The Cairns Indigenous Art Fair, which celebrates art, dance, music and theatre
- The Barunga Cultural and Sports Festival, held near Katherine each year in June
- The Garma Festival, held in north-east Arnhem Land in the Northern Territory, is one of the most famous Indigenous festivals. It's held at Gulkula, a beautiful stringybark forest with views to the ocean. It's a site of importance to the Yolngu. It's said that an ancestor, Ganbulabula, created the didgeridoo (yidaki) here. The festival celebrates Yolngu culture, including music and dance. It lets visitors experience all this on Yolngu country.

- The Laura Quinkan Aboriginal Dance Festival, held on Cape York Peninsula every second year to celebrate language, song, dance and stories
- Yabun, held on Australia Day — or Invasion Day or Survival Day — in Sydney, a family-focused day. It showcases Indigenous music, dance, history, politics and culture.
- The Coming of the Light Festival in the Torres Strait, marking the date of 1 July, the anniversary of the arrival of the London Missionary Society, bringing Christianity with them. Cultural ceremonies are on the islands and the mainland.

PROJECT

Write a short biography of an Indigenous singer mentioned in this chapter.

PROJECT

Watch a performance of the Bangarra Dance Theatre. (Many clips of their performances are available online via YouTube.) Write a short review highlighting what you saw in the movements and the story they tell.

Indigenous Literature: We've Always Been Storytellers

The past three decades have seen a new golden age in Aboriginal writing. Until colonisation, Indigenous languages were oral. Then, from the late 1800s, anthropologists and others began to record some of them as written languages. Sometimes they got the subtleties a little wrong, though. Indigenous people are no longer pleased to let others write down their languages or their stories for them. They are also no longer content to let others write about them.

Indigenous people are now using the written word to record their own lives, history and cultures. The written word may be in English, original languages and sometimes hybrids known as Aboriginal English, Kriol and Torres Strait Creole. They have also moved into writing in many genres. These include crime writing, women's fiction, memoir and academic papers. Some deeper thinking has happened about the rules that non-Indigenous people should use when writing about Indigenous peoples and their cultures. And, of course, much work is being done to improve literacy levels among the Indigenous community. This is particularly true among children.

In this chapter, I examine this move from oral to written languages. I cover some of the ways Indigenous people were written about in the past. I talk about some of the most notable Indigenous writers and poets, and their works. I also give a useful summary of the rules to protect Indigenous cultural content.

Moving from Oral to Written Traditions

Indigenous peoples have an oral tradition. The fact that storytelling is a big part of life isn't surprising. Cultural stories were told not for fun but to teach. These stories are often called *Dreamtime* or *Dreaming* stories. The stories had messages about morals, values, laws and duties. They explained how the world was made and how different natural features were formed. They also explained why animals had certain traits and where the boundaries of traditional lands were drawn. (Refer to Chapter 4 for more details.)

Many notes have been made about the conflict between traditional oral cultures and the written traditions of European cultures. Courts of law, for example, sometimes struggle. They don't know what weight to give oral history from Aboriginal witnesses against the written accounts of anthropologists and historians.

But the use of the written word as a new way of communicating about Indigenous experiences and cultures has been positive. Aboriginal peoples and Torres Strait Islanders have also used other ways of storytelling such as filmmaking (see the next chapter).

Many people feel this shift is positive. It allows Indigenous cultural stories and practices to be kept safely in archives. This became an important priority for Indigenous communities. The oral cultural tradition of older people handing down stories to younger people was disturbed by colonisation. It was particularly disrupted by the policy of removing Indigenous children from their families. Because of this history, Indigenous peoples have placed a great weight on the preservation of their cultures. Writing is a valuable way to make sure important cultural information isn't lost.

MYTH
BUSTER

While having an oral tradition, Aboriginal peoples and Torres Strait Islanders have embraced writing. They see it as a way of continuing the tradition of storytelling.

CULTURAL
PROTOCOLS

In traditional Indigenous cultures, the telling of a Dreamtime or cultural story carried with it cultural rules. Some stories had information that could only be told to people initiated into the clan. Others related to 'men's business' and 'women's business'. They couldn't be told to people of the opposite sex. For this reason, the telling of Dreamtime or cultural stories is still a sensitive area. It's important to get permission from the people who are the custodians of those stories before telling them to someone else.

Writing about the 'Aborigine' in Australian Literature

Many people have been interested in Indigenous peoples and their cultures. Both have been the subject of novels by non-Indigenous people.

Sometimes non-Indigenous authors had negative views about Indigenous peoples and their cultures. But on other occasions authors had good intentions. They wanted to make people aware about what Australia's Indigenous peoples have gone through.

Ever since Indigenous characters first appeared in novels written by non-Indigenous people, Indigenous people have had strong reactions to how they're shown. They felt that authors stereotyped Indigenous people and didn't correctly represent Indigenous cultures. This added to the desire of Indigenous people to write their stories themselves.

White people writing about black people

Indigenous people featured heavily in the notes of colonists in diaries and other non-fiction forms of writing. Exploring Indigenous characters in literature was something writers began to do more in the early 20th century.

Exploring the lives of Indigenous characters as part of a storyline was often sparked by sympathy from those writers. They felt sorrow about the way Indigenous people were forced to the margins in Australian society. They were sad about the poor conditions that many Indigenous people lived in. These authors hoped that their work would reach people and help them to deepen their understanding about the issues facing Indigenous people.

REMEMBER

Despite the good goals of the authors, Indigenous people have been critical of the way they've been shown in literature written by white Australians. They often believe that Indigenous characters are shown in shallow or racist ways.

Here's a list of some noteworthy authors and their books that feature Indigenous characters:

✏ **Arthur Upfield (1890–1964):** The Bony detective series by Arthur Upfield is made up of 29 books. They feature a 'half-caste' Aboriginal detective, Napoleon Bonaparte, known as 'Bony'. Bony was an orphan who was later initiated into his mother's tribe. He learned more about his heritage. He lived between the cultures of both black and white people. He used his skills to help the police solve hard cases.

In 1971, the books were made into a television series called *Boney*. There was a second series the next year. The producers of the TV show angered Aboriginal people. They used a New Zealander, James Laurenson, instead of an Aboriginal actor, to play the lead character. Laurenson was not aware of the controversy when he took on the role.

✏ **Katherine Susannah Pritchard (1883–1969):** Pritchard was a well-known journalist, feminist and founding member of the Communist Party of Australia. Pritchard wrote her novel *Coonardoo* in 1929 after visiting a cattle station in Western Australia. The novel is about the relationship between Hughie, the son and eventual owner of the property, and Coonardoo, an Aboriginal woman living on the property. The book comments on the way white cattle station owners treated Aboriginal women. It wanted to make a case that people had a duty to look after Aboriginal people in a kind way.

- **Xavier Herbert (1901–1984):** Herbert's first book, *Capricornia*, was published in 1938. It was based on his experiences as a Protector of Aborigines in Darwin. It takes place in a fictional place called Capricornia. The book follows the fortunes of a series of characters but comments on the attitudes and treatment of Aboriginal people by government bureaucrats. (In this book, the bureaucrats are unskilled, careless, uncaring and often cruel.)

  Herbert's later book *Poor Fellow, My Country* won the Miles Franklin award in 1975. (It's also often credited as the longest Australian novel. It's more than 1,436 pages!) This book, like *Capricornia*, deals with the treatment of Aboriginal people. It also deals with the relationships between black and white Australians. Herbert has been called 'a visionary defender of Aboriginal rights who enjoyed talking like a racist'.

- **Thomas Keneally (1935–):** Keneally is one of Australia's greatest writers. His novel *The Chant of Jimmie Blacksmith* was published in 1972. It tells the story of the title character, a 'half-caste' Aboriginal man who tries to fit in to white society. He becomes educated and marries a white woman. Jimmie constantly faces racism. In the end, he is trapped between two worlds. He snaps and goes on a killing spree. *The Chant of Jimmy Blacksmith* was short-listed for a Booker Prize. It was also made into a film in 1978 by Fred Schepisi. It stars Aboriginal actor Tommy Lewis as Jimmie Blacksmith.

  Keneally said in 2000 that he would take a different approach if he were writing the same book now. He said he wouldn't presume to write through the eyes of an Aboriginal person. Instead he'd tell it through the eyes of the white characters. This is because he thought it was tough, on reflection, to tell the story through the eyes of an Aboriginal person.

FINDING *THE SECRET RIVER*: KATE GRENVILLE

Australian author Kate Grenville's book *The Secret River* (2005) tells the story of William Thornhill. He arrives in the Australian colony as a convict and takes over land for farming. He does so despite the clear signs of Aboriginal occupation. He goes on to become a wealthy farmer and landowner. The story is inspired by Grenville's family history. It is told from Thornhill's point of view. But, due to Grenville's power as a writer, the book also gives proof of the deep connection the Aboriginal people have to their country and of the violence against them. Grenville can show this without creating an Aboriginal character to explain it.

The book was turned into a play by Andrew Bovell in 2013. It was also a television miniseries in 2015. In those, Aboriginal characters were introduced. They were developed by Indigenous creatives — writers, advisors and traditional owners — to include that point of view.

The sequel, *Sarah Thornhill* (2011), continues the family story from the viewpoint of William Thornhill's daughter. Grenville also explored the experiences of William Dawes in her 2008 book, *The Lieutenant*. He was an engineer in the early days of the colony and was also an astronomer. It includes the relationship Dawes had with the Aboriginal people living near the colony. Grenville goes back to the character of Dawes and the relationship the early colonists had with Aboriginal people in her book *A Room Made of Leaves* (2020). It is an historical novel based on the life of Elizabeth Macarthur, wife of pastoralist John Macarthur.

In *Searching for the Secret River* (2006), Grenville writes about researching her family history for the novel.

Black people writing about black people

The first Indigenous people to write their own stories were trail-blazers. They showed Indigenous people that writing from an Indigenous point of view was possible. They also showed that they could take back control of the image of Indigenous peoples and the portrayal of their cultures. They gave the wider community a chance to see a view of the world from an Indigenous perspective. Here are a few of those first Indigenous writers:

- **David Unaipon (1872–1967):** Unaipon was a Ngarrindjeri man, a preacher and an inventor. He is also credited as the first Aboriginal person to publish a book. He wrote Aboriginal cultural legends and published booklets under his own name: *Hungarrda* in 1927, *Kinie Ger: The Native Cat* in 1928 and *Native Legends* in 1929. Unaipon published poetry in the 1930s. Then he wrote more books about Indigenous legends in the 1950s and 1960s. Unaipon's collected legends were also published in 1930 by William Ramsay Smith as *Myths and Legends of the Australian Aborigines.* No note was included that it was Unaipon's work. Unaipon appears on the Australian $50 note.

- **Jack Davis (1917–2000):** Jack Davis wrote about Aboriginal life, working and living on the land, the bush and Australian society. His autobiographical works have won critical acclaim. They are *Jack Davis: A Life Story* (1988) and *A Boy's Life* (1991). He also wrote for the stage and wrote poetry.

- **Oodgeroo Noonuccal (1920–1993):** Oodgeroo Noonuccal was descended from the Noonuccal people of Stradbroke Island, Queensland. She published her first book of poetry in 1964. It was titled *We Are Going.* She was a trailblazer for Indigenous writing. She also played an active life in Aboriginal cultural and political matters. She was also known as Kath Walker.

- **Philip McLaren (1943–):** Phillip McLaren won the David Unaipon Award in 1992 for *Sweet Water: Stolen Land.* It was published the following year. He has written four more books, including *Scream Black Murder.* This book is a crime novel with an Aboriginal detective as the main character. It is set in the Aboriginal community of Redfern in Sydney.

- **Sam Watson (1952–2019):** Sam Watson wrote *The Kadaitcha Sung*, which was published in 1990. He also wrote for the stage and screen. Watson was active in political campaigns to protect the rights of Aboriginal peoples and Torres Strait Islanders.

  Watson's son, Samuel Wagan Watson, is an award-winning poet. His daughter, Nicole Watson, recently won the David Unaipon Award. (See the nearby sidebar 'David Unaipon Award winners'.)

- **Kerry Reed-Gilbert (1956–2019):** Kerry Reed-Gilbert was a poet. She was also an advocate for Aboriginal rights and culture, and an educator. She published several books of poetry. They included *Black Woman Black Life* in 1996 and *Talkin' About Country* in 2002. She also edited several collections of Indigenous writing and voices: *Message Stick: Contemporary Aboriginal Writing* (1997) and *The Strength of Us: Black Women Speak* (2000).

DAVID UNAIPON AWARD WINNERS

One of the most prestigious awards for Indigenous writing is the David Unaipon Award. This award is part of the Queensland Premier's Literary Awards. David Unaipon was the first Indigenous author to be published. It is fitting that the award in his name is for unpublished authors. The Unaipon Award began in 1989. The first winner was Graeme Dixon for *Holocaust Island*. Part of the prize is publication by the University of Queensland Press. The award has introduced many Indigenous authors to the Australian public. Here are the winners since 1999:

- 1999: *Of Muse, Meandering and Midnight* by Samuel Wagan Watson
- 2000: *Bitin' Back* by Vivienne Cleven
- 2001: *The Mish* by Robert Lowe

- 2002: *Home* by Larissa Behrendt (that's me!)
- 2003: *Whispers of This Wik Woman* by Fiona Doyle
- 2004: *Swallow the Air* by Tara June Winch
- 2005: *Anonymous Premonition* by Yvette Holt
- 2006: *Me, Antman and Fleabag* by Gayle Kennedy
- 2007: *Skin Painting* by Elizabeth Eileen Hodgson
- 2008: *Every Secret Thing* by Marie Munkara
- 2009: *The Boundary* by Nicole Watson
- 2010: *Purple Threads* by Jeanine Leane
- 2011: *'Mazing Grace* by Dylan Coleman
- 2012: *Story* by Siv Parker
- 2013: *Heat and Light* by Ellen van Neerven
- 2014: *It's not just Black and White* by Lesley Williams and Tammy Williams
- 2015: *The First Octoroon or Report of an Experimental Child* by Andrew Booth
- 2016: *Dancing Home* by Paul Collis
- 2017: *Mirrored Places* by Lisa Fuller (published as *Ghost Bird*)
- 2018: *Making of Ruby Champion* by Kirstie Parker (yet to be published)
- 2019: No award given
- 2020: *The Space Between the Paperbark* by Jazz Money (published as *How to Make a Basket*)

Establishing Indigenous Literature

Literature by Aboriginal people and Torres Strait Islanders is enjoying a golden age. A rich range of fiction, life stories and non-fiction are being written by Indigenous authors. Poetry has also been a popular form of writing explored by Indigenous people.

Not surprisingly, as Indigenous writing has grown, Aboriginal and Torres Strait Islander authors are writing in many different genres. These include crime novels and commercial women's fiction.

Indigenous writing has been a great way to draw attention to the issues of Indigenous Australia. Books such as *My Place* by Sally Morgan and *Follow the Rabbit-Proof Fence* by Doris Garimara Pilkington enjoy commercial success. The latter was also adapted for a movie. Indigenous writing often is on the reading lists of schools and universities.

REMEMBER

Indigenous content in books can help to engage Indigenous kids in reading.

Breaking through with Indigenous novels

Some books by Indigenous authors have broken new ground. They enjoy commercial or literary success like never before. Or they're in a genre that Indigenous writing hadn't gone into before.

Some important novels by Indigenous authors include these:

- **Doris Garimara Pilkington, *Follow the Rabbit-Proof Fence* (1996):** The book was made into the movie *Rabbit-Proof Fence* by Phillip Noyce in 2002 (see Chapter 15). It educated Australians and people all around the world about the policies that led to the Stolen Generations. They removed Aboriginal children from their families based on their race.

- **Kim Scott, *Benang: From the Heart* (1999):** *Benang* won the Western Australian Premier's Book Awards Fiction Award in 1999. It won the Miles Franklin Award in 2000. It was Scott's second novel. His 2010 novel, *That Deadman Dance*, also won the Miles Franklin Award.

- **Sally Morgan, *My Place* (1999):** Sally Morgan's book was about her family history and the way they came to terms with their Indigenous identity. It became a bestseller. It won a Human Rights literature award.

- **Alexis Wright, *Carpentaria* (2006):** *Carpentaria* won the Vance Palmer Award for Fiction, the top fiction prize of the Victorian Premier's Literary Awards, a Queensland Premier's Literary Award and the Miles Franklin award in 2007. *Carpentaria* is both funny and profound. It is told from the viewpoint of an Aboriginal Elder. Wright's style in this novel has been compared with Gabriel Garcia Marquez and Salman Rushdie. She also won much critical acclaim for her 2013 novel, *The Song Book.*

- **Tara June Winch, *Swallow the Air* (2006), *The Yield* (2019):** *Swallow the Air* won the David Unaipon Award in 2004. The book went on to win the Victorian Premier's Award for a first book of fiction in 2006 and the Nita May Dobbie Literary Award in 2007. Winch's book focuses on the struggles of an Aboriginal family. But most critics are drawn to the elegance of the writing. Her 2019 novel, *The Yield*, won the Miles Franklin Award.

- **Anita Heiss, *Not Meeting Mr Right* (2007), *Avoiding Mr Right* (2008), *Manhattan Dreaming* (2010), *Tiddas* (2014), *Barbed Wire and Cherry Blossoms* (2016), *Bila Yarrudhanggalangdhuray* (2021):** Anita Heiss is an author and an active promoter of Indigenous writing. She has created the unique genre of commercial women's fiction with Indigenous women as her main characters. Written for women, these books explore relationships. But they also deal with serious issues around racism and Aboriginal identity. Anita is an active champion for Aboriginal literacy projects.

- **Tony Birch, *Blood* (2011), *Ghost River* (2016), *The White Girl* (2019):** Tony Birch is a poet, essayist and writer of short stories and novels. He writes of the bravery of Aboriginal people facing tough life circumstances. He creates strong, colourful characters. He is also known for his strong depictions of country. Tony also writes about environmental issues and is an historian. In 2017 he became the first Indigenous writer to win the Patrick White Award.

- **Melissa Lucashenko, *Mullumbimby* (2013), *Too Much Lip* (2018):** Melissa Lucashenko is a novelist and essayist. Her stories of Aboriginal history and experience also explore connection to country and the strength of culture and family. *Mullumbimby* won the Victorian Premier's Literary Award for Indigenous Writing. *Too Much Lip* won the Miles Franklin Award. She is a founding member of Sisters Inside. She works to protect the rights of women prisoners. She is also a strong voice for the rights of Indigenous people.

Putting it into verse: Aboriginal poetry

Indigenous writers seem comfortable in the genre of poetry. It's a popular form of written expression. Poetry is like songwriting, which is another form of expression popular with Aboriginal people and Torres Strait Islanders. So it's not surprising that Indigenous poets have thrived. Some of these poets include Jack Davis, Oodgeroo Noonuccal and Kerry Reed-Gilbert. (See the earlier section 'Black people writing about black people'.) Here are just a few more of the popular Indigenous poets:

- **Herb Wharton (1936–):** Watson was a former stockman, drover and labourer. He turned to writing in the 1980s. He wrote novels, short stories and two books of poetry. *Kings with Empty Pockets* and *Imba (Listen): Tell You a Story* were both published in 2003.

- **Alf Taylor (1947–):** Alf Taylor was a member of the Stolen Generations. He worked as a farm labourer before joining the armed services. He came to writing later in life and found acclaim as a poet. He released his most recent book of poetry, *Long Time Now*, in 2007.

- **Ali Cobby Eckermann (1963–):** Eckermann is an accomplished poet. Her first poetry collection, *Little Bit Long Time*, was released in 2009. Before then she had won several awards. These included first prize in the ATSI Survival Poetry Competition in 2006 and the Dymocks Red Earth Poetry Award in the Northern Territory Literary Awards in 2008. She published a memoir, *Too Afraid to Cry*, in 2013. Another collection of poems, *Inside my Mother*, came out in 2015. In 2017 she won the Windham-Campbell Literature Prize for poetry.

- **Romaine Moreton (1969–):** Moreton is a writer of poetry, prose and film. She is also a well-respected performance artist. She first published *The Callused Stick of Wanting* in 1996. It was republished in 2000 as part of an anthology titled *Rimfire*. She published *Post Me to the Prime Minister* in 2004.

- **Samuel Wagan Watson (1972–):** Watson won the David Unaipon Award in 1999 for *Of Muse, Meandering and Midnight*. He went on to win the 2005 New South Wales Premier's Literary Awards Kenneth Slessor Prize for Poetry Book of the Year for *Smoke Encrypted Whispers*. Watson has written three other books: *Itinerant Blues* (2002); *Hotel Bone* (2001); and *Three Legged Dogs, and Other Poems* (2005). In 2018 Watson won the Patrick White Award.

- **Ellen van Neerven (1990–):** Van Neerven made a splash with their poetry collections *Comfort Food* (2016) and *Throat* (2020). They are also an accomplished writer. Their collection of short stories, *Heat and Light* (2014), won the David Unaipon Award and the NSW Premier's Literary Award.

- **Alison Whittaker (1993–):** Whittaker published her first book of poems, *Lemons in the Chicken Wire*, in 2016 to critical acclaim. She won the Judith Wright Poetry prize in 2017 for her poem 'Many Girls White Linen'. *Blakwork* (2018) is a powerful mixture of poetry, prose and reflective pieces. She has been described as a powerful and important new voice.

Not Putting Your Foot in It!

Sometimes non-Indigenous people have misused Indigenous cultural content without fully understanding the proper *protocols*. This term refers to ways of dealing with Indigenous cultural material and of interacting with Indigenous people and their communities. Protocols are designed to promote ethical behaviour. For example, some people have a false belief that Indigenous stories are in the public realm because they have no single 'author'. Therefore, they have a false belief that the stories require no permission for use or publication. This is definitely not the case. The stories are owned by their respective communities. Some people, however, have ignored both protocol and the law on purpose.

People have got into trouble writing about Indigenous cultures and characters in Australia in three ways:

- Pretending to be an Indigenous author — and so writing from an Indigenous perspective — when they are not. This behaviour is literary fraud.

- Telling Indigenous cultural stories without the proper cultural authority to tell them. Some cultural stories need to be told by the people who have the right to tell them. These are usually particular Indigenous people.

- Writing characters that continue stereotypes about Indigenous people and cultures. Writers get into trouble when they try to write from an Indigenous viewpoint but don't have enough experience with Indigenous cultures and worldviews to make the characters seem real.

REMEMBER

Aboriginal authors such as Lisa Fuller (author of *Ghost Bird*) also warn against writing about Indigenous stories as containing myths and legends, when these stories are actually about cultural and spiritual beliefs.

CULTURAL
PROTOCOLS

Guidelines to help authors writing about Indigenous issues have been created by the Australia Council for the Arts. You can download the publication from the website at www.australiacouncil. gov.au. Search for **Protocols for Producing Indigenous Australian Writing**. This publication gives useful case studies and discussion. The writing protocols identify nine principles for dealing with Indigenous cultural material and knowledge:

- **Respect:** Use the material respectfully. Local community protocols relating to particular material should be understood and respected.

- **Indigenous control:** Respect the principle of self-determination. Make sure that Indigenous people keep control over cultural material. Going to the appropriate individual or community about the use of their cultural heritage is important.

↙ **Communication, consultation and consent:** Work closely with Indigenous people. Talk with them. Make sure they're consulted and agree to any use of their material. Consultation can be a slow process. It needs a lot of time.

↙ **Interpretation, integrity and authenticity:** Make sure Indigenous cultural heritage is shown accurately. Also make sure Indigenous people won't be offended by the way the material is used.

↙ **Secrecy and confidentiality:** Understand that some cultural material is secret and shouldn't be made public.

↙ **Attribution and copyright:** Make sure that acknowledgement is given to people who have the rights to stories. Also make sure their copyright is protected.

↙ **Proper returns and royalties:** Make sure that the publication of work that includes the knowledge and cultural property of Indigenous people gives an equitable share in the profits and royalties generated by the work.

↙ **Continuing culture:** Maintain ongoing consultation about the use of material. Indigenous cultures are dynamic and changing.

↙ **Recognition and protection:** Understand that some legal protections of Indigenous cultural heritage have been introduced. In some instances, these may create issues over intellectual property to consider.

TIP

In seeking to build relationships or consult with Indigenous people about their culture and use of the culture in literary works, some key community organisations can be useful contacts. These include Aboriginal land councils, language centres and the Australian Institute of Aboriginal and Torres Strait Islander Studies.

FOUR QUICK FACTS ABOUT INDIGENOUS LITERATURE

Here are four facts about Indigenous literature that you might not know!

- Indigenous Literacy Day is celebrated on 1 September each year.
- The largest collection of Indigenous writing appears in *Macquarie PEN: Anthology of Aboriginal Australia*. It was published by Allen & Unwin in 2008.
- Several projects — such as the Indigenous Literacy Foundation — aim to help Aboriginal and Torres Strait Islander children to read. They donate books to their schools and communities. The Indigenous Literacy Foundation also produces and publishes books written by Indigenous people in multiple languages.
- Five novels by Indigenous authors have won the prestigious Miles Franklin Award: Kim Scott's *Benang: From the Heart* (2000), Alexis Wright's *Carpentaria* (2007), Kim Scott again for *That Deadman Dance* (2011), Melissa Lucashenko's *Too Much Lip* (2019) and Tara June Winch's *The Yield* (2020).

PROJECT

Read a poem by an Indigenous poet mentioned in this chapter and write a short response to it.

PROJECT

Write a short biography of an Indigenous author mentioned in this chapter.

PROJECT

Make a poster that celebrates the life and achievements of David Unaipon.

Performance Storytelling: Film, Theatre and Television

Indigenous culture has a strong storytelling tradition. So the leap by Indigenous people to use new methods and technologies to tell those stories was almost a given. Film, theatre, television and radio are all used successfully by Indigenous people for modern storytelling.

Not so long ago, Indigenous people felt the way they were shown in stories wasn't a true reflection of their lives, experiences, culture and worldviews. This was true even if the portrait was trying to be sympathetic.

Indigenous people prefer to tell their own stories their own way. Both electronic media and theatre have proved ideal methods. Indigenous storytellers often use humour to get their points across. But they aren't afraid to tell stories of tragedy as well. Through this work, Indigenous Australia has produced talented Indigenous directors, producers, writers and actors. You get to meet them in this chapter. These talented people give a voice to Indigenous people and educate the wider community about Indigenous experience, viewpoints and culture.

In this chapter, I also explore the more recent establishment of Indigenous media organisations. They make sure that Indigenous people have control over the content they're creating, as well as its spread.

Acting the Part: Indigenous People and the World of Films

Filmmakers have been interested in including Indigenous people and their stories in films since the early days of the industry in Australia. But early films showed Indigenous peoples and their cultures through the eyes of European directors. Over time, stories about Indigenous people became more sympathetic. Filmmakers worked with them on the stories.

Indigenous people were also secondary characters in films such as *Crocodile Dundee* and *Priscilla, Queen of the Desert.* They were meant to add a comic layer or to make a statement about Indigenous people's relationship with the land. But Indigenous people wanted to tell their own stories, in their own words, in their own style.

In the 1920s, movies were always from a non-Indigenous perspective. These movies tended to stereotype Indigenous people and their culture. They were often shown either as a threat or as mysterious and spiritual. In any case, they were one-dimensional and seen as inferior. *Heritage* (1935), for example, showed savage Aboriginal people attacking a homestead. In *Uncivilised* (1936) and *Bitter Springs* (1950), they were seen as a threat.

Many great Australian film directors have made a movie that has at its heart a story about Indigenous Australia. These include Fred Schepisi (*The Chant of Jimmie Blacksmith*), Baz Luhrmann (*Priscilla, Queen of the Desert* and *Australia*), Peter Weir (*The Last Wave*), Bruce Beresford (*The Fringe Dwellers*) and Phillip Noyce (*Backroads* and *Rabbit-Proof Fence*). These films weren't necessarily written to be critical of Indigenous people. But Indigenous people haven't always been happy with how they were portrayed.

Jedda (1955)

Jedda was the first movie with Indigenous people in its starring roles — Ngarla Kunoth (also known as Rosalie Kunoth–Monks) and Robert Tudwali. It was also the first Australian movie to be shot in colour. Australian filmmaker Charles Chauvel had shown negative images of Indigenous people in earlier films such as *Heritage* (1935) and *Uncivilised* (1936). *Jedda* was Chauvel's final movie. It had attention from around the world.

The film tells the story of Jedda, an Aboriginal girl born on a cattle station. She was raised by the wife of the white station owner and taught European ways. She was forbidden to learn the culture of her own people. As a young woman, Jedda is interested in Marbuck. He is an Aboriginal man living a traditional life. She is lured to his camp and he kidnaps her. Marbuck is punished by his clan for bringing Jedda to their camp and is *sung*. This was a mystical practice that places a sort of curse on the receiver. He goes insane as a result of his tribal punishment. He ends his life and Jedda's.

The audience is led to feel empathy with Jedda. But the ending hints that Aboriginal people and their culture couldn't be 'civilised'.

THIS STAR STILL SHINES: ROSALIE KUNOTH-MONKS

Rosalie Kunoth-Monks appeared as Ngarla Kunoth in the 1955 film *Jedda* at the age of 14. She was born in 1937 at Utopia Cattle Station in the Northern Territory. She's now a highly respected Elder of her community and a strong voice for her people. She has worked on many Indigenous issues. But she focuses on education. Kunoth-Monks is the Chancellor of Batchelor Institute of Indigenous Tertiary Education. This is an institution in the Northern Territory focused on the education of Indigenous people.

Walkabout (1971)

This film was adapted from James Vance Marshall's novel of the same name. Nicholas Roeg directed it. The story is about the journey of two children who are stranded in the Australian outback. They get help in finding their way back to civilisation from an Aboriginal boy. This boy is played by a young David Gulpilil.

Their journey is set against a backdrop of the violent legacy of colonisation. There is also the background of the mistreatment of the environment and Indigenous cultures. One of the strongest parts of the film is the cinematography. It showcases the Australian landscape.

Backroads (1977)

Phillip Noyce, who later went on to direct _Rabbit-Proof Fence_, directed this movie. _Backroads_ is a road movie that stars Aboriginal actors Gary Foley and Essie Coffey.

It tells the story of a white drifter, played by the iconic Australian actor the late Bill Hunter. He has a chance meeting with an Aboriginal man. Together they steal a car and keep stealing as they travel. They're joined on the journey by other characters. These include another Aboriginal man, the bored wife of a service station owner and a French backpacker. This crew is on the run from the police. The movie ends with a deadly mix of boredom and violence.

One of the unique things about the film is the dialogue between the characters. They talk about Indigenous political issues and Indigenous culture.

The Last Wave (1977)

The main character in Peter Weir's movie _The Last Wave_ is a white lawyer. He defends two Aboriginal men accused of murder related to a tribal punishment. There are a series of events and some strange dreams. Then he understands that the men are keeping a secret that relates to the major weather patterns that have started.

The film stars Richard Chamberlain as David Burton, the white lawyer, and David Gulpilil as Chris Lee, a member of the Aboriginal clan. The film has a strong Indigenous storyline. But the movie really relates to the main character, the white lawyer.

The Chant of Jimmie Blacksmith (1978)

Directed by Fred Schepisi, this movie was based on the 1972 novel by Thomas Keneally. The author was inspired by the life of Aboriginal outlaw Jimmy Governor. (Refer to Chapter 14 for more about this book.)

The film tells the story of Jimmie Blacksmith, a half-white and half-Aboriginal station worker. He was raised by a Methodist minister. He finds himself estranged from his family. He marries a white servant, who becomes pregnant. But he finds out later he isn't the father of her child. He is taught to try to attain the things that white society offers. But he is denied being treated as an equal. Eventually he snaps and goes on a rampage of revenge.

The film seeks to explain how an Aboriginal man, caught between white society and his traditional culture, could come to be so filled with rage. The movie was nominated for a Palme d'Or at the 1978 Cannes Film Festival. It stars Indigenous actors Tom E Lewis as Jimmie, Freddie Reynolds as his brother, Mort, and Steve Dodd as the wise Elder, Tabidji.

Manganinnie (1980)

Directed by John Honey, the film explores the Black Line of 1830. This was an attempt to kill all the Indigenous people of Tasmania (refer to Chapter 7). Separated from her family, Manganinnie travels across the country in search of her tribe. She is accompanied by a white girl. The two discover that the tribe has vanished. The film stars Mawuyul Yanthalawuy as Manganinnie.

The Fringe Dwellers (1986)

Acclaimed Australian director Bruce Beresford's first movie explores the difficulty faced by an Aboriginal family. They want to leave their life on the fringe and shift into mainstream society. They move to a respectable suburb. But the prejudice of the neighbours and the demands of kin responsibility make the change difficult.

The movie tries to explore the barriers to assimilation that Indigenous people faced. People were caught between two worlds. The cast includes Indigenous actors Justine Saunders, Kristina Nehm, Kylie Belling, Bob Maza and Ernie Dingo. The movie was based on a novel by Nene Gare.

Babakiueria (1986)

This movie was directed by Don Featherstone. The idea behind this satirical movie is that, instead of white people colonising Australia, the roles were reversed. The title is based on the word Aboriginal people believe the white people call their sacred space. It is, of course, the barbeque area. It stars Bob Maza as Minister for White Affairs. The movie uses humour to make a strong statement about the racist beliefs of dominant culture in Australia.

Yolngu Boy (2001)

This film was directed by Stephen Johnson and commissioned by the Australian Children's Television Foundation. It tells the story of three young men from Arnhem Land who flee the police and head to Darwin. It tries to highlight the modern issues facing Indigenous people. It also tries to show the way in which issues such as petrol sniffing are weakening the traditional cultural fabric of Indigenous communities. It stars Sean Mununggurr, John Sebastian Pilakui and Nathan Daniels. It also features music by Yothu Yindi (refer to Chapter 13).

Rabbit-Proof Fence (2002)

This film is based on the book *Follow the Rabbit-Proof Fence* by Doris Pilkington. It retells the story of Pilkington's mother and two other girls. In the 1930s, they ran away from an Aboriginal settlement to return to their families in the remote town of Jigalong. They walked for more than nine weeks, guided by a rabbit-proof fence, to return to their families.

In the movie, they are chased by a white constable and an Aboriginal tracker, Moodoo. But the skills they had learned from their Aboriginal families before they were removed help them not get caught. The film stars Everlyn Sampi, Daisy Kadibil and

Tianna Sansbury as the three girls, Ningali Lawford and David Gulpilil. It was directed by Phillip Noyce.

Australian Rules (2002)

This film is based on the book *Deadly Unna?* by Phillip Gwynne and is directed by Paul Goldman. It is set in an isolated fishing town. The story examines the relationship between Indigenous people and the rest of the community. It explores personal relationships and racial tensions. It focuses on the way that football was often the place where racially divided towns united. The Indigenous stars are Luke Carrol and Lisa Flanagan.

The Tracker (2002)

Directed and written by Rolf de Heer, *The Tracker* is set in the outback in 1922. It tells the story of a racist policeman. He uses the abilities of an Indigenous tracker, played by David Gulpilil, to find the Indigenous man accused of the murder of a white woman.

Ten Canoes (2006)

Rolf de Heer teamed up with Peter Djigirr to direct this film. It is the first feature film to be made entirely in an Aboriginal language, Yolngu Matha. But its narration, by David Gulpilil, is in English. (A Yolngu Matha version is also available.) Through switches between the present and the past, it explores the Yolngu relationship to land, as well as kinship and human flaws.

The film weaves together two stories. One is the adventures of a Yolngu man, played by Jamie Gulpilil, who covets his older brother's wife. The other is a story told to him about another young man whose desire for his brother's wife has tragic and unintended consequences. The wholly Indigenous cast are from the Arnhem Land communities of Ramingining and Maningrida.

High Ground (2020)

Directed by Stephen Maxwell Johnson, this film starts in 1919 in the Northern Territory. It stars Simon Baker as Travis, an ex-World War I sharpshooter who, 12 years after the events at the start of the film, is tasked with leading an expedition to arrest a Yolngu warrior, Baywarra (Sean Mununggur) who is resisting white colonists. With Travis as a guide is Gutjuk (Jacob Junior Nayinggul), a young Aboriginal man Travis saved years earlier when his family group was massacred by a group of white men. Baywarra, it turns out, is Gutjuk's uncle so the young man finds himself torn between the white community that adopted him and the community he was born into and is naturally drawn back to. Gutjuk is also drawn to the beautiful and powerful female warrior, Wak Wak, played by Magnolia Maymuru.

THE QUINTESSENTIAL ABORIGINAL ACTOR: GULPILIL

David Gulpilil was born in 1953 in Arnhem Land in the Northern Territory. He has become the most prolific Indigenous actor in Australia. A Yolngu man, Gulpilil was raised in the bush and at a mission school in Maningrida. He was initiated into his clan when he came of age. A skilled traditional dancer, it was this talent that caught the eye of filmmaker Nicolas Roeg. He cast Gulpilil in his 1971 film, *Walkabout.*

Gulpilil's screen presence brought him more attention. He went on to appear in many movies. These include *Storm Boy* (1976), *The Last Wave* (1977), *Crocodile Dundee* (1986), *Rabbit-Proof Fence* (2002), *The Tracker* (2002), *Ten Canoes* (2006), *Australia* (2008) and *Charlie's Country* (2013). He won the Best Actor award at the 2014 Cannes Film Festival for his role in *Charlie's Country*. Gulpilil also appeared on television, including in the series *Boney*, about an Aboriginal detective (1972 to 1973).

Gulpilil has also written two children's books based on Yolngu stories. He continues to perform traditional dance. Perhaps the greatest Aboriginal actor to date, Gulpilil has also kept strong connections with his country and heritage. He returned to his country to live a simple life as an Elder in his community. A documentary, *Gulpilil: One Red Blood*, was made about his life in 2003.

Taking Over the Camera

Storytelling is such a central part of Indigenous cultures. It was only a matter of time before Indigenous people took over the camera to tell their stories themselves.

In 2000, the Message Sticks Indigenous Film Festival was started to showcase Indigenous films in the categories of drama, documentary, comedy and shorts. It was curated by Indigenous filmmakers Rachel Perkins and Darren Dale. The festival was held at the Sydney Opera House. More recent festivals also celebrate Indigenous film. One example is the inaugural BIRRARANGGA Film Festival, held at the Australian Centre for the Moving Image (ACMI) in Melbourne in 2019.

Indigenous filmmakers

Indigenous directors are some of Australia's greatest storytellers. They use both documentary and drama. Here are just a few of them:

- **Wayne Blair** is an actor, writer and director. His first film was an adaptation of the play *The Sapphires.* It starred Deborah Mailman, Jessica Mauboy, Shari Sebbens and Miranda Tapsell. More recently, he directed *Top End Wedding* (2019) starring Miranda Tapsell. He has directed episodes of *Mystery Road* and *Cleverman* for television. He has also worked in theatre. He directed *The 7 Stages of Grieving*, written by Deborah Mailman and Wesley Enoch. (See the later section 'Must-see Indigenous plays' for more.) He also adapted Meme McDonald and Boori Pryor's award-winning novel, *Njunjul The Sun*, for Queensland's Indigenous theatre company.

- **Essie Coffey** was also known as the Bush Queen. She was from the town of Goodooga in north-west New South Wales. She was brought up in the bush and worked on cattle stations with her family. She married and lived on the banks of the Barwon River at Brewarrina. She later moved to Dodge

City, a reserve in West Brewarrina. There she raised eight children and ten stepchildren. She was a well-known country singer and songwriter. In 1976, she appeared in the Phillip Noyce movie, *Backroads*. She directed the documentary, *My Survival as an Aboriginal* in 1978 and a sequel, *My Life as I Live It*, in 1993. She passed away in 1998.

✔ **Tracey Moffatt** is a well-known Aboriginal artist and photographer. Her works are featured in art galleries around the world, including the Tate Gallery in London. (Refer to Chapter 12 for more on Moffatt's art.) Her first film was released in 1987. She made another short film, *Night Cries: A Rural Tragedy* in 1989. *BeDevil*, which she directed in 1993, is said to be the first feature film by an Aboriginal woman. She made several more short films, including *Heaven* (1997), *Lip* (1999), *Artist* (2000) and *Revolution* (2008).

✔ **Rachel Perkins** is a director, producer and writer. Her films include *Radiance* (1998), *One Night the Moon* (2001), *Bran Nue Dae* (2010) and *Jasper Jones* (2017). She also produced, directed and narrated the television series *First Australians* (2008). She directed on the television series of *Mystery Road* (series 1, 2018) and *Total Control* (2019–2021). She is the daughter of Indigenous activist Charles Perkins. Along with producer Darren Dale, Rachel founded the first Indigenous production company, Blackfella Films.

✔ **Ivan Sen** made his debut feature film *Beneath Clouds* (2002) after working on numerous short films. He also has many documentaries to his credit. His second feature-length movie, *Dreamland*, was released in 2009. *Toomelah* was released in 2011 to great critical acclaim. He wrote and directed the Western-inspired movies *Mystery Road* (2013) and *Goldstone* (2016).

✔ **Brian Syron** became the first Indigenous person to direct a full-length feature film. He made *Jindalee Lady* in 1992. Syron was born in Sydney. He ended up in Grafton Correctional Centre at the age of 14. So no-one suspected that he would go on to have such an extraordinary life. He went to acting school and ended up studying in New York alongside Robert de Niro and Warren Beatty. After returning home, Syron became a strong voice for Indigenous human rights. He helped start the National Black Theatre in Redfern. He also worked with Indigenous prisoners, encouraging them to write plays. He started the Aboriginal Theatre Company with Robert Merritt, an Aboriginal playwright who penned *The Cake Man*.

- **Warwick Thornton** is a cinematographer, director and screenwriter. His debut feature film *Samson and Delilah* (2009) was released to great critical acclaim. His film *Sweet Country* (2017) highlights his talents as a cinematographer and director. He directed on the first season of TV's *Mystery Road*. He also directed *The Beach* (2020). It is a documentary about his retreat to a remote location with no power.

A DYNASTY OF SCREEN PIONEERS

Freda Glynn was a co-creator of the Central Australian Aboriginal Media Association (CAAMA). Her son, Warwick Thornton, is one of Australia's most successful directors. He is known for his films *Samson and Delilah* (2009) and *Sweet Country* (2017). Freda's daughter, Erica Glynn, is also an accomplished director and producer. Her film credits include *In My Own Words* (2017). Freda's grandchildren are also talented. Dylan River is an accomplished director, writer and cinematographer. His film credits include *Buckskin* (2013), *Finke: There and Back* (2018), *The Beach* (2020) and the television series *Robbie Hood* (2019). Freda's grand-daughter, Tanith Glynn-Maloney, is a producer who has worked on *Robbie Hood* (2019) and *The Beach* (2020). Erica and Tanith produced a film, which Erica wrote and directed, on Freda Glynn's life story in 2019, *She Who Must be Loved*.

Noteworthy Indigenous films

The growing catalogue of Indigenous movies is a mix of different genres and styles. Here are a few noteworthy Indigenous films, directed by noteworthy Indigenous directors:

- *Jindalee Lady* **(1992)** — directed by Brian Syron — is the first full-length feature directed by an Indigenous person. It tells the story of an Indigenous fashion designer. She falls in love with another man during her unhappy marriage to a white husband. With a strong female lead, the story explores the struggle for Aboriginal women to find respect and success in Australian society. It stars Lydia Miller in the title role.

- *BeDevil* **(1993)** — written and directed by Tracey Moffatt — is a trilogy of ghost stories ('Mister Chuck', 'Choo Choo Choo Choo' and 'Lovin' the Spin I'm In'). They blend the imaginary and the real. It was the first full-length feature film made by an Aboriginal woman. Moffatt also stars in the movie, alongside Mawuyul Yanthalawuy, who also stars in *Manganinnie* (1980), *Women of the Sun* (1981), *We of the Never Never* (1982) and *A Waltz through the Hills* (1988).

- *Radiance* **(1998)** — directed by Rachel Perkins — tells the story of three sisters. They are successful opera singer Cressy, parental carer Mae, who looked after their ailing mother, and party girl Nona. The three unite for their mother's funeral and confront some family secrets. It stars Rachael Maza, Trisha Morton-Thomas and Deborah Mailman.

- *One Night the Moon* **(2001)** — directed by Rachel Perkins — tells the story of a white family living in the Flinders Ranges. Their daughter goes missing on the night of the full moon. They fail to use the skills of a black tracker, played by Kelton Pell, to help in finding her, due to their own prejudices. Singer Ruby Hunter also makes an appearance in the film. The story is based on a series of events that took place in 1932. They are depicted in a documentary, *Black Tracker*, made by Michael Riley in 1997.

- *Beneath Clouds* (2002) — written and directed by Ivan Sen — focuses on two teenagers who are leaving their country town for the city. They hope to find a better life. The film is a road movie and a coming-of-age movie that has universal themes that appeal to a broad audience. Its Indigenous star is Dannielle Hall.

- *Samson and Delilah* (2009) — directed by Warwick Thornton — shows the lives of two Indigenous teens, played by Rowan McNamara and Marissa Gibson. They live in a remote community. They steal a car and head to Alice Springs. The film takes a hard look at the issues facing Indigenous Australians, including the effects of petrol sniffing and violence. It was co-produced by Scarlett Pictures and CAAMA Productions. (See the later section 'Indigenous media organisations' later in this chapter.)

- *Stone Brothers* (2009) — directed by Richard Frankland — is a comedy and a road movie. It follows the adventures of Charlie (Leon Burchill) and Eddie (Luke Carroll) as they try to recover a sacred stone. It was entrusted to Eddie but Charlie has lost it. Frankland also wrote and directed the short film *No Way to Forget*, in 1996.

- *Bran Nue Dae* (2010) — directed by Rachel Perkins — is a musical set in Broome. It tells the story of an Aboriginal boy's journey from a Catholic boarding school in Perth to his homeland. Along the way, he searches for his identity. The movie is based on a musical written by Aboriginal playwright Jimmy Chi, from his own experiences. The stage play toured nationally from 1990. Jimmy Chi and local Broome band Kuckles wrote the musical score. It had influences from traditional music, rock, blues and the Roman Catholic Mass. The film's Indigenous cast includes Rocky McKenzie, Jessica Mauboy, Ernie Dingo, Deborah Mailman, Ningali Lawford, Dan Sultan and Stephen 'Baamba' Albert.

- *Toomelah* (2011) — directed by Ivan Sen — weaves together two stories. One is the story of a 10-year-old boy (Daniel Connors) living on the Toomelah Mission. His aim to be a gangster sees him caught up in a drug turf war. The other is the story of his aunt, a member of the Stolen Generations, who returns home. The film was shown at the Cannes Film Festival. The cast members were all drawn from the Toomelah community.

- *The Sapphires* (2012) — directed by Wayne Blair — is based on a true story. It tells the story of four Aboriginal singers in an all-girl group, The Sapphires. They travel to Vietnam to perform for the US troops. It stars Deborah Mailman, Jessica Mauboy and Shari Sebbins. The film speaks of the racism of the era but is also full of great musical numbers.

- *Mystery Road* (2013) and *Goldstone* (2016) — directed by Ivan Sen — are based around the outback cop, Jay Swan, played by Aaron Pedersen. In *Mystery Road*, he investigates the murder of an Aboriginal girl. In *Goldstone*, Swan comes to a town to investigate a missing person's case and uncovers a web of crime and corruption. Sen shot both films in the Western genre. This made most of the Australian landscape.

- *Spear* (2015) — directed by Stephen Page — shows the talents of the Bangarra Dance Theatre in magic realism style. It tells the story of an Aboriginal man navigating ancient traditions and modern society. It stars Hunter Page-Lochard in the role of Djali.

- *Sweet Country* (2017) — directed by Warwick Thornton — has a screenplay by Stephen McGregor and David Tranter. The film is set in the 1920s on the Northern Territory frontier. It follows the events after an Aboriginal farmhand shoots a white man in self-defence. It is based on a true story. It won the Special Jury Prize at the Venice Film Festival for Warwick Thornton.

- *Top End Wedding* (2019) — directed by Wayne Blair — stars (and is co-written) by Miranda Tapsell. The film follows the adventures of Lauren. After she is engaged to Ned, she must find her mother, who has gone travelling somewhere in remote far north Australia. She must reunite her parents, deal with her family and arrange her dream wedding.

Stephen McGregor is a talented writer and director. He has worked on a range of television shows. These include *Art + Soul* (2010–2014), *The Warriors* (2017), *Blue Water Empire* (2019) and *Black Comedy* (2014–2020). He also directed the documentary *Servant or Slave* (2016). He wrote the screenplay for *Sweet Country* (2017). He has also written on the television series *Redfern Now* (2012) and *Mystery Road* (2018–2020).

A new generation of Indigenous directors has also seen a new generation of Indigenous producers. They include Darren Dale, Mitchell Stanley, Dena Curtis, Pauline Clague and Tanith Glynn-Maloney. This means that the works are owned by Indigenous people. This ensures more Indigenous control of Indigenous storytelling.

Telling it like it is: Documentaries

Film has been an effective way to tell Indigenous stories. But it has also been a powerful medium for exploring Indigenous reality.

QUEEN OF THE SCREEN: JUSTINE SAUNDERS

Justine Saunders was one of the most prolific Indigenous actors to have worked on Australian stage and screen. She was the first Indigenous person to appear as a regular in a mainstream soap opera, *Number 96,* in 1976. She went on to appear in other television series, including *Prisoner* and *Heartland*. She also starred in the mini-series *Women of the Sun* and appeared in many movies. These include *The Fringe Dwellers, The Chant of Jimmie Blacksmith* and *Jindalee Lady.*

Justine Saunders received a Medal of the Order of Australia for her services to the performing arts in 1991. She returned it in 2000 in protest at the way the federal government at the time continued to deny the existence of the Stolen Generations (refer to Chapter 8). Saunders herself was removed from her family as a child. She died in 2007.

Essie Coffey's *My Survival as an Aboriginal* was the first documentary directed by an Indigenous person. It details the realities of life for Indigenous Australians. Documentary filmmaking soon became a powerful way to allow Indigenous people to highlight events and experiences that weren't being covered by the mainstream media.

Documentaries such as *Lousy Little Sixpence* uncovered issues like the impact of the policy of removing children from their families and the failure to pay wages to Indigenous people — including children — who were sent out to work. (Refer to Chapter 8 for more on the Stolen Generations.) They explore important key events, such as the freedom rides, the 1967 referendum, the Tent Embassy and the Mabo case. Indigenous documentary filmmakers have brought their viewpoints to a wider audience. Here's a sample:

- *My Survival as an Aboriginal* **(1978)** — directed by Essie Coffey in collaboration with Martha Ansara — was the first documentary to give an Aboriginal worldview. Coffey shares her culture and community, and the harsh realities of her life. She makes a powerful argument about the need to protect Indigenous cultures and rights.

- *Lousy Little Sixpence* **(1983)** — directed by Alec Morgan and Gerry Bostock — tells the story of five children, now all Elders. They were stolen from their families and used as unpaid labour. It includes their narratives, old film and photographs. It tells a heartbreaking story in a simple way. The film became a way for many Australians who didn't know about the removal policy to understand its devastating effects.

- *The Tent Embassy* **(1992)** — directed by Frances Peters-Little — is about this site of political activism outside Old Parliament House in 1972. The Tent Embassy still stands today. The documentary explores the goals and achievements of the Tent Embassy at the time and its legacy today.

✏ *Black Chicks Talking* (2001) — co-directed by Leah Purcell with Brendan Fletcher — is based on interviews with Indigenous women. They include actress Deborah Mailman and former Miss Australia and politician Kathryn Hay. Purcell also produced a book and a stage production from the project.

✏ *Vote Yes for Aborigines* (2007) — directed by Frances Peters-Little — is a documentary about the 1967 referendum and the campaign for Aboriginal citizenship rights that led up to it (refer to Chapter 9). It looks at the referendum's historical importance and modern legacy.

✏ *A Sister's Love* (2007) — directed by Ivan Sen — looks at the response of Aboriginal media personality Rhoda Roberts to the unsolved murder of her twin sister. Lois Roberts was last seen alive hitchhiking. Her body was later found in bushland. The film explores the power of family and the lasting impact of grief.

✏ *The Intervention: Katherine NT* (2008) — directed by Julie Nimmo — follows the impact of the Northern Territory intervention on one community over the first year it was rolled out. The documentary explores the lives of ordinary community residents and the government and business workers who come together to implement the intervention.

✏ *Servant or Slave* (2016) — directed by Stephen McGregor and produced by Mitchell Stanley —follows the experiences of women who were removed from their families as children. They were forced to work as domestic servants with no pay. They often faced abuse.

✏ *After the Apology* (2017) — directed by Larissa Behrendt (me!) — follows the fight of three grandmothers to regain custody of their grandchildren after they are wrongfully removed. The film looks at the structural racism that sees Aboriginal children removed from their families at a greater rate. It highlights the need to have greater community control in the child protection space.

    ✒ *Black Divaz* (**2018**) — directed by Adrian Russell Wills — follows six Aboriginal drag queens from around Australia as they compete in the inaugural Miss First Nations pageant.

REMEMBER

Two documentaries were released in 2019 that covered the relentless racial abuse by Australian Rules crowds of talented Aboriginal footballer Adam Goodes. *The Final Quarter* (2019) and *The Australian Dream* (2019) take complementary looks at this shameful episode. But they also highlight the quiet dignity with which Adam Goodes stands up to racism.

Treading the Black Boards

Performance has been a big part of traditional Indigenous cultures. Modern Indigenous playwrights have sought to bring their stories to an audience through theatre. It has been a way of telling powerful personal stories and exploring broader social issues.

In 1972, the National Black Theatre was started in Redfern. It marked a significant moment. Indigenous people were developing not only their own content but also their own theatre companies to showcase their work. Other Indigenous theatre companies have followed in recent years.

STALWARTS OF THEATRE: LESTER AND GERRY BOSTOCK

The Bostock brothers were both founding members of the National Black Theatre. Gerry became a playwright and Lester produced. Lester later worked to start Radio Redfern. He moved into filmmaking and television production. He taught at the Australian Film, Television and Radio School (AFTRS) and MetroScreen. Gerry went on to co-produce the influential documentary *Lousy Little Sixpence*.

The National Black Theatre

The Redfern community in Sydney was politically vibrant in 1972. The first Aboriginal medical service was being started. The first Aboriginal legal service had also begun. Four men from Redfern had gone to Canberra to set up the Aboriginal Tent Embassy.

At the time, street performance was part of the political movement of the community. Creative figures such as Brian Syron, Gary Foley and Gerry Bostock moved for the creation of a black theatre group. African-American dancer Carole Johnson also began classes.

This movement brought together a dynamic range of Indigenous people. Through workshops on modern and traditional dancing, acting and playwriting, the theatre helped develop a new generation of Indigenous talent.

The first performance of the National Black Theatre focused on the Gove land rights claim in the Northern Territory. It was performed in the street. Other early performances included a dance program focused on the Tent Embassy and its reestablishment. A political revue called *Basically Black* was written and performed by a group that included Bob Maza, Gary Foley and Bindi Williams. It was directed by Ken Horler. The revue later toured the country and made a television show of the same name. But the material had to be toned down for television.

The National Black Theatre became a hub of many activities and an umbrella for many groups, including a black casting agency. It also brought a focus on Indigenous arts policy.

In 1974, a building was provided and a 100-seat theatre built. It was given minimal funding from government. The first play to be performed there was Robert Merritt's *The Cake Man*, directed by Brian Syron. Merritt had written the play while in prison. He was let out, under guard, to attend the opening night. A television production of the play was aired by the Australian Broadcasting Corporation (ABC) in 1977.

With its funding cut in 1976, the Black Theatre closed the following year. But people involved with it went on to write and perform other plays, make films and form other arts groups. These include the National Aboriginal Islander Skills Development Association (NAISDA), the Bangarra Dance Theatre and the Eora Centre, which specialises in providing professional development in the visual and performing arts. (Refer to Chapter 13 for more on the Bangarra Dance Theatre.)

REMEMBER

The Redfern Aboriginal community pushed to have the site of the National Black Theatre redeveloped. This finally occurred in 2008. It now houses the Gadigal Information Service and National Indigenous Television. (See the later sections 'Indigenous media organisations' and 'National Indigenous Television'.)

Indigenous theatre companies

Since the start of the National Black Theatre in 1972, several Indigenous companies have also sprung up. Here are a few of them:

- **Nindethana Theatre** was started in Melbourne in 1972 by a group of Aboriginal people actively involved in the Aboriginal Advancement League. One aim was to create Indigenous performances. Another was to encourage and promote Aboriginal dance, music, art, literature, film production and other cultural activities in the community. The group produced a version of *The Cherry Pickers*, by Kevin Gilbert. But it broke up in 1973.

- **Ilbijerri Theatre Company** began in 1990, also in Melbourne. It's the longest running Indigenous theatre company. Rachel Maza Long is its artistic director. Ilbijerri is a Woiwurrung word that means 'to come together for ceremony'.

- **Yirra Yaakin** is a Perth-based theatre company formed in 1993. It stages performances of Indigenous plays. It runs workshops for dance and theatre in the Indigenous community. It also provides arts residences. Yirra Yaakin means 'stand tall' in the Noongar language.

✔ **Kooemba Jdarra** is a Brisbane-based company. Since its start in 1993, it has produced modern performances of the works of Indigenous people. These include Indigenous writer Sam Wagan Watson, among other Indigenous authors (refer to Chapter 14).

Must-see Indigenous plays

Indigenous playwrights and actors continue to write and perform on the stage. They tell moving, heart-warming stories about Indigenous experiences and worldviews.

Here are just some of the plays written by Indigenous people:

✔ *The Cherry Pickers* **(1971)** was written by Kevin Gilbert in 1968 while he was in prison. It's credited as being the first Indigenous play. The story is about rural workers and explores themes of dispossession, dislocation and family. It is also an honest exploration of issues such as alcoholism and violence.

✔ *The Cake Man* **(1975)** was written by Robert Merritt. It shows the difficulties of life on a mission in western New South Wales. The play was written while Merritt was in Bathurst Correctional Centre. It was first performed by the National Black Theatre in Redfern.

✔ *Box the Pony* **(1997)** was co-written by Leah Purcell and Scott Rankin. It is a semi-autobiographical play performed by Purcell. The one-woman show explores the life of an Indigenous woman growing up in Queensland.

✔ *Stolen* **(1998)** was directed by Wesley Enoch and written by Jane Harrison. It looks at the impact of the policy of removing children from their families on five Indigenous people who were taken away.

✔ *The Keepers* **(1988)** was written by Bob Maza and performed at the Adelaide Fringe Festival and at Belvoir Street Theatre. It explores the destruction of the Buandig people of South Australia. It won Maza the National Black Playwright Award.

✏ *What Do They Call Me?* **(1990)** was written by Eva Johnson. It is a one-woman show that explores the impact of the policy of removing Indigenous children from their families through the eyes of a mother and her two daughters. She wrote several other plays. They include *When I Die You'll Stop Laughing*, *Mimini's Voices* and *Faded Genes*.

✏ *The Sapphires* **(2004)** was directed by Wesley Enoch and written by Tony Briggs. It tells the story of The Sapphires, a singing group of four Indigenous women who tour Vietnam during the war. The original production included Deborah Mailman, Rachael Maza, Ursula Yovich and Lisa Flanagan. It was made into a movie by Wayne Blair.

✏ *Page 8* **(2005)** was co-written by David Page and Louis Nowra and performed by Page. It tells the story of his childhood as a singing and dancing child star growing up on a housing commission estate.

✏ *Rainbow's End* **(2005)** was directed by Wesley Enoch and written by Jane Harrison. It is set in 1950s northern Victoria. It creates a family snapshot through three generations, each represented by a richly developed female character. It also looks at the issues of housing and education.

✏ *Black Medea* **(2005)** was written and directed by Wesley Enoch. It is an adaptation of the classical Greek play by Euripides, with the gods replaced by ancestral spirits. Medea betrays her heritage for the love of Jason. She leaves her desert home to marry a handsome, ambitious Indigenous man from the city. In doing so, she violates the kinship rules of her own people. She makes her crimes worse by selling knowledge of her land to mining companies. Her husband goes mad from his own demons and throws Medea out of the house. Homeless and hopeless, she murders her son as an act of revenge and despair. The cast included Margaret Harvey, Aaron Pederson and Justine Saunders.

✏ *The 7 Stages of Grieving* **(2008)** was directed by Wayne Blair and co-written by Deborah Mailman and Wesley Enoch. It is a one-woman play, starring Mailman, that explores episodes in the life of a character who represents every Indigenous woman. It uses humour and irony. But it also tells the story of a life dealing with racism, grief and reconciliation.

- *Jack Charles v The Crown* **(2010)** is a one-man play that tells the story of Jack Charles' life. It is a hard look at racism, systemic prejudice, street smarts, addiction and an embrace of life. The play was developed by the Ilbijerri Theatre Company.

- *Kill the Messenger* **(2015)** was written and performed by Nakkiah Lui. This powerful tale of Aboriginal people slipping through society's gaps was told with poignancy and humour. It marked Nakkiah's arrival as a presence on the Australian stage.

- *Barbara and the Camp Dogs* **(2017)** is a play with a great soundtrack written by Ursula Yovich and Alana Valentine. It's about Barbara, an Aboriginal pub singer trying to make it in Sydney. Ursula played the title role of Barbara. Elaine Crombie played her foster sister, Rene. It won four Helpmann Awards including Best Musical.

- *City of Gold* **(2019)** was written by and starred Meyne Wyatt. It tells the story of the structural racism that defines life in a remote town like Kalgoorlie. It also explores racism in the performing arts sector. It was Meyne's first screenplay. The play was influenced by real events and experience.

TAKING THE STAGE: NAKKIAH LUI

Nakkiah Lui is an actor, comedian and writer. She has written a number of successful plays that have been put on by the larger theatre companies such as Sydney Theatre Company and Belvoir. These have included *Kill the Messenger* (2015), *Black is the New White* (2017) and *How to Rule the World* (2019). Nakkiah was a co-writer and starred in the sketch television show *Black Comedy* (2014–2020). She also wrote and starred in comedy television series *Kiki and Kitty* (2017). Nakkiah received the Nick Enright Prize for Playwriting in 2018 for *Black is the New White*.

Appearing on Mainstream Screens

In the 1950s and 1960s, more and more Australian households brought television into their lives. But Indigenous people weren't on Australian television. Indigenous actor and activist Gary Foley noted that at that time television spoke to 'the white, middle-class, patriarchal nuclear family and thereby excluded those that this audience saw as "other"'. Indigenous Australians and other parts of the community weren't seen on television unless they were on current affairs or news shows.

By the 1970s, Indigenous actors were on occasion on mainstream television shows, such as police dramas *Division 4* and *Homicide*. But Indigenous people were shown as victims or villains. They were one-dimensional rather than complex characters.

A production that was originally staged at the National Black Theatre in Redfern, *Basically Black*, used comedy to make important statements about Indigenous experience. It became the first all-Indigenous television show in 1972. But its sharper observations about racism in Australia had been cut.

Since then, Indigenous characters have started to appear in mainstream shows. Here are some of the Indigenous actors you may have seen regularly on television:

- **Jack Charles** is an actor, musician and writer. He is best known for the one-man play *Jack Charles v The Crown* (2010). It talks about his life as a member of the Stolen Generations and of crime. His life is recorded in the documentary *Bastardy* (2008). He has appeared on the screen in *The Chant of Jimmie Blacksmith* (1978), *Bedevil* (1993) and *Pan* (2015). He released an autobiography in 2020, *Jack Charles: Born-again Blakfella.*

- **Rob Collins** was in the television series *Cleverman* (2016–2017). He has built a career as one of Australia's busiest actors. He has had leading roles in *The Wrong Girl* (2016–2017), *Secret City* (2019), *Glitch* (2017–2019), *Total Control* (2019–2021) and *Mystery Road* (2020). He has also found the time to appear on the big screen in *Top End Wedding* (2019) and *Extraction* (2020).

- **Ernie Dingo** has many movie credits, including *Crocodile Dundee II* and *Bran Nue Dae*. But television is where he has most regularly worked. He has been in *The Flying Doctors*, *Heartbreak High* and *Rafferty's Rules*. He has also been a host of the television program *The Great Outdoors*. He appeared in the first series of *Mystery Road*.

- **Aaron Fa'aoso** is a Torres Strait Islander, Samoan and Tongan actor. He is known for his roles in *RAN: Remote Area Nurse* (2006), *East West 101* (2007–2011) and *The Straits* (2012). He also was in the sketch series *Black Comedy* (2014–2020). He has producing roles with *The Straits* and *Blue Water Empire* (2019).

- **Gary Foley** was in the television series *The Flying Doctors* and *A Country Practice*. He began his acting career with the National Black Theatre. He returned to the stage in 2011 with a play about his life simply titled *Foley*.

- **Ningali Lawford** was also known as Ningali Lawford-Wolf. She premiered her one-woman show, *Ningali*, in 1994. She made big screen appearances in *Rabbit-Proof Fence* (2002), *Bran Nue Dae* (2009) and *Last Cab to Darwin* (2015). Her work on the small screen included *Little J and Big Cuz* (2017) and *Mystery Road* (2018). She sadly passed away while touring overseas with the play *The Secret River* in 2019.

- **Bob Maza** was in many television series, including *Bellbird* and *Heartland*. Born on Palm Island in north Queensland, his father was a Torres Strait Islander and his mother Aboriginal. He was also a playwright. His work included *The Keepers*, as well as movie credits including *The Fringe Dwellers* and *Babakiueria*. He helped to start the Nindethana theatre company and the National Black Theatre. He died in 2000.

- **Deborah Mailman** was a regular in the popular television series *Love My Way*, *The Secret Life of Us* and *Offspring*. She also had movie credits for *Radiance* and *Bran Nue Dae*. She has more recently starred in the television series *Redfern Now*, *Cleverman* and *Total Control*.

- **Jessica Mauboy** rose to fame as a contestant on *Australian Idol*. She has become one of Australia's most successful pop stars of her era. She has also carved out a career as an actress starring in *The Sapphires* (2012) and in the television series *The Secret Daughter* (2016–2017).

- **Trisha Morton-Thomas** is an actress who wrote, starred in and produced the series *8MMM Aboriginal Radio* (2015). She played Mae in *Radiance* (1998) and Jan in the series *Total Control* (2019). She wrote and directed the documentary *Occupation: Native* (2017).

- **Aaron Pedersen** began his acting career in *Heartland*. He was in the popular television series *Water Rats* for two years. He then starred in *The Circuit* and *City Homicide*. He has defined the character of Jay Swan in the films *Mystery Road* and *Goldstone* and the later television series, *Mystery Road*.

- **Leah Purcell** is an accomplished actress who has worked steadily. She appeared on the big screen in films such as *Lantana* (2001), *Jindabyne* (2006) and *Last Cab to Darwin* (2015). On the small screen, she has appeared in series including *Fallen Angels* (1997), *Janet King* (2014–2017) and *Wentworth* (2018–2021). Leah also has had major success on the stage with her play *The Drover's Wife* (2016). She wrote and starred in it. She has also turned it into a feature film that she directed!

- **Justine Saunders** was the first Indigenous person to appear as a regular in a mainstream soap opera, *Number 96*, in 1976. She went on to appear in other television series, including *Prisoner* and *Heartland*. She also starred in the mini-series *Women of the Sun*, many films and on stage.

- **Miranda Tapsell** co-wrote and starred in the film *Top End Wedding* (2019). She also appeared as Cynthia in *The Sapphires* (2012). Her television credits include leading roles in *Love Child* (2014–2017), *Newtown's Law* (2017), *Little J and Big Cuz* (2017) and *Doctor Doctor* (2018–2021). In 2020 she released a memoir, *Top End Girl*.

⤳ **Meyne Wyatt** is an actor who wrote the critically acclaimed play *City of Gold* (2019). He has worked regularly on the stage including in the lead role of *Peter Pan*. He has also appeared in the television shows *Redfern Now* (2013) and *Mystery Road* (2018). In 2014, he joined the main cast of the show *Neighbours*. He was the first Indigenous actor to do so since it began in 1985. In 2020, he won the Packing Room Prize in the prestigious Archibald Prize for his self-portrait.

Shows focusing on Indigenous issues, with a news and current affairs format, were developed on publicly funded television. These have included the ABC's *Message Stick* and SBS's *Living Black*. Several television series also focused on dramatic narratives about Indigenous people and issues. They include *Burned Bridge*, also known as *Heartland*, *The Circuit* and *RAN: Remote Area Nurse*.

National Indigenous Television (NITV) is an initiative that Indigenous people involved with filmmaking and media pushed for. It has provided a chance for the development of more Indigenous content.

THE RIGHT DIRECTION: WESLEY ENOCH

Wesley Enoch is one of Australia's best known, most successful Indigenous playwrights and directors. Enoch trained at the Queensland University of Technology. There he earned a Bachelor of Arts (Drama) and started the QUT Bonsani Commedia Troupe.

Enoch has written several plays, including *Black Medea*, inspired by the play by Euripides. He has directed theatre productions at the Sydney Theatre Company and Company B of Belvoir St Theatre. These include *The 7 Stages of Grieving*, which he co-wrote with Deborah Mailman, and Jane Harrison's *Stolen*. He also debuted the work *I am Eora* at the Sydney Festival 2012. It brought together the stories of three Indigenous identities from

(continued)

(continued)

the time of the start of the colony at Sydney Cove. They are the resistance warrior Pemulwuy; Bennelong, who lived between the new colony and his own community; and his wife, Barangaroo. (All of these people are profiled in Chapter 6.)

Enoch's work explores issues of Aboriginal identity and culture. He has been a strong voice for the start of a National Indigenous Theatre Company. Enoch was the Artistic Director of Queensland Theatre Company from 2010 to 2015. From 2015 to 2020, he was the Artistic Director of the Sydney Festival.

Notable Indigenous television shows

Many television shows have brought Indigenous issues to a broad Australian audience. Here are some of them:

- *Basically Black* (1973) was the first Indigenous television show written and created by Indigenous people. It was based on a political review staged at the Black Theatre. Writers and actors included Gary Foley and Bob Maza. The series was a searing look at racism in Australia. It had cheeky humour with some elements censored by the ABC. It remains a classic.

- *Women of the Sun* (1981) was a ground-breaking television mini-series. It was originally broadcast on SBS television and later on the ABC. It had four stories set in different periods. They were looking at first-contact in the 1820s, frontier violence in the 1860s, life on the reserves in the 1930s and modern issues in the 1980s. It stars Naykakan Munung, Yangathu Wanambi and Gordon Lunyupi. There were also appearances by Essie Coffey, Justine Saunders and Bob Maza.

- *Message Stick* (1999 to 2018) showcased documentaries either made by Indigenous filmmakers or about Indigenous people. It aired on the ABC. Indigenous producers Grant Saunders and Miriam Corowa created the show. But it also showcased the work of other Indigenous producers such as Darlene Johnson and Kelrick Martin. Presenters also included Aden Ridgeway, Trisha Moreton Thomas, Rachael Maza and Deborah Mailman.

- *Bush Mechanics* **(2001)** originally screened on the ABC. This unique series was developed by Warlpiri Media. It was based in the Central Australian community of Yuendumu. It follows the adventures of a group of men from the community on their travels through the desert. In the last episode they drive to Broome in the Kimberley, across the Tanami Track. Along the way they have to solve their car troubles through innovative mechanical repairs. It also has stories and reflections of people from the area, giving a rich view of Warlpiri life. The show stars Francis Jupurrula Kelly, who co-directed it with David Batty. There was a cameo performance from Stephen 'Baamba' Albert, of *Bran Nue Dae* fame, as Jungala the Rainmaker in Episode 4.

- *Living Black* **(2003 to present)** is a current affairs program that focuses on the issues affecting Indigenous Australians. It is hosted by Karla Grant and airs on SBS. The program seeks to educate a broad audience about issues that don't always get an airing on mainstream television.

- *Heartland* **(2003)**, also known as *Burned Bridge*, is set in a small coastal town. It focuses on the mysterious death of an Aboriginal girl, the boyfriend accused of her murder and the two people who believe he is innocent. It stars Ernie Dingo, Cate Blanchett, Justine Saunders, Bob Maza and Rachel Maza. It includes appearances by Aaron Pedersen, Lillian Crombie, Lydia Miller and Luke Carroll.

- *RAN: Remote Area Nurse* **(2006)** is based in the Torres Strait Islands. It highlights some of the unique aspects of Torres Strait Islander culture. It follows the life of a remote area nurse working in the island communities. The show deals with cultural conflict, alcohol abuse, family dramas and the challenges of the environment. It aired on SBS. Its Indigenous stars include Charles Passi, Luke Carroll,

Margaret Harvey, Jimi Gela, Belford Lui and Dan Mosby. Locals also performed as extras and helped with production.

☑ *The Circuit* (2007) starred Aaron Pedersen as an Indigenous lawyer who moves to the Kimberley area to work on the court circuit. The series also has appearances from Kimberley actors Stephen 'Baamba' Albert and Ningali Lawford. Indigenous filmmaker Catriona McKenzie directed the series. A second series aired in 2009.

☑ *First Australians* (2008) is a landmark documentary directed by Rachel Perkins and Beck Cole. Producers include Darren Dale. Each episode covers a period of Australia's colonial history with a focus on the characters who experienced historic events.

☑ *8MMM Aboriginal Radio* (2015) is a six-part comedy series set at a local Aboriginal radio station. It looks at the issues that face the station along with the broader issues facing the community in Alice Springs. The series shows the tough, systemic issues facing the characters and their families. It also shows the way issues are faced with innovation and humour. The series stars Trisha Moreton Robinson, Shari Sebbins and Elaine Crombie. It was directed by Dena Curtis.

☑ *Black Comedy* (2014 **to present**) is a sketch comedy show that has been a showcase for Indigenous writing and comedy performance. It has included standout performances by Nakkiah Lui, Steven Oliver, Adam Briggs, Elizabeth Wymarra, Bjorn Stewart and Aaron Fa'aoso.

☑ *The Gods of Wheat Street* (2014) is more than just a family drama. It mixes social realism with magic realism to create a unique Indigenous story. Written by Jon Bell, it stars Kelton Pell as Odin Freeburn. It also stars Leah Flanagan, Shari Sebbens, Rarriwuy Hicks, Ursula Yovich and Miah Madden. It was directed by Wayne Blair, Catriona McKenzie and Adrian Russell Wills.

- *Art + Soul* (**2010–2014**) is narrated by curator Hetti Perkins. It explores modern Aboriginal and Torres Strait Islander art through the themes of Home + Away, Dreams + Nightmares and Bitter + Sweet. The show was directed by Warwick Thornton and Steven McGregor.

- *Redfern Now* (**2012–2013**) is a ground-breaking series. Each episode is a stand-alone story based around the inner-city suburb of Redfern. It provided a platform for Indigenous writers, directors and actors.

- *Cleverman* (**2016–2017**) was created by Ryan Griffin. It is set in the near future and sees creatures from ancient mythology seeking a way to co-exist in the modern world. The series cleverly explores ideas of racism and xenophobia. It was directed by Wayne Blair and Leah Purcell. It stars Hunter Page-Lochard, Rob Collins, Deborah Mailman, Rarriwuy Hick, Tasma Walton and Jada Alberts.

- *Mystery Road* (**2018–2020**) is a series based on the character Detective Jay Swan, played by Aaron Pedersen. It's a role he also played in the 2013 Ivan Sen film of the same name and its follow up, *Goldstone* (2016). The series was directed by Rachel Perkins, Wayne Blair and Warwick Thornton. Jay Swan's investigations go beyond the surface to uncover deeper systemic corruption and injustice.

- *Total Control* (**2019–2021**) stars Deborah Mailman as Senator Alex Irving. She is parachuted into parliament by Prime Minister Rachel Anderson, played by Rachel Griffiths. Alex struggles to get outcomes for her community as she navigates the shady world of political self-interests and corruption. Rob Collins plays her brother, Charlie. Rachel Perkins directed the first season of the show.

- *The Beach* (**2020**) is six-part television series that follows director Warwick Thornton as he retreats to a remote beach for several months. Without power, he has to go back to basics. The series also showcases the work of cinematographer Dylan River.

STAN GRANT JR: A GLOBAL VOICE

Stan Grant Jr is ABC's International Affairs Analyst. After beginning his career as a newsreader and radio presenter, he became a television presenter on Australian commercial and public broadcasters. He has worked around the world, including a period as a journalist and correspondent for CNN. His books *Talking to My Country* (2016) and *Australia Day* (2019) have been best sellers. He also wrote and narrated the documentary *The Australian Dream* (2019) about the racial abuse of AFL star Adam Goodes and wider racism in Australia.

Indigenous media organisations

Indigenous people have appeared more on Australian television screens. But Indigenous people were always interested in making their own content and controlling its distribution.

Urban communities such as Redfern had a great interest in developing media groups. Some remoter communities also saw the benefits of being able to broadcast their own content on radio or television.

A report requested by the federal government in 1984 was called *Out of the Silent Land*. It focused on the impact of satellite on remote areas in the central parts of Australia. As a result, the Broadcasting for Remote Aboriginal Community Scheme (BRACS) was introduced. Its purpose was giving people access to and control of their own media services by supplying basic equipment. Communities could receive mainstream content off satellites or produce their own instead. The scheme became the Remote Indigenous Broadcast Service in the mid-2000s.

Indigenous-controlled media companies have done well across Australia. They use both radio and television to tell their stories and maintain their culture and languages:

- **Central Australia Aboriginal Media Association (CAAMA)** was started in 1980 by John Macumba and Freda Glynn — both Indigenous — and Phillip Batty. CAAMA's vision is to promote Indigenous culture, language, dance and music. CAAMA's radio network is broadcast on 8KIN FM. It has a music label, CAAMA Music, as well as a film and television production company, CAAMA Productions. It produces programs about Indigenous culture and issues.

- **Goolarri Media Enterprises** was set up in 1991 and runs in Broome, Western Australia. It develops media content and supports Indigenous musicians in the area.

- **Imparja Television** broadcast its first show, an Australia versus Sri Lanka test cricket match, in 1988. Imparja is a private company owned by Indigenous people in the Northern Territory and South Australia. By 2008, its audience had grown to over 430,000. It now services over 700,000 people. It also broadcasts NITV (see the next section) on its second channel.

- **Pilbara and Kimberley Aboriginal Media (PAKAM)** is an association of Indigenous producers and broadcasters in the Pilbara and Kimberley regions of Western Australia. It supports 12 remote radio and television stations and 8 town-based radio stations. It covers an area of over a million square kilometres. PAKAM also has a training program that it runs with Goolarri media.

- **PY Media** started in the Ernabella community in north-western South Australia. It was first Ernabella Video and Television (EVTV). PY Media was developed in 1987 to deliver content developed by the local Indigenous community across the Anangu Pitjantjatjara Yankunytjatjara (APY) Lands.

- **Warlpiri Media** is based at Yuendumu in Central Australia. Warlpiri people began experimenting with video production and started the first Aboriginal television station in Australia in 1983. The community also started its own media group, the Warlpiri Media Association, to handle these activities. It created the popular, quirky television show *Bush Mechanics*, which aired on the ABC.

In remote communities that became involved with video production in the early 1980s, the community could decide whether to broadcast its own materials or material from elsewhere. From 1987, BRACS was rolled out to 103 communities to allow the transmission of locally produced radio and television. Today, 71 remote Indigenous communities have a community broadcasting licence that lets them broadcast their own radio and television content locally. Another 76 communities have a television licence that lets them retransmit material. Indigenous Community Television (ICTV) was started in 2001 as a way for remote communities across Australia to share their videos. It was one of the groups that supported the start of National Indigenous Television (NITV).

National Indigenous Television

In 2004, a committee was formed to oversee the creation of a national Indigenous television service. At the time, research estimated that only two hours per week of Indigenous programming aired on Australian television.

The idea was supported by Indigenous media groups such as Goolari Media Enterprises, ICTV, Warlpiri Media, CAAMA and Imparja. They wanted to see more Indigenous content created for and broadcast on television.

In 2005, the federal government funded the creation of NITV. On 13 July 2007, NITV was launched. It originally aired on Imparja's second channel. Then it was picked up by Foxtel and Austar, as well as several community television channels. It was re-launched in December 2012 by SBS as a free-to-air channel.

NITV has provided a platform for established talent and led to the rise of new talent within the industry. This talent includes new producers and new on-screen talent. Here are some of the television shows on NITV:

- *The Barefoot Rugby League Show* was a weekly show focused on rugby league. It was co-hosted by Brad Cooke and Tony Currie. It looked at the premier games in the NRL (National Rugby League) and at grassroots football competitions and their players. It paid tribute to Indigenous players of earlier years and the star players of today. The show ran until 2010.

In 2017, a new show was launched to cover NRL from an Indigenous perspective. *Over the Black Dot* is hosted by George Rose, Timana Tahu and Dean Widders.

✔ *Family Rules* is a reality television show featuring the Rule family, a charismatic and inspiring family of nine sisters — and one amazing mother! These women are great role models as they navigate the world and stay strong in their culture.

✔ *Letterbox* was a game show for children that taught spelling and grammatical skills. It focused on children between the ages of 10 and 12.

✔ *Little J and Big Cuz* is an animated children's show that teaches values of community, family and self-respect. Little J is five and Big Cuz is nine. They live with their nan and Old Dog. The characters are voiced by high-profile Indigenous actors, including Deborah Mailman, Miranda Tapsell, Aaron Fa'aoso, Shari Sebbins and Ningali Lawford. Episodes are also dubbed in Indigenous languages to help with bilingual education.

✔ *The Marngrook Footy Show* was a weekly show that discussed the news in Australian Rules Football. The show was first developed for radio by Grant Hansen in the mid-1990s. It lent itself to being turned into a television show when the opportunity arose. It was seen on NITV, ABC2 and SBS, still co-hosted by Grant Hansen, until 2019. It included general commentary about the sport with a focus on the performance of Indigenous players. The show ran for 12 years.

✔ *The Point* is a current affairs show that was originally anchored by Stan Grant Jr when it first aired in 2016. It remains an important source of news from an Indigenous perspective.

✔ *Yaarnz* told unique stories in short vignettes from all over the country. It was hosted by Paul Sinclair. It provided a platform for people to get their stories, achievements and points of view to a larger audience.

THE NEWS PRESENTERS AND PRODUCERS

Karla Grant presents *Living Black*, SBS's Indigenous news and current events program. She has hosted the show since 2004. Before then, from 1994, she was a producer, reporter, director and presenter on the SBS show *ICAM*. This was SBS's first Indigenous current affairs show.

Brooke Boney started as a political reporter for NITV and SBS before becoming a newsreader on ABC's Triple J. In 2018, she became the entertainment reporter on the popular morning program *Today*, on Channel 9. She was the first Indigenous Australian to land such a high-profile job on a mainstream show.

Miriam Corawa is a broadcaster, producer and presenter. She joined the ABC in 2021 as co-host of the ABC News Weekend Breakfast program. She is the weekend presenter of ABC News at Noon, and has worked on programs across the ABC and SBS, including *World News Australia* and *Message Stick*. She has co-hosted special events such as the 2008 Apology to the Stolen Generations.

Lorena Allam is a journalist who was a producer and presenter with the ABC for over 20 years. She then became the Indigenous Affairs editor at *The Guardian Australia*. She presented and produced the Indigenous arts and culture program *Awaye!* for over 14 years. She also worked on other Radio National Shows. Lorena Allam also worked outside of broadcasting at the Australian Human Rights Commission on *Bringing Them Home*, the report of the National Inquiry into the Separation of Aboriginal and Torres Strait Islander Children from Their Families, released in 1997. Since moving to *The Guardian Australia*, Lorena has been nominated for several Walkley Awards. She won the All Media: Innovation category in 2018 as part of the team who worked on the *Deaths Inside: Indigenous Deaths in Custody* project.

PROJECT

Write a biography of an Indigenous actor, filmmaker or journalist mentioned in this chapter.

PROJECT

Watch a show on NITV and write a short report on what you found interesting about it and what you learnt.

PROJECT

Watch a movie directed by an Aboriginal person and create a poster showing the themes in it.

Part 5
Dealing with Current Issues

In This Part . . .

☐ Explore some of the past reasons for Indigenous disadvantage — including lower levels of literacy, higher levels of unemployment and imprisonment, higher levels of poverty, overcrowded houses and lower levels of home ownership.

☐ Look at some real examples of programs and policies that have worked to improve Indigenous disadvantage — most of them simple but clever ideas that have been devised by Indigenous communities working to solve problems themselves.

Closing the Gap and the Way Forward

IN THIS CHAPTER

- Looking at past policies
- Understanding the Close the Gap approach
- Exploring Indigenous health issues
- Thinking about the role of housing
- Stepping up the education ladder
- Studying employment
- Keeping Indigenous children with their families

Indigenous people make up 3.3 per cent of the Australian population. Yet, on all social measures, they don't have the same chances or living standards as other Australians.

Australian governments have created policies in relation to Indigenous people. But none of these strategies has been successful in creating equality. The key strategy now is to Close the Gap on Indigenous disadvantage.

All the factors that affect the lives of so many Indigenous people create a cycle of poverty. These factors include poor health, literacy, housing, education and income. Poor health can be made worse by poor-quality housing and overcrowding. It affects the ability to take part in education and jobs. This, in turn, leads to lower incomes. That makes housing and health care harder to get.

Indigenous people continue to search for and use the best solutions to these tough problems. They are looking for effective ways to break the cycle. These include

✓ Starting Indigenous medical services to better provide more targeted health care to Indigenous people and their communities

✓ Training more Indigenous doctors

✓ Using programs designed to keep children interested in school

✓ Giving support to Indigenous businesses

In this chapter, I look at the key federal government policies of the past that have been used in relation to Indigenous people. I look at some numbers and show the differences between Indigenous and non-Indigenous Australians. I also look at the huge efforts by Indigenous people to make positive change.

Looking Back at Past Government Policies

The British government had trouble controlling how policies were used across their different colonies such as Australia. Local opinions and the settlers' priorities shaped the government's approach to Indigenous peoples. But across the country, an era of protection and assimilation was created. Policies included removing Indigenous children, denying the right to vote and refusing to grant equal wages. This happened through both the 19th and 20th centuries.

It wasn't until the 1967 referendum that Indigenous policy became a national focus. That's when the duty of Indigenous policy was also given to the federal government. (See Chapter 9 for more information.)

The Whitlam government started a policy of self-determination in 1972. This policy remained in various forms (although never the way Indigenous people wanted) until the election of the

Howard government. The policy of self-determination was then replaced. The focus moved to addressing the differences between Indigenous and non-Indigenous Australians.

Moving from 'amity' to 'practical reconciliation'

The following provides a little more detail on how the various policies relating to Indigenous peoples played out:

- ✔ **'Amity and kindness':** Governor Phillip was ordered by his bosses in Britain to deal with Aboriginal people in the new colony with 'amity and kindness'. Phillip was given no direct instructions to make treaties. He got no details on the rights of Aboriginal people. Colonial law was put into place. Aboriginal people had to follow it. The colonies were left to have polite relationships with the Aboriginal people. But they were much more affected by local factors rather than policies created in Britain. The relationship with Aboriginal people focused on conflict over land and resources. The Aboriginal population was also heavily hurt by disease. Numbers went down significantly. (See Chapter 7 for more on how Aboriginal people were affected in the first decades of colonisation.) This broke up traditional practices and kinship systems.

- ✔ **Protection:** By the 1880s, large pieces of land had been taken from Aboriginal people. They had been pushed onto reserves, as part of the *protection* policy. Governments believed that Indigenous people had to be protected. At the time, governments thought that Indigenous peoples were dying out. This belief was based on the large drops in Indigenous populations since 1788. (Chapter 9 talks about protection in more detail.)

The reserves were heavily regulated by white managers. The food and housing were poor. Education was limited. Marriage, work and movement around the country were all regulated. The policy of removing Indigenous children from their families was used on a larger scale. (Refer to Chapter 9 for more about the Stolen Generations.) Of course, Indigenous populations didn't die out. Instead, they began to grow.

- **Assimilation:** This became a formal government policy in the 1950s. But *assimilation* policy had actually been influential well before then. The policy stated that the best way for Indigenous peoples to fit into Australian society was to demand that they give up their cultures, languages and traditions. The policy stated that Indigenous peoples should live like white people. (Chapter 9 gives more detail.) The policy focused on Indigenous children, especially 'half-castes'. It removed children from their families. It either sent them to institutions where they could learn 'white ways' or adopted them into white families. Removing Indigenous children from their families was the most obvious and cruellest part of assimilation (refer to Chapter 8). Racism and exclusion ran so deep in society that many Indigenous people were denied the benefits of citizenship that other Australians had. This was much the same as under the protection policy.

REMEMBER

Indigenous people were told that they had to behave more like white people. But they never got basic rights. 'Behaving more like white people' was impossible. Also, Indigenous people were proud of their identity and culture. They didn't want to give it up. Towards the end of the 1960s, governments started to talk about *integration* instead of assimilation. This was the idea that Indigenous peoples could keep their cultures and still fit into broader Australian society. Non-British immigrants had done this in growing numbers since the end of World War II.

- **Self-determination:** The 1967 referendum results meant that the federal government now had some duty for Indigenous issues. It began to create national policies. (Refer to Chapter 9 for more on the referendum.) Self-determination was introduced as a policy by the Whitlam government in 1972. (It was a reaction to the assimilation policy). *Self-determination* is defined as the right of all peoples to 'freely determine their political status and freely pursue their economic, social and cultural development'. It affected government policy on Indigenous people until the Howard government was elected in 1996. Self-determination, in Australia, was taken to mean that Indigenous people should be part of creating policies that affected them. They do this most effectively by creating community organisations that work on specific issues such as health, education, employment, training and housing. (See Chapter 17 for more details on Indigenous self-determination.)

✔ **Practical reconciliation:** The Howard government came to power in 1996. It didn't have the same views on Indigenous affairs as the previous Labor governments. John Howard said that his government would adopt a policy of *practical reconciliation.* The focus for his government was on improving practical issues such as health, housing, education and job outcomes. To achieve this, the government embraced ideas of shared responsibility and mutual obligation. An example of this was services or infrastructure being offered to Indigenous communities in exchange for behavioural changes, such as sending children to school.

Closing the gap

Kevin Rudd came to power in 2007 as the leader of the new Labor government. He set the stage for a change of Indigenous policy by making an important symbolic statement. He made an apology for the removal policy (refer to Chapter 10).

The focus of the Rudd and Gillard Labor governments (2007 to 2013) was on 'closing the gap' between Indigenous and non-Indigenous Australians on many social measures. A report card on closing the gap was presented during the first sitting week of each year's parliament.

The original Close the Gap target areas were:

- ✓ Halve the gap in child death rates for Indigenous children under five by 2018

- ✓ Ensure 95 per cent of all Indigenous four-year-olds enrolled in early childhood education by 2025

- ✓ Close the gap between Indigenous and non-Indigenous school attendance by 2018

- ✓ Halve the gap for Indigenous children in reading, writing and math within a decade by 2018

- ✓ Halve the gap for rates of Indigenous Australians aged 20 to 24 attaining Year 12 or equivalent by 2020

- ✓ Halve the gap in job outcomes between Indigenous and non-Indigenous Australians by 2018

- ✓ Close the life expectancy gap by 2021

By 2020, only the targets for early childhood education and Year 12 attainment were on track.

REMEMBER

The Close the Gap agenda was a new approach to Indigenous Affairs. But in other ways, the Rudd and Gillard government's policies didn't change from those of the previous government. Examples included continued support for welfare quarantining and other aspects of the Northern Territory intervention. (See Chapter 10 for more on the intervention.)

A NOTE ON STATISTICS

Collecting data from Indigenous people is hard. The Australian Bureau of Statistics (ABS) conducts the Australian census. It says that it has problems in getting Indigenous people to fill in the forms that let them be counted in the figures. To make matters harder, Indigenous people weren't carefully counted for the purpose of figuring out the total population until 1971. This makes comparative figures tough to establish.

Closing the Gap Reboot

Making any major headway on most of the Close the Gap targets failed repeatedly. The Morrison government revealed new and bigger Close the Gap targets in 2020.

As part of this reboot, a National Agreement on Closing the Gap was developed. This agreement was created between the Australian government and Aboriginal and Torres Strait Islander peak bodies. This means a closer relationship between government and Indigenous community-controlled groups. It was seen as a positive step in making better progress.

The new targets include

- Close the gap in life expectancy within a generation by 2031

- Increase the proportion of Aboriginal and Torres Strait Islander babies with a healthy birthweight to 91 per cent by 2031

- Increase the proportion of Aboriginal and Torres Strait Islander children enrolled in early childhood education (the year before school starts) to 95 per cent

- Increase the proportion of Aboriginal and Torres Strait Islander children assessed as developmentally on track in different areas (such as health and language skills) to 55 per cent by 2031

- Increase the proportion of Aboriginal and Torres Strait Islander people aged 20 to 24 attaining Year 12 or equivalent qualification to 96 per cent by 2031

- Increase the proportion of Aboriginal and Torres Strait Islander people aged 25 to 34 years who have completed a tertiary qualification (Certificate III and above) to 70 per cent by 2031

- Increase the proportion of Aboriginal and Torres Strait Islander youth (15 to 24 years) who are in employment, education or training to 67 per cent by 2031

✔ Increase the proportion of Aboriginal and Torres Strait Islander people aged 25 to 64 who are employed to 62 per cent by 2031

✔ Increase the proportion of Aboriginal and Torres Strait Islander people living in appropriately sized (not over-crowded) housing to 88 per cent by 2031

✔ Reduce the incarceration rate of Aboriginal and Torres Strait Islander adults by at least 15 per cent by 2031

✔ Reduce the rate of Aboriginal and Torres Strait Islander young people (10 to 17 years) in detention by 30 per cent by 2031

✔ Reduce the rate of over-representation of Aboriginal and Torres Strait Islander children in out-of-home care by 45 per cent by 2031

✔ A significant and sustained reduction in violence and abuse against Aboriginal and Torres Strait Islander women and children towards zero

✔ Significant and sustained reduction in suicide Aboriginal and Torres Strait Islander people towards zero

✔ A 15 per cent increase in Australia's landmass subject to Aboriginal and Torres Strait Islander people's legal rights or interests and a 15 per cent increase in areas covered by Aboriginal and Torres Strait Islander people's legal rights or interests in the sea by 2030

✔ A sustained increase in number and strength of Aboriginal and Torres Strait Islander languages being spoken by 2031

To help with reaching the Close the Gap targets, four Priority Reforms were also outlined:

✔ Strengthen and create formal partnerships and shared decision-making

✔ Build the Aboriginal and Torres Strait Islander community-controlled sector

✔ Transform government organisations so they work better for Aboriginal and Torres Strait Islander peoples

✔ Improve and share access to data and information to let Aboriginal and Torres Strait Islander communities make informed decisions

PRE-CONTACT LIFESTYLES WERE HEALTHIER

Historians believe that Indigenous Australians had better levels of health before 1788. Indigenous peoples had traditional diets made up of food that was hunted, fished or gathered. Much of this food was rich in vitamins and minerals. No processed food was included in the diet. There was little fat, only unprocessed sugars and no alcohol. Hunting and gathering involve a lot of physical activity. They also include many natural remedies. (Refer to Chapter 4 for more details.)

Many of the diseases in European countries at the time didn't exist in Australia. These include scarlet fever, tuberculosis, syphilis and measles. So, when the Europeans arrived, these new diseases had a terrible effect on the Indigenous peoples. They couldn't fight these diseases because they had not developed immunity to them. Smallpox, measles, whooping cough and influenza were particularly deadly.

The impact of these diseases led to a huge drop in numbers in the Indigenous population. This meant that the social structures of Indigenous communities were weakened. Health was also affected by the impact of European settlement. In particular, farming practices destroyed traditional food bases. So, from the earliest days of the colony, a cycle of poor health began in Indigenous communities.

Examining Health Issues

A key measure of the difference between the health of Indigenous and non-Indigenous people is the difference in life expectancy between the two groups. The life expectancy for Indigenous males is 71.6 years, while it's 80.2 years for non-Indigenous males. For Indigenous females, life expectancy is 75.6 years; it's 83.4 years for non-Indigenous females. Part of the reason for the difference is that the health of Australians as a whole has improved over recent decades. This is due in part to better medicines and treatment of diseases. But the health of Indigenous peoples hasn't improved at the same rate.

MYTH
BUSTER

✔ **Alcohol:** Overall, the Indigenous population drinks less alcohol per capita than the general Australian population. But there is a higher level of excessive drinking among the group that does drink. In fact, Indigenous people are more likely to stay away from alcohol than the general Australian population. This is especially true in more remote areas.

✔ **Obesity:** Of Indigenous people aged 15 and over, 69 per cent are overweight or obese. The rate for men is about the same as for the general Australian community. Indigenous women are one and half times more likely to be overweight or obese than other Australian women.

✔ **Smoking:** The proportion of smokers in the Indigenous population is almost three times that of the non-Indigenous population. Rates of smoking have decreased among Australians overall in the last three decades. But the rate of smoking among Indigenous people remains high.

Inequality in standards of health is partly a result of lack of access to primary health care. Historically, Indigenous people weren't given enough access to doctors. They were, for example, only given medical attention on the verandahs of hospitals. They were not allowed in the beds in the wards. The long-term effect of this discrimination meant that Indigenous people had poorer health levels. This was made worse by poorer access to doctors and hospitals.

By the 1970s, Indigenous communities were interested in starting their own medical services. This would be a way around the racism they faced in the mainstream health system. People also believed that Indigenous health services were better able to target the health issues unique to Indigenous communities. They were staffed by Indigenous people and skilled doctors and nurses.

The first Indigenous-controlled medical service opened in 1971 in Redfern. The service has grown quickly since then. As with other Indigenous medical services, the Aboriginal Medical Service Cooperative in Redfern has grown to include primary and preventative health care programs and a dental clinic. Specific programs target nutrition, health-worker education and immunisation. Many services are also in remote and regional communities. This is often a result of the work of local communities.

These Indigenous community-controlled medical services and health groups started the National Aboriginal Community Controlled Health Organisation (NACCHO). It started in 1976 as the National Aboriginal and Islander Health Organisation (NAIHO). Today it represents over 140 health services. (You can visit the website at www.naccho.org.au.) The Torres Strait Islander community has also started its own health services to meet the community's needs.

REMEMBER

Aboriginal women were trained as nurses from the 1960s. But the growing number of Indigenous people trained as doctors is a more recent change. The Australian Indigenous Doctors Association (AIDA) was started in 1998. It had the aim of improving the health and life outcomes of Indigenous people. AIDA fights for improvements in Indigenous health. It gives expert advice to government and health bodies. It encourages Indigenous people to become doctors. It also gives support to Indigenous medical students and works closely with medical schools within Australian universities.

FRED HOLLOWS AND THE TRACHOMA PROJECT

Fred Hollows was originally from Dunedin in New Zealand. He graduated from the medical school at Otago University. He then studied ophthalmology in the United Kingdom and went on to work for three years as an Ophthalmic Registrar in Cardiff, Wales.

In 1965, Hollows moved to Sydney. He became Associate Professor of Ophthalmology at the University of New South Wales. He visited towns in rural New South Wales. He was shocked by the poor eye health among Indigenous people in those communities, particularly from trachoma.

He helped start the Aboriginal Medical Service in Redfern in 1971. He began travelling to Indigenous communities with a team of colleagues to survey and provide eye care services. Hollows started the National Trachoma and Eye Health Program (NTEHP) to carry out this work. He and his team visited over 465 communities, screened 100,000 people, treated 27,000 people for trachoma and performed 1,000 eye operations. In 1992, the Fred Hollows Foundation was started to ensure his work would continue. Hollows passed away in 1993 but left a lasting legacy.

Looking at Housing Problems

Good housing is an important part of having a healthy environment. Some health problems in Indigenous communities are caused or made worse by poor-quality housing and overcrowding. In some cases, poor hygiene and poor water and sewerage infrastructure are common. (See the preceding section for more details on health.)

An important part of housing and its links to health is the number of people living in a dwelling. Overcrowding is a problem in the Indigenous community. This brings many connected health and social problems. The statistics show that, on average, 3.4 people live in Indigenous households. This is compared with 2.6 people in total Australian households. The number increases in remote areas. In these areas, Indigenous households have an average of 5.3 people per household. Across Australia, 78.9 per cent of Indigenous people are adequately housed. This is compared to 92.9 per cent of non-Indigenous people.

Over 29 per cent of Indigenous Australians aged over 15 have been homeless at some time. This is compared to 13 per cent of non-Indigenous Australians.

Figures from 2018 showed 38 per cent of Indigenous people owned their own home. This is compared to 66 per cent of non-Indigenous people. Figures also showed that 57 per cent rented (36 per cent were private renters and 21 per cent were in social housing).

A few factors explain the lower rates of home ownership among Indigenous Australians. In some remote communities, large numbers of houses don't exist. (Indigenous people in remote areas are even less likely to own their own homes than in urban or rural areas.) Housing is also expensive everywhere. Being able to afford to buy a home in relation to income is an issue. Also, Indigenous people are more likely than other Australians to have irregular work or income streams. This makes home ownership tough.

In addition to overcrowding, poor infrastructure in housing can also cause health problems. Examples of poor infrastructure are sewerage and water problems, leaking roofs and rising damp. In a 2014–2015 National Survey, one in five Indigenous Australians were living in a house that did not meet acceptable standards. In remote areas, 27 per cent lived in houses that didn't have basic household facilities. And 31 per cent were in dwellings that did not meet acceptable standards.

REMEMBER

Health problems can occur with overcrowding or poor-quality sewerage and no clean water. It's worrying that over 16 per cent of houses where Indigenous children live have been classed as being of poor quality. Children have trouble studying and being school-ready in places that are overcrowded or have poor infrastructure. For example, poor water quality and sewerage can lead to problems with hygiene. Poor hygiene can lead to a greater risk of infectious diseases. Ear infections can hurt the ability for children to hear in class. They make it harder for them to engage in school and to learn.

Overall the Australian Institute of Health and Welfare has noted that compared to all other Australians, Indigenous Australians are

- Half as likely to own their own home

- Ten times as likely to live in social housing

- Three times more likely to live in overcrowded housing

- Nine times more likely to access services for homelessness

TRADITIONAL (AND NOT-SO-TRADITIONAL) HOUSING

Indigenous communities around Australia had different forms of traditional housing. These ranged from lean-tos made of stringybark to round dwellings made of thatched grass, trees or spinifex. Stone huts were used in the colder climates of the country. Traditional communities knew where the closest water sources were. But they also knew how to collect water by evaporation. Techniques were also developed to filter water such as by straining it through spinifex grass.

Towns and pastoral properties were built as European settlement spread through Australia. Camps of Indigenous people grew around the fringes of settlements. (They had been pushed off their traditional lands.) Dwellings were made of any available material, such as bark, hessian bags, wood and corrugated iron. The floors were either dirt or made of pieces of linoleum or carpet. This type of housing and living arrangement was common up until the 1960s. (Indigenous people were still excluded from entering towns during certain times then.)

Learning about Education Issues

Good education is a pathway to employment. It is important for being able to fully participate in many levels of society. But on this measure, Indigenous children fall behind non-Indigenous children. They have poorer levels of literacy and math skills. They have poorer attendance rates at school and poorer achievement rates. They're less likely to finish high school and much less likely to attend university. These differences start early in the educational pathway. The differences only become greater as students move through the education system.

REMEMBER

Much thought has been given to why Indigenous children don't go to school as regularly as non-Indigenous children and why they don't have the same levels of academic achievement. The main reasons Indigenous children don't stay in school include

▸ A curriculum that doesn't engage them

▸ Health problems making hearing and learning difficult

▸ Not enough books, chairs, desks and teachers in schools in certain areas

▸ Overcrowding at home (no environment in which to study and be school-ready)

▸ Poor quality of teaching in certain locations

▸ Teachers having low expectations of Indigenous students

▸ An unfriendly culture at the school that makes students feel bad

In the following sections, I look at problems in Indigenous education at each of the three levels of schooling (primary, secondary and tertiary). I also look at the benefits of vocational education and training for Indigenous youth.

ALICE SPRINGS TOWN CAMPS

Several town camps developed around Alice Springs for Indigenous people who had been left out of mainstream services in the town. The camps were often groups of people from the same language area. Over time they turned into permanent communities. The residents of the 18 camps started a community group called Tangentyere Council to advocate on their behalf in the 1970s. The council worked to get the residents legal ownership over the land they were camping on. It also worked to help in getting needed services such as water and electricity. The council also runs a range of services. These include a breakfast program at Yipirinye school, a night patrol, an art centre, a community banking facility and a 'work for welfare' employment program. The population of the town camps averages around 2,000. But it can reach up to 3,500 when certain events are held, such as sports events or meetings.

Primary education

Indigenous students fall behind non-Indigenous students early on. This gap in learning begins in the earliest years. Some headway has been made on closing this gap. This is partly because Indigenous preschool enrolments have grown to 84.6 per cent in 2018 from 76.7 per cent in 2016. This is also partly because rates for Australian students overall have dropped, from 91.9 per cent in 2016 to 88.8 per cent in 2018.

The Close the Gap target to halve the gap for Indigenous children in reading, writing and math skills within a decade had not been met by 2018. But some improvement had been made in this area. The gap narrowed across all year levels by between 3 and 11 percentage points. Between 2008 and 2018, the number of Indigenous students in Year 3 exceeding the national requirements in reading increased by 20 per cent.

Even so, by 2018, one in four Indigenous students in Years 5, 7 and 9 and one in five in Year 3 were below the national minimal standards in reading. Between 17 and 19 per cent of Indigenous students were below the minimum standards in numeracy.

REMEMBER

Literacy rates are poorest among Indigenous students in remote areas. This is due to many factors. One is the difficulty of attracting and keeping teachers. Another is the lack of investment in educational needs such as classrooms and desks. In remote areas, adults often don't have good levels of literacy. This makes it hard for parents to support their children through their education.

Attendance issues also occur early on. About 88 per cent of Indigenous five year olds attend school regularly. This is compared with 95 per cent of non-Indigenous children. In 2019, the attendance rate for Indigenous primary students overall was 85 per cent. This is compared with 94 per cent of non-Indigenous children. Very few Australians have never attended school (just 0.9 per cent). But 2.5 per cent of Indigenous people have never been to school.

BILINGUAL EDUCATION

Children learn best when taught in the language they speak at home. For some Indigenous children, English is their second language. This is a challenge for their teachers.

Just one example is the school community at Areyonga, west of Alice Springs and the most northern Pitjantjatjara community. Children are first taught to read and write, speak and listen in Pitjantjatjara. But at the same time, they're taught in English. When they're older, they have half their lessons in reading and writing English. The rest of the time focuses on Pitjantjatjara literacy. From the age of 13, students then study only in English. Local Elders are a consistent part of the program. They teach in the school.

(continued)

(continued)

In 2008, the Northern Territory government, supported by the federal government, ordered that all schools must give instruction in English for the first four hours of the day. This decision effectively closed bilingual education in remote Indigenous schools. The challenges facing bilingual education stem from their resource-heavy nature. This includes the time that teachers need to develop their skills in the local Indigenous language (meaning spending time in the community). But it has been hard to attract teachers to remote communities in the Northern Territory. On average, teachers posted to those communities stay about 15 months.

Secondary education

More Indigenous students stay on to Year 10 and Year 12 than a generation ago. But the retention and completion rates are much lower for Indigenous Australians than for all other Australians. A gap still exists: 63.2 per cent of Indigenous 20 to 24-year olds had a Year 12 equivalent in 2016 (up from 39.4 per cent in 2001). This is compared to 88.5 per cent for their non-Indigenous counterparts (up from 77.6 per cent in 2001).

Attendance rates for Indigenous students are lower for non-Indigenous students (82 per cent compared to 92 per cent in 2019). By Year 10, Indigenous students go to school 72 per cent of the time on average. This is a gap of around 17 percentage points.

REMEMBER

The key to keeping children in school and improving attendance rates is to build up the relationship between the community and the school. A great example of how this works comes from Chris Sarra. He was the principal of Cherbourg State School, Queensland, in the late 1990s. The school had over 250 students. Many of them were from disadvantaged Indigenous backgrounds. Sarra changed the performance of students through programs to improve school attendance and to increase the community's involvement in the school. Sarra went on to start the Stronger Smarter Institute at the Queensland University of Technology. The institute continues this work on a larger scale. Sarra's work runs on the belief that Indigenous children need to understand that they can achieve academic excellence. But they must be confident. The program builds self-esteem through helping children be proud of their Indigenous heritage. The institute also delivers leadership programs to school principals and other educators. It supports leadership in education in Indigenous communities. In this way, the institute focuses on building up teachers and schools on the one hand, and communities and parents on the other.

Another program that helps Indigenous youth is the Australian Indigenous Mentoring Experience (AIME). AIME was started by Jack Manning Bancroft, an Aboriginal man. It provides a six-year mentoring program for Indigenous students while they're attending high school. Students start in Year 7 and can stay in the program all the way through to Year 12. AIME links university student volunteers with Indigenous students so they can form one-on-one mentoring relationships.

REMEMBER

PROVIDING TERTIARY INDIGENOUS EDUCATION

Two education providers stand out for their commitment to Indigenous tertiary education.

Tranby Aboriginal College was started in Glebe, Sydney, in 1958. It is the oldest Indigenous education provider in Australia. Tranby delivers courses in a cultural environment that's friendly for Indigenous students, who come from across the country to study there. Courses include leadership programs for women and young people, community management, Indigenous history and culture, and legal studies. Tranby specialises in teaching Indigenous people who have had a limited secondary education. It provides these students with a chance to study again.

(continued)

(continued)

Batchelor Institute of Indigenous Tertiary Education was started in 1999 in the Northern Territory. But it had its origins back in the 1960s. It started teaching programs as Batchelor College in 1982. It attracts Indigenous people from all over the country. But it has a particular focus on students from rural and remote parts of Australia. Batchelor has created a process of teaching that's culturally appropriate for people who may have had little chance to complete secondary education. Batchelor also focuses on teaching traditional knowledge, especially Indigenous languages. The institute is located at Batchelor, about 100 kilometres south of Darwin. But it also holds classes in Alice Springs, Katherine and Tennant Creek.

Tertiary education

Between 2008 and 2018, the number of Indigenous students enrolled in Universities doubled.

In 2001, 18 per cent of Indigenous Australians aged 25 to 34 had a qualification of Certificate III or higher. This was compared to 49.2 per cent of the total Australian population. By 2016, 42.3 per cent of Indigenous people in that age group had a tertiary qualification. This was a large increase but still behind the 72.0 per cent of the total population.

The number of Indigenous people studying at university keeps growing. In 2009, 10,440 students were enrolled. By 2013 there were 13,781. But the total number of Australians attending universities has grown at an even greater rate.

Fewer Indigenous students completing high school means that fewer Indigenous students are ready to be accepted into university. But larger numbers of mature-aged Indigenous students have come back to study after leaving school early.

REMEMBER

Most universities have programs that note that Indigenous students in the past weren't encouraged to complete high school and go to university. They provide bridging courses designed to give Indigenous people a pathway into university. Whereas 82 per cent of all Australian university students enter tertiary education through their previous education, only 46 per cent of Indigenous students enter tertiary education this way. The remainder gain entry through bridging courses.

Today, Indigenous students study in all areas. But they are more likely to be studying in the areas of law, social sciences, education and health.

Indigenous students' overall degree completion rates have increased. But these rates still sit at less than 50 per cent. In comparison, 74 per cent of their non-Indigenous peers complete their studies. Most Indigenous students note financial and academic reasons for leaving university. Many also have children, which can increase financial pressures. Universities have responded to this lower completion rate. They have programs that give support to Indigenous students and create a space within the campuses that's culturally welcoming.

Also increasing is the number of Aboriginal people and Torres Strait Islanders enrolling in and completing postgraduate studies at Australian universities. Table 16-1 shows Indigenous tertiary enrolments by course level.

Table 16-1 Indigenous Tertiary Enrolments by Course Level

Level of Course	2008	2017	Growth
Enabling course	871	1,749	101%
Non-award qualification	50	97	94%
Bachelor degree	6,352	13,528	113%
Post graduate course work	1,138	2,372	108%
Post graduate research	393	590	50%

Interestingly, the Indigenous student population at university has a higher percentage of mature-age women than the general student population. Of the total number of Indigenous students, 64 per cent are women. In the general student population, women are 55 per cent of all students.

Importantly, the number of Indigenous people who work in universities has also grown by 72.6 per cent between 2005 and 2017. Academic staff grew by 55 per cent over that period. This has meant the inclusion of more Indigenous viewpoints across all fields. But Indigenous staff still make up only about 1 per cent of the workforce at universities.

Vocational education and training (VET)

Indigenous people are much more likely to study at a tertiary institution such as TAFE and agricultural colleges rather than a university. They are more likely to take a TAFE pathway than their non-Indigenous counterparts (19.8 per cent compared to 9.8 per cent). One of the main functions of the vocational education and training (VET) sector is to train apprentices.

Indigenous students make up 3.7 per cent of the student population in the VET sector. They study in areas as diverse as plumbing, horticulture, hairdressing and hospitality. The learning pathway through VET doesn't always need completion of high school. But the VET sector can be a pathway to further studies. Within the VET sector, Indigenous students are less likely to be studying for higher level qualifications. Of Indigenous students in VET courses, 44 per cent are studying for Certificate I or II qualifications (compared with 22 per cent of non-Indigenous students). But only 13 per cent are studying for Certificate IV qualifications (compared with 21 per cent of non-Indigenous students).

About 28 per cent of young Indigenous graduates studying Certificate I and II go on to further study.

Education as a step up the ladder

Education leads to better opportunities. Indigenous people with higher levels of schooling are more likely to be in full-time employment than those with lower levels. The percentage of Indigenous youth (aged 15 to 24) in education, employment or training is 57.2 per cent. This is compared to 79.6 per cent for their non-Indigenous counterparts.

Indigenous people who have completed Year 12 are more likely to have good health and lower levels of mental stress. Completing Year 12 means a person is less likely to smoke and drink large amounts of alcohol. They're also less likely to have many diseases than Indigenous people who leave school before Year 10. These include diabetes, kidney disease and heart disease.

And each Indigenous person who graduates from university is changing the future for themselves, their family and their community.

Working on Employment Problems

Indigenous people have higher levels of unemployment than non-Indigenous Australians. Unemployment for Indigenous people traditionally sits at 8 per cent. This is compared with 3 per cent unemployment for non-Indigenous Australians. Employment for Indigenous people is at just 51 per cent (with 46 per cent not in the workforce). This is compared with 65.7 per cent employment (and 34 per cent not in the workforce) for non-Indigenous people. The Close the Gap target is to increase Indigenous employment to 62 per cent by 2031.

Indigenous employment strategies try to increase the number of Indigenous people in the workforce. Programs have been put into place in parts of the country — particularly remote areas — where not enough jobs are available for everyone. For example, many Indigenous people were employed under work-for-welfare schemes such as the Community Development

Employment Projects. But the end of these schemes has increased Indigenous unemployment rates, particularly in remote areas.

When they have jobs, Indigenous people are much more likely to work in low-skilled occupations (78 per cent), such as labouring and trades, than other Australians in the workforce (60 per cent). They are twice as likely to work part-time (75 per cent) compared with other Australians in the workforce (39 per cent). You can see a notable gender difference within the statistics of Indigenous employment. Indigenous women are much more likely to be working in professions (15 per cent) than Indigenous men (8 per cent). But this difference is not quite as notable in the non-Indigenous workforces (23 per cent of women and 17 per cent of men).

Realising why job issues exist for Indigenous people

Indigenous people had a long history of being left out of the workforce. They were often paid with food and kept as a pool of cheap labour. Indigenous girls were trained to become domestic staff. Boys were trained to do manual labour.

In the 1960s, laws were finally introduced that Indigenous people had to be paid equal wages in the pastoral industry. Many lost their jobs. Indigenous employment statistics from the 1970s to the 1990s show that the levels of employment for Indigenous people actually got worse. Statistics show that they were much more likely to be long-term unemployed. Sadly, Indigenous labour trends often run counter to the economic cycle. When the economy gets better, Indigenous employment levels don't automatically follow.

Several factors are behind the high levels of unemployment in Indigenous communities. These include poor skill levels and low levels of education. They also include health problems, contact with the criminal justice system and geographical remoteness from jobs. Indigenous people are much less likely to be employed in rural and remote communities, especially by private businesses.

Systemic racism has also caused issues with employment. In the past, Indigenous people were left out of getting quality health services. They couldn't attend school. They weren't allowed to live in towns. They were overlooked by employers because of the colour of their skin. This racism was particularly firm in rural and remote areas. In the 1970s, discriminating against people on the basis of their race became illegal in providing medical, housing and other services, and in employment.

More recent times have seen a greater push to grow the numbers of Indigenous people working in the private sector. Indigenous people have also started their own businesses to take part in the economy (see the next section).

Running Indigenous businesses

In recent years, Indigenous people have taken part in the economy by starting their own businesses. In 2016, a conservative estimate placed the number of Indigenous owned businesses at 17,900. Figures also show that the number of Indigenous people running their own businesses is growing.

In the Australian workforce, 17 per cent of people are self-employed. Of the employed Indigenous workforce, 6 per cent are self-employed (just under 7,000 people). Of those self-employed Indigenous people, 89 per cent are based in the major cities or rural areas, and 11 per cent are in remote areas.

One way communities have often become successful in business is by starting community stores to offer better quality food and other products. Art collectives are another way to find business success. Indigenous people are also pursuing opportunities in areas such as mining, eco-tourism, fashion and textiles, legal services, cultural consulting and land management.

BLACK LIVES MATTER: INDIGENOUS PEOPLE AND THE CRIMINAL JUSTICE SYSTEM

Aboriginal people and Torres Strait Islanders have a complicated relationship with the criminal justice system. They are over-represented in custody and also over-represented as victims of crime. The problem for Indigenous people is that police tend to use arrest for minor offences. They also tend to use it more frequently when first dealing with Indigenous people than they do with non-Indigenous people. Additional issues arise when Indigenous offenders appear before the courts and are sentenced.

Examining the Royal Commission into Aboriginal Deaths in Custody

The Royal Commission into Aboriginal Deaths in Custody was established in 1987. It reported to the federal parliament in 1991. The Commission was generated because of calls from Aboriginal organisations, Aboriginal Legal Services, and the families of those who had died in custody and their supporters.

The Royal Commission came up with 339 recommendations to improve the justice system, including some broader ideas for improving the relationship between Indigenous people and the criminal justice system. These recommendations included

- Better education of police and judicial officers, including judges, about the most appropriate way to deal with Aboriginal people and Torres Strait Islanders
- Educational programs that would teach the wider Australian population about the issues facing Aboriginal people and Torres Strait Islanders, as well as improve understanding about their culture and history
- Empowerment of Indigenous people through self-determination and reconciliation

✔ Improved educational and employment opportunities

✔ Improved health care and housing conditions

Stopping the cycle

Targets in the 2020 Close the Gap reboot (see earlier in this chapter) also looked at ways to decrease imprisonment rates of Indigenous adults and children.

Several reform proposals are aimed at reducing the over-representation of Indigenous people in the criminal justice system and deaths in custody. These include:

✔ Implementing the recommendations from 1991 of the Royal Commission into Aboriginal Deaths in Custody

✔ Introducing strategies that move government funding away from prisons and to programs that will prevent crime or offer alternatives to putting Indigenous people in prison. (Check out Just Reinvest for a good example of this type of approach: www.justreinvest.org.au.)

✔ Ensuring adequate funding of Indigenous legal services and community-controlled child protection agencies

✔ Creating an independent body to oversee investigations into Indigenous deaths in custody

✔ Providing culturally appropriate support for Indigenous victims of crime

✔ Removing the practice of imprisonment for smaller offences, including not paying fines, and providing a medical support for substance addiction rather than criminalising it

✔ Providing alternatives to prison, such as community service

✔ Increasing support for treatment of mental health issues

No New Stolen Generations: Keeping Indigenous Children with Their Families

An apology was delivered to the members of the Stolen Generations in 2007. But the rates of Aboriginal children being removed from their families have increased. It has almost doubled in the ten years since then. By 2018, Indigenous children were 5.5 per cent of the total number of Australian children. But they made up 37.3 per cent of the children in out-of-home care. They are 10.2 times more likely to be in out-of-home care than non-Indigenous children. When Indigenous children are removed, they are increasingly less likely to be placed with Aboriginal and Torres Strait Islander family members or carers. In 2018, only 45 per cent of Indigenous children who were removed were placed with family. (This was down from 49.4 per cent in 2017.) These are alarming trends. So much information is available now about the negative impacts on Indigenous children brought up away from their culture.

A key explanation for the statistical trend is that Indigenous children have been deemed neglected because they live in poverty. A household being overcrowded or short on food is equated with neglect. Another issue is that many child protection workers are still not Indigenous. They make cultural assumptions where they assume neglect. For example, Indigenous children are often brought up communally and then judged as neglected because they spend nights at the homes of different family members. These workers can also sometimes make biased decisions. For example, a child who is underweight is thought neglected but later found to have had a medical condition. The linking of neglect with poverty is troubling since one in three Aboriginal children live in poverty and 25 per cent of Indigenous people facing homelessness are children.

Another systemic problem is that state child protection services often don't have enough resources. Most of the effort goes into child removal. Little effort goes into supporting families in crisis or restoring children to families after a period of crisis.

REMEMBER

The Aboriginal Child Placement Principle states that where an Indigenous child needs to be removed from their family, they should be placed with an extended family member. If that isn't possible, they should be placed with another Indigenous family within their community. Where that isn't possible, they should be placed with an Indigenous family. Finally, if that isn't possible, the child should be placed with a non-Indigenous family but a cultural plan should be in place. This is great as a principle. It has been put into legislation or the rules of each Australian state and territory. But child protection agencies struggle to practise it.

TECHNICAL STUFF

The Indigenous community–controlled sector is really important in the child protection space. Child protection is a state-based issue. So state bodies such as the Victorian Aboriginal Child Care Agency (VACCA), AbSec in NSW and the Queensland Aboriginal and Torres Strait Islander Child Protection Peak (QATSICPP) play an important role. A national coalition of these groups exists in SNAICC: National Voice for Our Children. This sector is better able to understand the family and cultural circumstances of Indigenous children. It is also better placed at finding extended family and community placements for children who do need to be removed. They also focus on family support and family reunification.

The Indigenous community-controlled groups have fought for policy changes through their Family Matters campaign (www.familymatters.org.au). A key strategy for changing the trend is to use the Aboriginal Child Placement Principle. Another strategy is to further use the recommendations of the *Bringing Them Home* report, particularly the recommendation of self-determination.

REMEMBER

Some positive steps have been taken in trying to turn the statistics around. After much lobbying from the Aboriginal community–controlled sector, a measure was included in the 2020 Close the Gap targets. It focuses on ensuring children are not over-represented in the child protection system. Child protection is a state issue. But this inclusion has made the issue national.

Also, both Victoria and South Australia have a dedicated Commissioner for Aboriginal Children and Young People. Victoria and Queensland have made the strongest commitment to giving more control over to community-controlled groups. In Queensland, 33 Family Well-being Services and 12 family participation programs are now delivered by the community-controlled sector. In Victoria in 2019, 46 per cent of Indigenous children on a care order were managed by a community-controlled group.

PROJECT

Identify a Close the Gap target and write a quick report on some strategies to address it.

PROJECT

Check out the Family Matters website (`www.familymatters.org.au`) and make a poster from the information the website gives on the issue of Indigenous child protection.

Doing It for Ourselves

From the moment the First Fleet arrived in 1788, Indigenous peoples have continued to clearly state their identity as distinct peoples. They have stated their right to be responsible for and control their own lives and the policies that affect them. They have organised community and national groups to stand for their interests. This chapter goes into more detail on the idea of *self-determination.*

elf-Determination: More Than Principle

The belief that Aboriginal peoples and Torres Strait Islanders are sovereign peoples flows from the fact that Indigenous peoples have never formally given up their land. They feel distinct identities and histories. But in their political language and goals, Indigenous peoples have a unique understanding of the term *sovereignty.* This differs from what the term means under international law.

The Indigenous Australian understanding includes concepts such as

✔ Representative government and democracy

✔ The recognition of cultural distinctiveness

✔ Ideas of the freedom of the individual

These claims seek a new relationship with the Australian state. This relationship would have increased self-government and power for Indigenous peoples. But it wouldn't mean the creation of a new country.

Self-determination is a human right and a political goal of Indigenous people. Research shows that the more Indigenous people take the lead on working out priorities in their community, the better the outcomes. This also includes leading policy development, service delivery and program design. Indigenous people best understand the issues in their communities and the solutions that will work the best. They can use their informal networks to work across agencies and services. They can make sure the most helpless in the community are involved rather than falling through the cracks.

TECHNICAL
STUFF

Many Indigenous peoples across the world haven't been thought of as 'peoples' within the principle of self-determination under international law. They still find it hard to fit their claims into the definition that makes them show distinct land boundaries. That is because much of their land was stolen during colonisation. They also can't say that the principle of non-intervention has been broken. Why? Most live in countries that have recognised, legitimate governments. So Indigenous peoples are under the control of their colonising state for rights protection and steps towards more power.

Groups for Self-Representation

Aboriginal peoples and Torres Strait Islanders have formed several groups to stand up for them and provide a shared voice. Some groups were created by legislation but used by Indigenous people. Others have been created outside of government. Here's a look at each group:

- ✐ **The Aboriginal and Torres Strait Islander Commission (ATSIC)** was started in 1990. It was formed under legislation that was passed through federal parliament the year before. ATSIC set up a national board and a system of regional bodies made up of elected representatives. It had a lot of responsibilities. These included support for Indigenous peoples, checking the work of government and running a housing, infrastructure and work-for-welfare program. The Howard government started reducing ATSIC's powers when it came to office in 1996. ATSIC was shut down in 2005 after a political agreement between the Howard government and the then-leader of the opposition, Mark Latham.

✔ **The National Congress of Australia's First Peoples** was started in 2009. Its first election was in 2011. It started as a lobbying group to represent its members. Its stated aims were to stand up for Indigenous rights and to work towards the social, economic, cultural and environmental future of Australia's Indigenous peoples. The Congress was a non-government body with over 2,000 members. But it got money from the federal government to help run it until 2013. It then had to run on its own economically. It stopped operations in 2019. (See Chapter 10 for more on the Congress.)

✔ **The New South Wales Aboriginal Land Council** was started in 1983. It was formed as part of state land rights legislation. This legislation let Aboriginal people in New South Wales claim back traditional land now owned by the Crown and not needed for an essential public use. The state land council is made up of elected representatives from across New South Wales. The system also has a network of 121 local land councils that deal with local issues and hold land for local communities. (The local land councils are all elected by the local membership.) It has a $2 billion portfolio of land and a $680 million capital fund. This fund pays for its operations and gives scholarships to its members and their children. It also gives money for repairs and infrastructure on Aboriginal reserves in New South Wales.

Today, the Land Council has over 23,000 members. One in three Aboriginal people in New South Wales are members. This means that the largest representative group with elected representatives is not a national body. It's a state one! The land council is also a strong supporter of Indigenous issues. It goes to United Nations forums to stand up for the views of its members.

The regional council structure in ATSIC worked well and was heavily used. Working at the regional level lets a large enough group have an impact. But it also makes sure the focus is local enough to understand the distinct local cultures and needs. Some examples of regional groups are

- **The Gunditjmara Nation:** These traditional owners have developed their own system of decision-making. This system focuses on the ideas of nation building and creating systems of self-governance. It also fits in with the cultural values of the nation. The traditional owners started the Gunditj Mirring corporation under the *Native Title Act 1993 (Cwth)*. This group is governed by Full Group meetings. These meetings bring together the traditional owners every month for talks and decision-making. This binds the Gunditj Mirring in representing the interests of the whole nation. The corporation also runs culturally important sites at places such as Lake Condah Aboriginal Mission and Lake Gorrie.

- **The Murdi Paaki Regional Assembly:** This group represents the members of 16 communities in north-west NSW. Its membership of Community Working Parties and the MPRA figures out the priorities in their area. It works with government and service providers. It grew out of the ATSIC Murdi Paaki Regional Council, led by the Community Working Parties. Check out their work at www.mpra.com.au.

- **The Ngarrindjeri Regional Authority:** This is an example of a community-designed self-governance model. It was started in 2007. The Ngarrindjeri nation in South Australia designed the structure with no help from government. It includes the values that the Ngarrindjeri want to be ruled by. One of those principles is the NRA Yarluwar-Ruwe Program. This program guides the direction of the NRA. It makes sure that cultural and environmental ideas are included in its work. It has created a lot of caring for country projects and cultural and education programs. The Ngarrindjeri have also come up with their own rules for making agreements or contracts with people. Kungun Ngarrindjeri Yunnan means 'listen to what Aboriginal people have to say'. The principles include the recognition of Ngarrindjeri rights and interests and the importance of cultural knowledge.

These regional structures allow regional communities and individual Indigenous nations to focus on the issues important to them. They also provide an important link between the community and state and federal governments. Governments can be sure that they are working in a proper consultative process.

Working within the Existing Process

Indigenous people have also tried to make change by working within the political process. They have joined political parties and been elected to Parliament. Neville Bonner was the first Indigenous person to enter Parliament. He became a senator for Queensland in 1971. First, he was a member of the Liberal Party. Then he became an Independent in 1983. That was his last year in Parliament.

Here are some other important Indigenous politicians:

- In 1999, Aden Ridgeway was elected to the Senate, representing New South Wales. He was a member of the Australian Democrats.

- Ken Wyatt was the first Indigenous person to be elected to the House of Representatives. He became the Member for Hasluck in 2010.

- The first Indigenous woman in federal parliament was Nova Peris. She became a senator for the Northern Territory in 2013 as a member of the Australian Labor Party. She left the parliament in 2016.

- Linda Burney became the first Indigenous woman in the House of Representatives. She became the member for Barton in 2016. She is a member of the Australian Labor Party.

In 2021, federal parliament included five Indigenous members:

- Ken Wyatt

- Linda Burney

- Senator Malarndirri McCarthy (for the Northern Territory; ALP)

- Senator Patrick Dodson (for Western Australia; ALP)

- Senator Jacqui Lambie (for Tasmania; Independent)

Representation has also grown in state and territory governments. Of note are the following:

- Adam Giles became Chief Minister of the Northern Territory in 2013. He led the Country Liberal Party government.

- Ernie Bridge was the first Indigenous Cabinet minister in an Australian government. He became the Western Australian Minister for Water Resources, the North-West and Aboriginal Affairs in 1986.

- Marion Scrymgour was the first female minister in 2003. She was part of the Northern Territory government.

- John Ah Kit and his daughter Ngaree Ah Kit were the first Indigenous father and daughter to serve in a parliament, both in the Northern Territory. John Ah Kit served from 1995 to 2005. Ngaree Ah Kit was elected in 2016.

LINDA BURNEY: WORKING INSIDE AND OUTSIDE THE SYSTEM

Linda Burney has had a long career as a politician in both the NSW state and federal parliaments. She was the first Indigenous person to serve in the NSW parliament. She was elected as the Member for Canterbury in 2003. In 2011, after the Australian Labor Party lost government in NSW, she became the NSW Deputy Leader of the Opposition. She became the National Vice President of the ALP in 2006, and was National President in 2008 and 2009.

She moved from state to federal politics in 2106. She was elected the Member of Barton in a by-election. She became the first Indigenous woman elected to the House of Representatives.

Before her career as a politician, Linda Burney had been active in the reconciliation process. She was an Executive Member of the National Council for Aboriginal Reconciliation. But she also worked at the community level on education policy. She became President of the Aboriginal Education Consultative Group in NSW. Then she became Director-General of the NSW Department of Aboriginal Affairs. She's worked hard inside and outside the system. And she's still going strong!

PROJECT

Write a biography of an Indigenous politician mentioned in this chapter.

PROJECT

Make a poster that celebrates the concept of self-determination for Indigenous peoples.

Part 6

The Part of Tens

In This Part . . .

☐ Explore a list of ten important cultural sites that are must-sees.

☐ Look at ten of the exciting 'firsts' achieved by Indigenous people in Australia.

☐ Help debunk ten myths about Indigenous people and their cultures.

Ten Important Indigenous Cultural Sites

Australia's Indigenous peoples have sacred sites all over the country. Visitors can't reach many of them. The sites listed in this chapter, though, can be visited for a unique cultural experience. These sites are as naturally beautiful as they are spiritually important. They are deserving of a visit if you have the chance. Most of these sites have Indigenous-owned tourism businesses operating. These businesses can give you information on the cultural importance and particular bush tucker and medicines in the area. They are a great way to meet local Indigenous people and learn about their culture. In this chapter, I've included sites from all over Australia.

Uluru, Northern Territory

Uluru is a huge sandstone outcrop 335 kilometres south-west of Alice Springs. It's about 9.4 kilometres around the base, 3.6 kilometres long, 2 kilometres wide and about 345 metres high. According to the Anangu people, the traditional owners of the area, Uluru represents the rainbow serpent, a creation spirit. It is thought to be a site of fertility. It's seen as both a male and female spirit, and thought to be both mother and father. Caves inside the rock are covered with paintings that show that this is an area of special spiritual meaning.

The best time to see Uluru is at sunset, when the colours of the rock change from red to purple. The rock is also stunning after heavy rain. That's when large amounts of water cascade off the sides.

REMEMBER

Uluru is a sacred place to Aboriginal people, and they found it offensive that people climbed over it. The area was returned to the Anangu in 1985 but is leased back as a national park. (Chapter 3 has more details.) The Uluru climb closed for good on 26 October 2019.

Kata Tjuta, Northern Territory

About 40 kilometres to the west of Uluru is another stunning natural outcrop, Kata Tjuta. (It is also known by the European name of 'the Olgas'.) Kata Tjuta — and Uluru — started as sediments in an inland sea. Kata Tjuta covers an area of over 22 square kilometres and has 36 domes. The highest point is Mount Olga, over a kilometre above sea level and over 546 metres above the surrounding plateau.

More than 300 million years ago, the sediments were pushed upwards above sea level. During this shift in the landscape, the force created cracks and fissures. Erosion over millions and millions of years has left the formations that look so stunning today. Like Uluru, the formations are especially beautiful at sunset. That's when the colours of the rocks change dramatically as the sun sinks below the horizon. They are thought to be 500 million years old.

Nitmiluk, Northern Territory

In 1978, the Jawoyn people of the Katherine area made a land claim over country that included the Katherine Gorge National Park. After talks between the Jawoyn, the Northern Land Council and the Northern Territory government, the land was leased back to the government and the Nitmiluk (Katherine Gorge) National Park started. Nitmiluk, also known as Katherine Gorge, is a series of 13 gorges carved by a river over a billion years, creating an amazing natural landscape with dramatic cliffs and sandy beaches. *Nitmiluk* means 'cicada place'. The area has spiritual importance for the Jawoyn people.

Windjana Gorge, Western Australia

Windjana Gorge is in the Kimberley region of north-western Australia. It was carved out of the Napier Range by the Lennard River over 300 million years. The walls are 30 to 100 metres high and the gorge is over 100 metres wide. The name of the gorge is believed to be a misspelling of Wandjina, an important spiritual being of the Kimberley region. The traditional owners, the Bunuba, tell a creation story of how a large serpent carved the gorge. The gorge also gave protection for Bunuba resistance fighter Jandamarra in the late 1800s (refer to Chapter 7). The area is now part of a national park that was created in 1971. It is home to freshwater crocodiles.

Daintree Rainforest, North Queensland

The Daintree Rainforest is more than 135 million years old. It's the oldest tropical rainforest in the world. The area has a rich history of Indigenous culture that dates back thousands of years. The area is also rich with wildlife and natural beauty. It contains 30 per cent of the frog, reptile and marsupial species in Australia. It also has 65 per cent of Australia's bat and butterfly species. Situated north of Mossman, Queensland — and about 100 kilometres north of Cairns — the area was made into a national park in 1981. It was given World Heritage Site listing in 1988. Many of the natural features that appear on the landscape have spiritual significance for the traditional owners of the area, the Eastern Kuku Yalanji. So do the areas that provide sources of water or constant supplies of food.

Mungo National Park, New South Wales

Some 900 kilometres west of Sydney, near Mildura in Victoria's north-west, lies the World Heritage–listed Willandra Lakes region. It's made up of 17 dry lakes, including Lake Mungo. In 1969, a skeleton, given the nickname of 'Mungo Lady', was found. In 1974, a second skeleton, 'Mungo Man', was found and added to other proof that showed that Aboriginal people had lived in the area for thousands of years. Scientists have used various dating methods for the remains. This process gave different guesses of their age, though it was found that both were ritualistically buried. An agreement was made through a group effort in 2003, dating the skeletons at around 40,000 years. Since then, children's footprints have been found in solidified clay and sand, and dated to over 40,000 years ago. Three Aboriginal nations are actively involved with the management of Mungo National Park — the Mutthi Mutthi, the Paakantyi and Ngyiampaa nations.

Yeddonba, Victoria

Yeddonba Aboriginal Cultural Site sits near the twin New South Wales and Victorian border towns of Albury and Wodonga, about 300 kilometres north of Melbourne. The site showcases artworks of the Duduroa clan of the Pangarang. The area, including several important water sources, had special meaning to the Pangarang clans. The Yeddonba area is related to a Dreamtime story about the Tasmanian tiger, the totem of the people here. Rock art shows images that relate to this story. The paintings have been dated to about 2,000 years ago. The Tasmanian tiger (the thylacine) is shown in ancient rock art way up in Arnhem Land. So finding the animal related to a Victorian site is perhaps unsurprising, as the island state of Tasmania was once linked by a land bridge. On another interesting note, the ochre in the paintings has been sourced to South Australia. This shows past trade connections between the two regions.

Ngaut Ngaut, South Australia

The Ngaut Ngaut Aboriginal Site is near Mannum in South Australia, on the land of the Nganguraku people. It is the place of the Black Duck Dreaming. The area is rich with Aboriginal rock art and cultural stories. Today, the site has a boardwalk that lets visitors walk over land occupied tens of thousands of years ago.

Wybalenna, Tasmania

Wybalenna is on Flinders Island and of special cultural meaning to the Palawa people. Unlike other places that have a long cultural history, the importance of Wybalenna has grown over recent times. In the 1830s and 1840s, more than 200 Aboriginal people from Tasmania were kept on the island in terrible conditions. Although the area has a tragic history, many Aboriginal people see it as an important spiritual place. The area was handed back to the Palawa in 1999. They believe that the return of the land can let them make sure that this spiritual resting place will be cared for and its history never forgotten.

The Aboriginal Tent Embassy, Canberra

On Australia Day in 1972, four Aboriginal men who had travelled from Sydney set up a protest camp on the lawns of Parliament House and declared it to be the Aboriginal Tent Embassy. Over the next few months, thousands of people — black and white — came from all over the country to join their demonstration. This protest got national and international attention. They were dispersed by police in July. The site was re-established in 1992 and is a reminder of an important historical political movement. Makeshift buildings still exist on the original site.

PROJECT

Research more about the sites mentioned in this chapter. Focus particularly on the Indigenous Elders from the area. Make a poster of images of the area and the information you find.

Ten Indigenous Firsts

Some firsts are great achievements for any Australian. But in the Indigenous community, each time someone breaks through a new barrier to achieve a first, that person becomes a role model to others in the community, especially young people. They show what's possible. In this chapter, I list ten significant firsts for Indigenous peoples.

The First Indigenous Australian to Visit Great Britain: 1793

The first Aboriginal person to make the long trip to Great Britain was Bennelong. He sailed there with Governor Phillip, leaving in December 1792. Bennelong's first contact with Phillip was Bennelong's capture in 1789. That was when Phillip had grown impatient with the slow progress of building relationships with the local Aboriginal community.

Bennelong stayed in the colony and took on some habits and customs of the British. He dressed in their clothes and learned their language. He went back to his clan in 1790 and often appeared at Sydney Cove to ask after the Governor. In 1791, a hut was built for him at what is now Bennelong Point. It is the site of the Sydney Opera House.

Bennelong and another Aboriginal man called Yemmerrawanne went with Governor Phillip on his return to London. There they met King George III. The stay in England didn't appear to be really happy for Bennelong. He suffered from the cold and homesickness. He went back to the Sydney colony with Governor Hunter in 1795. He died in 1813. See Chapter 6 for more on his life.

The First Indigenous Cricket Team Tour: 1868

In 1868, a team of 13 Aboriginal cricketers from Victoria sailed to England. They were, in fact, the first Australian cricketers to tour England as a representative team. In a tour that lasted six months, they played 47 two-day games. At the end of each game, the team showed off their skills at throwing spears and boomerangs.

The coach and manager of the team was Charles Lawrence. The star was perhaps Muarrinim (sometimes referred to as Unaarrimin), a player also known as Johnny Mullagh. He scored 1,698 runs and claimed 245 wickets on the tour. He went on to play for the Melbourne Cricket Club. But most of the other players on this tour didn't continue with professional cricket.

The team impressed the English with their staying power. It was noted in one newspaper, *Sporting Life*, that 'no eleven in one season ever played so many matches so successfully — never playing less than two matches in each week, frequently three, bearing an amount of fatigue that now seems incredible'. See Chapter 11 for more on this sporting feat.

The First Indigenous 'Pop Star': 1963

Musician Jimmy Little was said to be the first Indigenous pop star when his song, 'Royal Telephone', went to the top of the music charts in 1963. Little is a Yorta Yorta man who grew up on Cummeragunja Reserve. He moved to Sydney in 1955 and began his recording career in 1956.

He started to record hit songs with 'Danny Boy' in 1959 and 'El Paso' the following year. After 17 singles, 'Royal Telephone' reached number one on the charts. He continued to record songs, with his final hit from that era in 1974, 'Baby Blue'.

He turned to acting and then released his 14th album in 1994. In 1999 he was inducted into the ARIA Hall of Fame. In 2004, he released *Life's What You Make It*, featuring covers of modern songs. Little passed away in 2012.

The First Indigenous Person to Be Australian of the Year: 1968

Champion boxer Lionel Rose was named Australian of the Year in 1968 — at the age of 20. He was the first Indigenous person to receive that honour. He was awarded a Member of the Order of the British Empire (an MBE) that same year!

Born in the town of Warragul, in Victoria, Rose became a bantam-weight boxer. In another first, he was the first Indigenous Australian to win a world title in the sport. Rose had developed his skills when he joined his father on the boxing tent show circuit.

He won his first Australian title — amateur flyweight — in 1963, at the age of 15. He won the Australian bantamweight title in 1966. He won the world title in 1968 when he challenged Fighter Harada in a match in Tokyo. After his boxing career was over, Rose started a singing career. He passed away in 2011.

The First Indigenous Person to Be Elected to the Australian Parliament: 1971

Neville Bonner was the first Indigenous Australian to take a seat in the federal parliament. Elected from Queensland, Bonner was a senator from 1971 until 1983. He was born at Franklin Island, a small settlement on the Tweed River in northern New South Wales, in 1922. He started out doing labouring jobs — stockman, canecutter and ringbarker.

He spent 16 years on the Palm Island Aboriginal Reserve after he married and moved there with his wife in 1943. Many say that this experience gave him many skills that helped him in political life. It certainly made him want to change the circumstances in which Aboriginal people were living.

He left Palm Island and joined OPAL — the One People of Australia League. OPAL focused on the welfare, housing and education of Indigenous people. Bonner entered politics in 1967, when he joined the Liberal Party. After his death in 1999, he gained many honours. These included a scholarship in his name to support Indigenous Australians studying politics or a related field.

The First Indigenous Lawyer: 1976

The first Indigenous Australian to become a lawyer was Patricia O'Shane. She graduated from the University of New South Wales and became a barrister in 1976. In 1981, she moved from legal practice to run the New South Wales Department of Aboriginal Affairs. But she went back to the law when she was appointed as a magistrate in 1986.

O'Shane was born in northern Queensland, in the town of Mossman. She often talked about the way in which she saw and experienced discrimination. It shaped her resolve and her work. She was a gifted student. O'Shane went to school in Cairns and won a Teacher Scholarship at the Queensland Teachers Training College and the University of Queensland. She graduated and taught at primary and high schools. Then she won a federal government study grant to study law in 1973.

The First Indigenous Person to Make a Feature Film: 1992

The first Indigenous person to make a feature film was Aboriginal actor and teacher Brian Syron. His movie *Jindalee Lady* starred two Aboriginal actors, Lydia Miller and Michael Leslie. Born in Sydney, Syron went on to have an amazing life for someone from humble beginnings.

In 1961, Syron went to Europe and worked as a model for designers such as Dior and Cardin. Later that year, he moved to New York after he got into the respected acting school run by Stella Adler. Classmates included Robert de Niro and Warren Beatty. He then spent a year studying his craft in London. Later he went back to the United States to work in theatre and to teach.

Syron was drawn home to work with Aboriginal people. He went back to Australia in 1967. Syron kept acting in theatre, film and television. He directed theatre productions. He taught acting to younger Aboriginal actors and worked with Aboriginal writers. Syron helped start the Aboriginal Theatre Company in 1981.

He spent two years making *Jindalee Lady*. It came out in 1992. In another first, Syron asked Bart Willougby to write the score for the movie. This made Willougby the first Indigenous person to compose, play and direct the music track to a feature film. Chapter 15 has more on Indigenous filmmaking.

The First Indigenous Surgeon: 2006

Dr Kelvin Kong, a Worimi man from the Newcastle area, became the first Indigenous person to be qualified as a surgeon. In 2006, at the age of 32, he became a fellow of the Royal Australasian College of Surgeons. He graduated from the University of New South Wales. Kong helped to start a pre-medical program there for other Indigenous people to study medicine.

Based at the University of Newcastle's School of Medicine and Public Health, he has run clinics for various Aboriginal medical services. He helped to start a professional body for Indigenous doctors — the Australian Indigenous Doctors Association (AIDA). He also has worked on health policy advocacy for Indigenous Australians. His twin sisters, Marilyn and Marlene, are also doctors!

The First Indigenous Senior Council (SC): 2015

Tony McAvoy SC became a barrister in 2000 and did a lot of work in the area of native title. He has also worked in environmental law, human rights, discrimination law, criminal law and coronial inquests. He was appointed Senior Council in 2015, the first barrister to reach that high position. Tony was the co-Senior Council helping the Royal Commission into the Protection and Detention of Children in the Northern Territory in 2016. He has been a strong supporter of the protection of Indigenous rights in the legal system.

McAvoy is active in trying to improve the profession from the inside. He co-chairs the Indigenous Legal Issues Committee of the Law Council of Australia. He is the Chair of the NSW Bar Association's First Nations Committee. He also is a trustee of the NSW Bar Association's Indigenous Barristers Trust.

The First Indigenous Minister for Indigenous Australians: 2019

Ken Wyatt, a member of the Liberal Party, became the first Indigenous person to be elected to the House of Representatives. He came to politics after a career in Indigenous education and health. His electorate, Hasluck, is in Western Australia. After the election in 2019, he became the first Indigenous person to hold the Ministry for Indigenous Australians. He also became the first Indigenous person to sit in the Cabinet, the focal point of decision-making in government. Wyatt has kept his interest in Indigenous health and education as a Minister. He has also been active in the Aged Care portfolio.

REMEMBER

In 2016, Linda Burney became the first Indigenous woman to sit in the House of Representatives. She is a member of the Australian Labor Party. She represents the seat of Barton in New South Wales. Burney is the Shadow Minister for Indigenous Australians and Shadow Minister for Families and Social Services.

PROJECT

Can you find five more Indigenous 'firsts'? Make a list of these firsts, and include a note on why you think they are significant.

Ten Myths about Indigenous People

Many stereotypes about Indigenous people exist. Some are surprisingly well rooted in some parts of the Australian community. Many of the people who hold these views have possibly never met an Indigenous person. They have possibly never understood the issues that Indigenous people deal with every day.

These stereotypes are offensive. As with most generalisations, they aren't true. So, in this chapter, I debunk a few myths.

'Indigenous People Have a Problem with Alcohol'

Indigenous people drink less than the general Australian population. Among Indigenous men, 35 per cent don't drink at all. Only 12 per cent of the total Australian population stays away from alcohol. In the Northern Territory, 75 per cent of the Aboriginal population doesn't drink alcohol.

Among the population that drinks, some people do have problems with too much drinking. This causes further problems for their communities. However, no proof exists that Indigenous people are less biologically able to handle alcohol.

'Indigenous People Are Dying Out'

Indigenous populations are growing. Compared with the rest of the Australian population, Indigenous people have more children. Their populations also have a much larger proportion of young people. See Chapter 2 for more details.

Also, more Indigenous people are choosing to identify themselves as Indigenous. This has happened as discrimination against Indigenous people goes down. In earlier times, this choice may have seen them kept to reserves and needing permission to work and to marry.

'Indigenous People Who Live in Urban Areas Have Lost Their Culture'

Even in big cities, Indigenous people have strong memories and oral histories of their stories, history and culture. In Sydney, for example, there are many rock paintings and carvings around the harbour. The local community remembers where the important sites for traditions are. Also, they still have the same values that are a strong part of Indigenous cultures. These values are respect for country, respect for the wisdom of Elders and a belief in the ideas of reciprocity and connection.

'Indigenous People Were Killed Off in Tasmania'

It was believed that the Indigenous people of Tasmania died out with the death of an Aboriginal woman, Truganini, in 1876. She was thought to be the only person who came back from the

Flinders Island mission. This was where Tasmanian Aboriginals were sent for resettlement.

The removal of Aboriginal people from Tasmania ended up in a strong break of traditions and languages. But an Aboriginal population has survived. The group reminds the larger population of their lives, history and culture. Chapter 7 has more details.

'Indigenous People Are Addicted to Welfare'

Growing employment is a widely shared goal in Indigenous communities around Australia. But unemployment among the Indigenous population is around three times the national average. Not surprisingly, in remote areas there are not as many jobs as in more populated areas. Unemployment rates tend to be higher in remote areas too. In these areas, where work-for-the-dole schemes have been started, the chances created have had a high take-up.

Another factor that is part of the high level of unemployment in the Indigenous community is the low levels of education in some Indigenous communities. Yet another factor is leftover prejudice among some non-Indigenous employers who don't want to hire Indigenous people. See Chapter 16 for more details.

'Too Much Money Is Spent on Indigenous People'

The Australian government released the Australian Productivity Commission report on Indigenous expenditure in 2017. The report said about $6 billion was spent by federal, state and territory governments on targeted programs for Aboriginal and Torres Strait Islander Australians. In comparison, non-Indigenous people cost governments $522.7 billion.

Given the low education levels, the overcrowding and the lower life expectancy of Indigenous communities, this amount isn't enough to meet those pressing needs. And the remote location of some communities increases costs further.

Groups such as the Australian Indigenous Doctors Association and the Australian Human Rights Commission agree. Indigenous people say that money needs to be spent properly. Less of it should go into costly government red tape. Find more details on policies in Chapters 10, 16, and 17.

'Real Indigenous People Live in Remote Areas'

The largest Indigenous populations are in the cities. Of the total population of Indigenous people in Australia, 31 per cent live in major cities. 22 per cent live in inner regional Australia and 23 per cent live in outer regional Australia. Only 8 per cent live in remote Australia, while 16 per cent live in very remote Australia.

People don't stop being Indigenous because they live a more western life. Cultures can exist together. The legal definition from the Federal Court says a person is Indigenous when that person:

✔ Is of Aboriginal descent or Torres Strait Islander descent

✔ Identifies with the culture

✔ Is accepted as being Indigenous by the community in which he or she lives

This definition is used whether an Indigenous person lives in the city or the country. Where people live doesn't make them more or less Indigenous. Chapter 2 has more information.

'Indigenous Groups Don't Handle Money Well'

Accountability rules for Indigenous corporations, statutory authorities and grants are often greater than their non-Indigenous counterparts.

Indigenous groups such as the New South Wales Aboriginal Land Council manage a portfolio of more than $700 million and $2 billion worth of land. Strong rules are in place to ensure clearness in decision-making. All members of its elected arm have training. They know the difference in responsibilities between a board member and a staff member.

'Indigenous Culture Is Violent'

Sexual abuse of women and children has never been a part of traditional cultural practices. Abuse is considered evil by Indigenous men and women of all ages. Sexual abuse and violence are behaviours that are learned. Studies and reports have found them to be generational and cyclical; in other words, abusers have often been victims of abuse themselves. Today, many initiatives speak out against violence towards and abuse of Indigenous women and children. Some of these initiatives are led by Indigenous men.

'Indigenous Self-Determination Has Been Tried but It Has Failed'

Self-determination is a human right. It is the ability of people to determine their own future. It's measured by how much people feel they have control over the political processes that affect them. See Chapters 10 and 17 for more information.

For a brief period, Indigenous affairs in Australia had the title of 'self-determination'. But the Australian government officially stopped using that title. During this brief period, the approach was one of top-down decision-making. Governments were in charge of policy-making and programs. Indigenous people had no say in the decisions made about them. They were also not encouraged to find solutions to the problems in their communities. But many communities came up with answers apart from government funding and meddling.

REMEMBER

Self-determination is about Indigenous people leading policy creation and putting programs into action. The top-down approach of governments seems to go against this idea.

Self-determination has never been properly tested in Australia. But previous governments have used the term to describe their approach. This has created the myth that self-determination has been tried but failed.

PROJECT

Using examples from this book, write a reflection on how what you've read provides arguments against one of the myths included in this chapter.

Glossary

Aboriginal English: A version of English that encompasses some regional Aboriginal words but also applies particular meaning to other words of English, spoken across Australia.

Aboriginal person: A person who is of Aboriginal descent, identifies as Aboriginal and is accepted as Aboriginal by the Aboriginal community in which he or she lives. See also *blood-quantum*, *Indigenous person*, *Torres Strait Islander*.

acknowledgement of country: A common custom whereby an Aboriginal or non-Aboriginal person holding an event acknowledges the *traditional owners* of that land. See also *welcome to country*.

ALS: Aboriginal Legal Service.

AMS: Aboriginal Medical Service.

Anangu: An *Aboriginal person* from Central Australia.

assimilation: The argument that the best way for Indigenous peoples to fit into Australian society was to demand that they give up their cultures, languages and traditions and live like white people.

ATSIC: The Aboriginal and Torres Strait Islander Commission, established in 1990 as a nationally elected body to represent and support Indigenous regional communities; abolished in 2004.

ATSIS: Aboriginal and Torres Strait Islander Services, established in 2003 to administer *ATSIC* programs, replaced in 2004 by the Office of Indigenous Policy Coordination (OIPC).

blood-quantum: An outdated method of categorising Aboriginal or Torres Strait Islander people according to the proportion of Aboriginal or Torres Strait Islander heritage they have, using such terms as 'half-caste' and 'quadroon', which may be considered offensive. See also *Aboriginal person*, *Indigenous person*, *Torres Strait Islander*.

boomerang: A curved wooden tool used for hunting or as a weapon; returning and non-returning varieties were used.

bush tucker: Plants and animals gathered for food.

canoe tree: A tree with a visible scar in the bark from where a canoe was carved out of the bark.

clan: Small extended family group of about 40 to 50 people, part of a larger language group called a *nation*.

clapstick: A musical instrument made up of two wooden sticks, usually of different shapes, that are banged together to create a rhythmic beat.

coreeda: A traditional Indigenous game encompassing dance and combat.

corroboree: An important cultural or spiritual event celebrated through music and dance at a gathering of clan groups or nations.

Day of Mourning: The 1938 Australia Day protest in Sydney that marked the beginning of the Indigenous rights movement; later known as Aborigines Day and overseen by *NAIDOC*.

Dreaming tracks: The pathways taken by spiritual ancestors as they travelled across the landscape, creating its features, during the *Dreamtime*. See also *songlines*.

Dreamtime: Also called the Dreaming, the term given to the period when the world was created, with spiritual ancestors journeying across the landscape, along *Dreaming tracks*, creating its features; central to Aboriginal worldviews and spirituality.

Elder: An *Aboriginal person* or a *Torres Strait Islander* who has earned and is afforded the respect of the community, often then referred to as Aunty or Uncle.

firestick farming: The systematic use of fire to clear undergrowth and encourage regrowth to attract fauna.

freshwater people: Those who live by the rivers in inland areas.

gubba: An *Aboriginal English* term used to refer to white people; from 'governor'.

history wars: Also called the culture wars; refers to a period in the 1990s when historians and others became embroiled in debate over Aboriginal history, particularly the number of people killed on the frontier after colonisation.

Indigenous Land and Sea Corporation (ILSC): A body set up in 1995 to assist *Indigenous people* to acquire and manage land through a land fund; originally known as the Indigenous Land Council (ILC).

Indigenous person: Used in Australia to describe *Aboriginal peoples* and *Torres Strait Islanders* together. Some people prefer the term 'First Nations'.

karma songs: Traditional songs about the totems, history and mythology of a particular *clan*, used to educate children approaching puberty.

kinship system: A social division within some clans that defines the relationships between the people of the clan, usually giving a specific name to all members of that group. See also *skin name*.

Koori: An *Aboriginal person* from New South Wales or Victoria; also spelled as Goori.

Kriol: A hybrid language comprising English and a local Aboriginal dialect.

land rights legislation: Legislation enacted in states and territories in response to a social and political movement that evolved from the 1960s to the 1980s to include people from a broad spectrum of society. See also *native title legislation*.

marngrook: A traditional game involving kicking and leaping for a ball of possum skin encasing pounded charcoal and/or grass; believed to be the precursor to Australian Rules Football.

Murri: An *Aboriginal person* from Queensland or northern New South Wales.

NACCHO: National Aboriginal Community Controlled Health Organisation; the national leadership body for Aboriginal and Torres Strait Islander health.

NAIDOC: Originally NADOC, the National Aborigines Day Observance Committee (it became NAIDOC in 1991 to recognise Islanders too) was formed to celebrate Aborigines Day, as the *Day of Mourning* became known. It is now a week-long celebration held from the first Sunday in July each year and the whole week is known as NAIDOC.

nation: A large language group with responsibility for a specific area of country. See also *clan*.

National Sorry Day: A day of acknowledgement of the tabling in parliament of the *Bringing Them Home* report of the inquiry into the *Stolen Generations*, celebrated on 26 May since 1998.

native title legislation: Federal legislation enacted through the judicial recognition of native title in the Mabo case in 1992. See also *land rights legislation*.

1967 referendum: Referendum to change the Constitution to give the federal government the ability to make laws for *Indigenous people*, under the *races power*, and for Indigenous people to be counted in the census.

Noongar: An *Aboriginal person* from southern Western Australia.

Nunga: An *Aboriginal person* from southern South Australia.

Palawa: An *Aboriginal person* from Tasmania.

pastoral lease: A form of land tenure, unique to Australia, where land settled by *squatters*, for the purpose of agriculture or sheep or cattle breeding, is converted by the government to a lease agreement, with the government retaining ownership.

Protector of Aborigines: A powerful position, also often incorporating a Chief Protector, created from the late 1830s in each of the states and the Northern Territory under the auspices of protection of Aboriginal rights and welfare (but in practice used to control the lives of Aboriginal people).

races power: Section of the Constitution that gives the federal government the ability to make laws for any specific race; changed in the 1967 *referendum* to remove the exclusion of *Indigenous people*, so the federal government could make laws for Indigenous people.

rasp: A musical instrument made up of a notched stick that is scraped by a second smaller stick to produce a rhythmic sound.

saltwater people: Those who live by the sea in coastal areas.

self-determination: The right of all peoples to decide for themselves their political status and freely pursue their economic, social and cultural development.

Shared Responsibility Agreement: A type of agreement between government and *Indigenous* communities, endorsed by the *National Indigenous Council*, based on the idea that to receive services, communities had to agree to certain behavioural changes or standards.

skin name: A name given to every member (often with variations for male and female) of a kinship group within a *clan*; also called a kinship name.

songlines: The routes taken for cultural exchange of ideas, songs and ceremonies between *nations*, often following *Dreaming tracks*.

sorry business: Ceremonial practices surrounding a funeral.

Stolen Generations: The generations of children removed from their families as a result of government policies that promoted assimilation.

Survival Day: Term given by many people to Australia Day, commemorated on 26 January as the anniversary of the proclamation of the first British colony at Sydney Cove in 1788; also known as Invasion Day.

terra nullius: A phrase applied in legal terms in Australia until 1992 that implied Australia was vacant and without government at the time of possession by the British, later acknowledged as a 'legal fiction'.

Torres Strait Islander: A person of the Torres Strait Islands north of Cape York Peninsula in Queensland. See also *Aboriginal person*, *Indigenous person*.

totem: An animal, plant or landform believed to be ancestrally related to a person.

traditional owner: An *Aboriginal person* or a *Torres Strait Islander* who's acknowledged as being of direct descent of the original custodians of an area of land. See also *acknowledgement of country*, *welcome to country*.

welcome to country: A common protocol whereby *traditional owners* welcome people onto their land. See also *acknowledgement of country*.

woomera: A particular type of spear-thrower used as a multipurpose tool for hunting, chopping wood, cutting tree branches or chopping meat.

Yolngu: An *Aboriginal person* from central or eastern Arnhem Land in the Northern Territory; the nation of that region.

Index

About the Author

Larissa Behrendt AO is of Eualeyai and Kamillaroi descent, peoples of the north-western New South Wales. She is Distinguished Professor of the Jumbunna Institute of Indigenous Education and Research at the University of Technology, Sydney.

She graduated with a Bachelor of Laws and Bachelor of Jurisprudence from the University of New South Wales and was the first Aboriginal Australian to graduate from Harvard Law School when she gained her Master of Laws in 1994 and Senior Doctorate of Jurisprudence in 1998.

Larissa is a member of the Academy of Social Sciences of Australia and of the Australian Academy of Law.

She is the author of several books on Indigenous legal issues. She won the 2002 David Unaipon Award and a 2005 Commonwealth Writers' Prize for her novel *Home*. Her novel, *Legacy*, won a Victorian Premier's Literary Award in 2010. She is also a filmmaker and won the Australian Director's Guild award for Best Direction in a Feature Documentary for her film *After the Apology* in 2018.

Larissa is a Board Member of the Australian Museum, the Sydney Community Fund and Sydney Festival. She is Chair of the Cathy Freeman Foundation and is a former Chair of the Bangarra Dance Theatre. She was the inaugural chair of National Indigenous Television Ltd.

She was named as 2009 National Aborigines and Islanders Day Observance Committee (NAIDOC) Person of the Year and 2011 New South Wales Australian of the Year. Larissa was awarded an AO in 2020 for her work in Indigenous education, law and the arts.

Author's Acknowledgements

With thanks to everyone at Wiley (especially Ingrid Bond, Francesca Tarquinio, Charlotte Duff and Lucy Raymond). Special thanks to editor Kerry Davies for the expertise she provided in the first edition of the book. Thanks also to Amanda Porter and Terry Priest. Also sincere thanks to Michael McDaniel, my mother Raema Behrendt and my husband Michael Lavarch.

Dedication

To my mother, Raema Behrendt, who taught me the importance of knowledge and education, encouraged me to dream big and supported me when I did.

Publisher's Acknowledgements

Some of the people who helped bring this book to market include the following:

Acquisitions, Editorial and Media Development

Project Editor: Tamilmani Varadharaj

Acquisitions Editor: Lucy Raymond

Editorial Manager: Ingrid Bond

Copy Editor: Charlotte Duff

Production

Graphics: SPi

Proofreader: Penny Stuart

Indexer: Estalita Slivoskey

The author and publisher would like to thank the following organisations for their permission to reproduce copyright material in this book:

- **Cover image:** © Myra Nungarrayi Herbert / Copyright Agency, 2021
- **Pages 38-39:** Unpublished paper 'Aboriginal Citizenship Conference' by Professor Peter Read, ANU, February 1996
- **Page 89:** National Archives of Australia. NAA: A6135,K10/12/74/9. © Commonwealth of Australia National Archives of Australia 2019.
- **Page 105:** NLA.PIC-AN24526893 Engraving by James Neagle. Reproduced with permission from the National Library of Australia. © Commonwealth of Australia National Archives of Australia 2019.
- **Page 108:** State Library of Victoria; Accession No: 30328102131553/7, Image No: pb000329
- **Page 110:** © Keith Barnes / Shutterstock.com
- **Page 118:** State Library of Victoria; Accession Number: H14164; Image Number: b28462
- **Pages 158-159:** From Prime Minister Kevin Rudd, MP — Apology to Australia's Indigenous peoples; Wednesday, February 13, 2008, Parliament of Australia, Department of Parliamentary Services
- **Page 193:** *Charles Perkins returning home after studying at Sydney University, circa 1963.* Copyright photograph by Robert McFarlane, courtesy Josef Lebovic Gallery.
- **Pages 212-214:** Uluru Statement, https://ulurustatement.org/
- **Page 260:** © Newspix / Brenton Edwards
- **Page 269:** © Newspix / Mark Calleja

Every effort has been made to trace the ownership of copyright material. Information that enables the publisher to rectify any error or omission in subsequent editions is welcome. In such cases, please contact the Permissions Section of John Wiley & Sons Australia, Ltd.

Printed and bound by CPI Group (UK) Ltd, Croydon, CR0 4YY
07/01/2022
03102764-0001